Landscapes and Languages

Exploring the Linguistic and Spatial Contours of La Florida and Beyond

Landscapes and Languages

Exploring the Linguistic and Spatial Contours of La Florida and Beyond

EDITED BY TIMOTHY J. JOHNSON

Academy of American Franciscan History
San Diego, California
2025

Library of Congress Cataloging-in-Publication Data

Names: Johnson, Timothy J., editor.
Title: Landscapes and languages : exploring the linguistic and spatial contours of La Florida and beyond / edited by Timothy J. Johnson.
Description: San Diego, California : Academy of American Franciscan History, 2025. | Includes bibliographical references and index. | Summary: "This book, a collection of essays from a conference held at Flagler College in St. Augustine, Florida in 2023, continues a strong tradition of inquiry into the relationships between Native people and the Spanish religious and secular forces in the early colonial era. It becomes abundantly clear to the reader of these essays that simplistic dichotomies between Native and European attitudes must give way to more subtle explorations of these complex encounters. Instead of thinking of either Catholic or Indigenous culture as uniform, the authors of these chapters show us that whether we look at text, performance, or land use we find complex entanglements of interpretation and practice." — Provided by publisher.
Identifiers: LCCN 2025007217 | ISBN 9780883823156 (cloth)
Subjects: LCSH: Franciscans—Relations—Indians. | Catholic Church—Relations—Indians. | Indians of North America—Florida (New Spain)—Languages. | Indians of Mexico—Languages. | Indians of North America—Florida (New Spain)—Religion. | Indians of Mexico—Religion. | Indians of North America—Missions—Florida (New Spain) | Indians of Mexico—Missions. | Indians of North America—Florida (New Spain)—Languages—Influence on Spanish. | Indians of Mexico—Languages—Influence on Spanish. | Florida—History—Spanish colony, 1565-1763. | Mexico—History—Spanish colony, 1540-1810. | LCGFT: Conference papers and proceedings. | Essays.
Classification: LCC E78.F6 L35 2024 | DDC 975.9004/97—dc23/eng/20250510
LC record available at https://lccn.loc.gov/2025007217

Academy of American Franciscan History
San Diego, California

Table of Contents

Section Two

Introduction

GEORGE AARON BROADWELL, *University of Florida*

This volume of papers from a conference held at Flagler College in St Augustine, Florida in 2023 continues a strong tradition of inquiry into the relationships between Native people and the Spanish religious and secular forces in the early colonial era. It becomes abundantly clear to the reader of these essays that simplistic dichotomies between Native and European attitudes must give way to more subtle explorations of these complex encounters. Instead of thinking of either Catholic or Indigenous culture as uniform, the authors of these chapters show us that whether we look at text, performance, or land use we find complex entanglements of interpretation and practice. And as this book represents the fourth volume of a series sponsored by the Academy of American Franciscan History and Flagler College, it is clear that new historical, anthropological, and linguistic scholarship continues to be inspired by the fertile interaction of scholars from different continents and academic traditions.

This introduction draws on a few themes that unite the volume. First are the papers which focus on text, context, and performance. The authors of these chapters base their work on close readings of Native language texts and attempt to contextualize how the language of the texts is related to religious observance.

Viviana Díaz Balsera examines the ways in which Movilla's 1635 book, *Explicación de la doctrina*, addresses a Timucua audience. The work is a monolingual Timucua translation of Bellarmine's 1598 defense of Catholic doctrine against Protestantism, and thus perhaps to European eyes contains nothing particular to the Indigenous people of La Florida. Yet a close reading of the Timucua text shows the multiple ways in which the European original was edited and altered to make it suitable for a Native audience. These adaptations, carefully considered, provide considerable insight into Timucua religious agency and understanding.

Mark Christensen also touches on an issue of performance, this time focusing on the Deposition, or lowering of Christ's body from the cross. Religious plays that deal with this element of the Passion were present in Europe from the tenth century onward. Native versions of the Deposition were performed in Mexico from the sixteenth century onward. In his essay Christensen examines in careful detail an early nineteenth-century Maya sermon about the Deposition. This sermon describes a ceremony performed in the Yucatán that likely began early in the colonial period and was contemporaneous with similar performances in central Mexico at the time.

John F. Schwaller continues the theme of text and performance by examining the Stations of the Cross. Although rooted in medieval European devotion, performances of the Stations of the Cross became particularly popular in seventeenth-century Mexico. Franciscans used public stations and humilladeros (roadside shrines) to link local religious structures, making the Stations of the Cross an accessible form of communal worship. Fr. Agustín de Vetancurt's *Via crucis*, a 1680 Nahuatl translation, was an important text which served as a bridge between European and Indigenous traditions.

George Aaron Broadwell and Alejandra Dubcovsky focus on a particularly important Timucua word *Utina*, which in previous historical and archaeological accounts has variously been described as the name of a person, of various places, or even a region. By careful reading of Timucua Christian texts, they show that *Utina* is instead a label for people and things regarded as venerable. The widespread incorporation of *Utina* into the names of various places and as an epithet for one powerful Timucua leader allows us a better understanding of how veneration worked in traditional society. At the same time, the use of *Utina* as an epithet for the Christian God shows how Franciscans adapted earlier systems of veneration to the new religious landscape of Colonial Florida.

A second theme for the volume involves conflicts in the use, adaptation, and understanding of land and its resources. European and Native people had conflicting practices of using, understanding, and adapting the land and natural resources around them.

As Denise I. Bossy and Keith Ashley argue in their insightful work, Native people were active participants in shaping the land around them to meet their needs for burial structures, places of governance and ceremonial spaces. Mocama council houses are a locus of the tension between traditional spaces of governance and the necessity of adapting traditional governance to the reality of Spanish colonialism.

Helmut Flachenecker looks carefully at another arena of conflicting uses of land and space in the colonial Southwest, focusing on the status of the kiva as a site of traditional worship. The kiva thus seemingly stands in opposition to a mission church, yet as Flachenecker notes, the situation is more complex than this. At times, Franciscan missionaries showed tolerance toward Indigenous practices, and in some places, kivas were even integrated into mission spaces. Pecos Pueblo, built in 1617, is a key example of the partially conflicting and partially intertwined relationships between traditional and Catholic uses of ritual space.

Jennifer Scheper Hughes examines the Franciscan conception of the sacred geography of the world, and how prior conceptions were shaken and reimagined in the face of the New World. As Hughes writes, landscapes are not merely backdrops of human action, but are actively constructed by humans. Examination of diverse sources reveals a Franciscan vision of a sacred geography shaped by both colonial conquest and Indigenous resistance, offering insights into how the order sought to re-anchor itself in Mexican lands amid chaos.

Lee Newsom focuses on the culture of food in Franciscan missions, where there was a complex mix of food systems from Europe and from Native America. The Franciscans were dependent on Native people to understand Native food resources, including knowledge of local food systems, horticultural and agricultural practices, and environmental adaptation. The missions consumed a mix of local (fish, maize) and imported (pigs, cattle, wheat) resources. This fusion of Native and settler foodways was essential to the success and survival of both the missions and the broader Spanish colonial enterprise in the region.

Jennifer R. Saracino examines how Franciscan missionaries and the Indigenous Nahua depicted and experienced the landscape of New Spain post-conquest. Saracino shows that there is considerable dissent and conflict in understandings of the land. Some sources, such as Fray Toribio de Motolinía's *Historia de los indios de la Nueva España* and engravings by Diego de Valadés in his *Rhetorica Christiana* show a familiar European view of the progress and order of Spain and Christianity. Another source, the remarkable Uppsala Map, offers a counter-narrative, showing churches coexisting with Indigenous structures and practices, emphasizing community identity beyond Christianity.

A final theme for the volume deals with texts and their interpretations. This is a particularly rich and challenging area for investigation, since it requires careful understanding of the ways in which ideas of patriarchy, grammar, biography, and the epic changed in the face of the encounter between European and Native traditions.

Timothy Johnson's intriguing chapter focuses on a close reading of the 1627 *Catecismo en lengua timuquana y castellana* looking at the contrast between the matrilineal society of the Timucua and the predominantly patriarchal European traditions of the Franciscans. As Johnson notes, despite Catholicism's traditional emphasis on patriarchal and masculine roles, Franciscan missionaries frequently went beyond these roles. Franciscans positioned themselves as both mothers and servants to their congregations, influenced by mystical theological traditions, particularly those of pseudo-Dionysius.

Seth Katenkamp and Doug Henning complement Johnson's analysis of the 1627 *Catecismo* with a close reading of Pareja's 1614 *Arte y pronunciacion de la lengva timvqvana y castellana*. Unlike other documents in the Timucua corpus, the *Arte* is intriguing as a work in progress. The surviving manuscript is partially type-set and partially hand-written, with corrections and insertions in Pareja's hand. By comparing printed and corrected material, we can see Pareja's process, where he repeatedly modified his understanding of Timucua grammar. Given Pareja's use of a Latinate model for the *Arte*, some non-European grammatical categories were challenging for his description, but the corrections allow us insight into his progressive understanding of Native grammatical categories.

Jane Tar's examination of the life and influence of the Spanish abbess Luisa de la Ascensión focuses on her influence on the Franciscans of the colonial period. The abbess was a passionate defender of the Eucharist and the doctrine of the Immaculate Conception. Given the undetermined status of this doctrine during the colonial period, Luisa de la Ascensión had an influence on the ways in which doctrine was presented in missionary encounters.

Francisco Javier Rojo-Alique gives us important information about the intellectual backgrounds of the Spanish religious who came to the New World to learn indigenous languages and preach the gospel. Despite the fact that Franciscans of this era were divided on the value of higher education (with some holding it to be incompatible with humility), those who came to the New World were among the most intellectually trained of their time. Among their accomplishments was the establishment of the Colegio de Santa Cruz de Tlatelolco, a site of higher education for Native students in Mexico, and a training ground for many Native people who went on to play important roles in writing dictionaries, grammars, and translations of religious treatises.

Thomas Hallock's chapter examines *La Florida* by Alonso Gregorio de Escobedo, an epic poem set in colonial Florida which is often neglected in modern studies. As Hallock shows, the form of the poem reflects European standards of the time, but its subject matter intertwines descriptions of Native Timucua practices with Christian allegories. Although a reader might expect the poem to reflect a thoroughly colonial point of view, Hallock argues the epic is essentially dialogic—capturing multiple perspectives, including Native resistance and accommodation to Spanish rule. A rereading of *La Florida* is thus part of an ongoing, open-ended process of interpretation and translation and thus connects nicely with the new interpretations and translations of Timucua texts discussed in the chapters by Díaz Balsera, Johnson, and Broadwell and Dubcovsky.

Anna M. Nogar's *Early Modern Global Stagings of Sor María de Jesús de Ágreda and La mística ciudad de dios* explores the global influence of the seventeenth-century Spanish nun Sor María de Jesús de Ágreda and her work, *La mística ciudad de dios*. Sor María's work focused on the Virgin Mary and St. Joseph and impacted devotional practices worldwide. Nogar looks at Mexican and Indian examples of this influence. Nogar's analysis reveals how Sor

María's writings spurred a global Josephine cult and contributed to the religious practices of diverse communities.

In conclusion, the essays that make up this volume represent a new standard for research into Native and Spanish encounters in the colonial period. As the authors gathered in this volume show, such research requires extensive background knowledge of the complexities of European and Indigenous traditions, as well as proficiency in linguistic, historical, interpretive, or archaeological inquiry. By exploring these entangled histories, this volume sets a promising foundation for future research, offering a richer, more nuanced understanding of early colonial interactions.

Acknowledgments

TIMOTHY J. JOHNSON, *Flagler College*

The gathering in March of 2023 at Flagler College for the fourth international conference *Landscapes and Languages: Exploring the Linguistic and Spatial Contours of La Florida and Beyond* confirmed the extraordinary ability of the college community to foster an engaging, interdisciplinary forum for scholars and the interested public to explore the nexus of languages and landscapes within Indigenous and Spanish Colonial cultural dynamics. While Henry Flagler's stunning Ponce de Leon Hotel, now Flagler College, dominates the landscape of Saint Augustine and the European architecture and languages associated with colonialism are visible and audible on many a street corner, the memory of the earlier Mocama-Timucua inhabitants of Northeast Florida is emerging as the contours of their landscapes and language garners ever-increasing attention from scholars and laypersons alike thanks to the generous support of the Academy of American Franciscan History. To this end, the Academy has published three earlier conference volumes available to the public through the University Press of Florida: *Facing Florida: Essays on Culture and Religion in Early Modern Southeastern America*, 2021; *Franciscans and American Indians in Pan-Borderlands Perspective: Adaptation, Negotiation, and Resistance*, 2018; and *From La Florida to La California: Franciscan Evangelization in the Spanish Borderlands*, 2013. Jeffrey M. Burns, the academy director and co-editor of two volumes, has guided this long-standing research project with enthusiasm and expertise. My ever favorite Franciscan, Prof. Agnieszka (Aggie) Johnson, was a continual source of encouragement and guidance throughout the inception and completion of this project. Several Flagler College campus entities played a crucial role in assuring a successful outcome, among them the Offices of the President, Academic Affairs, and Institutional Advancement. The conference was bittersweet in that Jan Cheney served for the last time as conference coordinator. From the first gathering in 2011 to the fourth in 2023, her organizational expertise and hands-on enthusiasm assured a smooth and enjoyable experience for all in attendance. This volume is dedicated to her.

Section One

Chapter One

Unearthing Mocama Landscapes, Writing Mocama History

Denise I. Bossy, *University of North Florida*
Keith Ashley, *University of North Florida*

Introduction: Mocama Landscape Construction

This chapter examines how the Mocamas understood and designed their landscape both by incorporating pre-existing Indigenous monuments and by engineering their built environment. Mocama homelands encompassed the saltmarshes, barrier islands, rivers, and mainland tidewater coast between the St. Johns (FL) and Satilla (GA) rivers of northeast Florida and southeast Georgia (Figure 1). The Mocamas had a well-developed concept of territory and understood their landscape as simultaneously sacred and political. Sand mounds and council houses in particular functioned as gateways linking This World to those Above and Below—the three realms of existence, as the Mocamas understood it. The Mocamas' sacred built architectural spaces were crucial nodes in both internal and external Indigenous networks where people near and far gathered for religious and diplomatic ceremonies and discussions. They were also key markers of sovereign territory. In these places the Mocamas and their ancestors defined who they were, connected with their broader sacred landscape, and confirmed their relationship to their homelands.

Northeast Florida has a deep and complex Indigenous history that remains poorly understood. Prior scholars have often engaged in what historian Jean O'Brien terms "firsting," effacing Indigenous actors, histories, and territoriality in favor of promoting colonial origin stories.[1] Instead, we center the Mocamas in their own histories and stories through our research partnership, combining Ashley's work in Mocama (1450–1600+) and St.

---

1. On the concept of firsting, see Jean M. O'Brien, *Firsting and Lasting: Writing Indians Out of Existence in New England* (Minneapolis: University of Minnesota Press, 2010).

Figure 1. Mocama homeland, and select Mocama towns discussed in this chapter.

Johns II (940–1300) archaeology with Bossy's work in interpreting French and Spanish colonial sources through ethnohistorical and Native American Indigenous Studies methodologies.[2] In this way we capture a fuller picture of the deep history of the Mocamas and their ancestors and situate the intrusions of French and Spanish colonial settlers in a longer and continuous Mocama history.

Focusing on what is often referred to as the "First Coast" makes our work all the more meaningful, for we are reconceptualizing a region that has long been proclaimed as the place where the French established the "first" Protestant colony (1564–65) and the Spanish established the "first" and "oldest

2. Denise I. Bossy and Andrew K. Frank, "Charting a Path toward an Indigenous History of Florida," *Florida Historical Quarterly* 100 (Summer 2021): 1–22.

city" (1565) in the present-day United States.[3] By taking stock of the many centuries of Indigenous history that preceeded these events, we can see that for the Mocamas these experiences fit into a much longer history of religious, political, social, and material encounters and change. We offer three case studies over the past millennium that illustrate how we are thinking about writing the Mocamas' deep history in part through landscape.

MILL COVE COMPLEX (940–1300 C.E.)

The Mocamas' predecessors began to build what archaeologists call the Mill Cove Complex around 940 C.E.[4] Within a century it became a major civic-ceremonial center along the lower St. Johns River, approximately ten miles west of the Atlantic Ocean. Indigenous architects constructed two major sand monuments: a large typical-shaped conical burial mound and another more intricately constructed mortuary monument located 750 yards to the east, respectively called Grant and Shields mounds by archaeologists.[5] Their Indigenous designers created these two mounds to serve as sacred spaces that anchored the community's spiritual views and reinforced their connections with the broader cosmos.[6] Throughout the Southeast, Indigenous communities endowed features of the natural and built landscape with sacred, other-

3. Denise Bossy, "Indigenous Digital Humanities and "Firstings": Situating French-Fort Caroline in Mocama History," *The American Historian* (January 2024): 24–29. Jonathan DeCoster's work is a notable exception to this, "Entangled Borderlands: Europeans and Timucuans in Sixteenth-Century Florida," *Florida Historical Quarterly*, 91 (Winter 2013); "'Aid from the Indians Themselves': Native Rivalries, Spanish Precedent, and French and English Colonialism," *Terrae Incognitae*, 51 (2019): 111–30.

4. Predecessors here should not be taken to mean ancestors in a genealogical sense. The Indigenous population of present-day Northeast Florida had a diverse and dynamic history as a result of episodic migrations and coalescences. Archaeological evidence suggests that around 1450 C.E. Timucua speakers moved south into the Mocama region from modern Southeast Georgia.

5. Keith Ashley, "Early St. Johns II Interaction, Exchange, and Politics: A View from Northeastern Florida," in *Late Prehistoric Florida: Archaeology at the Edge of the Mississippian World*, eds. Keith Ashley and Nancy Marie White (Gainesville: University Press of Florida, 2012), 104–107.

6. A commonly shared cosmology in the Native South during the Mississippian period (ca. 1000–1500+ C.E.) is a cosmos consisting of three intricately conceived levels or worlds, often depicted in art and iconography. The living world of humankind (This or Middle World) balanced the powerful spiritual forces of the sky (Above or Upper World) and under-earth/water (Beneath or Under World) realms. The Above World signaled order, expectedness, perfection, and present time, while the Below World marked disorder, chaos, and future time. See Charles Hudson, *The Southeastern Indians* (Knoxville: University of Tennessee Press, 1976), 122–32.

worldly, and animate qualities. Their monumental constructions in the form of buildings, mounds, and other earthworks often functioned as powerful referents to sacred beliefs and social orders, whereby Indigenous architects imprinted aspects of the cosmos on This World.[7] For them, religion as much as politics guided mound building.[8] Laboring with a conscious plan in mind, residents of Mill Cove engineered an expansive sacred landscape at Shields consisting of a large mortuary mound, a distant pond, and a connecting embankment-lined avenue, unlike anything else in far northeast Florida.[9] Mt. Royal—a contemporaneous St. Johns II center approximately 60 miles to the south along the St. Johns River—also exhibits a novel mound-pond-embankment combination.[10] Both Shields Mound and Mt. Royal appear to have been designed as a bridge between the Above and Below worlds. At Shields, Indigenous engineers transformed a natural sand ridge into a burial mound with a long hook-shaped extension through years of communal construction.[11] From there, they built two closely spaced earthen embankments that ran for hundreds of yards before terminating at the edge of a pond (Figure 2). We can reasonably deduce that the burial mound, which was a resting place for venerated ancestors, symbolized connections to the Above World, whereas the pond embodies a mystic portal to the watery Below World.[12] Because of the

---

7. Cameron B. Wesson, "Mississippian Sacred Landscapes: The View from Alabama," in *Mississippian Towns and Sacred Spaces: Searching for an Architectural Grammar*, eds. R.B. Lewis and C. Stout (Tuscaloosa: University of Alabama Press, 1998), 97–101.

8. David G. Anderson, "Mississippian Beginnings: Multiple Perspectives on Migration, Monumentality, and Religion in the Prehistoric Eastern United States," in Mississippian Beginnings, ed. Gregory D. Wilson (Tuscaloosa: University of Alabama Press, 2020), 301.

9. Ashley, "Early St. Johns II Interaction," 111–15; Keith Ashley and Robert L. Thunen, "St. Johns River Fisher-Hunter-Gatherers: Florida's Connection to Cahokia," *Journal of Archaeological Method and Theory* 27 (2020).

10. Clarence B. Moore, "Certain Sand Mounds of the St. Johns River Florida, Part I," *Journal of the Academy of Natural Sciences of Philadelphia, Second Series* 10 (1894), 18–19; William Bartram, *Travels of William Bartram*, rpt. ed. Mark Van Doren (New York: Dover, 2007), 101–102; Helen G. Cruickshank, ed., *John and William Bartram's America: Selections from the Writings of the Philadelphia Naturalists* (New York: Devin-Adair Co., 1957).

11. Clarence B. Moore, "Certain Sand Mounds of Duval County," *Journal of the Academy of Natural Sciences of Philadelphia, Second Series* 10 (1895), 452–56. Figure 2 adapted from William M. Morgan, *Precolumbian Architecture in the Eastern United States* (Gainesville: University of Florida Press, 1999).

12. Among the Timucuas, the Below World was associated with sacred pollution whose symbols (death, disease, menstrual and childbirth blood) "had the power to alter a person's state of being in bringing them closer to the Under World." Death was a "transformative process" that ritually transitioned an individual from a human member of the

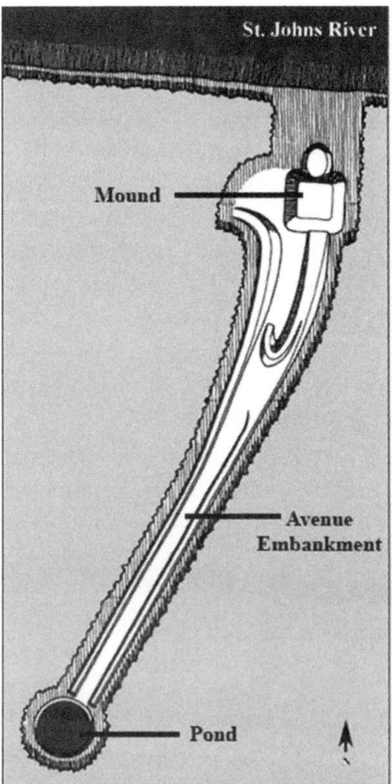

Figure 2. Idealized Shields Mound diagram adapted from CB Moore diagram and description (see Morgan, 1997, 210).

disorienting powers associated with the Below World the pond was intentionally placed at a distance from daily life.[13]

---

community to a venerated ancestor now associated with the Above World. Shields and Grant mounds each housed hundreds of human burials rendering them dwellings of the ancestors and storehouses of memories, with perpetual connections to the Above World. For the Timucua, the physically dead were not socially dead in that the deceased in the form of ancestors were honored, given new kin designations, as they assumed an active presence in the lives of the living. See Tamara Shircliff Spike, "Death and Death Ritual Among the Timucua of Spanish Florida," in *From La Florida to La California: Franciscan Evangelization in the Spanish Borderlands*, eds. Timothy J. Johnson and Gert Melville (Berkley; The Academy of American Franciscan History, 2013), 188; Tamara Spike, "To Make Graver This Sin: Conceptions of Purity and Pollution among the Timucua of Spanish Florida" (Ph.D. diss., Florida State University, 2006), 56–62.

13. Hudson, *The Southeastern Indians,* 130, 133.

Just off the northwest flank of Shields Mound, archaeologists have unearthed deposits of periodic social gatherings, rituals, and feasts that brought together people and objects from nearby settlements and faraway communities.[14] Among the broken pieces of pottery and discarded food remains, revelers deposited whole and fragmented exotica in the form of copper, galena, and stone in this ritual midden, as they did in the Grant and Shields mounds.[15] Most prized were a pair of copper long–nosed god maskettes, biconical ear gauges, and distinctive stone points originating from Cahokia. This urban and cosmopolitan city was located along both sides of the Mississippi River near modern-day St. Louis and thrived between 1050–1350 C.E.[16] Cahokia was but one node in a vast and complex network of religious, economic, and sociopolitical connectivity across Indigenous southeastern and midwestern North America, a broad landscape known to archaeologists today as the Mississippian world (Figure 3). At that time, travelers carried objects significant distances on spiritual journeys, diplomatic and alliance building ventures, pilgrimages, and religious missions.[17]

The movement of people, objects, and ideas across the Mississippian world sparked change and played a role in the tenth century founding of Mill Cove, as groups from the middle St. Johns migrated north to the river mouth. Immigrants to Mill Cove may have selected a naturally prominent landform for siting the Shields Mound because it recalled the massive Archaic period shell monuments upon which they constructed sand burial mounds in their homeland along the middle St. Johns.[18] Builders might also have sculpted the

---

14. Archaeologists refer to this area of the Mill Cove Complex as Kinzey's Knoll, a special event midden that lies about 150 feet northwest of the Shields Mound. It is a roughly oval-shaped shell deposit measuring 100-×-60-feet, with a maximum thickness of three feet.

15. The funerary objects (exotica) from Grant, Shields, Mt. Royal, and other mortuary mounds mentioned in this chapter were excavated in the 1890s, and the authors did not take part in any burial mound excavations. We support the sovereign rights of Indigenous Nations to protect their cultural heritage, including all rights under NAGPRA concerning ancestral remains, funerary objects, sacred objects, and items of cultural patrimony.

16. Timothy R. Pauketat, *Ancient Cahokia and the Mississippians* (Cambridge: Cambridge University Press, 2004).

17. Keith Ashley and Vicki Rolland, "Ritual at the Mill Cove Complex: Realms beyond the River," in *New Histories of pre-Columbian Florida*, eds. Neill J. Wallis and Asa R. Randall (Gainesville: University Press of Florida, 2014), 269–78; Ashley and Thunen, "St. Johns River Fisher-Hunter-Gatherers: Florida's Connection to Cahokia."

18. Keith Ashley, "Moving to Where the River Meets the Sea: Origins of the Mill Cove Complex," in *Reconsidering Mississippian Households and Communities,* eds. Elizabeth Watts Malouchos and Alleen Betzenhause (Tuscaloosa: University of Alabama Press), 193; Asa Randall, *Constructing Histories: Archaic Freshwater Shell Mounds and Social Landscapes of the St. Johns River, Florida* (Gainesville: University Press of Florida, 2015), 172, 256.

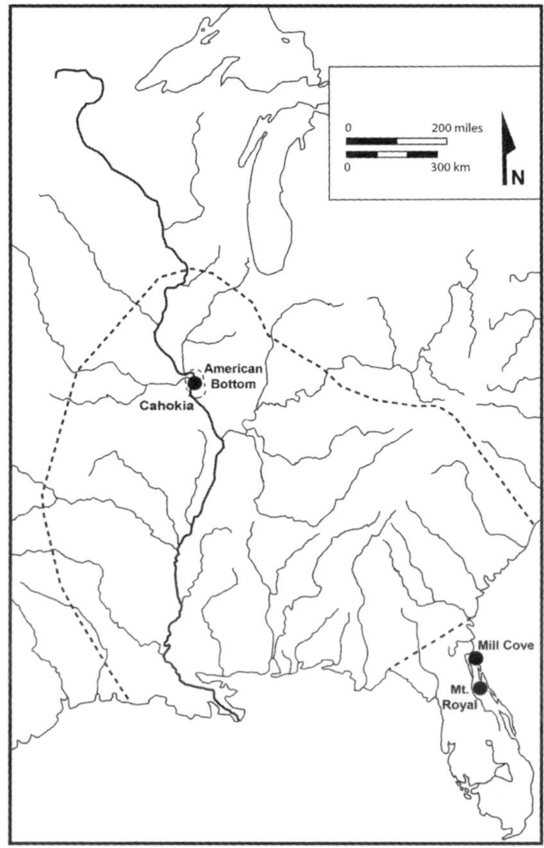

Figure 3. Location of Mill Cove Complex, Mt. Royal, and Cahokia (Mississippian world denoted by dotted line).

natural formation to some extent to make it look more like ancient monuments back home. Through their heightened and broadened interactions spheres the diverse residents of Mill Cove learned of new and differing lifeways, politics, and ideologies that they distilled locally transforming their worldviews, rituals, and built environments.[19]

The Mill Cove Complex is not the only engineered architecture from the St. Johns II period in northeast Florida. On Big Talbot Island, about 12 miles east of Mill Cove and near the mouth of the St. Johns River, new arrivals there

19. Charles Cobb and Michael Nassaney, "Domesticating Self and Society in the Woodland Southeast," in *The Woodland Southeast*, eds. D.G. Anderson and R.C. Mainfort (Tuscaloosa: University of Alabama Press, 2002), 526.

one thousand years ago built a shell ring and surmounting sand burial mound.[20] Measuring nearly 210 feet in diameter and 3 feet in height, this roughly annular shell formation enclosed an area some 100 feet in diameter. Construction of the shell ring began some two thousand years after those of the late Archaic era, including the nearby Rollins Shell Ring, which is among the largest late Archaic shell rings along the Atlantic coast.[21] There seems little doubt that the residents of Grand Shell Ring were keenly aware of this ancient monument and may have used it as inspiration for constructing their own shell ring, as a commemorative reenactment of ancestral practices. Shell debris and other refuse amassed during both daily activities and feasting events may have contributed to the formation of the ring in community promoting practices. This interpretation takes into account the historical past and considers "ritualization of the mundane," where everyday garbage was redefined in ritual contexts and put to special use to reconstruct a past monument.[22] The shell ring at Grand may have served as a "structuring structure," in that its ongoing construction afforded a tangible link to the past that frames and constrains future social action. The shell ring's surmounting sand burial mound confers a heightened aura of sacredness, rendering it more than a mere pile of food refuse.[23]

By the late thirteenth century, the rippling effects of broader geopolitical changes across the Mississippian world altered the landscape and networks of those along the St. Johns River. Mill Cove was largely abandoned but not forgotten.[24] Over the next century and a half, the Indigenous population of northeast Florida displayed a less sedentary trend in settlement marked by increased residential mobility and the discontinuation of burial mound building. By the mid-fifteenth century, the ancestors of the Mocamas began to

---

20. Keith Ashley, "The Grand Shell Ring: Public Architecture Commemorating the Past?," in *Methods, Mounds, and Missions: New Contributions to Florida Archaeology*, eds. Ann S. Cordell and Jeffrey M. Mitchem (Gainesville: University Press of Florida, 2021), 95–121.

21. The heyday of shell ring construction along the Atlantic coast was during the late Archaic period, ca 2000–1000 BCE. For an overview of Rollins Shell Ring, see Rebecca Saunders, "The Stratigraphic Sequence at the Rollins Shell Ring: Implications for Ring Function," *The Florida Anthropologist* 57 (2004).

22. Ian B. McNiven, "Ritualizing Middening Practices," *Journal of Archaeological Method and Theory* 20 (2013): 553.

23. Ashley, "The Grand Shell Ring," 116.

24. Portions of the area's thirteenth-century population may have left the region and headed south, while others stayed and welcomed Timucua allies from the north. See Keith Ashley and Robert Thunen, "Before the Churches: Precontact Mocama History, Culture, and Religion," in *Facing Florida: Essays on Culture and Religion in Early Modern Southeastern North America*, eds. Timothy J. Johnson and Jeffrey M. Burns (Oceanside, CA: The Academy of American Franciscan History, 2021), 191.

revive their use of those ancient burial mounds even as they developed a new type of built architecture: the council house.[25]

MONUMENTS AND FRENCH COLONIALISM

Through both archeological and historical archives, we know that the sixteenth-century Mocama landscape consisted of a dense web of towns, villages, and hamlets. The Mocamas connected their independently governed towns by developing a new political association, a networked polity formed through processes of confederation.[26] To link their towns, the Mocamas built and maintained robust local networks between their settlements through diplomacy, ceremony, exchange, and kinship. The Mocamas did not engage in the same intensity of long-distance networking with Cahokia and other Mississippian polities as their predecessors had centuries earlier. All the same, they preserved the deep historic connections between their region and other Timucua speaking communities along interlocking overland trails and waterways of present-day northern peninsular Florida and southern Georgia (Figure 4). For centuries, the Mocamas' predecessors and Timucuas of modern interior Georgia had a particularly strong relationship. This is evidenced centuries earlier by the presence of pottery imported from the Ocmulgee River Big Bend region at Mill Cove between 940 and 1300 C.E.[27] The Mocamas maintained this network into the seventeenth century. In 1602, for example, Franciscan friars bemoaned the frequent two-way flow of Indigenous people between Mocama and inland Timucua communities in present-day Georgia to visit "friends and relatives."[28] We can also see these relations archaeologically in

25. Ashley and Thunen, "Before the Churches: Precontact Mocama History, Culture, and Religion," 197–99.

26. Jennifer Birch, "Premodern Confederacies: Balancing Strategic Collective Action and Local Autonomy," *Frontiers in Political Science* 4 (February 2022): 1–13.

27. A distinctive cordmarked pottery from the area near the confluence of the Ocmulgee, Oconee, and Altamaha rivers, Georgia, See Keith Ashley, Neill J. Wallis, and Michael D. Glascock, "Forager Interactions on the Edge of the Early Mississippian World: Neutron Activation Analysis of Ocmulgee and St. Johns Pottery," *American Antiquity* 80, no. 2 (2015): 290–94.

28. John H. Hann, A History of the Timucua Indians, and Missions (Gainesville: University Press of Florida, 1996), 155; Baltasar López, "Letter to Blas de Montes, September 15, 1602," Archivo General de Indias (Seville), Santo Domingo 235, Woodberry Lowery Collection, Library of Congress, reel 2, trans. John Hann, Tallahassee, Florida Bureau of Archaeological Research, 3; Francisco Pareja, "Letter to Blas de Montes, September 14, 1602," Archivo General de Indias (Seville), Santo Domingo 235, Woodberry Lowery Collection, Library of Congress, reel 2, trans. John Hann, Tallahassee, Florida Bureau of Archaeological Research, 8.

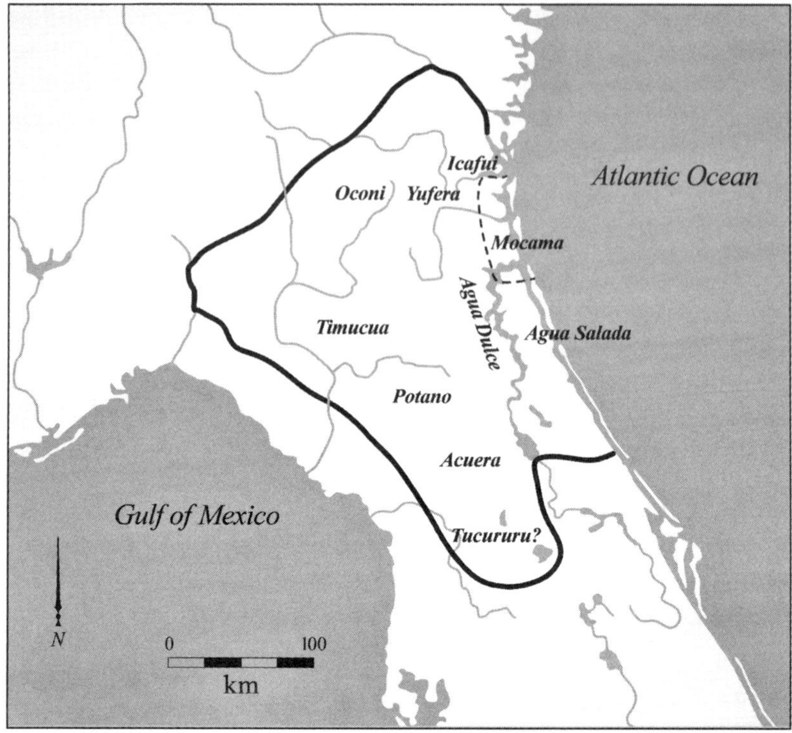

Figure 4. Homeland of Timucua speakers, with location of Timucuan dialects.

the marked similarities in pottery styles between Mocamas, Potanos, and hinterland Timucuas, interconnecting communities across a broad swath of modern northern peninsular Florida and southeast Georgia.[29]

As first the French (1564–65) and then the Spanish (beginning in 1565) tried to establish colonial settlements in the heart of Mocama country, they found themselves struggling to master what remained a profoundly Indigenous landscape defined by both Indigenous networks and sacred spaces. In present-day Jacksonville (Florida), archaeologists have uncovered nearly 100 pieces of Indigenous pottery and burned corn cobs that date to the late fifteenth to early sixteenth century—all of it lying adjacent to Grant Mound,

29. The Mocamas' "San Pedro" pottery type is strikingly similar to the Potano's "Alachua" pottery type in exterior surface decorations, particularly cobmarked styles. See Keith H. Ashley and Vicki L. Rolland, "Grog-Tempered Pottery in the Mocama Province," *The Florida Anthropologist* 50 (1997); Jerald T. Milanich, "The Alachua Tradition of North Central Florida," *Contributions of the Florida State Museum, Anthropology and History* 14 (1971), 29–36.

one of the large monumental sand mounds at the Mill Cove Complex in use between 940 and 1300 C.E.[30] What this tells us is that the Timucua-speaking Mocamas of the sixteenth century intentionally lived in eyesight of what was to them already an ancient religious monument several hundred years old at the time. The sixteenth-century Mocamas did not construct large mortuary monuments themselves. Sometime around 1300 C.E. their predecessors had also stopped building mounds.[31] Yet those mounds—as well as even earlier monumental architecture including late Archaic (2000–1000 B.C.E.) shell rings—remained religiously significant to future generations.

By 1450 C.E. the Mocamas' ancestors began to integrate pre-existing monuments into their own living landscapes.[32] More than a century before the Jesuits and Franciscans attempted to engage their communities, ancestral Mocamas established towns near these ancient sacred centers and interred elites in the ancient burial mounds that already dotted the landscape. For example, the Mocamas built their principal town of Alimacani adjacent to a Woodland period (500–900 C.E.) burial mound in their territory and reused the mound for elite burials likely in the late fifteenth to early sixteenth centuries.[33] By appropriating these earthly expressions of otherworldly or spiritual places that linked This World to the Above World and were also inhabited by ancestral spirits, the Mocamas and their ancestors announced their deep and historic connection to these places—and underscored that those lands were theirs.[34] Thus, by the time that colonizers began to enter Mocama communities in the mid-sixteenth century, the Mocamas had already long engaged in a fascinating revival of burial mound reusage that persisted well into the sixteenth and possibly seventeenth centuries—one that deepened their claims to their territory by grounding it in the sacred, historic, ancient landscape.

---

30. In addition to San Pedro pottery, local residents also have collected more Mocama sherds and fragments of Spanish olive jar near Grant Mound.

31. Ashley and Thunen, "Before the Churches: Precontact Mocama History, Culture, and Religion," 191, 196–97.

32. On Native Southerners' deep and often continuous mound usage to the present see Christina Snyder, "The Once and Future Moundbuilders," *Southern Cultures* 26 (2020): 96–116.

33. Ashley and Thunen, "Before the Churches: Precontact Mocama History, Culture, and Religion," 197–99. This is all the more significant because the Mocamas permitted the Spanish to erect a small mission (San Juan del Puerto) in Alimacani in 1587. Their engagement with their own deep religious past and Spanish Catholicism, we might reasonably conclude, demonstrates that the Mocamas fit Catholicism into their pre-existing religious framework and practices rather than understanding themselves as exclusively Catholic.

34. Ashley and Thunen, "Before the Churches: Precontact Mocama History, Culture, and Religion," 201.

Yet, historians of the French and Spanish contestation over La Florida in the second half of the sixteenth century have largely erased Mocamas from this clash of empires—a clash that occurred in and over Mocama homelands. At the same time, it is worth emphasizing that both the French and Spanish openly acknowledged Mocama territorial sovereignty. They also sought to coopt Mocama lands by erecting their own memorials and adding their own built architecture to the Mocama landscape. The Mocamas so overtly articulated their sovereignty through their landscape practices, military authority, and pronouncements of land ownership that they forced colonizers to recognize their territoriality. In 1564, for example, when the French came a second time into Mocama homelands, they reported that "some chieftains approached our captain and gave him to understand that they were subjects of a certain powerful chief named Satouriwa, whose territory we were in, whose residence was near to us, and who could put into the field so many thousand men."[35] At the time, the town of Saturiwa was the paramount community in the Mocama confederacy. The town's leader—who assumed the name Saturiwa after his community—was the most influential of the Mocamas' many distinct holatacare (chiefs). He further took on the title of parucusi or military commander heightening his status (see Broadwell and Dubcovsky in this volume).[36]

Focusing on the struggle between Mocamas and French settlers in their homelands through the lens of landscape practices reveals how the Mocamas expressed and maintained their territorial sovereignty in the mid-sixteenth century in part through built architecture. In turn, the French engaged in two different forms of architectural marking, as they tried to establish a foothold in Mocama homelands. On both occasions, the Mocamas undermined French claims to their territory by coopting these French colonial demarcations.

In 1562 the French spent just two days in Mocama territory during an exploratory expedition sent to identify a future settlement site. During this brief encounter, the Mocamas kept the French away from their towns, containing them to the mouth of the St. Johns River. The Saturiwas opened their first encounter with the French by appearing in military formation "with bowes and arrows in there hands . . . right souldier like with as warlike a bouldnes as might be."[37] They clearly communicated that the French were now in Mocama territory and that they would defend their people

35. Paul Hulton, ed., "Narrative of Jacques Le Moyne de Morgues," *The Work of Jacques Le Moyne de Morgues: A Huguenot Artist in France, Florida, and England* (London: British Museum Publications Limited, 1977), I: 120.

36. For more on the Timucua language see https://www.webonary.org/timucua/; https://hebuano.wordpress.com/.

37. H.P. Biggard, ed., "Jean Ribault's Discoverye of Terra Florida," *The English Historical Review* 32 (April 1917): 261.

and lands. On their second day in Mocama, the French planted a stone pillar emblazoned with the king's seal near the coastline squarely in Saturiwa homelands. For the French, this pillar laid the foundation of a myth that they now had some rights to what they themselves readily acknowledged was Saturiwa territory.[38]

The Saturiwas, however, interpreted this column very differently. The French pillar fit into the deeper history of their engagement with sacred objects. Like the Cahokian maskettes, the French pillar symbolized Mocama access to spiritually powerful networks that stretched beyond their homelands. This pillar was a gift of what we call spiritual diplomacy, not a colonial symbol of possession. To the Mocamas it communicated that the French recognized Mocama geopolitical authority and honored that with a sacred gift. The pillar's spiritual significance was made more potent by the great distance it had traveled and the regional rarity of the stone from which it was made. The pillar itself thus laid the possibility for a future relationship between the two communities, one grounded in French acknowledgment of Saturiwa territorial sovereignty.[39]

When the French returned in 1564 to request Mocama permission to establish a fortified settlement in their homelands, Parucusi Saturiwa orchestrated a ceremony at the pillar to emphasize the vastness of his domain, the power he wielded through his matrilineage, and his community's interest in opening diplomatic dialogue with the French. Guiding the French to the pillar, Saturiwa showed the French "how far up the [St. Johns] river" ran "the limits of his authority." Using both the built and natural landscape—the pillar and the river—Saturiwa instructed the French of his territorial and political power, telling them to call him "Paracousi Satouriona" and underscoring that his heirs (his sororal nephews and nieces in this matrilineal society) also bore this title. Instrumental to this ceremony was Mocama preparation of the pillar. In keeping with their ritual arrangement and construction of other architectural spaces for diplomatic meetings, the Mocamas had already dressed the

38. Frank Lestrigant, "A Staged Encounter: French Meeting Timucua in Jacques Le Moyne de Morgues," *Journal of Transnational American Studies* 8 (2017): 1–15; Scott D. Juall, "The Columns of (Dis)possession: Totem and Territory in French Colonial Expeditions to Florida (1562–1565)" in *Odysseys: Travel Narratives in French,* ed. Jeanne M. Garane (Boston, Brill, 2017), 16–41.

39. Ribault's language here is sexually suggestive "carrying with us a pillar or column of hard stone, our kings arms graven therein . . . upon a little hill" with "sweet pleasant smelling shrubs, in the middle whereof we planted the first bound or limit of his majesty." Ribault, "Discoverye of Terra Florida," 263. European colonizers frequently twinned the conquest of American territory with the sexual conquest of Indigenous women. John Gilbet McCurdy, "Gender and Violence in Early America," *The Cambridge World History of Violence*, III: 255–73, eds. Robert Antony, Stuart Carroll, and Caroline Dodds Pennock (New York: Cambridge University Press, 2020), 255–73.

pillar with laurel "crowns" (couronnes) and placed small baskets of maize around its base.[40] The Mocamas conventionally used both laurel and palm to build pergolas and seating areas for diplomats during their conferences. Maize was commonly part of feasts organized by Mocama women who played a significant role in fostering peaceful exchanges through hospitality. These were not simply raw materials but served an important function in making the space ready for the discourse to come.[41]

As a result of this diplomatic meeting, the Mocamas initially allowed the French to establish a small military outpost in their territory. The Mocamas understood the French outpost to be what we call a satellite village within Mocama—not a distinct and separate colony, but one under Mocama stewardship, control, and oversight. Indigenous communities across the Native South had long forged closer relationships by permitting outsiders access to their territories. Resident communities allowed groups of foreign Indigenous allies to live among them—sometimes in pre-existing host towns and sometimes in their own settlements within the larger host's territory. Some of those outsiders functioned as ambassadors who bridged their discrete communities by living among their hosts for a period of months or years, others more permanently joined their hosts as new residents who would build kinship ties over time either from their discrete towns or by moving into host communities.[42]

The Mocamas would have understood their relationship with the French as a temporary and primarily military alliance. This is because the French were only capable of establishing a military alliance and did not have the means to establish a functioning society within Mocama. They had sent some three hundred men and only one woman to establish La Caroline; moreover, many of those men were soldiers.[43] The establishment of an almost entirely male satellite

40. The French reported that Saturiwa's "enfants" bore the title of *parucusi*. In this matrilineal society these would have been Saturiwa's nephews and nieces. René de Laudonnière, "L'Histoire notable de la Floride," in *Les Français en Amérique Pendant la Deuxième Moitié de XVI Siècle*, ed. Charles-André Julien (Paris: Presses Universitaires de France, 1958), 88. For the English, see Sarah Lawson, trans., *A Foothold in Florida: L'Histoire notable de la Floride* (Somerset, England: Castle Cary Press, 1992), 50.

41. Le Moyne, "Narrative of Jacques Le Moyne de Morgues," 120; Laudonnière, "L'Histoire notable de la Floride," 52.

42. John H. Blitz and Karl G. Lorenz, "The Early Mississippian Frontier in the Lower Chattahoochee-Apalachicola River Valley," *Southeastern Archaeology* 21 (2012): 125–30; Maureen S. Meyers, "The Role of the Southern Appalachian Mississippian Frontier in the Creation and Maintenance of Chiefly Power," in *Archaeological Perspectives on the Southern Appalachians: A Multiscalar Approach*, eds. Ramie A. Gougeon and Maureen S. Meyers (Knoxville: University of Tennessee Press, 2015), 125–30.

43. John T. McGrath, *The French in Early Florida: In the Eye of the Hurricane* (Gainesville: University Press of Florida, 2000), 98–99.

community within Mocama was uncommon because only women could create lasting kinship ties between different nations in the Mocamas' matrilineal society. But an alliance forged through common military goals was not out of the norm. Indeed, one of the primary factors that linked the many Mocama towns together was their shared commitment to protecting their homelands and to organizing joint military expeditions against common enemies.

To emphasize that the French were subordinate guests in Mocama territory, Parucusi Saturiwa directly oversaw the French, establishing a military treaty and closely monitoring the French construction of a wooden fort in his peoples' territory. The terms of the military alliance were straightforward. The Mocamas expected the French to join them in their war against their "most ancient and natural enemies," the Thimogonas who lived to the southwest, on the middle St. Johns. Their holata was Outina, an especially powerful leader as Broadwell and Dubcovsky examine in the next chapter. In exchange for their military assistance, the Mocamas would permit the French to stay in their territory. Saturiwa enticed the French further to agree to these terms of alliance by reporting that the gold and silver his people wore had been taken by force from the Thimogonas. He proposed to help the French secure this mineral wealth when they joined in Mocama military expeditions against their now common enemies. The French commander reported that he "understood what they wanted" and "promised" French forces would, indeed, accompany the Mocamas on future strikes against the Thimogonas.[44] Parucusi Saturiwa would soon remind the French of "the treaty they had entered into between them" and call on the French to "stand by the terms of the agreement, specifically by proving that he was a friend of the chief's friends and an enemy of his enemies."[45]

Having allowed the French limited access to Mocama territory, Saturiwa closely monitored the French construction of La Caroline, a wooden fort with associated domestic buildings. "[E]very day," Parucusi Saturiwa "sent scouts . . . to see what we were doing," the French reported. Saturiwa also engaged in strategic military displays to emphasize his control over the French. When the French broke ground on their triangular fort, for example, Saturiwa organized a major martial procession to reinforce that the French were on Mocama homelands. He sent an advance guard two hours before his own arrival, "an officer with a hundred and twenty strong men brandishing bows, arrows, clubs, and spears and laden (after the Indian fashion) with their valuable feathers, necklaces of shell, bracelets of fish teeth, girdles of silver balls, pearls on their legs and some with discs of gold, silver, copper on their legs that sounded like little bells." The Mocama officer instructed his men to build a pergola for Saturiwa out of "palms, laurels, mastics, and other aromatic

44. Laudonnière, "L'Histoire notable de la Floride," 93-94.

45. Le Moyne, "Narrative of Jacques Le Moyne de Morgues," 121.

trees" on the ridge where the parucusi could observe "whatever was going on inside our [French] defenses." When Saturiwa himself arrived, he came with a full military escort of seven to eight hundred "strong, hardy, athletic" men "carrying their weapons as they usually do when about to go to war," fifty "youths carrying javelins or spears," "twenty pipers," and his primary religious and political advisors.[46] Through this remarkable military display, Saturiwa communicated Mocama military control over their territory.

La Caroline quickly became a flashpoint of contention, as the French progressively destroyed their relationship with Saturiwa and other Mocama communities. The French lived in a Mocama world, were guests in Mocama territory, and were expected to adhere to the terms of their treaty which recognized the primacy of Mocama political agendas—most notably French consent to provide military aid in the ongoing Mocama war with the Thimogonas. Instead, the French knowingly and deceitfully directly undermined the military aims of their hosts, allying with Outina and the Thimogonas in the belief that this would expand their access to gold and silver resources.[47] As they did so, they also began to cut off Mocama access to the fort by altering the built architecture so that there was just one way into the French fort through an "extremely narrow" guarded "entrance." Saturiwa discovered this, to his surprise, after the French failed to commit troops to a Mocama expedition against the Thimogonas. Heading a Mocama military corps of twelve to fifteen hundred men to forcefully remind the French of the terms of their treaty, Saturiwa was barred from entering La Caroline by French soldiers. Only after reluctantly agreeing to bringing just twenty of his men was Saturiwa granted entry into the fort. Once the parucusi was inside, the French captain orchestrated a military display of his own in a vainglorious attempt to cow Saturiwa; he just further inflamed the situation. Creating a "din" of "drums, trumpets" and cannon firing, the French engaged in a sensorial display intended to "thoroughly" frighten the Mocamas. But Saturiwa stayed put, and yet again reminded the French of their commitment to provide military aid.[48]

The Mocamas were well aware that the French were both violating their military treaty and simultaneously attempting to annex the territory on which La Caroline sat, communicating their intended possession of Mocama lands through their military display. The Mocamas not only claimed the landscape on which La Caroline sat but also had an overlapping claim to the French

---

46. Le Moyne, "Narrative of Jacques Le Moyne de Morgues," 120. Le Moyne claimed the French began construction of La Caroline before agreeing to the treaty with Saturiwa, but Laudonniere's account contradicts this. Laudonnière, "L'Histoire notable de la Floride," 93–94.

47. Laudonnière, "L'Histoire notable de la Floride," 101–104.

48. Le Moyne, "Narrative of Jacques Le Moyne de Morgues," 121–22.

architecture itself. Saturiwa had provided the labor and resources to finish the construction of the fort. For two days, eighty Mocama roofers had woven a palm leaf roof for the French munitions storage facility and likely the surrounding French homes as well.[49] While the French interpreted this Mocama labor as generosity, the Mocamas would have understood this quite differently—as assistance to guests that reinforced Mocama authority over the landscape and built environment. This is evidenced by how Saturiwa had already expressed his territorial sovereignty by using the 1562 French pillar. It is further demonstrated by how the Mocamas more generally responded to French territorial and treaty violations. Most Mocama towns discontinued French access to their food and information networks in a bid to drive the French out of their homelands. The French had broken not only the terms of their specific treaty with Saturiwa (to war with their enemies the Thimogonas/Outina) but also the standard protocols of a satellite diplomatic town in another's territory. They had attempted to annex the territory of their hosts.

By February 1565, the French had irrevocably destroyed their relationships with the Mocamas. They ravaged nearby Indigenous communities for supplies and soon realized that they had no choice but to abandon La Caroline and began to take their fort apart in July, preparing to return to France. Having tried and failed to master Mocama territory through the built environment and political manipulation, the French leader proclaimed, "What I feared most" was "that the Indians would rise against us." To the now starving French, it seemed "that the earth and water fought against us." What they did not recognize was that the "river was less abundant with fish than normal" by Mocama design. The Mocamas had intentionally permitted the French to establish La Caroline in a location without marsh creeks thereby rendering the French dependent on them for food from the start. Despite French efforts to seize part of Mocama territory, this remained an entirely Mocama curated landscape—one they understood, shaped, and claimed. Well before the Spanish arrived to finish off their small military colony, the French had already failed in their effort to transform Mocama into French lands. Despite promising the Mocamas that they would leave the fort and domestic buildings intact, in July 1565 the French began to dismantle La Caroline, destroying "all their houses that were outside the fort," "breaking down the palisade" on the riverbank, and making plans to set fire to the fort when they departed for France. In so doing, they continued to betray their hosts who had reiterated their claim to the built landscape when the French announced they were leaving.[50] When

49. Laudonnière, "L'Histoire notable de la Floride," 98; Le Moyne, "Narrative of Jacques Le Moyne de Morgues," 121.

50. They also claimed a French boat to "make war against their enemies." Laudonnière, "L'Histoire notable de la Floride," 158, 164.

French colonial relief ships and a Spanish armada arrived a month later, they warred over a site that was not French but still squarely in Mocama hands.

Mocama Resiliency: The Council House at the Mocama Town of Sarabay

The Spanish quickly picked up where the French had failed, claiming La Caroline as theirs by right of conquest after defeating the French in an epic battle on September 20, 1565. The Mocamas had wittingly stayed clear of this colonial wrangling, believing the Spanish would simply bring a swifter end to their French problem. Instead, the Spanish established their own fort atop La Caroline, sparking decades of colonial violence as the Mocamas defended their territory. In 1568, for instance, "several hundred Indians" from the Mocama communities of Saturiwa and Tacatacuru assaulted the Spanish fort and seriously wounded the garrison's general before being repelled. They were aided by an unsanctioned corps of Frenchmen who had briefly come to avenge their countrymen. The Spanish subsequently repaired San Mateo and reinforced the fort with an additional fifty soldiers, and the war over Mocama raged on.[51]

By the late 1580s the Spanish had shifted tactics, replacing soldiers with Franciscans on the frontlines of Mocama colonization projects. Seeking respite from the violence, some Mocama holatacare began to build tentative networks to the Spanish. When analyzed from Mocama perspectives, these nascent alliances largely adhered to Indigenous diplomatic protocols and involved gift giving, mutual defense pacts, and the residency of a few Spanish spiritual ambassadors in Indigenous towns who were under the authority of the Indigenous leadership.[52] Among the twenty or so settlements that populated the Mocama homelands of Atlantic coastal northeast Florida and southeast Georgia, at this time, lived just two missionaries. One dwelled in the Mocama town of Alimacani and another in the community of Tacatacuru, and these two friars comprised the total resident Spanish population in the Mocama territory (Figure 1).[53]

51. Eugene Lyon, "Forts Caroline and San Mateo, Vulnerable Outposts." Report submitted to Fort Caroline National Memorial (PX532090219), Jacksonville, FL (1982): 54; Archivo General de Indies [AGI] Patronato 254,5 (14 September 1565).

52. There was also an important religious dimension to these alliances. For more on what we call spiritual diplomacy in La Florida, see Denise I. Bossy, "Spiritual Diplomacy: Reinterpreting the Yamasee Prince's Eighteenth-Century Voyage to England," in *The Yamasee Indians: From Florida to South Carolina*, ed. Bossy (Lincoln: University of Nebraska Press, 2018), 131–62.

53. The Spanish came to refer to Alimacani as mission San Juan del Puerto and Tacatacuru as mission San Pedro de Mocama. At this time, the Spanish garrison community of St. Augustine had a population of less than 200 individuals. See John R. Dunkle,

Archaeological excavations in northeast Florida are helping to piece together how the Mocamas navigated the subsequent intrusion of Spanish Franciscans into their communities beginning in the late sixteenth century.[54] Most relevant to this study, Mocama built landscapes—especially the physical structure of Mocama towns—appear to have remained largely intact. Mocama matrilineages continued to spread out their households across the community's territory, and council houses continued to tether these dispersed matrilineages to a sacred-political zone highlighted by the presence of a council house. These public buildings persisted as indispensable features of Timucua towns and continued to serve as beacons by which social, religious, and political information was publicized within and between towns, at times over great distances. How the Mocamas actually configured their settlements contrasts markedly with how Theodor de Bry mistakenly depicted their towns in a series of engravings published in 1591. De Bry's flawed and overused image of a circular, walled village with a tight huddle of domestic houses and a rectangular council house looks nothing like actual Mocama towns from the period. Yet scholars continue to use the de Bry images, unwittingly perpetuating this visual colonization of Mocama built landscapes in the process.[55]

The endurance of Mocama built landscapes despite Spanish missionization efforts is exemplified by archaeological testing at the Mocama town of Sarabay on the southern end of Big Talbot Island (Florida). Spanish docu-

---

"Population Change as an Element in the Historical Geography of St. Augustine," *Florida Historical Quarterly* 37 (1958): 6.

54. Keith Ashley, "Grafting onto the Native Landscape: The Franciscan Mission System in Northeastern Florida," in *From La Florida to La California: Franciscan Evangelization in the Spanish Borderlands*, eds. Timothy J. Johnson and Gert Melville (Berkeley: The Academy of American Franciscan History, 2013), 154–63; Keith Ashley, "Distribution of Contact and Early Mission Period sites in the Mocama Province," *Florida Anthropologist* 67 (2014): 164–71.

55. The de Bry family printed a series of illustrated books on the Americas, depicting various Indigenous peoples of the Americas. In 1591 Theodor de Bry published 42 engravings on the Timucua, images purportedly based on the lost paintings of Jacque Le Moyne, a French painter and cartographer who spent 15 months at La Caroline in 1564–65. Theodor De Bry never left his workshop in Europe and relied on the writings and sketches of others for inspiration. Archaeologists and historians with a deep understanding of the de Bry engravings and detailed knowledge of the realities and circumstances surrounding their production have convincingly demonstrated that the accuracy of the de Bry images are greatly overestimated. See Christian F. Feest, "Jacques Le Moyne Minus Four," *European Review of Native American Studies* 1 (1988): 33–38; Jerald T. Milanich, "The Devil in the Details," *Archaeology* (May/June 2005): 26–31; William C. Sturtevant, "The Sources for European Imagery of Native Americas," in *New World of Wonders: European Images of the Americas, 1492–1700*, ed. Rachel Doggett (Washington, DC: Folger Shakespeare Library, 1992), 25–33.

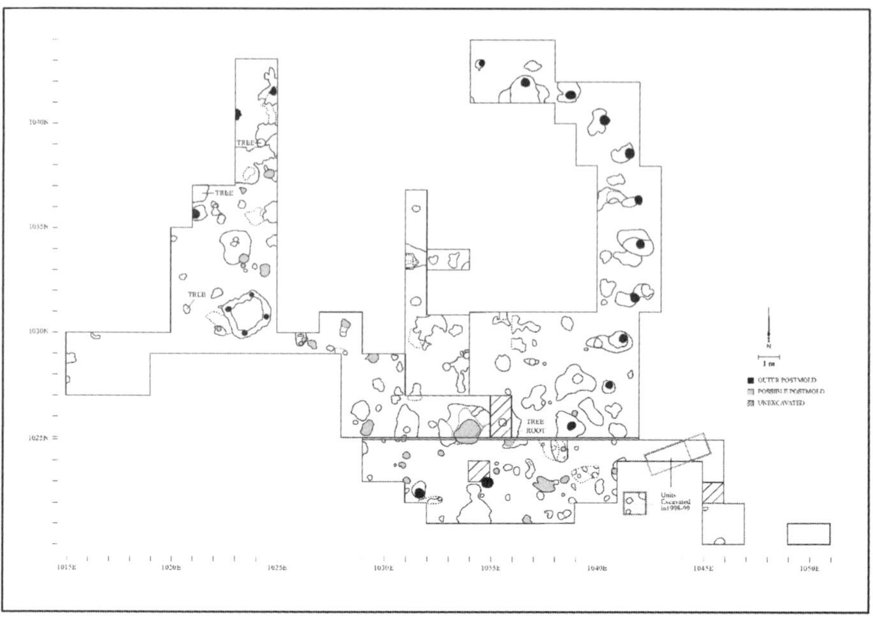

Figure 5. Block C at the Armellino site (Sarabay) showing postmolds outlining potential council house.

ments place Sarabay adjacent to Fort George Island and the Mocama town of Alimacani (San Jun del Puerto) where a lone friar resided between 1587–1702.[56] In the late 1990s archaeologists identified and revealed that this community, like other Mocama settlements, was spread along the island edge, fronting expansive tidal marshes (Figure 1).[57] This broadly dispersed Mocama town layout—tied to a central precinct, housing a council house, plaza, and elite residences—persisted throughout both the French invasion and the more than century long attempt at Spanish missionization. Early French and Spanish writers rarely referred to Sarabay. Yet, ongoing excavations by the University of North Florida (UNF) allow us to fill in this significant archival gap—

56. Pareja, "Letter to Blas de Montes," 7.

57. The importance of Sarabay lies in its history as a Mocama town that thrived during the opening decades (ca. 1580–1620) of Spanish missionization in the Mocama homelands. It is worth noting that the center of Sarabay lies several hundred yards south of the previously discussed Grand Shell Ring. Archaeological excavations at Sarabay or the Armellino site (8DU631) have taken place in 1998–99 and 2020–23. See Keith Ashley, Vicki Rolland, and Robert L. Thunen, "Excavations at the Armellino Site (8DU631): The Proposed Mocama Village and Visita of Sarabay," *Florida Anthropologist*, 69 (2016): 52–54.

offering a porthole into the Sarabay landscape and daily life during the late sixteenth and early seventeenth centuries.

In fall 2020 and summers of 2021 through 2023, UNF students uncovered the outline of a large Indigenous post-in-the-ground building, some 60–70-feet across and circular in shape (Figure 5). The sandy barrier island soils still preserved the mottled soils of large postholes and the darker circular stains of rotted posts (postmolds). Inside the outer ring of posts were additional postmolds and pits of assorted sizes and shapes. One pit, more than 3 feet in diameter and three feet deep, was replete with Indigenous pottery, animal bone (including 5 shark teeth from 3 separate species), and a complete wing of a northern gannet, which laid atop the trash filled pit. Another unusual interior feature was a donut-shaped trench ring about 2 m in diameter that housed four equally spaced postmolds, possibly representing a platform or storage facility. This impressive array of postholes, postmolds, and pits is surely the Sarabay council house, dating to ca. 1580–1620s.[58]

Built of perishable wood and palmetto, documented Timucua council houses were cone shaped with large interior support posts and a floor diameter of 50–80 feet.[59] Encircling the community's central sacred fire—the symbol of the sun in This World—Mocama architects constructed one or two concentric rows of benches. Seventeenth century accounts further describe painted murals and small compartments along the outer inside wall.[60] Council houses, innovative corollaries to the mounds of their predecessors, served as religious and political anchors of their communities. From town centers, council houses and their associated plazas communicated religious and political authority across the landscape of their domain.

Less than 25 yards away from the proposed Sarabay council house is what was presumably a high-status family's residence with wall-trench construction, uncovered by UNF in 1998.[61] Along the inside wall of the house laid a com-

---

58. This date range is based on a combination of radiometric assays, archival information, Indigenous pottery types, and the presence of certain European-made artifacts. The recent recovery of a brass medal of Saint Teresa de Avila, suggests a post-canonization date of 1622. If true, the Sarabay council house would be only the second Indigenous council house to be uncovered by archaeologists in the present state of Florida. The other is the council house of San Luis in present-day Tallahassee, Florida. See Gary N. Shapiro and John H. Hann, "The Documentary Image of the Council Houses of Spanish Florida Tested by Excavations at the Mission San Luis de Talimali," in *Columbian Consequences, Volume II*, ed. David Hurst Thomas (Washington, D.C.: Smithsonian Press, 1990), 518–21.

59. Shapiro and Hann, "The Documentary Image of the Council Houses of Spanish Florida Tested by Excavations at the Mission San Luis de Talimali," 512–13, 521.

60. Shapiro and Hann, "The Documentary Image of the Council Houses of Spanish Florida Tested by Excavations at the Mission San Luis de Talimali," 512.

61. Ashley, Rolland, and Thunen, "Excavations at the Armellino Site," 61–65.

plete San Marcos pot, damaged by eighteenth century plantation-era plowing. Charred corn cobs, numerous fragments of Spanish olive jar, and a brass scabbard tip point to a structure of some importance. An area of little Mocama refuse southwest of the council house probably represents a plaza. The residents of Sarabay included European-produced goods in their materiality, but this does not spell a loss of Mocama identity. Rather it points to their ingenuity in adding new things and foreign (non-local) ideas to existing traditions, a characteristic seen repeatedly in the archaeological record of Indigenous northeast Florida well before the coming of Europeans.

All said, it appears that UNF excavations have unearthed the center of the town of Sarabay. Like other known Mocama communities, Sarabay's religious and political center connected Indigenous households widely dispersed across the southern end of the island. Mocama council houses predated European colonization efforts and continued for more than one-hundred and fifty years after first contact. As much, or perhaps more, attention was given to maintaining the upkeep of council houses as afforded Catholic churches. A case in point is the church at the 1603 town of Tacatacuru (San Pedro de Mocama) that the Mocamas had allowed to fall into great disrepair, seemingly an expression of their ambivalence toward Spanish ritual space.[62] Catholic worship was led by a friar in the church. While council houses were the exclusive domain of Native community members, not the Spanish. Precontact protocols and rituals were enforced, as attendees sat on benches positioned by rank during formal meetings to hold councils. At these closed-door meetings Mocamas surely discussed how to navigate Franciscan colonization, ranging from rejecting those elements of missionization that did not serve the community to engaging in armed warfare against the Spanish. The persistence of Mocama council houses as the primary religious and civic centers of their communities in both the archaeological and documentary records of Indigenous northeast Florida underscore the deep and historic ingenuity of the Mocamas in navigating the challenges posed by religious and political colonialism in part through their built landscapes.

Conclusion

Over the seventeenth century, Mocamas and other Timucua speakers allowed the French and Spanish some access to their landscape and Indigenous-centered networks. Mocamas built architecture, curated environments, and participated in interaction networks that, in turn, shaped the contours of intercultural diplomacy, trade, and Spanish missionization. The presence

62. Governor Gonzalo Méndez de Canço, Visitation of Mocama and Guale, February 1603, Archivo General de Indies, 54-5-9, Mary Ross Papers, folder 46, item 22, 17–19.

of Franciscan missions did not erode the institutional authority of Indigenous council houses as the religious and political centers of their towns, sacred architecture that Mocamas designed and used for religious and diplomatic networking at local and regional scales. Instead, Franciscan friars stood on the literal margins of a dynamic and deep-rooted Indigenous world anchored by built and cultivated landscapes. Throughout the seventeenth century, official visitations to mission towns by Spanish governors or other bureaucrats routinely transpired in town council houses attended by Indigenous leaders and community members in sacred political spaces constructed by the Mocamas to connect This World to the Above World. The Spanish sought to overlay their mission system atop this preexisting Indigenous networked landscape. But even at the supposed height of Spanish missionization, Mocamas and other Indigenous Floridians continued to express their autonomy, to define and make their landscapes their own, and to proclaim their rights to their homelands.

Chapter Two

Who (or What) Is Utina? *Understanding Timucua Names and Titles*

George Aaron Broadwell, *University of Florida*
Alejandra Dubcovsky, *University of California-Riverside*

Spaniards visited *Utina*. Or maybe they met *Utina*. The French did as well. Or did they? Competing evidence for *Utina* the person, *Utina* the place, and *Utina* the town appears in sixteenth- and seventeenth-century Spanish and French records. To make matters more complicated, irregular spelling, mistranslations, and ongoing misunderstandings about the meanings and usages of Timucua words created different and, at times, contradictory notions of what, where, or who *Utina* was. On the surface, confusion over the word *Utina* hardly seems surprising or even noteworthy. It is almost a truism to state that sources produced by European explorers and settlers are riddled with mistakes and incorrect assumptions when it comes to describing Native people. Afterall, as Inga Clendinnen explained, relying on Spanish sources to learn about Native history is complicated because: "Alien soldiers rarely make sensitive ethnographers."[1] Clendinnen's assessment is certainly true for early Florida, where European explorers were far more concerned with recording their own struggles and mandates than with producing "sensitive" or even adequate accounts of Native people. The uncertainty surrounding the meaning of *Utina* seems to reveal little more than the limited understanding Spanish conquistadores and French colonists had of the peoples, places, and languages of early Florida.

But European sources were not the only ones that mention *Utina*. Timucua language materials also make use of this word. In Timucua texts, *Utina*

1. Inga Clendinnen, *Ambivalent Conquests: Maya and Spaniard in Yucatan, 1517–1570*, Cambridge Latin American Studies (Cambridge: Cambridge University Press, 1987), 131.

was neither a person or a place. Instead, this word was connected to Timucua ideas about veneration and worship. By tracing the manifold appearances of the word *Utina* in European sources and then examining its uses and meanings within Timucua language materials, we explore the multivalency underlying this important Native concept. When relying on Timucua language materials and on Timucua's own linguistic logic, the seemingly small question about who or what is *Utina* becomes much larger and opens up new avenues for investigating Timucua ideas and beliefs. Privileging Native knowledge over European confusion requires working with Native language sources and reckoning with all the possibilities as well as ambiguities afforded by these historical materials. The word *Utina,* in all its varieties and with all its potential meanings, shows some of the conceptual frameworks that Timucua people relied on to translate, express, and represent religious beliefs.

Early Spanish Chronicles

One of the earliest, if not the earliest record, of the word *Utina* comes from Hernando de Soto's violent and devastating expedition through the Southeast in 1540. There are three surviving narratives of the expedition, two written and published in Spanish—"Relation of the Island of Florida," by Luys Hernández de Biedma, and "Account of the Northern Conquest and Discovery of Hernando de Soto," by Rodrigo Ranjel—and one published in Portuguese—"The True Relation of the Hardships Suffered by Don Hernando de Soto" by Gentleman from Elvas. There is a fourth, if we include the far more literary rendering from Garcilaso de la Vega's *La Florida del Inca.* Published in Lisbon in 1605, the text appeared forty-five years after the expedition and, though written by someone who had access to many first-hand accounts, Garcilaso had not personally traveled to the region.[2]

The word *Utina* appears as a placename in the accounts of both Rodrigo Ranjel and the Gentleman from Elvas. For Ranjel, *Utina* was a town hardly worth noting. Ranjel, who served as de Soto's secretary, chronicled the expedition's arrival to Potano and explained that the "Indians of that land are very warlike and wild and strong." De Soto's forces then made their way to the town of Utinamocharra, also known as Utinama, but then departed to a much bigger town the Spanish came to call Mala Paz (Bad Peace). Ranjel's account describes in some detail the events that took place in the town of Mala Paz,

2. Other scattered manuscript materials are compiled and translated in Edward C. Moore, Lawrence A. Clayton, and Vernon James Knight's incredibly useful two-volume anthology: *The De Soto Chronicles*, Vol 1 & 2: "The Expedition of Hernando de Soto to North America in 1539–1543" (Tuscaloosa: University of Alabama Press, 1993). See also Doug Henning and Seth Katenkamp, "Language Learning in Pareja's 1614 *Arte*," in this volume, 43–64.

in particular the extraordinary violence with which de Soto's forces retaliated against Native people who did not want to aid or labor for the Spanish expedition.[3] In this context, it is easy to miss the reference to *Utina*. *Utina* was a town or, more precisely, part of a town name, quickly mentioned in Ranjel's narrative and even more quickly rushed through by de Soto's men.

The "Account by a Gentleman from Elvas" includes the word *Utina* in a very similar way. "On the eleventh day of August, in the year 1540," the Elvas narrative reads, "the governor left Cale and went to sleep at a small town called Ytara, the next day at another called Potano, and the third at Utinama. He arrived at another town to which they gave the name Mala Paz."[4] Once again, *Utina* was mentioned by name and, once again, it was described only in passing. Though none of the de Soto chroniclers uttered the word Timucua, it seems clear that the towns and places the Spanish expedition entered were in the Timucua language. For example, around the area of Utinama/Utinamocharra, de Soto's men also visited the towns of Itaraholata, Uriutina, and Cholupaha. These town names contain Timucua words: *holata* means chief and *paha* means house; the suffix *-ma* (at the end of the word *Utina*) is also clearly Timucua. Though it is hard to extract much information from placenames alone, taken together, these towns seem to indicate that de Soto's men were traveling through an area where Timucua was spoken or, at the very least, was utilized for placenames.

The word *Utina* made several other appearances in the narratives of de Soto. Ranjel described how a month after leaving Utinamocharra, the Spanish had met a "principal Indian, who was named Guatutima." He served "as guide, because he said that he knew much of what was farther on and gave very great news about it."[5] Guatutima directed the Spanish forces to "Uriutina, a town of pleasant view and with much food." Neither Ranjel nor any of the other chroniclers commented on this word. Though this Timucua word was repeated often and it formed part of both placenames and proper names, early Spanish sources offer no discussion of its frequency, use, or meaning. These early Spanish texts contain very little reflection on Native words and languages, except for the occasional complaint about the difficulty of

---

3. "Account of the Northern Conquest and Discovery of Hernando de Soto," by Rodrigo Ranjel in *The De Soto Chronicles,* Vol. 1 (Tuscaloosa: University of Alabama Press, 1993), 262–63.

4. "The True Relation of the Hardships Suffered by Don Hernando de Soto" by Gentleman from Elvas, *The De Soto Chronicles,* Vol. 1 (Tuscaloosa: University of Alabama Press, 1993), 66.

5. "Account of the Northern Conquest and Discovery of Hernando de Soto," by Rodrigo Ranjel in *The De Soto Chronicles,* Vol. 1 (Tuscaloosa: University of Alabama Press, 1993), 262–63.

finding reliable guides and translators. Spanish conquistadores did not really understand or particularly care about what the word *Utina* meant.

The Timucua people, unimpressed with de Soto and deeply concerned for his penchant for violence, encouraged the conquistador to travel quickly through their towns and head towards the supposedly wealthier region of Apalachee. Timucua tactics worked and de Soto headed west, convinced that his wealth and glory was just beyond the horizon. But even in his hurried journey, more focused on what was to come than what was before him, the word *Utina* makes a repeated appearance. If de Soto was troubled that *Utina* was the name of a place (or rather the name of several places) and *Utina* was also the name of a person, he kept those concerns to himself. Nonetheless, the slippery usage of the word *Utina* serves as a simple reminder that de Soto's chroniclers were trying to narrate complex Native worlds they did not fully understand and, perhaps even more importantly, did not understand that they did not fully understand.[6]

French Accounts

Jacques le Moyne de Morgues, who was an artist and part of the 1564 French expedition to North America, produced an early map of Florida that contains clear demarcations for a town called *Utina*. Morgues' drawings provide some of the earliest depictions of Native people in Florida, and include many details Morgues observed first hand in the region. But while he depicted *Utina* as a place, other French sources from the sixteenth century argued that *Utina* was a person, and a very important one at that.

In his *L'Histoire Notable de la Floride* published in 1586, René de Laudonnière recounted his experiences and struggles on the Florida coast. Laudonnière participated in three Huguenot expeditions to the region. During the first expedition in 1562 he served as second in command to Jean Ribault; in 1564 he led the expedition and established Fort Caroline, as the French garrison would come to be called; and in his final voyage in 1565, he attempted to resupply the small French colony before Spanish forces led by Pedro Menéndez de Avilés reached the area and challenged French dominion over the region. Laudonnière's efforts in Florida proved short-lived. Violence, hunger, and disease plagued the colony from the start, and relations with nearby Native groups became increasingly bellicose over the colony's short life. Laudonnière's accounts, coupled with the depositions of captured settlers, accounts of escaped soldiers, and a handful of letters and poems that survive from Fort Caroline describe the colony's truly precarious hold on the region

6. Christina Snyder, "The Once and Future Moundbuilders." *Southern Cultures.* 26, no. 2, 2020, 96–116.

Figure 1. Le Moyne's broad triangle version of Florida. Jacques Le Moyne de Morgues, Floridae Americae provinciae recens & exactissima descriptio, 1591. Geography & Map Division, Library of Congress.

and the centrality of Native people—allies and, more importantly, enemies—to the fate of the colony.[7]

Outina first entered French sources as the enemy. Laudonnière heard about Outina from Saturiwa, a leading chief who controlled territory near the mouth of the St. Johns River and present-day Jacksonville. Saturiwa identified Outina as "Thimogoua," a word that possibly hints at the elusive meaning of the word "Timucua," but more immediately sought to convey Saturiwa's relationship to Outina. Saturiwa and Outina were not on friendly terms; Saturiwa described how he "ordinarily made warre upon him [Outina]" and now

7. Jonathan DeCoster, "Entangled Borderlands: Europeans and Timucuans in Sixteenth-Century Florida," *Florida Historical Quarterly* 91, no. 3 (2013): 375–400. Céline Carayon, *Eloquence Embodied: Nonverbal Communication among French & Indigenous Peoples in the Americas* (Williamsburg, Virginia Chapel Hill: Omohundro Institute of Early American History and Culture University of North Carolina Press, 2019), 193–222. Denise I. Bossy and Keith Ashley, "Unearthing Mocama Landscapes, Writing Mocama History," in this volume, 3–26.

Figure 2. Detail of town Utina, in Le Moyne's broad triangle version of Florida. Jacques Le Moyne de Morgues, Floridae Americae provinciae recens & exactissima descriptio, 1591. Geography and Map Division, Library of Congress.

sought French support for his military advances. Though he did not want to offend Saturiwa, Laudonnière could also not risk alienating Outina, described as "a great king," an *holata* (chief), and a *paracoussi*, a Timucua word referring most likely to an important military position/commander.[8]

Laudonnière first tried to use the rivalry of Saturiwa and Outina to his advantage, but the commander of the starved and woefully ill-supplied Fort Caroline soon realized he was in no position to make demands. The French, who had hoped to avoid the dangers and entanglements of inter-Indian politics, soon found their soldiers and weaponry fighting in Outina's battles. Several engravings made by Theodor de Bry in the 1590s commemorate Outina's military prowess. At least four of de Bry's drawings mention Outina by name: "Outina, going at the Head of His Army, Against the Enemy, Consults a Sorcerer on the Event," "Outina, With the Help of the French, Gains a Victory

8. René Goulaine de Laudonnière, *A Notable Historie Containing Foure Voyages made by Certayne French Captaynes Vnto Florida Vvherein the Great Riches and Fruitefulnes of the Countrey with the Maners of the People Hitherto Concealed are Brought to Light, Written all, Sauing the Last, by Monsieur Laudonnière, Who Remained there Himselfe as the French Kings Lieuetenant a Yere and a Quarter: Newly Translated Out of French into English by R.H. in the End Is Added a Large Table for the Better Finding Out the Principall Matters Contayned in this Worke* (Histoire notable de la Floride, Selections) (London: 1587), https://www.proquest.com/books/notable-historie-containing-foure-voyages-made/docview/2240927220/se-2. 26.

over His Enemy Potanou," "Order of March Observed by Outina on a Military Expedition," and "How Outina's Men Treated the Slain of the Enemy."[9]

If the titles of these illustrations make clear that Outina was a savvy political and military leader, their captions leave no doubt:

> When King Satourioua left for war, his soldiers advanced in no particular order, scattered on all sides. On the other hand, his enemy Olata Outina, of whom I have already spoken, and who is considered the king of kings, superior to all others in his number of subjects and his riches, marches with his troops in military formation. He goes alone in the middle of his ranks, painted red. The wings of the army, in the order of march, are composed of young men, the fittest of whom, also painted red, are used as runners and scouts to reconnoiter the enemy troops.[10]

Olata Outina was "the king of kings." In these French sources, the word *Utina* clearly referred to a prominent person.

SPANISH ACCOUNTS

In 1565, Spanish forces returned to Florida. The *adelantado* Menéndez de Avilés attacked Fort Caroline and established San Agustín, a permanent Spanish settlement in La Florida. Though San Agustín was located far from where de Soto and his men had traveled two decades earlier, the words Outina and *Utina* once again flowed back into Spanish sources. And though Laudonnière and Menéndez de Avilés agreed on little, these rival colonial leaders wrote about Outina as a person, not a place. He was the king, chief, *holata*, or *paracoussi* who oversaw a territory east of the Suwannee River, north of the Santa Fe River, and close to the St. Johns River.

The word *Utina* appears and reappears with persistence in Spanish sources in the seventeenth century. As Franciscan missionaries expanded their evangelizing activities from the coastal region into the interior of La Florida, Spanish sources made note of how people from the regions of Potano and *Utina* sought alliance with San Agustín and conversion into the Catholic faith.[11] In these sources Potano and *Utina* were both identified as large areas with size-

---

9. For a good overview and reproductions of all the engravings, see "Theodor de Bry's Engravings of the Timucua," Florida Memory, State Library and Archives of Florida. https://www.floridamemory.com/discover/historical_records/debry/.

10. Theodor de Bry, 1528–1598, *XIV, Order of March Observed by Outina on a Military Expedition*, 1591, State Archives of Florida, Florida Memory. <https://www.floridamemory.com/items/show/294780>, accessed 21 January 2023.

11. John H. Hann, "Summary Guide to Spanish Florida Missions and Visitas. With Churches in the Sixteenth and Seventeenth Centuries," *The Americas* 66, no. 4 (1990): 417–513.

able numbers of Timucua speakers. Timucua people were described as friendly and eager for conversion, especially in contrast to the coastal Guale people who in 1597 expelled and killed five Franciscans in their towns.[12] And though the word "Timucua" first entered European records as spoken by Chief Saturiwa to describe his enemies, it is clear that by the 1600s, the word Timucua was referring to something more than a foe.

In these seventeenth-century Spanish sources, Timucua gradually became the name for both a language and a people and the word *Utina* once again enters into Spanish sources. Andrés de Sotomayor, a soldier in San Agustín, explained that "he knows that there are Christians in the Rio Dulce of which Anlonyco is cacique, and in the villages of Tocoy Julian, and Nyautina."[13] Alonso Sancho Sáez de Mercado and Francisco López, two other Spanish settlers of San Agustín, reiterated many of the details of Sotomayor's 1602 testimony. These men mentioned several Timucua town names that contained the word *Utina*. Almost thirty years later, as Franciscan friars compiled a list of all Timucua missions in the area, they included mention of San Isabel Utinahica. By the early seventeenth century, the word *Utina* could be found in a myriad of Spanish sources; *Utina* referred to a person, a group of people, and was even part of many Timucua placenames.

Utina, as Friar Luis Gerónimo de Oré soon discovered, also meant something more.[14] Friar Oré surveyed the missions in Florida briefly in 1614 and for a longer period in 1616, and around 1618 published *Relación de los mártires que a avido en las provincias de la Florida*, an important text that documented early Franciscan efforts in the region, and in particular focused on the Franciscan struggles with the Guale people. Oré's text also included some descriptions of the nascent Timucua missions in the interior of Florida. Oré praised Timucua loyalty and commitment to the Catholic faith by contrasting it with Guale rebelliousness. The friar recalled how several prominent Timucua chiefs had traveled to San Agustín and had asked for Franciscan missionaries to be sent to their towns.

Oré recorded the speech of these Timucua chiefs:

---

12. For Franciscan expansion into Timucua, see John E. Worth, *The Timucuan Chiefdoms of Spanish Florida, Volume 1: Assimilation* (Gainesville: University of Florida, 1998), 3–43. For Guale, see Francis J. Michael, Kathleen M. Kole, and David Hurst Thomas, *Murder and Martyrdom in Spanish Florida Don Juan and the Guale Uprising of 1597*, American Museum of Natural History Anthropological Papers, vol. 95, 2011.

13. Andrés de Sotomayor, *September 2, 1603*. AGI Santo Domingo, 2533. Cited MS 006: Fernando de Valdés Inquiry (1602), P.K. Yonge Library of Florida History, University of Florida, 76–80.

14. For an overview of Oré and his efforts in Florida, see Noble David Cook and Alexandra Parma Cook, *Luis Gerónimo de Oré: The World of an Andean Franciscan from the Frontiers to the Centers of Power* (Baton Rouge: Louisiana State, 2023), 149–90.

> Father, we have a house for you and a church; come and instruct us for the Christians have already told us it is of prime importance for us to go and see the *Utinama*, who is in heaven above; besides the caciques there, who are most *orobisi*, which means learned, [they] tell us that they have become Christians. We also desire to become such and to be guided by that which they do and say, instructed by you.[15]

The Timucua chiefs were ready to "do and say" as the Franciscan instructed. They were eager to "become Christians." They thus knew it was "of prime importance" that they "go and see the *Utinama*." *Utinama* was not a place. *Utinama* was also not a person. Oré claimed *Utinama* was, if not the Christian version of God, a higher power of sorts. *Utinama* was "in heaven above." It is interesting to note that Oré does not use the Spanish word for God or Jesus. Instead, the friar, who had been born in Peru and had extensive experience producing catechetical works in Aymara and Quechua, leans on a Timucua word to express a Christian concept.[16] For Oré, *Utinama* and *orobisi* (the only other Timucua word included in his writings) were words filled with positive connotations and represented Timucua willingness and capacity—intellectual as well as linguistic—for conversion.[17]

But in Oré's writings, the words *Utinama* and *orobisi* were removed from their Timucua context. Much like the place names de Soto listed or the chief mentioned in the early French and Spanish accounts, the Timucua words in Oré's text were understood only through his concerns and preoccupations. Luckily, sources in European languages are not our only way to grapple with Timucua people, ideas, or language.

Utina in the Timucua Language

Reading the Timucua language has been a long and collaborative endeavor. Until very recently, there was no reliable dictionary or grammar of the Timucua. In collaboration with student volunteers, George Aaron Broadwell has built a corpus of approximately 148,000 words of Timucua. The

15. Luis Jerónimo de Oré, and Maynard J. Geiger, *The Martyrs of Florida (1513–1616),* Franciscan Studies (New York: J. F. Wagner, 1937), 107. Emphasis added.

16. Noble David Cook, "Beyond the martyrs of Florida: The Versatile Career of Luis Gerónimo de Oré." *The Florida Historical Quarterly* 71, no. 2 (1992): 169–87. Giuliana Miranda Larco, "Misiones y Catequesis en el Perú del XVI: Fray Luis Jerónimo De Oré (1554–1630), El Symbolo Catholico Indiano," *Allpanchis* 39 (2007),15–82. For more on Timucua language conversion, see Viviana Díaz Balsera, "The Timucua as Implied Audience in Fr. Gregorio de Movilla's Explicacion de la Doctrina, 1635," in this volume, 99–116.

17. For a parallel discussion in a different context, see Gili Kliger, "Translating God on the Borders of Sovereignty," *The American Historical Review* (2022): 1102–130.

corpus now contains every word recorded in the Timucua language.[18] When we examine the corpus for instances of the word *Utina*, we find that it is most frequently used in combination with the Spanish loanword *Diosi* (God) to form the phrase *Dios(i) Utina*, which means "the venerable Dios." Consider example (a), which includes the Timucua language version in the top line, a linguistic analysis in the second line (which breaks down the meaning of each word or word component), and is followed by a literal translation in English.

a.

Caqi	*Dios*	*Utina,*	*inibiti,*	*nùma*	*yahangala,*	*inemi*
This	God	Utina,	important	heaven	eleven	all

mine	*ayehibuano,*	*hibua-ni-ma*
3:resp	chair	sit-hon:pass-def

This important Dios *Utina*, all the eleven heavens are the chair that he sits on.[19]

While "Dios *Utina*" often appears in Timucua texts to refer to the Christian God, it is unusual to see the Christian God referred to only as *Utina*, without the Spanish word Diosi also included. In contrast, the word Dios/Diosi does appear independently without the word *Utina*. This suggests that for Timucua Christians, the primary way to refer to God was Diosi, with *Utina* added as an additional epithet, comparable to words such as "holy," "venerable," or "all-powerful." Simply put, it does not seem that Timucua people used the word *Utina* by itself to translate the Spanish notion of God—regardless of what Friar Oré detailed in his 1619 writings.

One of the most enlightening passages for understanding the word *Utina* is the portion of Pareja's 1627 *Catecismo* that discusses notions of "idolatry." Consider the following passage (b) that discusses non-Christian worship among Native people in Florida.

b.

Apalachi-co,	*vtina,*	*eyo,*	*oca,*	*can-te-la*	*anoquayaqe*
Apalachee-alter	Utina	other	this	be-tns-dec	Anoquayaqe

18. A working dictionary of the language, based on this corpus, is available at http://timucua.webonary.org.

19. Francisco Pareja, *Catecismo en lengua timuquana y castellana en el qual se instruyen y cathequizan los adultos infieles que an de ser Christianos* (Mexico City: Imprenta de Iuan Ruyz, 1627), 11v. Glossing conventions. The glosses in this chapter use the following abbreviations: 1 = 1st person, 3 = 3rd person, abs = absolutive, alt = alternative, ben = benefactive, caus = causative, cop = copula, dec = declarative, def = definite, desid = desiderative, ds = different subject, erg = ergative, foc = focus, hon = honorific, ins = instrumental, neg = negative, nmlz = nominalizer, part = participial, pass = passive, pl = plural, poss = possessive, pres = present, rem = remote past, resp = respect, top = topical, vsuff = verb suffix of uncertain function.

nan-te *Timuqua-co,* *anoco-mitota-te,* *naquos-ta-qe,*
called-tns Timucua-alter lord-3:pl:poss-foc do:so-part-ds

vti-reqe-ma *hica-reqe-ma,* *vtina* *eyo-cote,*
land-every-def town-every-def Utina other-also

naquoso-ta-qe
do:so-part-ds
'The Apalachees have another *Utina* that is called Anoquayaqe and the Timucua make their lord and every country and every town makes another *Utina*...'[20]

While the Apalachee had one *Utina* (Anoquayaqe), the Timucuas had another. Example (b) suggests that "every country and every town" had their own *Utina*. There were many and different *Utinas.* The Timucua people, as Example (c) shows, used the word *Utina* to refer to their multiple objects of veneration.

c. *Ca,* *inemi-mano,* *ano* *yoqua-reqe* *cumele-so-ta,*
thus all-top person other-every decide-caus-part

ela-co *anoco-mitota,*
sun- lord-3:pl:poss

vtina *chie-ta,* *aparò-ta,...* *Acu-co,* *vtina-le,*
Utina make-part worship-part moon-alter Utina-cop

aparo-ta, *naqua,* *mos-ta-chiqe*
worship-part therefore do-part-conj

chapi-co, *cuiu-co,* *abay-co* *acu* *naqua* *mos-ta*
icon-alter fish-alter manatee-alter this therefore do-part

hachi-qe, *mo-qe* *hachipile-co,* *Utina-la* *mo-qe.*
ceremony-desid say-ds animal-alter Utina-dec say-ds
Furthermore every other person says that the sun is their lord, they prepare *Utina* and worship it, . . . or the moon is *Utina*, and therefore they worship it. They say, the chapi [icon?], the fish, the abay [manatee?] are all [Utina] they believe; they say there should be ceremonies, and they say that an animal is *Utina.*[21]

---

20. Francisco Pareja, *Catecismo en lengua timuquana* (1627), 13r–15v.

21. Francisco Pareja, *Catecismo en lengua timuquana* (1627), 13r–15v. *Abay* and *chapi* are words of uncertain meaning, but probably *abay* means "manatee" and *chapi* means "religious icon." See George Aaron Broadwell, "The Things They Formerly Worshiped: Timucua Christian Texts on Native Worship," in *Facing Florida: Essays in Culture and*

In example (c) *Utina* refers to objects or animals that are venerated. This Timucua example makes clear that *Utina* alluded to non-Christian veneration (though later examples make clear that *Utina* could also be connected to Christian veneration as well). Example (d) offers an important insight into Timucua understanding of this concept. The text contrasts Timucua confessants' earlier veneration practices with their newly adopted Catholic religious practices:

d.

anta-mano	*vtina*	*eyo*	*eten-ta*
earlier-top	Utina	other	adore-part

yno-s-ta-n-chu	*heqe-no*	*Christiano*
work-ben-part-1:sg:erg-rem	now-top	Christian

le-ta	*vtina*	*nocomi*	*aco-na*	*eten-ta-tiyacu*
cop-part	Utina	true	great-1:sg:poss	adore-part-vsuff

chapi-co	*eten-ta-n-tiqua*
icon-alter	adore-part-1:sg:erg-neg

Diosi	*vtina*	*nocomi-ma*	*eten-ta-ni-co.*
God	Utina	true-def	adore-part-1:sg-alter

Previously I adored and worked for other *Utina*; now I am Christian and I adore my great true *Utina*. I do not adore chapi [icons?], but I adore Dios the true *Utina*.[22]

This example makes clear that *Utina* was a general object of worship or veneration. In fact, there were many and "other *Utina*" in the past. But Franciscan missionization had led to an important shift: from the worship of multiple *Utina* in many different places to the adoration of a singular, *nocomi* or "true" *Utina*.

The Meanings of *Utina*

The extensive writing and examples from Timucua language texts make clear that considering *Utina* solely as the personal name of a chief or as the name of a particular territory cannot account for the ways that the word is used in religious contexts. The word *Utina* had a broader meaning, encompassing the application of the word to refer to a particular powerful chief, various towns, the Christian God, and other Native objects of veneration (including trees, ani-

---

Religion in Early Southeastern America, eds. Timothy J. Johnson and Jeffrey M. Burns (Oceanside, CA: Academy of American Franciscan History, 2021), 51–62.

22. Francisco Pareja, *Cathecismo y examen para los que comulgan. En lengua castellana y timuquana* (Mexico City: Imprenta de Iuan Ruyz, 1627), fol. 50r.

mals, and chapi).[23] To understand how these broad definitions of *Utina* actually worked within the Timucua language, we must turn to Timucua grammar.

Like most languages, Timucua distinguishes between proper nouns and common nouns grammatically. One simple distinction between common and proper nouns in Timucua is that whereas the former can have possessive markers, the latter cannot. In Timucua, the first-person plural possessive (our) is shown with either the suffix *-nica* or *-mile*. Consider the examples in (e):

e. nasi-nica
son:in:law-1:pl:poss
Our son-in-law

chito-mile
Head-1:pl:poss
our heads

While the common nouns in this example ("heads" and "son-in-law") can have a possessive suffix, Timucua does not have any examples where the possessive suffix appears on a proper noun. For example, we do not find phrases like *Jesusmile* or *Mariamile,* with hypothetical meanings of "our Jesus" or "our Mary." However, the word *Utina* can have possessive suffixes as shown in example (f).

f. Diosi *Utina*-mile
God *Utina*-1:pl:poss
God our *Utina*[24]

Because only common nouns allow possessive suffixes, this example shows that *Utina* is a common noun. Slightly more complex examples of possessive suffixes attached to the word *Utina* follow similar grammatical rules. In the two examples shown in (g), the honorific morpheme *ano~ani* is contracted onto the beginning of the possessed noun.

g. An-*Utina*-nica
hon-*Utina*-1:pl:poss
Our (honored) *Utina*[25]

---

23. For a parallel discussion of the shifting meaning of the word *teotl* in Nahua, see Louise Burkhart, *The Slippery Earth: Nahua-Christian Moral Dialogue in Sixteenth-Century Mexico* (Tucson: University of Arizona, 1989), 36–42; Camila Townsend, "Burying the White Gods: New Perspectives on the Conquest of Mexico," *The American Historical Review* 108, no. 3 (2003): 659–87.

24. Francisco Pareja, *III Parte del Catecismo, en lengua timuquana y castellana* (Mexico City: Imprenta de Iuan Ruyz, 1628), fol. 49v.

25. Pareja, *III Parte del Catecismo, en lengua timuquana y castellana*, fols. 39v–41v.

An-iti-nica
hon-father-1:pl:poss
Our (honored) father[26]

From the point of view of Timucua grammar, it becomes clear that *Utina* was not a proper noun, and thus not the name of a place or person.

Noun Incorporation in Timucua

An additional argument for the status of *Utina* as a common noun comes from a grammatical feature known as "incorporation." Noun-incorporation involves forming a complex verb unit composed of a verb + noun. English does not have productive noun-incorporation, but one might think of examples like "baby-sit" and "house-hunt" as comparable in structure. As in most languages, Timucua grammar only allows a common noun to be incorporated; names of people or places are never incorporated. Consider the examples of noun incorporation shown in (h) and (i):

h. Cruci-ma na-isi+pesa-ta
Cross-def ins-blood+flow-part
Blood flowing from the Cross[27]

i. Ni-hebano+eca-si-bile-tequa.
1:abs-word+teach-ben-prior-and:so
She taught me (words) and so. . .[28]

In Timucua, *Utina*, like other common nouns, may be incorporated into the verb. When the word *Utina* is incorporated into the verb it generally adds a meaning like "worthy of veneration" to the overall sense of the verb. Consider example (j), which shows *Utina* incorporated into the copula -le meaning "be":

j. Santissima, Trinidad mo-no, Diosi-ma, *Utina*+le-no, ano hapu-ta. . .
most:holy Trinity say-nmlz God-def *Utina*+cop-nmlz person three-part
It is called the Holy Trinity, God being *Utina* [worthy of veneration], is three persons. . .[29]

---

26. Pareja, *III Parte del Catecismo, en lengua timuquana y castellana*, fol. 96r.

27. Francisco Pareja, *Cathecismo y examen para los que comulgan. En lengua castellana y timuquana* (Mexico City: Imprenta de Iuan Ruyz 1627), fol. 217v.

28. Gregorio de Movilla, *Explicacion de la Doctrina que compuso el cardenal Belarmino, por mandado del Señor Papa Clemente 8. Traducida en Lengua Floridana: por el Padre Fr. Gregorio de Movilla* (Mexico: Imprenta de Iuan Ruyz, 1635), fol. 157r.

29. Pareja, *III Parte del Catecismo, en lengua timuquana y castellana*, fol. 22v.

In this example, *Utina* is incorporated into the verb "being" to signify that Diosi (God) should be afforded great respect. Because proper nouns are never incorporated in Timucua (or in any other language), this grammatical evidence strengthens the argument that the word *Utina* is not a proper noun.

Analysis of the grammar and the contexts in which the word appears provides us with a new way to understand the meaning of *Utina*. We claim that the core meaning of this common noun is: "person or thing which is venerable, worthy of worship, or divine." Thus, the Chief *Utina*/Outina mentioned in French and Spanish historical sources was not a chief with *Utina* as a personal name. Instead, Timucua grammar rules suggest that *Utina* was one of his epithets, like chief, *holata*, or *paracoussi*. *Utina* likely signaled the chief's high social position and/or his religious status.

But what about all those *Utina* references as part of town or placenames? The definition of *Utina* as "venerable, worthy of worship, divine" still holds. These placenames with the word *Utina* perhaps allude to a venerable person, animal, or object located at or near that town. We can compare this Timucua practice of placenames with English language placenames like Christchurch or Saratoga Springs. In both of these English examples, the city is named after a notable feature (a church, a mineral springs) that is located in that place.

To further unpack the way the word *Utina* fits into placenames, we return to Timucua grammar. The great majority of Timucua placenames that use the word *Utina* are compounds. The meaning of a Timucua compound is dependent on the order of its elements, and the second element of the compound determines its overall semantics. To see this pattern, consider two examples. *Mucu ibine* means "tears" and it is made of two parts: *mucu* "eye" and *ibine* "water/fluid." The whole compound means literally: "water/fluid of the eye." Because the second element of the compound is *ibine* "water/fluid," the meaning of the entire *mucu ibine* compound refers to a type of fluid and not to a kind of eye. In a similar fashion, the compound *ahanaye* "oak tree" is made up of two parts: *ahano* "acorn" and *aye* "tree." Taken together, the compound refers to a type of tree, and not to a type of acorn.[30]

Thus, in accord with the general properties of compounds, when *Utina* is the second element of the compound placename, the placename narrows down the kind of venerable person or thing located at that place. For example, the placename *Niaautina* is made up of two parts, *nia* "woman" and *Utina*. The meaning of this placename is thus "a place associated with a venerable woman." The placename Uriutina is harder to understand, since we do not know the meaning of *uri*. However, based on Timucua grammar and com-

30. George Aaron Broadwell, *The Timucua Language: A Text-Based Reference Grammar* (Lincoln: University of Nebraska Press, 2024).

pound construction, the placename likely meant "the place associated with a venerable *uri*."

When *Utina* is the first element in a compound placename, the overall compound refers to a place associated with something venerable. Take for example, the placename Utinahica, which is made up of the components *Utina* and *hica* "town." This placename seems to mean "a town associated with a venerable [person, animal, or object]." In a less explicit manner, the placename Utinama is made up of the word *Utina* and the definite suffix *-ma,* "the." The overall meaning of the placename is "a place associated with the venerable [person, animal, or object]." Somewhat obscure to analysis is the placename Utinamocharra. We can identify the first part of this name, but we do not know what *mocharra* means. Thus, the best analysis we can currently provide for this placename is "a place associated with a *mocharra* (which is) a venerable [person, animal, or object]."

Conclusion

In conclusion, *Utina* is a word with complex semantics in Timucua, used to refer to individuals, deities, animals, and objects that are considered worthy of worship or veneration. In the religious texts produced in the context of missionization, *Utina* was primarily used in combination with the word *Diosi* to refer to the Christian God. In the names of people, *Utina* functioned as an epithet for highly venerable individuals. In town names, *Utina* was used metonymically to mean something like "place where a person, animal, or object worthy of worship or veneration is located." By studying Timucua grammar and language, we can conclude that *Utina* was not a proper noun, and thus not likely the name of a person or place in Timucua. And that corrective, while small and specific, speaks to a much larger story of misunderstanding and simplification. By working exclusively with Spanish language materials or English translations, we have missed the complex ways Timucua people have used their language. The word *Utina* was versatile, but it followed clear Timucua grammar rules. Centering Native constructions and usage of their own language gives us insight into the religious and cultural practices of Timucua people in the sixteenth and seventeenth centuries.

Chapter Three

~~The Corrections~~: Language Learning in Pareja's 1614 Arte

Doug Henning, *University of North Florida*
Seth Katenkamp, *Yale University*

Introduction

Speakers of the Timucua language of northeastern Florida first came into intensive contact with the Spanish beginning with the founding of St. Augustine in 1565.[1] It was not until the arrival of the Franciscan missionary Francisco de Pareja, however, about three decades later that the earliest known documentation of this extinct language isolate began. The first stage of Pareja's work with Timucua speakers culminated in 1614 with the partial publication of *Arte y pronunciacion de la lengva timvqvana y castellana*, containing 150 folios of grammatical analysis with sentences extracted from translations of catechistical material into Timucua, as well as a selection of vocabulary. Along with the other ten known texts in Timucua, largely religious in nature, the *Arte* is invaluable as a record of the Native South in the seventeenth century, although it is hampered by the rudimentary linguistic terminology and Eurocentric conceptual apparatus available to Pareja at the time.

Like many of his missionary contemporaries encountering Native North American languages in the early decades of colonization, Pareja was overwhelmed by Timucua's cornucopia of grammatical forms, remarking "although this language is considered barbaric, it is very fecund."[2] Nevertheless, he initially applied a procrustean approach, struggling to squeeze this Southeastern language into a European, explicitly Latinate model, albeit one which he would eventually partly abandon in the process of writing his gram-

1. George Aaron Broadwell, *The Timucua Language: A Text-Based Reference Grammar* (Lincoln: University of Nebraska Press, 2024).

2. "*...aunque esta lengua se tiene por barbara, es muy fecunda*" in Francisco de Pareja. *Catecismo en lengua timuquana y castellana en el qual se instruyen y cathequizan los adultos infieles que an de ser Christianos* (Mexico City: Emprenta de Ioan Ruyz, 1627), f. A, vii.

mar. The *Arte* is a unique, hybrid book consisting of printed pages up to folio 79 and manuscript pages thereafter, and so the process of Pareja learning and reworking his understanding of Timucua grammar is made visible through his corrections, additions, emendations, alterations, and outright excision of entire pages in the manuscript portions of the book.

Why was the printing process interrupted? Did Pareja discover so many errors that he began to write the remainder of the manuscript anew? These and other questions are raised by this document, which is most aptly described by the linguist Albert Gatschet in his review of the 1885 edition as an "extraordinary jumble of rules, exceptions, paradigms, examples thrown out pell-mell in the greatest disorder; not the editors, but the author Pareja himself, is to be held accountable for this disorder, and it will require heroic efforts from future linguists to disentangle the present chaos."[3]

While only scratching the surface of the "enormous complexity" of both Timucua itself and Pareja's approach, this paper, by documenting something of his process learning the language, is a contribution to this effort of disentanglement. We begin in the next section, providing historical context for Pareja's *Arte*, as well as a timeline of its provenance and relevant modern academic work. In the third section, we discuss the medium of both the original manuscript and its 19th century reprinting, including how the recent digitization of the original manuscript has revealed numerous handwritten edits absent from the reprinting. The fourth section then describes the evolution of Pareja's methods as he investigated and documented Timucua grammar, using examples from the text and from Pareja's handwritten corrections.

History of Pareja's *Arte*

The Arte *as genre*

The *Arte* stands out among other Native language grammatical descriptions for the early date of its publication. It is not, however, without forebears: Pareja's work follows in the genre of Spanish colonial *artes* (grammatical descriptions) that began with the Nahuatl *Arte de la lengua mexicana* by de Olmos in 1547.[4] This was soon followed by the *Arte de la lengua mexicana*[5] of Molina and the *Arte mexicana*[6] by Rincon. Several other languages spoken in New Spain received study before the end of the 16th century, including

3. Albert Gatschet, "Linguistic Notes," *The American Antiquarian and Oriental Journal* 8, no. 3, 1886: 186–89.

4. Andrés de Olmos, *Arte de la lengua mexicana* (Mexico: UNAM, 2002 [1547]).

5. Alonso de Molina, *Arte de la lengua mexicana y castellana* (Mexico City: Emprenta de Pedro Ocharte, 1571).

6. Antonio del Rincon, *Arte mexicana* (Mexico City: Emprenta de Pedro Balli, 1595).

Quechua in the *Grammatica o arte de la lengua general de los indios de los reynos del Perú*,[7] Zapotec in the *Arte en lengua zapoteca*,[8] and Otomí in the *Arte de la lengua otomí*.[9] No *arte* was written of Taíno or other Caribbean languages closer to Florida. A grammar and catechism of the nearby Guale language spoken to the north of Timucua territory on the Georgia coast were produced by Jesuit Fr. Domingo Agustín Báez but they have not survived.[10] This leaves Pareja's *Arte* as the earliest extant grammar of a language Indigenous to what is now the United States and Canada.

Outside the Spanish world, the seventeenth century saw other grammars published: John Eliot's *Massachusett Bible*[11] and *The Indian Grammar Begun*,[12] as well as the anonymous *Grammatica huronica*, a description of the Huron-Wendat language usually attributed to Jesuit priest Pierre-Joseph-Marie Chaumonot, who lived in Huronia from 1639 on, and which was the first grammar of an Iroquoian language.[13] These and other grammatical texts of the period understand the structure of the language largely through the lens of a Latinate approach, with its attendant tables of declensions and conjugations. Moreover, these grammars were often followed by other works, particularly in the case of Nahuatl. Materially, the early grammars survive either as handwritten documents or fully printed and published. By contrast, Pareja's *Arte* survives in both printed and manuscript form, which uniquely provides a window into Pareja's process of learning and revision of his grammatical understanding.

Chronology

The circumstances leading to the unfinished state of the *Arte* are evident from the chronology of Timucua studies, inherently linked to the *Arte* as it is

7. Domingo de Santo Tomás, *Grammatica o arte de la lengua general de los indios de los reynos del Peru* (Francisco Fernandez de Cordoua, 1994).

8. Juan de Córdoba, *Arte en lengua zapoteca* (Mexico City: Casa de Pedro Balli, 1578). Available online at https://ticha.haverford.edu/en/arte/.

9. Alonso Urbano, *Arte breve de la lengua otomí*, ed. René Acuña (México: Universidad Nacional Autónoma de México, 1990 [1580]).

10. John Worth, "Guale" in *Handbook of North American Indians, Volume 14: Southeast* (Washington, DC: Smithsonian, 2004), 238.

11. John Eliot, *Mamusee Wunneetapanatamwe Up-Biblum God* [trans. of the Bible into Massachusett] (Cambridge, MA: Marmaduke Johnson, 1663).

12. John Eliot, *The Indian Grammar Begun* (Cambridge, MA: Marmaduke Johnson, 1666; Massachusetts Historical Society Collections Series 2:9, 243–312, 1822).

13. Wouter Mercelis, Andy Peetermans, and Toon Van Hal, "10. Comparing the three extant grammars of Wendat," *Anchored in ink* (2023), 409 passim; Megan Elizabeth, *The Elaboration of Verbal Structure: Wendat (Huron) Verb Morphology* (University of California, Santa Barbara, 2018), 27.

the only known grammar. We discuss first its composition in the colonial era, then provide an account of its rediscovery in the late nineteenth century, and conclude with a brief overview of modern academic work on Timucua and this text in particular.

Colonial Era

Fray Francisco de Pareja was born in an unknown year in Auñón, Guadalajara, Spain, and left for Mexico in 1569 in the company of 32 other Franciscans from Sanlúcar de Barrameda. In the quarter-century between his arrival in Mexico and departure for St. Augustine, he had learned Nahuatl and become familiar with the aforementioned *artes* and others of the genre. It is also possible that Pareja's Timucua catechisms are not his first experience with translating an Indigenous language of the Americas, if, as Luis Resines Llorente has argued, Pareja was the author of the anonymous Nahuatl *Doctrina cristiana muy útil y necesaria* published in Mexico in 1578.[14]

Twenty-five years after his arrival in Mexico, Pareja was sent in 1594 with other missionaries to La Florida among the Guale, before fleeing the 1597 uprising.[15] Around 1600, he relocated to San Juan del Puerto (modern Ft. George Island, Jacksonville) in the Saturiba chiefdom, where he began to learn the local Mocama dialect of Timucua and introduced a common written form of the language for the first time to promote Christian literacy.[16]

The arrival of writing in Timucua Florida was followed by its rapid spread, and Jerónimo de Oré reported that from Pareja's works "many *indio* men and women have easily learned to read in less than two months, and write letters in the language to each other."[17] Early work by Pareja included completing and publishing his first translations of a catechism and an exposition of Christian doctrine, both in 1612, as well as the 1613 *Confessionario*, all three

---

14. Luis Resines Llorente, "Sobre el autor de la Doctrina Christiana," *Nueva época* VII, nos. 1 y 2 (México: Boletín del Instituto de Investigaciones Bibliográficas, 2002): 53–54.

15. Timothy J. Johnson, "A Rediscovered Catechism: Fray Francisco Pareja's Literary Works and the IIII. parte de catechismo en lengua timuquana y castellana en que se trata el modo de oyr missa, y sus ceremonias" in *L'épaisseur du temps: Mélanges offerts à Jacques Dalarun* (Turnhout: Brepols Publishers, 2021), 585, 583–98.

16. Alejandra Dubcovsky and George Aaron Broadwell, "Writing Timucua: Recovering and Interrogating Indigenous Authorship," *Early American Studies* 15, no. 3 (Summer 2017): 420.

17. "*...con facilidad [h]an deprendido muchos indios e indias a leer en menos de dos meses, y escriben cartas en la lengua los unos a los otros*" from Jerónimo de Oré, *Relación de Los Mártires de La Florida Del P. F. Luis Jerónimo de Oré: Estudio Preliminar, Cronología, Edición Modernizada Y Anotada, Y Bibliografía*, ed. Raquel Chang-Rodríguez (Lima: Fondo Editorial de la PUCP, ca. 1619 [2014]), 24v.

of which were mentioned in 1619 by Oré.[18] We know only the years of publication in Mexico City, but not the order or date of composition of these works while in Florida, much less the unnamed Timucua coauthors who performed the translations. It is probable that some or all of these texts were composed soon after his arrival and circulated in shorter manuscript form during literacy and conversion efforts before being compiled for publication.

By 1614, twenty years after his arrival in *La Florida*, Pareja had partially completed publication in Mexico City of his *Arte* to describe the grammar of the language. A *vocabulario* (dictionary) is also mentioned in the sources but has been lost. Soon after the publication of the *Arte*, Pareja was elected as *provincia* of Santa Elena in 1616. Following a lull in his output, the next known catechistic documents appear in publication more than a decade later. It is likely that Pareja's promotion and new responsibilities disrupted his grammatical and catechistical work until that later period.[19] The last known document, the *IIII. Parte del cathecismo*, was published in 1628, the year of his death.

Pareja's *Arte*, however, would never be completed and the book remains unfinished. Although a detailed paleographic study has yet to be conducted, inspection of the majority of the additions and corrections suggests it is in a single hand, that of Fray Pareja himself. Hence, the marginalia may tentatively be attributable to his own re-edition of the text following the printing of the initial 79 folios, as undoubtedly can the subsequent manuscript pages written "in the hand of the author according to Fr. Aix" per the *Arte*'s own overleaf. The exact chronology of these marginalia is unclear though, as they could have been written at any time after printing.

Besides Pareja's work, the only Timucua documents known are two catechisms by Gregorio de Movilla and two letters from 1651 and 1688 written to Spanish authorities. Movilla, writing in the 1630s after Pareja's death, worked to collate and translate more catechisms, with linguistic guidance from six skilled *atiquis* (i.e., translators, from Timucua *tiqi* "ear").[20] However, most of their later efforts have been lost due to a decline in interest in bilingual documents for suspicions of heterodoxy and the decline of the Timucua language itself. The last remaining Timucua speakers within the mission system at St. Augustine evacuated to Guanabacoa in Spanish Cuba upon the English takeover of Florida in 1763.[21] Other Timucuas still living outside the missions

---

18. Jerónimo de Oré, *Relación de Los Mártires de La Florida Del P. F. Luis Jerónimo de Oré*, 24v.

19. Timothy Johnson, personal communication.

20. "*seys Atiquies consumados*" in Gregorio de Movilla. *Explicacion de la doctrina que compuso el Cardenal Belarmino, por mandado del Señor Papa Clemente 8. / Traducida en lengua Floridana* (Mexico City: Imprenta de Iuan Ruyz, 1635), f. 145v.

21. Jerald T. Milanich, *Timucua* (Cambridge, MA: Blackwell, 1996), 212–16.

likely fled westward or to southern Florida, driven down to the Keys by English slaving raids, but the Timucua language itself is thought to have become extinct by the early nineteenth century at the latest.

Modern Era

More than two hundred years passed before another attempt at understanding Timucua grammar was undertaken. By the late nineteenth century, Pareja's early Timucua work was known to scholarship, as was the fact that he had written a grammar to accompany them. Whether it had survived the vicissitudes of the centuries, however, remained unknown until 1881, when an *intéressante épave* ("interesting derelict," in the words of Julien Vinson) surfaced from an old convent on the Iberian Peninsula and was acquired by Charles LeClerc, editor of the *Bibliotheca Americana*.[22] It turned out to be the unique copy of the *Arte* and was presented in Madrid at the *Congrès des américanistes* in 1884 by Vinson. Two years later, Vinson and Lucien Adam edited the text for publication in Paris, and this edition went on to serve as the primary source for late nineteenth and twentieth century descriptions of Timucua by Gatschet, Müller, and Swanton.[23] A rather idiosyncratic grammar and dictionary based on the *Arte* and Swanton's notes were published by Julian Granberry in 1993,[24] but comprehensive study of Timucua would await the development by George Aaron Broadwell of a digitized Timucua language corpus in 2008 using Fieldworks Language Explorer (FLEx). This corpus contains all attested Timucua texts encompassing 148,000 words[25] and development continues today. It also serves as the basis for Broadwell's reference grammar.

Spurred by the compilation of this corpus, Timucua studies have continued to accelerate in recent years. In 2019, the previously unknown *IIII.*[26] *Parte del cathecismo* was rediscovered by Timothy Johnson of Flagler College, the

22. Francisco de Pareja, *Arte de la lengua timuquana, compuesto en 1614 por el padre Francisco Pareja, y publicado conforme al ejemplar original único*, eds. Lucien Adam and Julien Vinson (Paris: Maisonneuve Frères et Ch. Leclerc, 1886), v.

23. Albert S. Gatschet, "The Timucua Language," *Proceedings of the American Philosophical Society Held at Philadelphia for Promoting Useful Knowledge,* 17 (1878): 465–502; Friedrich Müller, "Die Sprache der Timukua," in *Grundriss der Sprachwissenschaft* (Wien: A. Hölder, 1876–88); John R. Swanton, "Terms of Relationship in Timucua," in *Anthropological Essays Presented to William Henry Holmes* (Washington, DC: J.W. Bryan Press, 1916), 451–63.

24. Julian Granberry, *A Grammar and Dictionary of the Timucua Language* (Tuscaloosa: University of Alabama Press, 1993).

25. George Aaron Broadwell & Alejandra Dubcovsky, "Hearing a Faint Voice: Timucua Words in a Catholic Miracle Story," *The New American Antiquarian 1* (Fall 2022): 21.

26. Broadwell, *The Timucua Language*, 2024.

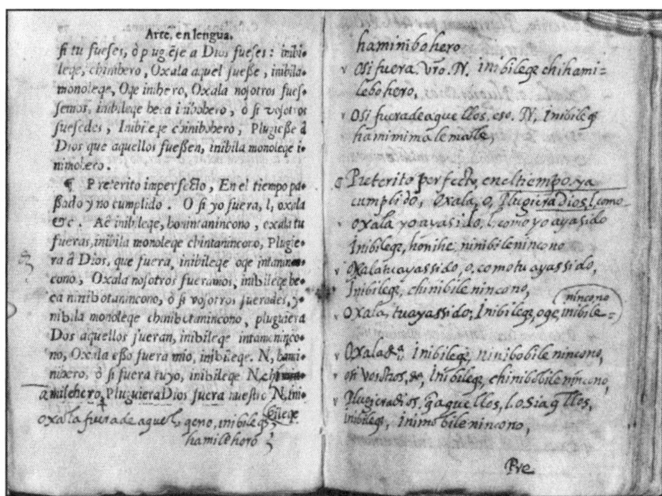
Arte, en lengua.
si tu fueses, ò plugèse a Dios fueses: inibileqe, chimbero, Oxala aquel fuesse, inibilamonoleqe, Oqe inibero, Oxala nosotros fuessemos, inibileqe beca inibobero, ò si vosotros fuesedes, Inibileqe chinibobero, Plugiesse â Dios que aquellos fuessen, inibila monoleqe inimolero.

¶ Preterito imperfecto, En el tiempo passado y no cumplido. O si yo fuera, l, oxala &c. Ac inibileqe, bonintanincono, oxala tu fueras, inibila monoleqe chintanincono, Plugiera â Dios, que fuera, inibileqe oqe intanincono, Oxala nosotros fueramos, inibileqe beca ninibotanincono, ò si vosotros fuerades, ynibila monoleqe chinibotanincono, pluguiera Dos aquellos fueran, inibileqe intamenincono, Oxala esso fuera mio, inibileqe. N, baminicero, ò si fuera tuyo, inibileqe N. chi... amilehero, Pluguiera Dios fuera nuestro N. ini...

Figure 1. *Arte*, f. 79r–80v.

first new Timucua text since the nineteenth century, expanding the corpus further. In 2020, Alejandra Dubcovsky and Broadwell began the Hebuano Project to develop a website with Timucua language lessons and engage in community outreach.[27] Also in 2022, the complete *Arte* manuscript was digitized by the New York Public Library, for the first time allowing scholarly access to this work in a high-quality format and providing the impetus for our study.[28]

MEDIUM

A hybrid manuscript

The sole surviving copy of the *Arte* is a document of mixed type, both manuscript and print: 79 folios of printed text end abruptly mid-word on the verso (Figure 1). At the bottom of this page, there is one handwritten line, and the text continues entirely handwritten on the next page until the end of the manuscript. In addition, both parts of the manuscript have handwritten edits made in the form of notes in the margins, lines crossing out portions of the text, and so on.

27. Alejandra Dubcovsky, George Aaron Broadwell, et al. Hebuano: A Timucua Language Resource Guide. Accessed 27 May 2024, http://www.hebuano.com/.

28. As of this writing, the *Arte* manuscript held by the New York Public Library is not currently online at the NYPL Digital Collections website (https://digitalcollections.nypl.org/). We hope this will change soon.

In the manuscript passages, the formatting is structured less linearly than the printed portion. Presumably, Pareja's handwritten originals of the printed pages, when submitted to the printers, also had a similar appearance. There are sets of examples with two columns (for Spanish and Timucua) and other data laid out in tables that would have likely been rendered more straightforwardly if printed.

Both sections of the manuscript require difficult interpretive work on the part of the reader. While early pages aspire towards a hierarchical information structure (chapters with apparent subsections, etc.), all of this structure is absent from most of the text, making shifts in topic difficult to track. For example, Pareja generally explains a specific verb tense with a section header naming the tense—that is, *Preterito plus quamperfecto* (*Arte* f100)—followed by example sentences in Spanish and Timucua for each of the six person/number combinations in Spanish (*yo, tu, el/ella, nosotros, vosotros,* and *ellos/ellas*). This scheme is complicated by the fact that very often multiple Timucua sentences or parts of sentences are listed together, without indication of whether there is a difference in meaning between them, or even where one example starts and another ends. Consider the following:

1) *Quien lo dixo, Chitacoste, l, taco ise, l, iste?* (*Arte*, f. 068v)

In this quotation and others that follow, the printed abbreviation < l, > used by Pareja stands for Latin *vel* "or," derived from a medieval use of barred lowercase < ł > for the same.[29] Thus, we are presented here with three possible translations for the Spanish *Quien lo dixo* 'Who said it?,' which appear to be (1) *chitacoste*, (2) *taco ise*, and (3) *iste*. However, if we look at glosses of these three options, this appears to not be the case.

2) Glosses for Timucua translations of *Quien lo dixo*

a) *chitacoste*			b) *taco ise*			c) *iste*	
chitaco	*isi*	*-te*	*taco*	*isi*	*-e*	*isi*	*-te*
who	say	-tns	who	say	-?	say	-tns
'who says'	'who says'		'says'				

We can see here that the first two indeed appear to be full alternants, but the third alternant, *iste*, seems only to be a substitute for the second word in the sentence. Thus, the three possible translations are meant to be (1) *chitacoste*, (2)[*chi*]*taco ise*, and (3) [*chitaco*] *iste*. Such abbreviated sequences of synonymous forms are very frequent throughout the *Arte* and must be parsed with care.

29. Adriano Cappelli, *The Elements of Abbreviation in Medieval Latin Paleography* (Lawrence: University of Kansas Libraries, 1982), 19.

Additionally, the examples used by Pareja derive from a variety of sources. Searching through the digitized corpus, it is clear that some were taken from the translated doctrinal material Pareja was producing, but the precise authorship of these translations is unclear. Pareja likely used several different Timucua consultants, but the dynamics between him and these unnamed Native consultants are undocumented. Additionally, there are other words and clauses in the *Arte* that seem to be entirely artificial, created by Pareja *de novo* to explain the various grammatical points he was trying to make.

Pulling examples out of their original context in corpora, as with any loss of context, can result in misunderstanding. The situation is exacerbated by the nature of Timucua grammar, which, as is typical for Southeastern languages, often delays subject marking until the end of a discourse. As a result, the corpus contains many long sentences, from which Pareja often extracted his demonstrations of grammatical features. Unfortunately, it is often quite difficult to discern which noun in a sentence is the subject or object of a particular verb, even in complete Timucua sentences much less in mere fragments of a larger whole. These characteristics of Timucua, combined with Pareja's imperfect understanding of the translations, mean that example sentences were usually quoted and analyzed without significant contextual information that would affect the form and interpretation of the words. The loss of such context obfuscates the relationship between specific words and their translated meanings. Altogether these conventions, maintained throughout the *Arte*, make interpreting the data and evaluating the validity of Pareja's descriptions of Timucua grammar difficult for the modern scholar.

Comparing the original with the Adam and Vinson (1886) edition

The recent addition of the scanned text of the *Arte* to the Timucua corpus allows for a more fine-grained analysis of the edits made in Pareja's hand,[30] providing a window into his changing thinking. There are numerous instances of marginalia and changes in the printed text that were omitted in Adam and Vinson's edition. These emendations often reveal something of the limits to Pareja's understanding of Timucua, as in the example below:

inih[o]nti niniha > ninihanti l, niniha
No sea yo
"Let me not be" (f. 78r)

30. In Vinson's introduction, he claims to identify, in the corrections to printed editions "annotations of two or three hands" ("*des annotations de deux ou trois mains*"), associating them with the various owners of the book. Direct retranslations resembling the style of the manuscript portion are tentatively assumed to be in Pareja's hand. However, this requires further paleographic confirmation.

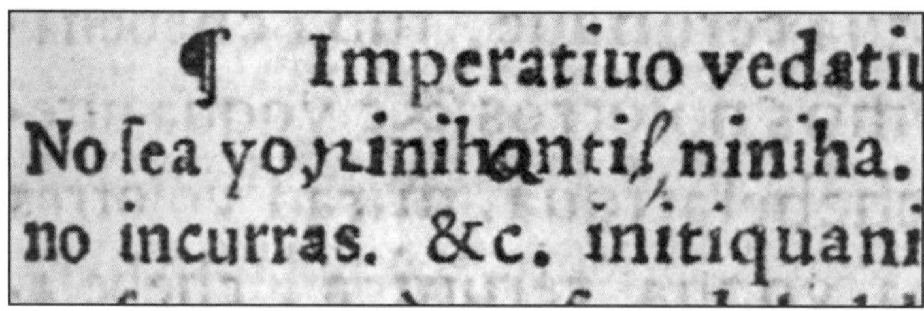

¶ Imperatiuo vedati
No ſea yo, ninihanti, l, niniha.
no incurras. &c. initiquani

Figure 2. *Arte* f. 78r.

Both words are given the same translation in the subjunctive mood, reflecting the lack of the Timucua declarative suffix *-la*. In the first printed sentence, *inihonti* has been corrected to *inihanti* and the first-person prefix *n-* has been added before the verb *ini*. The abbreviation *l*, has also been inserted to indicate that *niniha* is an alternative translation, perhaps intended to be read with the negative suffix *-ti*. From our understanding of the full Timucua corpus, we now know that a first-person marker *n(i)-* can variously precede or follow the verb in different sentence contexts, so that verbs suffixed with *-hanti* are better analyzed as *-ha* "future" + *-n* "first person" + *-ti* "negative." This means Pareja's edited sentence includes the first person in both pronoun slots! Effectively, he gave the following as translations: "Let I not be me" and "Let me (not) be"—which may not have been quite grammatical for speakers of Timucua.

As another illustration, consider the following sentence from a section about the particle *qere* used for emphasis and encouragement: *qerena guehasi* in the printed text. Previously, we had speculated that this was to be read as *qere* followed by a shortened form of *naquene*, a common verb that functions as an emphatic form of "to be." However, upon examining the annotations, we found that he reorganized the separation of the words, adding a comma, tilde, overline, and joiner, though he did not amend *gu-* to *qu-*:

3) qere, nã guehasi (f7r)
Assi sera mañana
"Thus it will be tomorrow."

Modern interpretation:

qere	*naquen(e)*	*-hasi*
exhortative	be:thus	-future:emphatic

This analysis not only better matches the given translation but also the segmentation given by Pareja's edits to the printed words. In this way, the ability to see Pareja's marginalia and corrections allows us to confirm or disconfirm our interpretations of his writings and Timucua grammar.

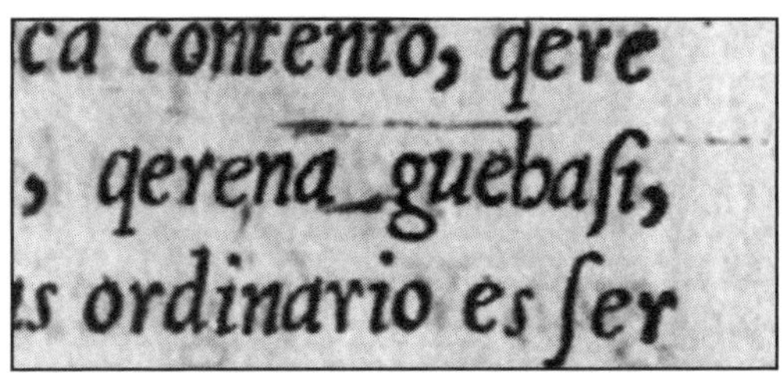

ca contento, qere
, qerena guebaſi,
s ordinario es ſer

Figure 3. *Arte* f. 7r.

EVOLUTION OF PAREJA'S APPROACH

Through the marginalia, we can also discern the overall trajectory of Pareja's approach, from one which closely adheres to the philosophy of language pedagogy in early modern Europe to one which is more dexterous and descriptive. To begin, we will describe more thoroughly the features of the "Latinate" grammatical template mentioned throughout this paper. Then, we will give an instance of Pareja realizing that at least one structure common to many Romance languages cannot be extended to Timucua, followed by a discussion of Pareja's analyses of Timucua verbal morphology and their progressive deviation from the Latinate model. We will then conclude by outlining the types of limitations to Pareja's work that remain, even after relinquishing that model.

The Latinate model

One of the most conspicuous failures of Pareja's Latinate model is its pervasive assumption of case marking. Unlike Latin, Timucua does not use case to indicate a noun's role in the sentence. Neither does Spanish, but the grammatical descriptions that Pareja most was familiar with were descriptions of Latin and Greek, which have extensive case-marking systems in multiple declensions, as well as other *artes* that had mistakenly applied case interpretations to Native languages. Like the writers of his model grammars, Pareja initially assumed that this was the appropriate way to describe grammar and tried to fit Timucua morphology into a Latinate declension.

4) An example of Timucua's supposed "case" system (adapted from f. 027r)

Case	Spanish phrase	Timucua translation		
Nom[inative]	*La casa de v.m.*[31]	*paha mitonoma*		
		paha	mitono	-ma
		house	2:poss:hon	-def
	'Your Mercy's house'	'your (honored) house'		

31. *v.m.* = *vuestra merced* "Your Mercy"

Gen[itive]	*De casa de v.m.*	*paha mitonomasi*
		paha mitono -ma -si
		house 2:poss:hon -def -emphasis
	'of Your Mercy's house'	'for your (honored) house'
Dat[ive]	*Para la casa de v.m.*	*paha mitonomabeta*
		paha mitono -ma -beta
		house 2:poss:hon -def -oblique
	'for Your Mercy's house'	'at/to your (honored) house'
Acc[usative]	*Su casa de v.m.*	*paha mitonoma*
		paha mitono -ma
		house 2:poss:hon -def
	'Your Mercy's house'	'your (honored) house'
Voc[ative]	*ò, l, â la casa de v.m.*	*paha mitonolechu*
		paha mitono -lechu
		house 2:poss:hon -pejorative
	'oh, Your Mercy's house!'	'your (honored) unfortunate house!'
Abl[ative]	*En casa de v.m.*	*paha mitonomaqua*
		paha mitono -ma -qua
		house 2:poss:hon -def -loc
	'in Your Mercy's house'	'at your (honored) house'

Another aspect of Pareja's Latinate approach appears in the verbal system. The prototypical use of Latin *amare* "to love" (and its descendants, such as Spanish *amar*) as an example verb inspires the use of *hubuaso* "to love" and *ho* + *mani* "to love, to desire much" in order to explain Timucua "conjugations" in three persons, singular and plural.[32] Molina's Nahuatl grammar likewise uses *tlazotla* "to love" as the primary example verb, and this may also have influenced his choice.[33] Pareja's preliminary adherence to the model of Latin and Greek, as in the other *artes*, leads him into trouble, due to the default assumption that the Timucua verbal system functions similarly to Latin and can be conjugated in the same manner.

A brief example

Now, let us turn to the section on "infinitival constructions," where the assumption of a Latinate framework causes Pareja some difficulties. He identifies

32. His choice of two primary love verbs for demonstrating the grammar of Timucua was potentially influenced not only by similar contrast in Spanish but also perhaps the Pseudo-Dionysian contrast between ἀγάπη (*hubuaso* "cause to be loved") and ἔρως (*ho* + *mani* "greatly desire"). See Timothy Johnson, "Eros, Ministry, and Motherhood: The Gendered Landscape of Franciscan Evangelization," in this volume, 77–97.

33. Molina, *Arte de la lengua mexicana*, f. 26v.

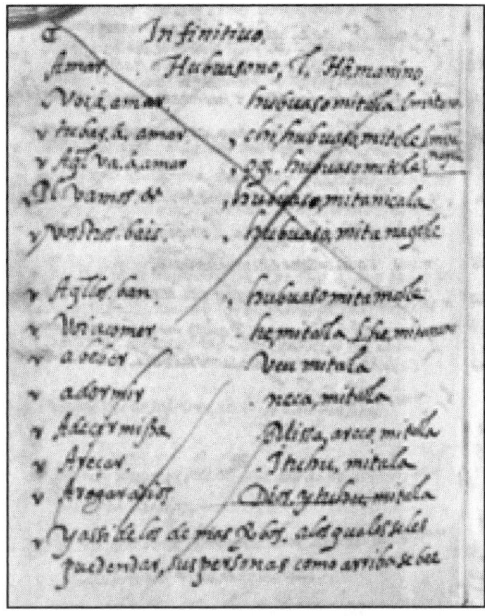

Figure 4. *Arte*, f. 105v.

a verb stem followed by the suffix *-no*, which we now analyze as a nominalizing suffix, as the "infinitive" in Timucua. Then, in folio 105v, Pareja tries composing Timucua sentences using what is a typical infinitival construction in Spanish: *ir a*… "to go to" when representing a future event (e.g., *voy a comprar un refresco* "I am going to buy a soda," with the reading that it is something I will do in the future, and not that there will necessarily be literal ambulation).

Consider the first Spanish-Timucua pair from Pareja's table on f. 105v:

5)	Spanish:				~Timucua:			
	voi a amar				*hubuaso mitala*			
	voy	a	am	-ar	hubuaso	mi	-ta	-la
	go.1s.pres	to	love	-inf	love	go	-pres.1s	-dec
	'I will love'				'I go (away) and love'			

There are two important problems with this Timucua datum. Firstly, it does not contain the expected "infinitival" form: instead of *hubuaso-no*, we have only a bare *hubuaso.* This is the case for all of the translations in this table; after the initial isolated "Hubuasono l. hômaníno" for 'amar,' the *-no* suffix is conspicuously absent. In spite of this, Pareja transcribes a translation for *ir a amar* for each person-number combination in Spanish and then tries the structure with six different verbs in the third person plural (the Spanish translations all beginning with "*Aqllos ban*…").

Secondly, though only the modern gloss reveals this, the Timucua sentence probably does not mean the same thing as the Spanish. While Spanish permits an idiomatic reading of the verb *ir* "to go" to mean that an event will take place in the future, we have no evidence that Timucua permits such a reading. In spite of the fact that *mitala* or *mitele* is the form of the Timucua verb *mi* "go" used in this table, it is rare elsewhere. Within the *Arte* there are twenty-six instances of *mitala* and *mitele* (eight of which are in the table in f. 105v) while there are only thirteen in the rest of the corpus, even though the rest of the corpus is more than fourteen times larger than the *Arte*.

6) Distribution of *mitala/mitele*

	total words in corpus	hits for *mitala/mitele*
Arte	9,372	26
non-*Arte* texts	137,119	13

Of the non-*Arte* instances of *mitala/mitele*, none seem to have a future reading; *mi* suffixed to another verb instead indicates motion away from the speaker. Given the rarity of this particular construction, combined with the fact that it does not seem to have been used to convey the idea of future action, it seems likely that the verb presented in Image 4 above is not a natural Timucua structure. It may not have been categorically ungrammatical to speakers, which is perhaps why Pareja wrote it down, but but he likely discovered eventually that this was not how native speakers of the language expressed the idea of future action, which is why this entire page is crossed out in the handwritten pages of the *Arte*.

The example of the false infinitival structure shows Pareja's capacity to go back and reflect on the quality of his documentation, but his long journey towards understanding person and tense marking in verbs best exhibits the process by which his documentary methodology evolved.

A less brief example

In most Indo-European languages, several features of the verb are conveyed through a simple morpheme (the verb "ending"). For example, in the Spanish *hablo*, the *-o* conveys present tense, indicative mood, and first-person singular subject marking. Typologically, this is known as fusional morphology. In other languages such as Timucua, however, these different features are separated, with each feature conveyed through its own separate morpheme, a language typology known as agglutinative, following Wilhelm von Humboldt and Edward Sapir. Additionally, there are often idiosyncrasies in the phonology or orthography of forms due to historical processes. Consider the examples below:

7)	infinitive		example of inflection	
"regular" verb:	*hablar*		*hablé*	
	habl	-ar	habl	-é
	speak	-inf	speak	-1s.pret.ind
orthographic alternation:	*electrificar*		*electrifiqué*	
	electrific	-ar	electrific	-é
	electrify	-inf	electrify	-1s.pret.ind
phonological irregularity:	***salir***		***saldré***	
	sal	-ir	**saldré**	-é
	leave	-inf	leave.fut	-1s.fut.ind

Because of these idiosyncrasies, centuries of learners have found it useful to separate verbs with slightly different inflectional paradigms into classes and to study, recite, and document them in tables showing each combination of tense and person/number. Thus, in the process of learning how to conjugate regular Latin verbs of the "first conjugation" (those with a theme vowel /a/), one might be presented with the following:

8) Present tense first conjugation in Latin, reproduced from D'Ooge.[34]

		amāre	(love)	monēre	(advise)
sing. {	1.	amō	I love	moneō	I advise
	2.	amās	you love	monēs	you advise
	3.	amat	he (she, it) loves	monet	he (she, it) advises
pl. {	1.	amāmus	we love	monēmus	we advise
	2.	amātis	you love	monētis	you advise
	3.	amant	they love	monent	they advise

This table describes the verb inflections for the present active indicative tense. A student would traditionally memorize its contents and then, if using D'Ooge's textbook or another like it, proceed to the tables for the imperfect active indicative, the future active indicative, and so on. Early on, Pareja's descriptions of Timucua verb inflection are evocative of these conjugation paradigms and the pedagogical philosophy behind them. However, Timucua verbs are not inflected like Indo-European verbs. Each feature is represented with its own affix, phonological irregularity is rare (if extant), and the meanings of affixes often do not map well to the features of European languages, which could be described and taught similarly to one another because they are mostly historically related and exhibit isomorphic idiosyncrasies. Thus, the "Latinate" model quickly runs into trouble with Timucua.

34. Benjamin L. D'Ooge, *Latin for Beginners* (Boston: Ginn and Company, 1911), 54.

Let us consider some of the indicative mood forms present in f. 075 of the *Arte*. All are in the first person singular and will be labeled with the verb tense Pareja believes them to represent.

9) Some indicative verb conjugations

Verb tense	Spanish	Timucua
present	*Yo soy*	*(honihe) nintela*
preterite imperfect	*Yo era*	*(honihe) nintequa*
preterite perfect	*Yo fuy*	*ninibila*
preterite pluperfect	*Yo auia sido*	*(honihe) ninechunu*
future imperfect	*Yo sere*	*(ho)ninihabela, ninihateno*
future perfect	*Yo abré sido*	*ninibilehabela*

While the data are somewhat messy, certain patterns are apparent. Resorting the rows and parsing some of the possible morpheme breaks makes them even clearer:

10) Reorganized visualization of the paradigm in (9)

Verb tense	Timucua
present	*nin-te-la*
preterite imperfect	*nin-te-qua*
future imperfect	*nini-ha-te-no*
preterite perfect	*nini-bi-la*
future perfect	*nini-bi-lehabela*
preterite pluperfect	*nini-chu-nu*

Using only these examples, one could posit *-chu* as a pluperfect suffix, *-bi* as a perfect suffix, and *-te* as an imperfect or elsewhere suffix. However, this analysis does not survive the subjunctive verb forms that follow:

11) Some subjunctive verb conjugations

Verb tense	Spanish	Timucua	issue
present	*como yo sea*	*niquenincoqua*	(no te)
preterite imperfect	*si yo fuera*	*ninihanimanacu*	(no te)
preterite perfect	*como yo aya sido*	*ninibileninconacu*	
preterite pluperfect	*como yo ubiera sido*	*ninibilebileninconacu*	(two bi, no chu)
future	*como hubiere sido*	*honihe ninihanima* *ninihanimano*	
second future	*aya de ser*	*ninihabele hanima*	
third future	*yo sere adelante*	*ninihabeletahabela*	
fourth future	*si sere yo esse*	*niniheco?*	("para preguntar dudãdo")
		ninintaheco	

Besides the fact that *-te* and *-chu* seem to have disappeared from their expected places and that *-bi* appears to have a different distribution than

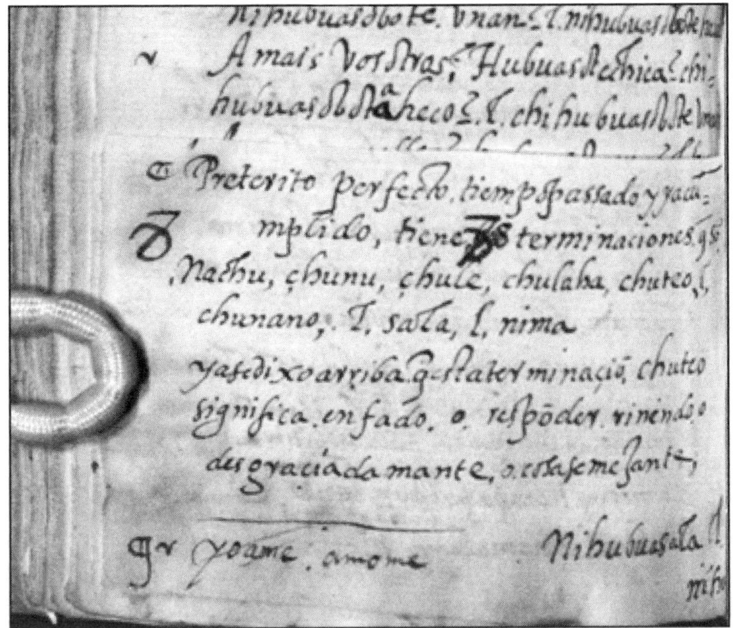

Figure 5. *Arte* eight suffixes with (not quite) the same meaning.

before, the most conspicuous element of this dataset is the four different types of future tense, one of which is labeled as being used to express doubt.

From the first dataset to the second, we observe a rapid decomposition of the Latinate model. Not only are there specific suffixes which do not seem to map onto Latin tenses, there also appear to be expressions for describing events that have not yet occurred which are more varied and specific in nature than the Latin future tense.

The most remarkable moment of incompatibility occurs on a partially cut-out folio between f. 089 and f. 090, where Pareja attempts to list endings of the "preterite perfect tense." The text originally reads '[the] preterite perfect, [the] past and already completed tense, has six endings' ("*Preterito perfecto, tiempo passado y ya cumplido, tiene 6 terminaciones*"), but in the handwritten manuscript the number "6" is crossed out and replaced with "7," and then replaced again with "8."

Here we see the suggestion that there may be eight suffixes with the same meaning, but a modern analysis of the usage in the corpus suggests more complexity.[35]

35. See Broadwell, *The Timucua Language.*

12)

Original	Modern Analysis	Gloss
nachu	*-nachu*	past:perfect? [unclear]
chunu	*-chu-nu*	remote:past (completive chu- with topic -no?)
chule	*-chu-le*	remote:past (completive chu- with copula -le?)
chulaha	*-chu-laha*	remote:past-emphatic
chuteo	*-chu-teo*	remote:past-anger
chunano	*-chu-na-no*	remote:past-first:person:ergative:topical?
sala	*[i]so-la > sa-la*	do-declarative = "It is done"
nima	*-nima*	conditional used for previous context

All of this morphology and its apparent incongruency with Latin grammar eventually inspires Pareja to set aside the Latinate model. Instead, in later portions of the *Arte,* we see Pareja reporting directly on observable properties of Timucua, rather than attempting to configure it to presuppositions of Romance structure. For example, we see the suffix *halaqua*, not in a table of paradigmatic inflection, but instead given its own section of prose, which explains that it attaches to different tenses to express compliance or willful action ("se dice por cumplimiento, otras de buena volũtad…").[36] Additionally, Pareja recognizes that the suffix *-chuteo* expresses anger and, in a section discussing the past tense, translates *Ame te* "I loved you" into the word *chihubuasobinchuteo* but (amusingly) adds *con enfado* ("with anger").[37]

This less restricted methodology leads to the documentation of phenomena which do not occur in the Romance languages, bringing his work closer to modern linguistic analysis. For instance, f. 132r has a table of suppletive plural verbs, in which a different verb root is used if one of the verb's arguments (usually the absolutive argument in Southeastern languages) is plural.[38] While suppletion can occur in Indo-European languages, typically it follows tense rather than number, such as in English present *they are* vs. past *they were* or, more dramatically, Latin present *ferō* "I carry" versus past *tulī* "I carried" and *lātus* "having been carried."

13) "Estos verbos sirben para solo singular, y en el plural sirben otros"

	singular	plural	English gloss
a.	*niocono*[39]	*oyosinino*	'run'

36. This suffix does not occur outside the *Arte*, making it difficult to determine how accurate Pareja's description is, although its component suffixes *-hala* "irrealis-declarative" and *-qua* "locative/auxiliary" are common.

37. *Arte*, f. 90v. Pareja seems to have mistakenly edited preterite *Ame* into present *Amo* despite the section's subject being the preterite perfect tense. This amendment is invisible in the Adam and Vinson edition.

38. Karen Booker, "Comparative Muskogean: Aspects of Proto-Muskogean Verb Morphology" (PhD diss., University of Kansas, 1980), 52.

39. Note how Pareja still uses verb forms ending with the nominalizer *-no* as the base form of verbs in an attempted parallel with the Latin infinitive.

b.	*meno/mi(te)no*	*tameno*	'go'
		yarino	'go "como emprocesion"'
c.	*alihono*	*abosinteno*	'walk'

Remaining limitations

While documenting suppletive plurals, a phenomenon without any precise analogue in the languages of Europe, is remarkable, limits to Pareja's documentation persist. Even without the restrictions of the Latinate model, there remains a paucity of terminology: in a sense, Pareja lacks the theoretical linguistic equipment necessary to observe or describe some phenomena which occur in Timucua. In particular, Timucua has a switch-reference system, whereby clauses are marked (via a verb suffix) for whether or not they have the same subject as the verb that follows. Switch-reference is widespread in the languages of the Americas, and also occurs in Australian and Pacific languages, but it has only relatively recently been formally documented in linguistics. Even as late as 1922, in his description of the grammar of the Hitchiti language, John R. Swanton makes no reference to switch-reference as a phenomenon, even though most verbs in that language carry switch-reference suffixes.[40] Ultimately, the term "switch reference" or "reference switching" was not coined until William Jacobsen Jr.'s 1964 grammar of the Washo language of California.[41]

As we would expect, Pareja does not notice switch-reference phenomena. That documentary gap is the result of his aforementioned paucity of linguistic terminology but also of his method of gathering data from existing texts produced by his native coauthors and presenting them without context.[42] Consider the following simple example from the *Arte* (f. 079v).

14) Spanish:
Oxala eſso fuera mio

ojalá	eso	fuera	mío
hope.for	this	be.subj.perf.s3	mine

"I wish that this were mine."

Timucua:
inibileqe N, haminihero

inibi	-leqe	N(oun)	hami (i)	ni	-hero
hopefully	-focus	(noun)	possession	be	-desid:ds

"(Somebody wishes) that hopefully (noun) were the possession (of somebody else)."

---

40. John R. Swanton, "A Sketch of the Hitchiti Language." Unpublished manuscript. BAE Archives, Washington, DC, 1921–22, 51.

41. William Jacobsen, Jr., "A Grammar of the Washo Language" (PhD diss., Berkeley: University of California, 1964), 665.

42. Dubcovsky and Broadwell, "Writing Timucua," 414–26 *passim*.

Here the suffix *-hero* has a switch-reference feature, specifically "different subject." Because it provides information about the subject of some following clause, it cannot be used sentence-finally (unlike what the *Arte* implies here), and by studying the rest of the Timucua corpus we can see that the desiderative suffixes are almost always followed by a verb of cognition, *mani/mane*. This is more obvious in the full sentence below, from Pareja's 1612 *Catechismo y breve exposición de la doctrina christiana*, f. 082r:

15) *inibileqe; honihe haminlehero manecono iniheti ynino istico inihe?*

inibi	*-leqe*	*honihe*	*hami*	*-n(a)*	*le*	*-hero*	*mani*	*-co*	*-no*
hopefully	-focus	I	possession	-my	-cop	-desid:ds	think	-alter	-topic

mani	*-co*	*-no*	*inihetiynino*	*istico*	*ini*	*-he?*
think	-alter	-topic	sin	bad	be	-fut

"Would it be a bad sin to think, 'I wish it were my possession'?" (-1612 Cat, f. 82r)

Notice that Pareja's example begins with *inibileqe* and ends with a form of *hami* followed by *-hero* but that this is only a portion of a clause complementing the verb *mani*. Observing discourse-related linguistic phenomena such as switch-reference requires attention to context, and Pareja's practice of pulling some of his examples from texts without regard for their context results in unintendedly stranded discourse markers. Similarly, it obfuscates the subordinating role these markers play, specifically how they are required when the clause is an argument of the auxiliary verb *mani*. This incomplete selection of grammatical forms also provides additional evidence for Pareja not being the primary author of much of the translated catechistical material used to write the *Arte*, as Broadwell and Dubcovsky have noted, because his partial understanding of the grammar would not have allowed him to produce translations that exhibit common Southeastern linguistic features unknown to him.

These are only a few examples that allow us to observe how Pareja's methodology for documenting the Timucua language and resultant understanding of the language's grammar evolved over the course of writing the *Arte*. However, Pareja's progress was limited by a poverty of terminology in the seventeenth century for precise language description, as well as the *Arte*'s fundamental data structure, although it is clear that he never stopped thinking about the problem. In a revealing passage from the 1627 Catechism, Pareja compares the difficulty of translating Timucua into Spanish to Romance languages' departures from Latin and differences between the Latin Vulgate and the Greek original of the Gospels.[43] Perhaps his difficul-

43. Pareja cites a characteristically monastic example of translation mismatch: *Exiit orare* for *ad orandum*, referencing Luke 6:12, which reads ἐξελθεῖν αὐτὸν εἰς τὸ ὄρος

ties with this incongruity can ultimately explain the abandonment of the *Arte*'s publication.

CONCLUSION

Drawing on plain textual evidence, marginalia newly revealed in the digital scans of the original, and a quantitative study of other Timucua texts in the corpus, we have seen that Francisco de Pareja's *Arte y pronunciacion de la lengva timvqvana y castellana* was an important early effort at understanding a Native North American language that stands out from the period's grammatical genre due to its incomplete, "work-in-progress" state. The recent digitization of the original printed and handwritten text provides an opportunity to reveal a dynamicity within the text that was invisible in previously published transcriptions.

It is instructive to compare this to some of the other contemporary grammars of Native languages discussed earlier, such as Molina's *Arte de la lengua mexicana* and the anonymous *Grammatica huronica*. The Nahuatl *Arte* is written in Latin and fully printed in blackletter, while the Wendat grammar is in manuscript and composed in a mixture of Latin and French. Both grammars follow a Latinate model: for example, Molina declines Nahuatl nouns into the five traditional "cases" despite all five forms being identical (Nominativo *teutl* "god," Accusativo *teutl*, etc.)[44] while the *Grammatica* describes Wendat as having a subjunctive and infinitive, categories alien to the Iroquoian verb system. Unlike Pareja, both of these grammars were preceded by earlier research and followed by later grammatical work: Molina was succeeded by Horacio Carochi's grammar, which greatly improved upon the language's description by marking vowel length and the glottal stop with diacritics, and the Wendat *Grammatica* served as the model for Potier's later *Elementa grammaticae huronicae*, primarily a retranscription of the *Grammatica*'s conjugation tables into an updated orthography.

Pareja's *Arte*, on the other hand, is a singular work, lying somewhere in between these poles: neither wholly printed nor manuscript, neither copied nor innovated upon. Like other *artes*, Pareja's scholarship is initially defined by the pedagogical methods of teaching Latin. However, as we can read

---

προσεύξασθαι, "He went out into the mountains to pray" in Greek while the Latin Vulgate has *Exiit in montem orare* rather than Latinically correct *ad orandum*. Here, the infinitive *orare* directly corresponds to the Greek aorist infinitive προσεύξασθαι "to pray" instead of the gerundive *orandum*, a construction that Greek lacks. Apparently, he had learned something from his own struggles with infinitives (Pareja, *Catecismo en lengua timuquana*, f. A vii verso).

44. Molina, *Arte de la lengua mexicana*, f. 7r.

(sometimes literally) between the lines of his manuscript additions, Pareja's methodology evolved and shows a capacity to relinquish those assumptions when they come into conflict with the reality of Timucua morphosyntax. In its later portions, the description of the Timucua language presented in the *Arte* is not as limited by adherence to a Latinate model but rather by the nature of Pareja's data and the fact that some of the phenomena present in Timucua grammar would not be understood or described by Western linguistic traditions until the late twentieth century.

Acknowledgments

We are grateful to the other members of the Hebuano Project—Denise Bossy, George Aaron Broadwell, Caxantino Corona, Alejandra Dubcovsky, and Ian Iglesias—for countless hours of productive conversations about Timucua history and grammar. (Special thanks to Dr. Broadwell for suggesting both our topic and our title!) We also wish to thank Timothy Johnson heartily for his guidance and for organizing and hosting the Languages and Landscapes conference at Flagler with the Academy of American Franciscan History, providing us with the opportunity to present there and contribute to this volume. Appreciation is additionally owed to Samopriya Basu, Bill Delaney, Erik Hamilton, William Petersen, Michael Powell, and Matthew Scarborough for their valuable comments on our draft. Finally, we are greatly indebted to Fray Pareja and his unnamed Timucua consultants for not finishing their book in a timely manner, an oversight with which we can sympathize and without which we would have had nothing to write about.

Chapter Four

Escobedo's La Florida: *Poetic Fruit or Dead on the Vine? A Parable for Literary Historians*

Thomas Hallock, *University of South Florida*

This is a parable of literary history. Among the countless poems from our extended past, some are savored today—many, many more die on the vine.[1] Not all literary works find their readers. Poems lose their topical edge, they sour with changing tastes, they wither in the archive. The reputation of any given genre or work will rise and fall over the centuries. This harvest—or neglect—points to the central task of a literary historian: what do we need, as living readers, for a poem to speak to us today? Alonso Gregorio de Escobedo's massive epic, *La Florida*, provides a classic example. Penned around 1600, this sprawling epic collects 37 *cantos* (or books), each about 500 lines, around the themes of missionizing Franciscans. Betraying the toponymic title, which seems to promise focus, Escobedo cuts a wide path: there are dedicatory sonnets to the benefactors of his home monastery in Andalucía, biblical and theological glosses, chapters on the early missions of the Canary Islands, observations from his experiences in North America, and most significantly, reflections on his tenure as priest from 1587 to 1593 at Nombre de Diós mission—a religious outpost near the Native village of Seloy, two crossbow shots north of St. Augustine. For generations, the poem has sat in the manuscript room of Spain's Biblioteca Nacional. Commentators have cited the poem (mostly in passing) for over a century, a scholarly edition

1. This essay, an exercise in literary recovery, argues that Escobedo's *La Florida* requires contextualization at three levels: cultural-religious, literary, and on the local historical landscape. On literary recovery, I am grateful for support from the New York Public Library; on the cultural-religious, to the John Carter Brown Library; and for archival research, to the National Endowment for the Humanities, which allowed me to conduct research at the Archivo General de Indias (AGI) in Sevilla, Spain, as well as to the University of South Florida, which supported foundational research into the Jeannette Thurber Connor Collection of Floridiana, on deposit at George A. Smathers Library, University of Florida.

has been heroically prepared by Elizabeth Sununu, and one canto of *La Florida* makes a long-overdue appearance in an American literature textbook. Yet Escobedo's sprawling verse epic remains largely unread, a footnote at best.[2]

Why? What factors render some literary works as distant—and others as accessible or familiar? What contextual bridges must one establish in order to access an overlooked book? Escobedo's *La Florida*, decidedly of its time, provides an opportunity to examine the root causes of neglect. Penned a generation before the earliest English-speaking colony in New England, *La Florida* is notable as the first epic poem in what is now the United States. As an ethnographic source, the author would conceivably be valued for his observations about Florida's first people. And as a local example of the proliferating Spanish epics from the time, Escobedo merits note in studies of settler-colonialism. Instead there is obscurity. Escobedo would seem to fit a classic dismissal of frontier mission writing, this from Herbert E. Bolton: "But most of what has been produced consists of chronicles of the deeds of the Fathers, polemic discussion by sectarian partisans, or sentimental effusions with literary, edifying, or financial intent." Of late, a "polemic" poet-priest such as Escobedo has experienced a modest revival, warranting further explanation. A translated canto has recently appeared in an undergraduate literature anthology; I am currently preparing a translated edition of colonial epics myself; research by others looms on the horizon.[3] As I have labored in the dark for over a decade, making futile argument for this walking-dead of a poem, I have become acutely aware of the broader challenges in understanding sixteenth-century, heroic-religious verse. This essay provides the core background needed to close the gap. My argument may be said to resemble nesting dolls, with one

---

2. For a definitive edition, see Alonso Gregorio de Escobedo, *La Florida*, ed. Alexandra Sununu (New York: Academia Norteamericana de la Lengua Española, 2015); for a prose translation of the poem, in excerpts, see *Pirates, Indians and Spaniards: Father Escobedo's La Florida*, ed. James W. Covington (St. Petersburg, FL: Great Outdoors Press, 1963). All references to Escobedo are from Sununu's edition; translations are my own. Earlier assessments of the poem include: Maynard Geiger, OFM, "An Early Poem on Florida," *The Fortnightly Review* 41, no. 12 (December 1934): 271–72; Fidel Lejarza, "Rasgos Autobiográficos de P. Escobedo en su poem *La Florida*," *Revista de Indias* 1, no. 2 (1940): 35–69; Alexandra Sununu, "Escobedo y Su Poema *La Florida*," *Boletín de la Academia Norteamericana de la Lengua Española* 8 (1992): 37–49.

3. Scott Cave et al. include Canto 26 of *La Florida* in *The Broadview Anthology of American Literature*, volume A, ed. Derrick R. Spires, et al. (Petersborough, Canada: Broadview Press, 2022), 79–84; I am currently preparing a selection for "The Epic of Florida: Selected Poems by Juan de Castellanos, Bartolomé de Flores, and Alonso Gregorio de Escobedo." Herbert E. Bolton's meme-worthy dismissal appears in "The Mission as a Frontier Institution in the Spanish-American Colonies," *The American Historical Review* 23, no. 1 (October 1917): 43.

point set inside the other: from the problem of translation, to translation and poetic form, to poetic form and empire, to empire and colonialism, and finally, colonialism back to the coopting of voice. I will move us from artistic conventions, to how and why those conventions surfaced when they did, and back to how the historical intersects with the aesthetic. In the end, I will leave the question to readers: Is this an undervalued poetic harvest? Or fruit better forgotten, left to wither on history's vine?

Before any judgements, first, some context.

One must always remember that Escobedo's poem is just that, a poem. The point merits emphasis because scholarship in early Florida has been typically empirical. Historian Michael V. Gannon celebrates an ever-growing "data bank" of information; his longtime colleague Jerald T. Milanich warily dismisses the "romance" of missions that has clouded scientific study, and like Gannon, relishes the "wheelbarrows" of information yielded with each archaeological dig.[4] What works for archaeology does not always work for literature, however, and a principal challenge to reading Escobedo's *La Florida* rests in the recovery of aesthetic form. As many others did in his day, the versifying Franciscan wrote in *ottava rima* (*octava real* in Spanish), a rhyme scheme of eight line stanzas, each stanza eleven syllables long, with alternating rhymed couplets in the first six lines followed by a closing rhymed couplet (ABABABCC). This poetic form, imported from Italy and the preferred mode during the years of Spanish imperial expansion, is far better suited to Romance languages than English. Escobedo and his contemporaries thrived with *octava real* because Spanish (obviously) holds a vast arsenal of words that end with an "a" or an "o" or the nouns ending "ión." The rhyming poses fewer challenges. Escobedo may describe Timucua practice of whale hunting off the Florida coast, for instance, with relative ease:

> Y aunque parece caso de aspereza
> lo que quiero decir al castellano,
> no me creer será mucha rudeza,
> pues por la fe lo afirmo de cristiano,
> por ser verdad y que hay desta proeza
> testigos con la firma de escribano,
> cuyo fiel signo certifica el hecho
> y da al que no lo sabe satisfecho.[5]

4. Michael V. Gannon, quoted from the introduction to *The Spanish Missions of La Florida*, ed. Bonnie G. McEwan (Gainesville: University Press of Florida, 1993), xiii; Jerald T. Milanich, *Laboring in the Fields of the Lord: Spanish Mission and the Southeastern Indians* (Washington, DC: Smithsonian Institution Press, 1999), 10, 16.

5. Escobedo, *La Florida* (27:305–11). Escobedo's account of whale hunting, in fact, corroborates with other sources; see José de Acosta, *Natural and Moral History of the Indies*

And while it may seem I am being unfair,
what I want to say to the Christian,
who unknowing, may not believe me,
which as a Christian I swear by my faith
that the feat I describe is the truth
there are notarized and sworn witnesses,
with signatures to certify as fact,
for those who still are not satisfied.

The same form, however, lends itself to insurmountable challenges in English. With a handful of exceptions (notably William Butler Yeats and George Gordon, Lord Byron), English-language poets avoid the meter far-better suited to Spanish or Italian. It's a dead practice, an exercise that surfaces occasionally in poetry circles as a curiosity or in shows of skill, but not considered worthy of serious efforts. Creative writing handbooks often include sample formats for students to try, but *ottava rima* rarely appears in these manuals; the Academy of American Poets website has an excellent searchable guide, though on the Academy's list of 42 formats, the once-flourishing *ottava rima* is notably absent.[6] This broader poetic problem trickles down to Escobedo. For decades the only translation of *La Florida* avoided verse altogether, presenting the book instead in prose form. Escobedo was not done a favor. Seen as a documentary source, the poem appeared without its central driver.

The vehicle of *ottava rima*, in fact, is an immediate product of the colonial culture that produced the poem in the first place. That is, outside its rhyme scheme, *La Florida* lacks its own raison d'etre. Originating from Italy (as noted), the verse style legitimated an upstart and rapidly expanding Spanish realm. With Spain still seen as a newer, borderline European power, poets in the language drew from examples such as *Orlando Furioso*, by Ludovico Ariosto, in order to seal their own credentials. The Spanish language still lacked the validity of Italian; the first Spanish translation of Ariosto set out to establish the less-prestigious language as a capable medium or mode. A Spanish edition of Virgil's *Aeneid* appeared in 1557; the success of *La Araucana* by Alonso de Ercilla y Zúñiga, describing the remote lands of Chile, made equally far-off corners of the empire—including St. Augustine—proper literary subjects. The expanding empire under Charles V and Philip II generated

(*Historia Natural Y Moral de las Indias*), trans. Frances M. López-Morillas, ed. Jane E. Mangan, with introduction and commentary by Walter D. Mignolo (Durham, NC: Duke University Press, 2002), 134–35.

6. Academy of American Poets, "Poems," consulted September 25, 2023 (https://poets.org/poems).

dozens, even hundreds of similar works.[7] These same works sought to archive contradictory rhetorical aims: often hierarchical, or top-down, they justified the more traditional interests of the realm; they were local, identifying with a place or legitimated by a knowledge of specific place, yet always considering the removed setting within the realm; and while foundational, the epic form was always allowing in conflict. Such were the ingredients of the colonial epic.

Escobedo's poem may be read, then, as a dispatch from the field in a global territorial war. As the resident priest at Nombre de Dios mission in St. Augustine, he had joined the ranks of an evangelizing army, advancing the truth of Christianity before—his contemporaries believed—the end of the world. His ethno-religious accounts of the Timucua Indians fell within a predicted apocalypse, in which a temporal history of Europeans' arrival to America synced with God's clock of Divine Revelation.[8] The Catholic-Franciscan concerns, in turn, interlocked with Spanish strategic interests along the Florida coastline. Although St. Augustine was considered to be a remote boondock, "una tierra mala" by all accounts, the proximity to the coastline gave the fortifications here tactical importance. Spain needed access to the Georgia Bight, the concave bend between north Florida and South Carolina, in order to protect valuable fleets that freighted mineral wealth from Meso- and South America back to Europe along the Gulf Stream. As has been well established, Spanish Florida missions—religious reasons aside—were designed to establish a human shield against rival efforts by the English and French. Escobedo arrived at St. Augustine in 1587, one year after English privateer Francis Drake leveled

7. Gregorio Hernandez de Velasco, *Los Doze Libros de la Eneida de Vergilio Principe de los Poetas Latinos, Traducida en Octava Rima y Verso Castellano* (Anvers [Amberes]: Juan Bellero y Halcon, 1557). For a classic study of the epic as lost genre, see *The Heroic Poem of the Spanish Golden Age: Selections*, ed. Frank Pierce (Oxford: Dolphin, 1947). Isaías Lerner reviews the epic's role in colonial letters in his introduction to Alonso de Ercilla y Zúñiga, *La Araucana* (Madrid: Cátedra, 1998), 9–13. Juan Bautista de Avalle-Arce argues that the colonial American epic collapsed history and poetic form in *La Épica Colonial* (Pamplona: University of Navarra, 2000), 13; Lucia Binotti maps the transfer of the poetic form from Italy to Spain in *Cultural Capital: Language and National Identity in Imperial Spain* (Woodbridge, Suffolk: Tamesis, 2012), 53–81; Elizabeth B. Davis emphasizes the legitimating role of the epic in *Myth and Identity in the Epic of Imperial Spain* (University Missouri Press, 2000), 4–5. A collection that helps to restore the epic alongside contemporary concerns is *Épica y colonia: Ensayos sobre el génerso épico en Iberoaméricano (siglos XVI y XVII)*, ed. Paul Firbas (Lima, Peru: University of Nacional Mayor de San Marcos, 2008); see also Raúl Marrero Fente, *Poesía Épica del Siglo XVI: Historia, Teoría y Práctica* (Madrid: Iberoamericana, 2017). Pedro Piñero Ramirez provides a succinct geneaology of the form in "Épica Hispanoamericana Colonial," from *Historia de la literatura hispanoamericana, Tomo 1* (Madrid: Cátedra, 1982), 161–86.

8. Mónica Ruiz Bañuls, "El fransciscanismo en el contexto evangelizador novohispano: raíces del mensaje misional," *Sémata*: *Ciencias Sociales e Humanidades* 26 (2014): 499.

the city; he left in 1593, three years prior to Juanillo's uprising (also known the the Guale Rebellion) of 1597; and in the years in which he completed his massive poem, probably around 1600, the future of the missions and St. Augustine itself were in question.[9]

The core of *La Florida*, given this political context, turns effectively on tactical versus spiritual needs of the rhyming priest's Timucua charge. In a series of Cantos, books 26 to 28, Escobedo dips into proto-ethnography, describing Florida's people through an ethno-allegorical lens. The rationale for this fusion of first-hand observation and the Gospels was to establish how the Natives could be converted, thus in Spanish eyes, justifying the continued mission effort. Escobedo finds his richest vein in the practices of Native people that resonates with scriptural precedent. His description of Timucua fishing, for instance, intersects with the familiar reference of Jesus as the "fisher of men." Details are specific:

Pesca de otra manera el ponentino
cuando trae una red en cada mano,
con que toma pescado de contino
en las saladas aguas del pantano.
Es éste un ejercicio peregrino,
pues no le puede lance salir vano
por causa de quedar seca la entrada
por donde entró en la balsa represada.

The western Indians have another way
of fishing, where they take up the net in
each hand, and with the same motion,
they trawl the brackish waters of the swamp.

---

9. The time of the poem's completion, circa 1600, corresponds with a crisis moment in St. Augustine's future, when the missions and colonial outpost were under debate; see Charles W. Arnade's classic study, *Florida on Trial: 1593–1602* (Coral Gables: University of Miami Press, 1959); on St. Augustine as a financial drain, and implicitly the need for Escobedo to defend the missions, see Amy Bushnell Turner, *Situado and Sabana: Spain's Support System for the Presidio and Mission Provinces of Florida* (Athens: University of Georgia Press), 45; on Florida as "tierra mala" [bad land], see Alonso de las Alas to the King (Dec. 11, 1595), Connor Papers (3:15), accessed at the University of Florida; on concerns following Francis Drake, coinciding with the arrival of priests, see Fernandez de Quiñones to the King (June 20, 1587), AGI, Santo Domingo, 126; on fortifications and priests arriving to St. Augustine, see Pedro Mendez Marquez to the King (July 17, 1588), AGI, Santo Domingo, 224; Bartolome de Arguelles registers complaints about St. Augustine in a letter to King (2 May 1591), AGI, Santo Domingo, 229; on Franciscans as instrument of pacification, see Francisco de Marrón to the King (July 6, 1594), AGI Santo Domingo 223; Francisco Pareja makes an internal case for strategic gain of missions to King (12 October 1599), AGI, Santo Domingo, 235.

Wandering like pilgrims in this manner,
they can keep the fish from escaping,
because a dry spot in the narrow gate
keeps fish from leaving these shallow pools.[10]

The poem provides a window into the actual industry, which clearly involved the manipulation of low-lying tidal flats, nets, and presumably mangrove weirs. The physical description leads into allegory, as the Timucua in a simile "wander like Pilgrims." In the next stanza, Escobedo entertains the potential of conversion: "If they converted to the Roman faith … / … their souls would be cleansed from their sorrow."[11] The meditation, in the following, continues to a broader reflection upon the need for missions:

Es tal la de esta gente infiel traidora
que sólo puede el sol de la justicia
con su divina luz que mi alma adora
dársela a sus tinieblas de malicia.
¿Pueblo que idolatrías atesora
y está alistado siempre en su milicia,
podrá gozar de Dios bien soberano?
Sí, con la fe y bautismo del cristiano.

It is so: that these traitorous infidels
who have been kept in shadowy darkness,
without the divine justice my soul adores,
may be brought to the light of justice.
Can a town that treasures idolatry,
and that is always preparing for war,
enjoy the solace of a sovereign God?
With baptism in the Christian faith: Yes.[12]

Fishing yields just one example, though Escobedo offers others, linking Indigenous farming to the parable of the vineyard and black drink (*Cacina* or yaupon holly) to the parable of the sower.

The translation in this instance occurs at a cultural level, with the missionary priest interpreting the customs and manners of Natives through a Christian lens. The Spanish needed the Timucuas, historians and anthropologists remind us, more than the Timucuas needed them; frontier culture was defined by accommodation and exchange. Cultural-material practices would support a need for translation, which turn, underscored a central paradox that

10. Escobedo, *La Florida*, 27:129–36.
11. Escobedo, *La Florida*, 27:149–50.
12. Escobedo, *La Florida*, 27:153–60.

intersected with the epic genre—and the colonial model in particular. The epic poem, as current scholarship notes, is dialogic.[13] While these narrative poems are foundational, telling the story of a beginning, they invariably nod to what is prehistorical or outside the historical record. In their attempt to recount foundational moments, in short, they leave traces of the very stories the poems seek to supplant. The West African epic, *Sundiata*, captures a tension between Islam (brought to the nation of Mali through Saharan trade routes) and animistic fetishes; although the emperor, Sundiata, is associated with Islam he is, like his rival, practiced in sorcery. Even though John Milton's great Christian poem *Paradise Lost* celebrates the coming of Jesus, as any undergraduate English major (or the movie *Animal House*) will remind you, Satan is the story's driving character. Beowulf's famed victory of Grendel followed a reckless indiscretion that cost the hero his best friend, and as most translations of *The Aeneid* shows, the poet Vergil reinvented the dubious bloodline of his patron Augustus Caesar, turning past failure to later greatness.[14] Escobedo's most immediate influence, Alonso de Ercilla y Zúñiga, writes the great Spanish poem of empire because he gives voice not so much to the invading Europeans, but to the Native people of Chile for whom his poem is named, the Araucanian people. Recent scholarship on the epic demonstrates that even as the genre is foundational, narrating a story of beginnings, the foundational moment never entirely erases the conflict, and the conflicts indeed establish a given poem's most memorable moments.[15]

---

13. On accommodation and exchange, see J. Michael Francis and Kathleen M. Kole, *Murder and Martyrdom in Spanish Florida: Don Juan and the Guale Uprising of 1697* American Museum of Natural History Anthropological Papers, 95 (2001), 25. Kathleen Deegan emphasizes in light of the population imbalance, Spanish colonizers were not in control; see "St. Augustine and the Mission Frontier," *The Spanish Missions of Florida*, 89.

14. On Satan in *Paradise Lost* and *Animal House* (1978), see the short clip featuring a lecturing Donald Sutherland (www.youtube.com/watch?v=Ciw1os85nz0&t=1s). A fascinating contrast of Islam versus animistic religions is drawn from comparing translations of the West African epic, *The Sundiata*; see *Sundiata: An Epic of Old Mali*, ed. D.T. Niane (Essex: Longman, 1965), 38–40; and griot Bambo Suso's telling of the Sunjata, ed. Gordon Innes, et al. (New York: Penguin, 1999), 3, 94 n12. On the poet Vergil's use of epic to clean up Augustus Caesar's bloodline, see *The Aeneid*, trans. Shadi Bartsch (New York: Modern Library, 2021), xxix–xxxi. I am indebted to my University of South Florida students, ENG 3103: Great Literature of the World, for these analogs.

15. The deconstructive move in an epic, in which the foundational narrative includes the very moments of resistance it seeks to illuminate, is described in various forms in *Epic Traditions in the Contemporary World: The Poetics of Community*, eds. Margaret Beissinger, Jane Tyles, and Susanne Wofford (Berkeley: University of California Press, 1999); Elizabeth B. Davis draws from trauma theory to examine shifting narrations in "Épica y configuración del canon en la poesía española del Siglo del Oro," *Torno al Canon: aproximaciones y estrategias*, ed. Begoña López Bueno (Sevilla: University of Sevilla, 2005), 318. David Quint

Case in point, *La Florida*. But with an important catch! Escobedo narrates the meeting, and purported triumph, of Christianity over Native practices that he considered ungodly. *La Florida* follows the allegorized descriptions of Native fishing, gift-giving and agricultural parables with a stanza that announces the conversion of one hundred Timucua souls. From today's vantage point, the poem provides a rich instance of the dialogic quality in mission culture, the interchange of traditional knowledges and practices with Christian ideals. Scholarship on Franciscan missions has been energized by what David Hurst Thomas describes as a "cubist" approach, a recognition of the range of perspectives, across stakeholders, resulting in a multiplicity of views. Kathleen Deegan emphasizes the "essential multivocality of the past," a fragmentation that aligns with the deconstruction tension embedded inherently within epic as genre.[16] Escobedo, at points that most interest readers, makes sense in this cubist framework. Elsewhere, the unshakeable convictions overwhelm his allegorical-ethnographic syncretism. With reference to the parable of the vineyard (Matthew 20:1–16), Escobedo emphasizes with that colonization the Native people of Florida (who hear Christianity last) may now be first. He writes:

El dueño de la viña al alborada
ya tercia, sesta y nona llevó obreros.
Y cuando está la gente descuidada
a mediodía en punto los postreros,
a quien por breve espacio les fue dada,
la paga como a todos los primeros,
y quejándose uno deste hecho
le dio el Señor del caso satisfecho.

The lord of the vineyard sent his workers
at dawn and *tercia*, between *sesta* and *nons*.
And when those careless people, arriving

sets tensions in the epic in historical context in his classic study, *Epic and Empire: Politics and Generic Form from Virgil to Milton* (Princeton, NJ: Princeton University Press, 1993).

16. See David Hurst Thomas's lead article, "Franciscan Florida in Pan-Borderlands Perspective: Adaptation, Negation, and Resistance" (plus essays that follow) in *Franciscans and American Indians in Pan-Borderlands Perspective: Adaptation, Negotiation, and Resistance*, eds. Jeffrey M. Burns and Timothy Johnson (Oceanside, CA: Academy of American Franciscan History, 2018), 1–15; Kathleen Deegan, "Introduction," *Facing Florida: Essays in Culture and Religion in Early Southeastern America*, eds. Timothy Johnson and Jeffrey M. Burns (Oceanside, CA: Academy of American Franciscan History, 2018), 8–9. Robert C. Galgano observes that while the Spaniards "had many advantages," the Native people of Florida (and New Mexico) decided for "themselves whether to accept, adapt or reject" what came their way; see *Feast of Souls: Indians and Spaniards in the Seventh-Century Missions of Florida and New Mexico* (Albuquerque: University of New Mexico Press, 2005), 9.

> at midday, put themselves ahead of others,
> despite the shorter time they had put in,
> the last were paid as if they had been first,
> leading the workers who had come before
> to complain and plead their case to the Lord.[17]

The emphasis on time captures what Francisco Rojo-Alique calls an "eschatological urgency," the papal bull *Cum hora undecima*, that was to suggest evangelization of Native people had arrived in the "eleventh hour." The Franciscans, Rojo-Alique notes, took the Parable of the Vineyard as a reminder in the urgency of completing the work of salvation before the return of Christ.[18] This biblical gloss situates Escobedo's use of Matthew in a more precise religious-historical context, yet does little to relieve the flat name calling and harsh judgment ("infiel traidora"). Today, the name-calling sticks. At other moments *La Florida* not only jars in its prejudice, but that same prejudice leads to basic factual errors. The product of patriarchal European culture, Escobedo overlooks the role of women in matriarchal Timucua society. Coming himself from a sedentary society, and vested in gathering his flock under the mission bell, he describes the Natives as shivering inexplicably through Winter homes on the coast. He has no sympathy for Native "witch doctors" or priests.[19] And so on, my point not being to fact check the literary record (one of the less rewarding forms of literary criticism, made possible only by reducing ambivalent and slippery texts to feed the empirically-driven data mill). From a cultural studies perspective, enough to say that the biases

17. Escobedo, *La Florida*, 27:161–68.

18. Francisco Javier Rojo-Alique, "The Old and New World of Spanish Observant Preaching," from *Preaching and New Worlds: Sermons as Mirrors of Realms Near and Far*, eds. Timothy J. Johnson, Katherine Wrisley Shelby, and John D. Young (New York: Routledge, 2019), 270–71.

19. Ample scholarship and primary sources allow scholars to gauge Escobedo's descriptions on the continuum between accommodation and prejudice. Milanich emphasizes that Escobedo's parish near Seloy (or Nombre de Dios) was inhabited by a relocated population, experiencing tremendous change; see *Laboring in the Fields of the Lord*, 109. Amy Turner Bushnell unpacks the sedentism that was prescribed by the Franciscans (and, ironically, is a source of criticism by Escobedo) in "The Sacramental Imperative: Catholic Ritual and Indian Sedentism in the Provinces of Florida," *Columbian Consequences, vol. 2, Archaeological and Historical Perspectives on the Spanish Borderlands*, ed. David Hurst Thomas (Washington, DC: Smithsonian Institution Press, 1990), 475–90. Those interested in situating Escobedo alongside his religious contemporaries should align his poetic descriptions against the probing questions by Francisco Pareja, *Confessionario en Lengua Castellana y Timuquana con Algunos Consejos para Animar el Penitente* (Mexico: Diego López Davalos, 1613); judgmental language that sounds excessive in a poem, in fact, aligns with the religious values framed by a confessional.

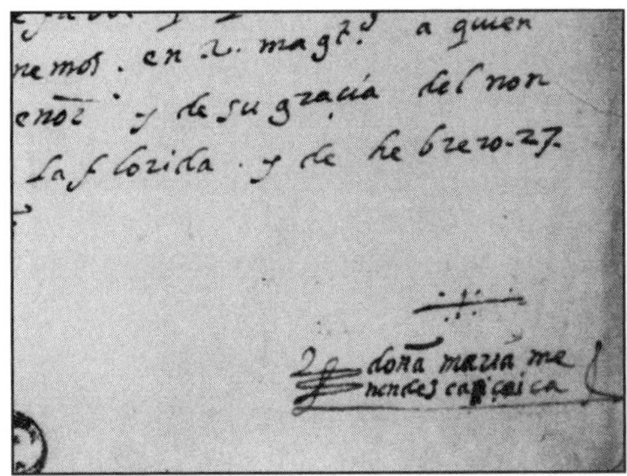
nemos . en v. mag.d a quien
enoz . y de su gracia del nor
la florida . y de hebrero . 27 .

doña maria me
nendes cacica

Figure 1. Cacica Doña Maria Menendez to King, 27 February 1958 (AGI, Santo Domingo, 232).

underscore an old truth about translation: *traduttore, traditore.* Any act of translation is also a treason, a betrayal. To translate is to erase.

And this erasure, to close, leads to a final step in the process of preparing a sixteenth-century epic for today's reader. That is, any edition outside its time must also stand outside the text. Beyond the range of Escobedo's verse, Native voices survive, fruitfully illustrating points of accommodation, resistance, and manipulation of European norms. In the decades after he left St. Augustine, Escobedo's near contemporary Francisco Pareja collaborated with Mocoma-speaking Timucua on a series of liturgical tracts and a linguistic guide. Luís Jerónimo de Oré's account of Juanillo's rebellion captures a Native mockery of European textual practice. The rebelling Guales tie Father Francisco de Ávila to a cross, threaten to burn him, adorn liturgical vestments, and mock his mass. Providing what literary critics would call a strong reading "against the grain," the Natives clock Ávila on the head with a book, striking him "with such a blow that it left me senseless."[20] In the aftermath to this same rebellion, meanwhile, some Natives advanced their own position from within, pitching their own performances to European expectations. After the 1597 uprising, the leadership of St. Augustine was in turmoil and a party of twenty-two area caciques presented themselves to the Crown, taking advantage of the uncertainty. The group

20. Timothy J. Johnson, "'Are They Damned?' Timucuans, Theology, and the Necessity of the Sacraments," in *Facing Florida*, 31; George Aaron Broadwell, "Shadow Authors: The Texts of the Earliest Indigenous Florida Writers," in *Franciscans and American Indians in Pan-Borderlands Perspective*, 161–74; Alejandra Dubcovsky and George Aaron Broadwell, "Writing Timucua: Recovering and Interrogating Indigenous Authorship," *Early American Studies* 15, no. 3 (summer 2017): 409–41; Luis Jerónimo de Oré, *Account of the Martyrs in the Provinces of La Florida*, eds. and trans. Raquel Chang-Rodríguez and Nancy Vogeley (Albuquerque: University of New Mexico Press, 2017), 124, 125.

included Doña Maria, from Escobedo's home parish, who pled poverty and sought goods "so the Indians" would become "more motivated to be Christians." Writing to the King, and following expectations to the letter, she writes:

> . . . my poverty and the frequency of the Indians, both Christians and infidels, who come seeking goods for their conversion, and others who are important and needed by the governor for the proper government of these provinces, compel me to ask your majesty to give me some short term help, so I can meet the expenses that I have incurred with them, as is evident from the information that goes with this. I beg your majesty to see and attend to this matter, so the result may be the Indians may be more motivated to become Christians, seeing that in this way those who keep the faith are protected by your Majesty; and so that I can do what I ask above, I beg your Majesty to send me a letter of Your favor, that can be taken to my Indians, that shows how your Majesty protects us and ours. . . .[21]

Given the other examples, the rebelling Guales and anonymous joint authors with Francisco Pareja, no internal motivation can be drawn from this petition. Doña Maria speaks to her audience: she pleads humility, sets the interests of her reader above her own stakes, and adheres closely to obsequious court record. The Crown rewards her with tribute.

But that is not my point. What matters is that we always see translation as an open-ended process. Doña Maria's petition bears directly on the poem because, as the Christianized cacica of Seloy, a parish served by the Nombre de Dios mission, she almost certainly knew the rhyming priests; almost certainly, she took communion from Escobedo's hand. The mistake in reading *La Florida* is in giving the poet-priest the last word. All translations are open-ended and ongoing. The most promising take on Escobedo situates his poem within a dialogic culture, as part of the multivocal past. Recent scholarship on the mission, in this way, may align with current interpretations of the epic, which emphasize how the foundational story seems to envelop an alternative past that never quite goes away. The work of Franciscans in sixteenth-century Florida lent itself to prerogatives of the epic genre. By situating this one epic within the religious and immediate historical context, we may at least understand the nature of an otherwise forgotten, astringent grape.

---

21. Doña Maria Menéndez to the King, 27 February 1598, AGI, Santo Domingo, 232; for a later and more polished letter, see Doña Maria Cacica to the King (20 February 1600), AGI, Santo Domingo, 231. On the delegation following the Guale rebellion, see Juan Mendez Marquez to the King (13 April 1601), AGI, Santo Domingo, 232; Gonzalo Méndez de Canzo to King (23 and 28 February 1598), AGI, Santo Domingo, 224. Mendez de Canzo describes Doña Maria as "una yndia buena cassada con un hespanol . . . muy buena y muy leal" (24 October 1598), AGI, Santo Domingo, 224.

CHAPTER FIVE

Eros, Ministry, and Motherhood: The Gendered Landscape of Franciscan Evangelization

TIMOTHY J. JOHNSON, *Flagler College*

INTRODUCTION

In the beginning, the God grounded gendered relations in ecstasy according to Francisco Pareja and his Timucua co-authors in the 1627 *Catecismo en lengua timuquana, y castellana*. Following Saint Augustine's reading of Genesis 2:21, they speak of the divinely induced slumber of Adam before the mysterious revelation of Eve as ecstatic.[1] The Bishop of Hippo argued Adam was caught up to the heavenly court of angels to fathom the magnitude of Eve's impending creation. His exclamation upon awakening, "This is bone of my bone, and flesh of my flesh," was not a biblical-anatomical statement, but a prophetic revelation of the gendered mystery of our scriptural primogenitors.[2]

The profound and ecstatic sleep of Adam—Eve's voice in the initial encounter with Adam is mute in Genesis—cannot be separated from Pareja's theological understanding of God as erotic. Educated within the Eastern and Western medieval tradition,[3] Franciscans and other missionaries like Pareja embarking for the Americas faced challenges that demanded unprecedented efforts to reimagine their pastoral practices without readily prepared theological guidelines or doctrines.[4] In the prologue of the 1627 *Secunda parte del*

1. Francisco Pareja, *Catecismo en lengua timuquana, y castellana, en el qual se instruyen y cathequizan los adultos infieles que an de ser christianos y no serà menos util para los ya cristianos* (Mexico: Iuan Ruyz, 1627), 39v.

2. St Augustine, *The Literal Meaning of Genesis*, vol. 2, trans. and annotated James Hammond Taylor (New York: The Newman Press, 1982), 95.

3. On this tradition, see Denys Turner, *Eros and Allegory: Medieval Exegesis of the Song of Songs* (Collegeville: Liturgical Press, 1995).

4. See the essay by Francisco Javier Rojo-Alique in this volume, 137–54.

Cathecismo, Pareja fleshes out a creative response to this new ministerial reality by appealing to Pseudo-Dionysius,[5] the enigmatic Christian writer from the late fifth to the early sixth century and favorite among Franciscans in the golden age of Spanish mysticism.[6]

Laboring within the matrilineal framework of Timucua culture, Pareja recasts pastoral ministry as a decidedly feminine-maternal dynamic driven by the ecstatic eros of God. This essay follows the trajectory of this claim by exploring the Franciscan option for a maternal hierarchy of service, gender construction, and erotic ministerial performance.

Francis of Assisi and Maternal Ministry

The noted Franciscan scholar, Jacques Dalarun, reminds us that when Francis of Assisi wrote to his close companion Brother Leo "Sicut mater" that is, "As mother," he was not simply expressing an appealing sense of maternal tenderness but revealing an institutional metaphor of governance.[7] This brief letter of goat parchment, which is now preserved as a relic in the Cathedral of Spoleto, reads:

> To Brother Leo your brother Francis, greetings and peace. Thus I say to you, my son, as mother, that all the words which we said on the road, briefly, in this word, I dispose them; and I counsel—and you must not come to me to take counsel, since I counsel you thus—: in whatever manner seems to you best to please the Lord God and to follow his footsteps and poverty, do this, with the blessings of the Lord God and my obedience! And if it is necessary to you that your soul return to me for another consultation of yours, and if you wish, come![8]

Despite Francis's reference to himself "as mother," there should be no illusions that governing and exercising power in the thirteenth-century church of Francis of Assisi was not a male prerogative. The saint himself unabashedly strove to secure the future of his burgeoning movement within the parameters of ecclesial power and the kingdom of God, the Father almighty.[9] This reality is foreshadowed when he renounced his human father in favor of his eternal

5. Francisco Pareja, *Secunda parte del Cathecismo por el mismo P. Francisco Pareja, ahora nuevo corregido en esta secunda Impressa* (Mexico: Iuan Ruyz, 1627), 1r–3v.

6. Jean Leclercq, introduction to *Pseudo-Dionysius. The Complete Works*, trans. Colm Luibheid with foreword, notes, and translation collaboration of Paul Rorem (New York: Paulist Press, 1987), 30.

7. Jacques Dalarun, *To Govern Is to Serve: An Essay on Medieval Democracy*, trans. and introduction, Sean L. Field (Ithaca, NY: Cornell University Press, 2023), 181.

8. Quoted in Dalarun, *To Govern Is to Serve*, 184.

9. Dalarun, *To Govern Is to Serve*, 197.

father before the bishop of Assisi.[10] Yet, the medieval understanding of pastoral responsibility necessitated some degree of gender reversal lest the divine mandate of care remain unfulfilled by the shepherd. Those in positions of ecclesial authority frequently evoke counterintuitive gender imagery to underscore a wholistic pastoral approach for the sake of encountering the gendered other; thus, the abbess becomes a father, the abbot a mother, and most strikingly, Jesus a mother to all.[11] As the French philosopher, Michel Foucault argued, the failure of the shepherd to guide the flock along the path of salvation risked the eternal loss of both the sheep and the shepherd.[12]

As Jacques Dalarun points out, for Francis of Assisi, the focus of gender reversal is first of all, institutional. Once "Sicut mater" is translated "as mother" instead of "as a mother" this is clear. The phrase does not denote a comparison, but Francis is Leo's mother because that term encompasses the saint's understanding of the service of those referred to as ministers and servants. Furthermore, he never uses the term "father" to designate himself or his brothers.[13] Instead of seeking the title of abbot or superior as found in monastic communities, Francis rejected the implication of dominance suggested by these titles and grounded his position of governance in the ground, that is to say, mother earth.[14] Within the gendered cosmos of the *Canticle of Creatures*, the Assisian's Umbrian poem, Sun, Wind, and Fire are brothers, and the Moon, Stars, and Water are sisters, with the Earth both sister and mother. Mother Earth models ministerial service, for she both sustains and governs: "Praised be to You, my Lord, through our Sister Mother Earth, who sustains and governs us, and produces diverse fruits with colored flowers and herbs."[15]

With the earth as mother, all creatures are subjects, not objects, and form a wide-ranging community marked by relationships of gendered equality with

---

10. On this event, see Marco Bartoli, *Francis' Nudity: Historical Reflection on the Stripping of the Poor Man of Assisi,* trans. Gilberto Cavazos-González (St. Bonaventure: Franciscan Publications, 2020).

11. Dalarun, *To Govern Is to Serve*, 197.

12. On Foucault and Franciscan pastoral practice in the mid-1260s, see Timothy J. Johnson, "Dispensations, Permissions, and the Narbonne Enclosure: The Spatial Parameters of Power in Bonaventure's Constitutions of Narbonne," in *Oboedientia: Zu Formen und Grenzen von Macht und Unterordnung im mittelalterlichen Religiosentum*, eds. Sébastien Barret and Gert Melville, *Vita Regularis*, 27 (2005), 295–304; Timothy J. Johnson, "'Ground to Dust for the Purity of the Order': Pastoral Power, Punishment, and Minorite Identity in the Narbonne Enclosure" in *Franciscan Studies*, 63 (2006): 295–304.

13. Optato van Asseldonk, "Madre" in *Dizionario Francescano* (Padua: Edizizioni Messggero Padova, 1983), col. 919.

14. Dalarun, *To Govern Is to Serve*, 167–68.

15. Francesco d'Assisi, *Scritti*, ed. Carlo Paolazzi (Grottaferrata: Frati Editori de Quaracchi, 2009), 122. All translations are by the author unless noted otherwise.

a shared source of life-giving vitality. The creation of this novel sibling structure elicits praise offered to the Lord, not in the guise of a distant *pater familias*, but the all-powerful, gracious God of Genesis who delights in creatures, at once useful, desirable, beautiful, and strong.[16] Among the brotherhood or fraternity of Francis's followers, the image of God as a father is evoked in line with the common hierarchy of power within the medieval family, but there is no doubt that the privileged relationship is between mother and sons.[17]

Francis urges his brothers to learn embodied service from Mother Earth in the *Salute of the Virtues*. He exhorts them, with mortified bodies in obedience to the spirit and their brothers, to place themselves as, ". . . subject and submissive to everyone in the world, and not only to people but even to all beasts and wild animals. . . ."[18]

The initial locus of this service, in imitation of Mother Earth, is the local fraternity of "fratres minores" or "lesser brothers" where the brothers relinquish any claim to the power and prestige associated with the "maiores" of the world who rule by domination. Among them, there was to be no "superior" but only ministers marked by humble maternal service.

A normative document that captures the fluidity of maternal ministry and gender is *A Rule for Hermitages* (1217–1221). These out-of-the-way dwellings with a handful of friars were reserved for contemplation. Two served as "mothers" who cared for one or two "sons" with alms and safeguarded their solitude. This relationship was fluid since "the sons may assume the office of the mothers as it appears to them to alternately arrange for a time. . . ."[19] This reversal of hierarchical governance underscored a new paradigm of fraternal relationships evinced in other normative documents such as the *Earlier Rule* (1209/10–1221) and the *Later Rule* (1223). When treating the question of begging for alms in the *Earlier Rule*, a salient aspect of early Franciscan life suggesting weakness and vulnerability, the intimate image of a sustaining mother is proposed, "Let each one fearlessly make known his need to another that the other might discover what is needed and minister to him. Let each one love and nurture his brother as a mother loves and nurtures her son. . . ."[20] The *Later Rule* (1223), approved by Pope Honorius III, extends the circle of those in need beyond the hungry to all those in need, especially the sick

16. Timothy J. Johnson, "Francis and Creation," in *The Cambridge Companion to Francis of Assisi*, ed. Michael J. P. Robson (Cambridge: Cambridge University Press, 2012), 145–46.

17. Jacques Dalarun, *Francis of Assisi and the Feminine*, trans. Paula Pierce and Mary Sutphin (St. Bonaventure: The Franciscan Institute, 2006), 55.

18. Francesco d'Assisi, *Scritti*, 50.

19. Francesco d'Assisi, *Scritti*, 344.

20. Francesco d'Assisi, *Scritti*, 258.

brothers ". . . For if a mother nurtures and loves her carnal son, how much more diligently should one love and nurture his spiritual brother?"[21]

FRANCISCO PAREJA AND GENDER CONSTRUCTION

Friar Francisco Pareja knew the *Later Rule* backward and forwards, inside and out—in Latin and Spanish. While the date of birth is uncertain, we do know that he was born in Auñón, Spain, and entered the Castilian Province of Franciscans. Before he died in 1628 in Mexico, he served as a pastor, custos, and later as the first provincial of the Province of Saint Helen (Florida-Cuba).[22] From the time of his novitiate, the *Later Rule* would have been studied, read aloud in chapter meetings, and cited in sermons. A normative text from this period, the *Book of the Rule and Constitutions of the Order of Our Father Saint Francis of the Observance*, includes Chapter Six of the *Later Rule* in Latin and Spanish:

Table 1. The *Later Rule of Saint Francis* on Mothers and Sons

Latin—English	Spanish—English
Quia si mater nutrit et diligit filium suum carnalem, quanto diligentius debet quis diligere et nutrire fratrem suum spiritualem? [23]	Porque si la madre ama y cria á su hijo carnal, quanto con mayor diligencia debe qualquiera amar and criar a su hermano espiritual.[24]
For if a mother nurtures and loves her carnal son, how much more diligently should one love and nurture his spiritual brother?	For if a mother loves and raises her carnal son, with how much more diligence should anyone love and raise his spiritual brother.

The nurturing imagery found in the *Later Rule* alludes to the Apostle Paul's description of his ministry among the Thessalonians (1 Thess. 2:7): ". . . while in your midst we were as children: as if a nurse were cherishing her own children. . . ."[25] The *Later Rule* explicitly uses the term "mother" and

21. Francesco d'Assisi, *Scritti*, 330.

22. On Francisco Pareja's life and work, see Timothy J. Johnson, "A Rediscovered Catechism: Fray Francisco Pareja's Literary Works and IIII. Parte de catechismo en lingua timuquana y castellana: En que se trata el modo de oyr missa, y sus ceremonias," in *L'épaisseur du temps. Mélanges offerts à Jacques Dalarun*, eds. Sean L. Field, Marco Guida et Dominique Poirel (Turnhout: Brepols, 2021), 587–602; esp. 584–89.

23. Francesco d'Assisi, *Scritti*, 330.

24. Luys de Rebolledo, *Libro de la Regula y Constituciones Generales de la Orden de Nuestro Sant Francisco de la Observancia* (Seville: Clemente Hildago, 1607), 6v.

25. 1 Thess. 2:7, *The Holy Bible: Translated from the Latin Vulgate with Annotations, References, and an Historical and Chronological Table* (New York: P.J. Kenedy & Sons, 1950), 267.

Pareja combines the two texts in the 1627 *Secunda parte del Cathecismo* prologue when describing the love ministers should display with those who are the subjects of their pastoral care:

> However, as they are servants of love they have to be together mothers and mistresses of their subjects by treating them like sons and caring for them as children, and providing them with the care that the mother has of the creature at her breasts in the manner the same Apostle says in 1 Thess. 2:7: "But we were gentle among you, like a mistress taking care of her children. . . ."[26]

To perform as a woman, that is, like a mother with a child does not track the dominant gendered image of masculinity among the friars cultivated by Franciscan writers of Francisco Pareja's era. In her study on the construction of gender roles in early modern Mexico, Asunción Lavrin understands masculinity and femininity as models of social behavior accompanied by psychological and moral qualities deemed appropriate for each biological sex. Furthermore, gender construction entails the intellectual-pedagogical process of creating forms of behavior that distinguish men and women in theory and practice embedded in malleable social and historical realities.[27] How this process played out among male religious such as friars comes into view presupposes an educational system that eliminates sexual virility as a model given the requisite vow of celibacy. Once in the Americas, however, the concept of conquest—be it martial or spiritual—emerged and called for qualities typically applied most frequently to men of the period. On the spiritual level, the friars were thus locked in a battle with the demonic that demanded strength, courage, the willingness to suffer any number of indignities and physical hardships, and even die as a martyr. Like other conquistadors, they were willing to offer their lives for the cause, but unlike their martial counterparts, the friars were to eschew aggressive behavior and humbly submit to their fate—a decidedly feminine characteristic according to the prevailing Iberian culture of "New Spain."[28]

Given the significance of humility for Franciscans, it is hardly surprising that the social-historical context for gender construction for Franciscan Pareja and his confreres was markedly hierarchical. This is visible in the images found of temporal and ecclesial hierarchies in *The Rhetorica Christiana* of Fray Diego

26. Francisco Pareja, *Secunda parte del Cathecismo por el mismo P. Francisco Pareja, ahora nuevo corregido en esta secunda Impression* (Mexico: Iuan Ruyz, 1627), 1v.

27. Asunción Lavrin, "Masculine and Feminine: The Construction of Gender Roles in the Regular Orders in Early Modern Mexico," in *Explorations in Renaissance Culture*, vol. 34, no. 1 (Summer 2008): 4.

28. Lavrin, "Masculine and Feminine," 7–9.

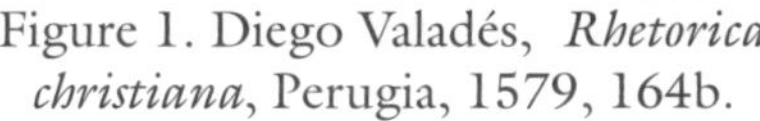

Figure 1. Diego Valadés, *Rhetorica christiana*, Perugia, 1579, 164b.

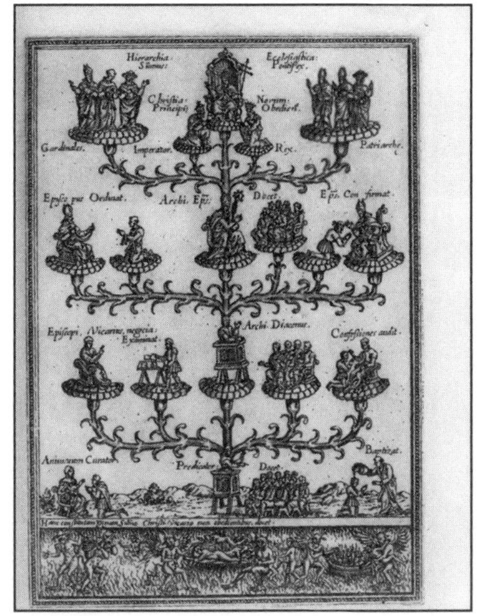

Figure 2. Diego Valadés, *Rhetorica christiana*, Perugia, 1579, 164d.

Valadés, the first book published in Europe by an author from the Americas.[29] A close examination of the tree of temporal hierarchy places the *pater familias* at the base of the trunk with the nursing *mater* to the right with the children at the left (Figure 1).[30] She is the only female appearing in this depiction and no females are readily identifiable in the tree of ecclesial hierarchy (Figure 2).[31] Except for the mother, women are invisible in this vertical world and the underworld where the disobedient are punished.

Women, designated as *puelle* (girls) and *mulieres* (women), do emerge on the left edge of the image in the depiction of an idealized concept of ecclesial place with their male counterparts of *pueri* (boys) and *homines* (men) on the right edge of the image. Together they anchor the four corners of the conven-

29. On the use of rhetoric and imagery in the *Rhetorica christiana*, see Rolando Carrasco M., "El *exemplum* como estrategia persuasiva en la *Rhetorica christiana* (1579) de fray Diego Valadés," in *Anales del Instituto de Investigaciones Estéticas,* vol. 22, no. 77 (2000): 33–62.

30. Diego Valadés, *Rhetorica christiana ad concionandi et orandi usum accommodata, utriusque facultatis exemplis suo loco insertis; quae quidem ex Indorum maximè deprompta sunt historiis. Unde praeter doctrinam, sum̃a quoque delectatio comparabitur* (Perugia: Petrus Jacobus Petrutius, 1579), 164b. For the text and images, see https://archive.org/details/rhetoricachristi00vala_0/page/n196/mode/1up.

31. Valadés, *Rhetorica Christiana*, 164d.

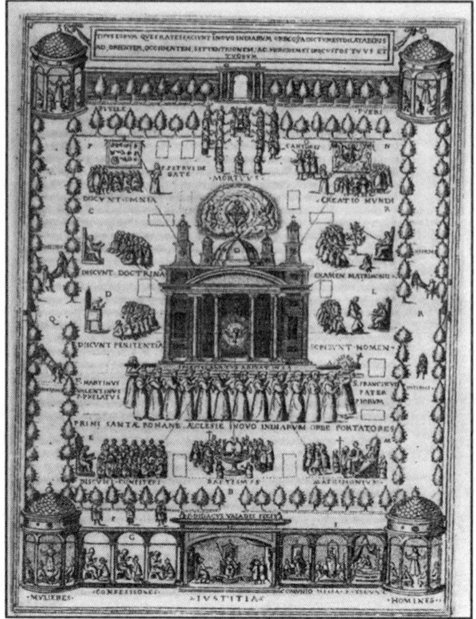

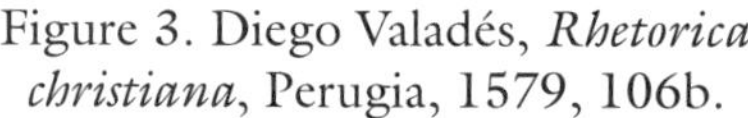

Figure 3. Diego Valadés, *Rhetorica christiana*, Perugia, 1579, 106b.

Figure 4. Diego Valadés, *Rhetorica christiana*, Perugia, 1579, 220c.

tual atrium of evangelization (Figure 3).[32] In what has been named the image of creation or the great chain of being, the ecstasy-driven emergence of Eve from Adam is represented in the center of the order of creation by Valadés with representatives of humanity stretching out to her left and right. The virgin Mary appears as well, notably on her knees in prayer like Eve, in the upper left-hand corner facing the Mercy Seat of the Trinity (Figure 4).[33]

The *Rhetorica Christiana* situates the girls and boys in separate rooms at the entrance into the cloister area where the initiation into Christianity begins by developing catechetical literacy and learning about the creation of the world. These children continue to undergo gendered instruction as adults, where they are introduced to the sacraments such as matrimony, which is preceded by an examination.

An analysis of the relationship between those men and women who are married and become fathers and mothers is found in Francisco Pareja's reflections on creation in the *Catecismo en lengua timuquana, y castellana*.[34] His views evince a long-standing medieval philosophical-theological perspective that encompasses those in sacramental marriages blessed by a priest as well as

32. Valadés, *Rhetorica Christiana*, 106b.

33. Valadés, *Rhetorica Christiana*, 220c.

34. Pareja, *Catecismo en lengua timuquana, y castellana*, 39rv–56r.

those in unions based on mutual consent alone.[35] Taking a cue from Thomas Aquinas, Pareja claims that children should love their fathers more than their mothers. This reason revolves around the theological claim that a child is an *imago Dei*, an image of God, and the process governing the creation of a wooden image mirrors what happens in the conception of a child.[36] The mother is the laborer who brings the "wood" to the father, who like an artisan, crafts the material per an image he holds in his mind. To whom is the image, in this case, the child, most obliged? Although Pareja acknowledges the strenuous work of the woman who offers the unformed material and at birth pulls the infant into the world; however, it is the man who forms, organizes, and arranges the material, resulting in the perfection of the image through the reception of the soul. In short, while the mother offers the "material," the father assures the "substance" of the child. Due to this debt that children owe to their fathers, they are obliged to love them more despite the great sufferings of their mothers. Furthermore, while fathers must provide the necessities of life for their children, they are even obligated to take care of their fathers before their children in times of grave necessity as both Scripture and Aristotle in *The Ethics* demonstrate.

When considering the order of charity within the family, Pareja asserts that in situations of extreme necessity, fathers, and then children should be

---

35. In the *Confessionario en lengua castellana, y timuquana con algunos consejos para animar al penitente* (Mexico: Diego Lopez Danalos, 1613), 184r, the question arises in the Spanish version regarding caciques who approved marriages according to Timucua customs without informing the local parish priest. The Timucua version asks if both parties have voluntarily given their consent, beginning with the women, to the marriage but makes no mention of the priest. For a translation of the Timucua, see George Aaron Broadwell, Fieldworks Language Explorer, Texts, Conf. f. 184r–184v (5). For friars such as Francisco Pareja, the possibility of offering the sacrament of marriage, or a blessing for those not married according to the Roman Catholic rite, is predicated on knowing if a pre-existing Timucua union was based on consent. For those seeking baptism, it was clear they had not been married by a priest due to the sequence of sacramental marriage, but it was essential to know if they had consented to marriage with their partner. For this reason, there is a divergence in the Spanish–Timucua questions. Regarding consent, see Philip L. Reynolds, *How Marriage Became One of the Sacraments* (Cambridge: Cambridge University Press, 2016). For a different take on this question, see https://www.smithsonianmag.com/history/with-their-powers-combined-two-scholars-may-have-deciphered-a-long-lost-native-language-180982118/. The focus on the voluntary consent of the two individuals—even if made in secret—mirrors the Roman Catholic teaching regarding the nature of sacramental marriage. The majority view of Franciscan theologians was that Indigenous marriages were valid. See Federico R, Aznar Gil, "La institución matrimonial en los autores franciscanos americanos," *Archivo-Ibero Americano*, no. 181–84 (1986): 793–95.

36. Pareja, *Catecismo en lengua timuquana, y castellana*, 43r–44r.

loved before mothers.[37] The reason is twofold: first, children are indebted to their fathers for their substance or being, and second, the union between fathers and children is based on their shared substance while the union between fathers and mothers is united by the principle of generation when they become one flesh according to Genesis 2:24. Despite the hierarchization of love in favor of the spirit over the flesh, the *Catecismo en lengua timuquana, y castellana* recognizes the beauty of marital love reflected in the bridal veil, the exchange of coins, and the wedding rings, which are fashioned from gold, the most precious of materials. Pareja confirms this reciprocal love exceeds all other loves on the human level of the flesh and the symbols are meant to convey this reality to Spanish and Timucua Christians alike. He also implies that in the quotidian, husbands often love their spouses more than their fathers and children by stating that these actions are by no means to be considered mortal sins. Notably, the *Confessionario en lengua castellana, y timuquana* never raises the question about the hierarchical obligations of love within the family, thus suggesting that while the issue was of theological import, it held little or no significance for him on the level of pastoral ministry.[38]

Eros and Ministerial Gender Performance

Francisco Pareja's hierarchical focus on fathers does emerge in the *Confessionario en lengua castellana, y timuquana* and elsewhere when he comments on the Fourth Commandment, "Honor your father and mother," found in Exodus 20:12. As early as 1612, the commentary on this text in the *Cathechismo y breve exposicion de la doctrina christiana*[39] is accompanied by an image identifying a Franciscan friar as a father together with another image of a father and mother (Figures 5 and 6).

Pareja's patriarchal stance in the case of ministerial governance is on display not only in image but also in writing. The Spanish text references the natural father although the mother is pictured along with the father.[40] He is expected to sustain, teach, and discipline his offspring. The spiritual father is also marked out for reverence.[41] Children are expected to honor and reverence

37. Pareja, *Catecismo en lengua timuquana, y castellana*, 44r–45r.

38. Francisco Pareja, *Confessionario en lengua castellana, y timuquana con algunos consejos para animar al penitente* (Mexico: Diego Lopez Danalos, 1613).

39. Francisco Pareja, *Cathechismo y breve exposicion de la doctrina christiana; muy vtil y necessaria, asi para los Españoles como para los naturales, en lengua Castellana, y Timuequana, en modo de preguntas, y respuestas* (Mexico: Pedro Balli, 1612), 68r.

40. Pareja, *Cathechismo y breve exposicion de la doctrina christiana*, 68r.

41. Pareja, *Cathechismo y breve exposicion de la doctrina christiana*, 68r–70r. See also Pareja, *Confessionario en lengua castellana, y timuquana*, 137r–39r.

Figure 5. Francisco Pareja, *Cathechismo y breve exposicion de la doctrina christiana*, Mexico, 68r.

Figure 6. Francisco Pareja, *Cathechismo y breve exposicion de la doctrina christiana*, Mexico, 68r.

both fathers, who generated life within them, be it naturally through marital relations or spiritually through the sacraments, beginning with baptism. The depth and breadth of the commandment are evident when Pareja reminds the readers that the godparents, teachers, and older members of the community are all worthy of honor and reverence.

Ministers, for their part, are to assume the role of fathers who govern and serve out love for those entrusted to their care according to the prologue of the 1627 *Secunda parte del Cathecismo*.[42] The pastoral paradigm is Jesus whose love was ecstatic, even erotic according to Pareja who anchors his argument in the theology of Pseudo-Dionysius, sometimes known as the Areopagite or simply Dionysius. This author, whose name and exact historical context remain an enigma, proposed a unique combination of Athenian Neo-Platonism and Syrian Christianity in a series of texts dating to the late fifth century.[43] Despite the obscurity surrounding the author, the influence of his major works, the *Divine Names*, *Mystical Theology*, *Celestial Hierarchy*, and *Ecclesial Hierarchy*, is evident in numerous authors in Western Christianity in subsequent centuries.[44] Franciscan authors of sixteenth-century Spain displayed a predilec-

42. Pareja, *Catecismo en lengua timuquana, y castellana*, 1v.

43. Paul Rorem, "The Uplifting Spirituality of Pseudo-Dionysius" in *Christian Spirituality: Origins to the Twelfth Century*, eds. Bernard McGinn, John Meyendorff, and Jean Leclercq (New York: The Crossroad Publishing Company, 1986), 132–33.

44. Rorem, "The Uplifting Spirituality of Pseudo-Dionysius," 144–49.

tion for the Areopagite's theological reflections they encountered in his collected works[45] and the writings of confreres like Bonaventure of Bagnoregio.[46]

The Pseudo-Dionysian corpus attracted friars due to an emphasis on what Paul Rorem terms "the uplifting spirituality" of the elusive writer from the fifth century. Affective contemplation was a central motif of those like Francisco Pareja who were members of the Observant or Reformed branch of the Franciscan Order. Dionysius proposed an ascent or "uplifting" of Christians from catechumens to clerics into divine darkness beyond words and thoughts through the interpretation of scriptural-liturgical symbolism at the perceptual-conceptual levels.[47] To affirm that God is "good" is proper yet there is a dissimilarity between what is understood as "good" by men and women and "good" as a divine attribute; thus, sensual perceptions of goodness in the world must be abandoned so that the interpreter can ascend to the conceptual idea. Since the divine is beyond all cognitive powers, even concepts of the "good" must be forsaken, so intellectual efforts proper to contemplation and the acquisition of biblical and liturgical insights may yield to the silent darkness of affective ecstasy. This ultimate encounter with the divine was marked by compassion and affections similar to those shared between mothers and sons, spouses, and enduring friends.[48]

As appealing as this experience is for those who seek the divine, the *Secunda parte del Cathecismo* includes a warning to those who delight in contemplation but neglect to care for their neighbors. Turning to the twelfth-century Parisian theologian, Richard of St. Victor, he cautions: "There are many poor in spirit, joyful in hope, fervent in charity, advanced in other effects of love and sanctity, however quite lukewarm in zeal for souls, with each one claiming their excuses even though they are rich enough to help those nearby. . . ."[49] Pareja finds a goad to action in his interpretation of God's ecstatic love revealed in the incarnation of Jesus. Some scholars have faulted the Areopagite's weak treatment of this central tenet of Christianity,[50] yet it foregrounds Pareja's hermeneutic of gendered ministry.[51]

---

45. For example, *D. Dionysii Areopagitae Scripta* (Alcalá: Brocar, 1541).

46. On Bonaventure and Pseudo-Dionysius, see Luke V. Tongi, "A Sweet Influence: St. Bonaventure's Franciscan Reception of Dionysian Hierarchy" (PhD diss., Marquette University, 2019).

47. Rorem, "The Uplifting Spirituality of Pseudo-Dionysius," 133–43.

48. Melquíades Andrés Martín, *La teología española en el siglo XVI* (Madrid: EDICA, 1977), 11.

49. Pareja, *Catecismo en lengua timuquana, y castellana*, 3v.

50. Rorem, "The Uplifting Spirituality of Pseudo-Dionysius," 144. On eros and incarnation in Pseudo-Dionysius, see John M. Rist, "Love, Knowing and Incarnation in Pseudo-Dionysius," in *Traditions of Platonism* (Ashgate, 1999), 375–88.

51. The cosmic coming forth and return of divine eros in the incarnation is best described by the Dionysian term, "philanthropia." See Rist, "Love, Knowing and Incarnation in Pseudo-Dionysius," 379.

The incarnation is a revelation of eros, in which God's ecstatic love for creation culminates in Christ's desire to come out of himself, to exceed himself, to go beyond himself to become a lowly servant in the flesh for the good of others.[52] Such love is both the impetus and model for the minister:

> And so that this teaching [which is well founded in Charity] God Our Lord teaches him [minister/prelate] the Spirit of the perfect prelate and minister, similar to his own that he holds the same love, according to what Saint Dionysius says in *On hierarchy*, 42. n. 41, which in a certain way draws forth from itself to do good to his creatures. By ruling them in delight and giving himself away in loving them and looking out for them, this love made him come out of himself to take the form of a servant to do good for his servants.[53]

Pareja notes the minister's service is initially understood as patriarchal, thus reinforcing the prevailing model found in his commentary on the Fourth Commandment, illustrated in *The Rhetorica Christiana* of Diego Valadés, and the conquistador model proposed by Asunción Lavrin. But there is more. This excessive love, which flows from the depths of divine eros, also draws the minister beyond the customary role of the father into the realm of gender performance and reversal:

> . . . for as the mistress raises her children, natural love draws out from her the mother who raises her son to take care of him, and for this reason [the minister/prelate] becomes a girl with a boy, takes the bite from the mouth to give it to him, loses sleep, tranquility, and his comforts, looks to wash him, dress him, take care of him, nurse him at his breast, and free him from all harms and dangers.[54]

As Jacques Dalarun notes, Pareja's spiritual father, Francis of Assisi, performed or played the woman and mother, in his attempt to avoid the position of dominance and power in relationship to the brothers of the community while retaining his respect for the ecclesial hierarchy of the Church. While Francis willingly speaks of God as "father," he longs to follow in the footsteps of Jesus like the Virgin Mary and gladly becomes a woman to care for the sons he birthed.[55] The image of Francis as mother extended beyond his fraternity according to the canonization documents of his Assisian companion in religion, Clare. One of the witnesses in Clare's cause for sainthood was

52. Pareja, *Catecismo en lengua timuquana, y castellana*, 1r–v.
53. Pareja, *Catecismo en lengua timuquana, y castellana*, 1r–v.
54. Pareja, *Catecismo en lengua timuquana, y castellana*, 1v.
55. Dalarun, *Francis of Assisi and the Feminine*, 268.

Sister Philippa, who testified Clare related a vision in which she nursed at the breast of Francis and found his milk to be delightfully sweet to the taste.[56]

The gender shift, exemplified by Francis of Assisi and promoted by Pareja reinforces what Judith Butler might affirm as the culturally constructed binary status of gender,[57] yet it is surprising at first glance given his identification of service in the same text as, ". . . surrendering to the fatherly and loving government of the inferior. . . ."[58] He maintains that given their hierarchical status, priests hold a superior rank, and like a gnarly fig tree display a grave external countenance to others, but inside is soft and spongy like cotton, they offer the tasty treats of example and doctrine.[59] Both Paul the Apostle and Bernard of Clairvaux support Pareja's maternal turn as the former reminded the young Christian community in Thessalonica, "But we were gentle among you like a mistress taking care of her children" (1 Thess. 2:7), and the latter taught his monastic brethren in a sermon on the *Canticle of Canticles* and *Letter 45 to Fulk* that those governing religious communities should be mothers to those in their care.[60]

The *Secunda parte del Cathecismo* is an ode to charity as the goad and goal of maternal ministry. With the divine mandate of "My word shall not return to me empty" (Isaiah 55:11), Pareja reminds his confreres that their praxis is informed by the endearing charity revealed in the life of Christ. In an excess of love, they are moved by charity. This "caritas" is linguistically feminine, and according to Bernard of Clairvaux, "she is the mother of men, and of the angels, pacifying and uniting all things that are in heaven and on earth. As she has a mother's spirit, entering the heart of the minister, she clothes him with this spirit, and with the companionship of zeal that does everything well and gently."[61] Charity determines the ebb and flow of the contemplative/active aspects of Franciscan life, as "she" animates the prayers offered for those in the care of the friars and draws them out of their contemplation as any mother would give up her rest for the sake of her children.[62]

---

56. On this dream, see Gerard P. Freeman, "Clare of Assisi's Vision of Francis: On the Interpretation of a Remarkable Dream," in *Dreams as Divine Communication in Christianity: From Hermas to Aquinas*, ed. Bart J. Koet (Leuven: Peeters Publishers, 2012), 225–54.

57. Judith Butler, "Performative Acts and Gender Constitution: An Essay in Phenomenology and Feminist Theory," in *Theatre Journal*, vol. 40, n. 4 (1988): 524–28.

58. Pareja, *Catecismo en lengua timuquana, y castellana*, 1v.

59. Pareja, *Catecismo en lengua timuquana, y castellana*, 3r.

60. Pareja, *Catecismo en lengua timuquana, y castellana*, 2v.

61. Pareja, *Catecismo en lengua timuquana, y castellana*, 2r.

62. Pareja, *Catecismo en lengua timuquana, y castellana*, 3r.

THE MATERNAL MATRIX OF MINISTRY: FUTURE DIRECTIONS AND PRELIMINARY CONCLUSIONS

The maternal matrix of ministry in the *Secunda parte del Cathecismo* elicits further study in the context of Northeast Florida where Francisco Pareja and his confreres had been working since as early as the 1570s within the matrilineal culture of the Timucua inhabitants. He arrived in 1595 and was stationed in San Juan del Puerto near current-day Jacksonville. Several Spanish sources note the agency of Timucua women as early as 1602 when Doña Maria, Doña Inez, and Doña Ana are listed as the *cacicas* (female chiefs)[63] at the pivotal missions of Nombre de Dios, San Juan del Puerto, and San Pedro de Mocama, respectively.[64] While conquistadors were taken aback in their first encounters with cacicas,[65] over time Spanish officials may have preferred to deal with them rather than their male counterparts.[66] Friar Alonso de Jesus, the custos of the Franciscan province of Saint Helen, confirms in 1630, that Timucua women, like the men, were tribal leaders and in this capacity could enter the community house. The Timucua gloss on Eve's role in the "Fall" claims she ate the fruit first because she wanted to be a "paracusi" or female warrior chief with limitless knowledge.[67] Despite their status, desired or deter-

63. Cacica is an elastic Spanish term used to designate female Indigenous leaders from male caciques in Spanish colonial areas of the Americas. On the history of these leaders, see: *Cacicas: The Indigenous Women Leaders of Spanish America 1492–1825*, eds. Margarita R. Ochoa and Sara Vicuña Guengerich (Norman: University of Oklahoma Press, 2021).

64. John E. Worth, *Timucuan Chiefdoms of Spanish Florida: Resistance and Destruction*, vol. 1 (Gainesville: University of Florida Press, 1998), 58.

65. Pekka Hämäläinen, *Indigenous Continent: The Epic Contest of North America* (New York: Liveright Publishing Corporation, 2022), 46.

66. Ida Altman, "Cacicas in the Early Spanish Empire," in *Cacicas: The Indigenous Women Leaders of Spanish America 1492–1825*, 6.

67. ". . . wanting to be a God without delay, she [Eve] forgot the one that she always loved, her husband, and without loving him, thought 'If I give it to him after I eat it, I will be a woman war-chief (parucusi), knowing all things, my heart wants this; [but] if Adam my husband is a strong man, a king, a chief, then I will serve him." Thinking 'I will not waste time and I want to be the boss of my husband,' she took and ate it." George Aaron Broadwell, 1627 Cat f. 55v–56v [Why did Eve eat first?) Texts, Field Works Language Explorer 9. Pareja and his Franciscan confreres like Bonaventure would not be surprised to encounter women with aspirations like Eve since women like Deborah (Judges 4) could lead armies in battle and dominate men in temporal-secular arenas. Still, they were to be excluded from hierarchical positions of spiritual domination. See Alistair Minnis, *From Eden to Eternity: Creations of Paradise in the Later Middle Ages* (Philadelphia: University of Pennsylvania Press, 2016), 107. Another powerful woman in a time of war was Judith, who killed the proud Holofernes. For the Timucua, see https://hebuano.wordpress.com/beginner-lessons/. The female artist, Artemisia Gentileschi dramatized this scene in the 1612–

mined, Pareja lamented that the agency of some women was too strong for his taste; they were "bossy" and held sway over their homes and husbands, thus disrupting his ministry.[68] Nevertheless women functioned as catechists in La Florida, were instrumental in a broad range of missionary efforts, and may have been among Francisco Pareja's coauthors. Women very well could have been catechists in places like Mission Nombre de Dios, where an image of Our Lady of La Leche was venerated and a confraternity to honor her was established by Native Americans as early as the 1630s.

Another area to explore Pareja's maternal matrix of ministry is linked to the Franciscan devotion to Mary, the mother of Jesus, and the feminine landscape of the colonial city of Saint Augustine. The *Secunda parte del Cathecismo* gestures in this direction in the prologue which evokes the apocalyptic vision of Mary, the woman clothed in the sun in the Book of Revelation (12:1). As Scripture relates, John saw her in a vision, pregnant, and she cried out in labor as she gave birth to the child she bore in her womb (12:2). Afflicted and fatigued, suffering in travail, she brings the savior into the world. Those who minister with love enter into her experience, and with prayers, tears, and sighs, suffer painfully, for the salvation of others. Visible reminders of Mary's ministerial role surrounded Pareja and his confreres, as the landscape around them included the parish church of the city founded in 1572, Our Lady of the Remedies, whose footprint has been uncovered by archaeologists between Aviles Street and Avenida Menendez.[69] In 1702 the parish community moved to Our Lady of Solitude, whose devotion recalls the loneliness of Mary before Easter Sunday.[70] The chapel was attached to the first hospital in the continental United States and the temporary home for the Franciscan friars.[71] In 1604 the friars moved to their reconstructed convent, which was dedicated to Our Lady of the Immaculate Conception in 1592 and is now the site of the Florida National Guard Headquarters.[72] Friars from the convent served the mission and church of Our Lady of the

---

1613 painting now found in the Museo Capodimonte in Naples, Italy. For another take on the "Timucua Eve," see Alejandra Dubcovsky, *Talking Back: Native Women and the Making of the Early South* (New Haven, CT: Yale University Press, 2023), 1–3.

68. Pareja, *Catecismo en lengua timuquana, y castellana*, 54v.

69. Kathleen Deagan, "Death and Burial in Spanish Saint Augustine," in *Catholicism and Native Americans in Early North America: Parish, Church, and Mission*, ed. Kathleen Deagan (Notre Dame: Notre Dame Press, 2024), 30–33.

70. Deagan, "Death and Burial in Spanish Saint Augustine," 33–37.

71. Elsbeth Gordon, *Heart and Soul of Florida: Sacred Sites and Historic Architecture* (Gainesville: University Press of Florida, 2013), 88–90.

72. Kathleen Hoffman, "The Archaeology of the Convento de San Francisco" in *The Spanish Missions of La Florida*, ed. Bonnie G. McEwan (Gainesville: University Press of Florida, 1993), 63.

Figure 7. Francisco Pareja, *Cathechismo y breve exposicion de la doctrina christiana,* Mexico, 48r.

Figure 8. *Our Lady of the Milk and Good Birth*, Cathedral Museum, Campeche, Mexico.

Rosary of the Point, which was established in the 1720s primarily for Christian Yamasee refugees.[73] Finally, the mission church of Nombre de Dios, with the later Shrine of Our Lady of the Milk and Good Birth, best incarnates Pareja's maternal theology within the context of a small Timucua community where female leadership was evident from the first days of the Spanish arrival in the area of contemporary Saint Augustine.[74]

The third possibility for further research lies in an admittedly speculative but intriguing arena: the maternal matrix of ministry as the locus of gender permeability and reversal. Already in the early decades of the sixteenth century, the Spanish explorer Álvar Núñez Cabeza de Vaca related his encounter with men in the area of the Gulf of Mexico whom he regarded as repulsive since they dressed like women and performed their traditional tasks. Nevertheless, his admiration for their arguably male qualities is clear as he claims they are stronger and taller than other men, capable of carrying great burdens, and skilled with

73. Deagan, "Death and Burial in Spanish Saint Augustine," 40–43.

74. On Nombre de Dios and the attendant shrine, see Kathleen Deagan, "Nombre de Dios: The First and Last Franciscan Mission in Spanish La Florida," in *Facing Florida: Essays on Culture and Religion in Early Modern Southeastern America*, eds. Timothy J. Johnson and Jeffrey M. Burns (Oceanside, CA: The Academy of American Franciscan History, 2021), 203–20.

the bow.[75] René Laudonnière was less than laudatory when commenting on the Timucua "hermaphrodites" he saw on the French expedition to Northeast Florida some three decades later in 1564. They made themselves repulsive to the eye, often ate despicable food, and carried provisions for warfare.[76] Referred to by the French with the disparaging term "berdache," these individuals were often highly regarded in Native American cultures according to some scholars and even seen in some circles as a third or fourth gender.[77] This designation *mutatis mutandis* has been proposed for Franciscan friars and other members of the clergy and religious orders.[78] Generalizations and false equivalencies must be avoided, but the visual cues of the friars, with their tonsured heads and dress-like clothing, when accompanied by their economic-political dependency on Indigenous and secular rulers, may have marked them as "other" in both Spanish and Timucua circles. The possible "shamanic status" of some Franciscan friars may also have fostered a perception of gender permeability.[79] When

---

75. *The Journey of Alvar Núñez Cabeza de Vaca*, trans. Fanny Bandelier, ed. Ad. F. Bandelier (New York: A.S. Barnes and Company, 1905), 126.

76. René Laudonnière, *Three Voyages*, trans., intro., and notes, Charles E. Bennett (Tuscaloosa: The University of Alabama Press, 2001), 13. On their possible role in ritual burials, see Tamara Shircliff Spike, "Death and Death Ritual among the Timucua of Spanish Florida," in *From La Florida to La California: Franciscan Evangelization in the Spanish Borderlands*, eds. Timothy J. Johnson and Gert Melville (Berkeley: The Academy of Franciscan History, 2013), 196.

77. Will Roscoe, *Changing Ones: Third and Fourth Genders in Native North America* (New York: Saint Martin's Press, 1998).

78. R.N. Swanson, "Angels Incarnate: Clergy and Masculinity from Gregorian Reform to Reformation," in *Masculinity in Medieval Europe,* ed. Dawn M. Hadley (London: Addison Wesley Longman, 1999), 60–77.

79. On Timucua shamans, see Jerald T. Milanich, *The Timucua* (Oxford: Blackwell Publishers, 1999), 178–81. While the "two-spirited" Timucua do not appear to be explicitly honored, similar individuals in other Indigenous groups were often considered shamans with considerable spiritual power; see Thomas A. Dubois, *An Introduction to Shamanism* (Cambridge: Cambridge University Press, 2009), 79–81, and mediated the invisible spirits of the material world, 82–86. Francis of Assisi's "shamanic powers" are a staple of medieval hagiography and are intimated in the countless statues of him with animals around the globe. When Pareja's confrere, Luis Jerónimo Oré, visited Florida he heard a story from another friar, Martín Prieto, with shamanic echoes. His efforts to catechize the Timucua village named Santa Ana in Spanish were due, according to the resident "witch doctor," to the resistance of the cacique. Hernando de Soto had held him captive as a boy and treated him horribly. Not surprisingly, the cacique wanted nothing to do with Christians. When Prieto was thrown out of the cacique's house, a sudden thunderclap and wind destroyed everything in the village except an upright cross and the church. Soon the cacique was baptized and four hundred people followed suit. See Luis Jerónimo Oré, *Account of the Martyrs in the Provinces of La Florida*, eds. and trans. Raquel Chang-Rodríguez and Nancy Vogeley (Albuquerque: University of New Mexico Press, 2017), 142–43.

Francisco Pareja in the *Secunda parte del Cathecismo* "becomes a girl with a boy" in ministry, he invites readers, intended or not, to consider the fluidity of gender constructs.

In conclusion, Francisco Pareja drew from the writings of Pseudo-Dionysius, medieval authors, and his Franciscan tradition to construct a strikingly innovative maternal model of ministry in his "new world" of Florida grounded in the ecstatic power of divine eros. Far from the lecture halls of Spanish convents and universities, he worked within a hierarchical system distant from Francis of Assisi's desire for a maternal model of governance and even reinforced the paternal structure when commenting on the Fourth Commandment. Yet, in light of the pastoral perspective he gleaned in Florida, Pareja, like Francis of Assisi, argued that the mother-child relationship paradigm for ministry displaced the father-child relationship. This theological proposal for pastoral care, while influenced by Christian sources and having produced numerous cachectical texts, emerged in the maternal-matrilinear Timucuan culture where women were agents in tribal government and ecclesial ministry. For Pareja, the ecstatic experience of Adam as Eve was drawn from his side, was repeated when the same divine eros drew a woman out of a man so to speak for the sake of a companion in ministerial care.

Appendix Translation 1: Francisco Pareja on Eros, Ministry, and Motherhood

Second part of the Catechism by Fr Francis Pareja himself, again corrected in this second printing

In which the Catechumen is instructed how to receive the Holy Sacrament of Baptism and some of its influences. It also talks about matters of the Faith. To this end, the minister of the Gospel resorts to the meekness of Christ our Lord imitating his love, and endearing charity, asking and responding lovingly, with the desire to take advantage of and to draw fruitful works from his labor by sowing the word of God. Isaiah, says the same, "My word will not return empty"; that is, it should not cease to affect souls, nor return empty-handed nor without profit, for by it many nations have been converted to our Holy Faith.

And so that this teaching [to that one who is shown is well founded in Charity], God Our Lord teaches him the Spirit of the perfect prelate and minister, similar to his own that he holds the same love, according to what Saint Dionysius says in *On hierarchy*, 42, n. 41, which in a certain way draws forth from itself to do good to his creatures. By ruling them in delight and giving himself away in loving them and looking out for them, this love made him come out of himself to take the form of a servant to do good for his servants. So then in this way by divine love he must come out of himself, surrendering to the fatherly and loving government of the inferior in a manner that they are not rightfully his to consider his own, but his subjects. As servants, they should apply to serve them, and provide them as necessary for the good of their souls in the way that Saint Paul says in 1 Cor. 9:19. 2. / 2 Cor. 4:5: "As I was free, I made myself a servant of all to gain all."

However, as they are servants of love they have to be together mothers and mistresses of their subjects by treating them like sons and caring for them as children, and providing them with the care that the mother has of the creature at her breasts in the manner the same Apostle says in 1 Thess. 2:7: "But we were gentle among you, like a mistress taking care of her children," for as the mistress raises her children, natural love draws out from her the mother who raises her son to take care of him, and for this reason becomes a girl with a boy; takes the bite from the mouth to give it to him; loses sleep, tranquility, and his comforts; looks to wash him, dress him, take care of him; nurse him at his breast, and free him from all harms and dangers. Thus, divine love draws from itself the loftier, and the holy minister devotes himself to the care of his sheep and subjects, and [as Saint Bernard says in Sermon 23 on the Canticle) gives him a mother's spirit so for them he can be a child with the children, sad with the saddened, happy with the happy, doing his best by giving them the milk of good doctrine, and spiritual sustenance of the virtues, with good advice, and better examples even if he might lose his comforts, and defend them from all temptations, and works that do not conform to God's law as some are founded on the greed they give them. And what is worse, if his work does not satisfy them, some people if not with bad words, call them dogs as if it were not a serious sin, and it is one of those who cries out to God against such a person who will not lack punishment. And for not paying them for his work he insults them with the word to see them poor and miserable, as if God did not shed as much blood for them, as for the Pope, and the King, and the others, confounds such as these, and they do not call themselves old Christians for their works deny God.

And they make him blaspheme as Saint Paul said, and if they have zeal, they should be like God's own, he is one of those whom the divine scriptures call zealots. Zealous not to be vindictive but as Saint Dionysus says, from an excess of love. And the ministers must be zealous for the good of their sheep not with anger, but with love in all that they do because the same Charity moves all of them.

Bernard says of this in his second letter, "O how good is Charity," which takes care of the sick, now exercises various duties, and among various people loves everyone as children; when she reprehends, it is meek when she orders, it is affable when she is strong, it is with piety, she is generous without duplicity, she knows how to be angry with humility, she is the mother of men, and of the angels, pacifying and uniting all things that are in heaven and on earth.

As she has a mother's spirit, entering the heart of the minister, she clothes him with this spirit, and with the companionship of zeal that does everything well and gently. So those who consider the above-said Charity and love of others, already offer themselves to follow as servants and to care as mothers, and during their rest pray for their subjects and sheep, do not neglect them, and if need be leave their sleep, prayer, and contemplation to come to them because the same Charity itself awakens and provokes them to do it.

And all who fervently come to this work receive from the Lord this loving spirit of mothers for their neighbors for as the same Savior said in Math. 12, whoever did the will of his eternal Father would not only be his brother but his mother, giving him spiritually in the souls of others with whom he would be a spiritual mother. And the minister is compared to the good shepherd and the shepherd is compared to the fig tree, because the fig tree is in the vineyard as a lady looking from above at the humble vines and branches. Similarly, the Prelate, minister, or Pastor looks down from the highest and most honored place at those others. Thus, Saint Gregory in his *Pastoral* says that the Crown of the Kings and Diadem of the Princes is not as high as that of the Priests because everything is included in his prayer. And as the fig tree has rough leaves and very soft fruit, so the shepherd has to have a grave exterior countenance to maintain the respect due to the excellence of the priesthood, but the works must be tasty as figs. Although the wood of the fig tree seems rough and gnarled, inside it is soft and spongy, and looking into the heart or bowels, it is a little like cotton. And so, the Prelate, or minister, or Pastor seems rough sometimes with words, his bowels must be soft as silk. As St. Gregory says in Book 20, 6 of *Morals*, authority, gentleness, piety, and discipline must live together in the bosom of the shepherd and he draws on the example in Job c. 29. *When I sat as a King, nevertheless I was a comforter of the suffering*, who has the gravity of the king, but the bowels of sadness and comforts others who are sad. And just as the fig tree bears two fruits, one being the early figs that Micah c. 7. called the first ripe figs. *My soul desired the precocious fig*, and another fig, so too the shepherd should bear the fruit of example and doctrine and it is not much to ask him for two fruits because they bring forth twice the honor.

Translation and editing of appendix by Ms. Mariana Marquez, Prof. Agnieszka Johnson, Prof. Timothy J. Johnson, and Fr. Francisco Javier Rojo.

Chapter Six

The Timucua as Implied Audience in Fr. Gregorio de Movilla's Explicacion de la Doctrina, *1635*

Viviana Díaz Balsera, *University of Miami*

The Franciscan Timucua missions were the earliest and longest occupied missions in La Florida existing for almost two centuries since the founding of the first *doctrina* in 1587 in Nombre de Dios. As had been their missionary practice in central Mexico, Guatemala, the Andes, and the Philippines the Franciscans set themselves to the task of learning and transcribing the spoken languages of the Indigenous peoples they served and to produce or co-produce written texts in those languages. The Franciscans in Florida were no different, and as a result, Timucua is the first Native American language in present day United States recorded in Latin script. Two Franciscan missionary-philologists, with unrecognized bi- or multi-cultural Indigenous intellectuals and fellow linguists, co-produced at least nine major Timucua/ Spanish imprints during the first three decades of the seventeenth century in the attempt by the Friars Minor to evangelize their Indigenous charges. These texts amount to at least two thousand pages; no Native American Indigenous language north of Mexico has such a rich and extensive corpus as the Timucua at this early period.[1] As Timothy J. Johnson has

1. Alejandra Dubcovsky and George A. Broadwell, "Writing Timucua: Recovering and Interrogating Indigenous Authorship," *Early American Studies: An Interdisciplinary Journal* 15 (2017): 419–21. For all extant imprints and documents as of 2013 comprising the Timucuan corpus, including Movilla's two works as well as two letters from Timucua caciques written in Timucua and translated into Spanish by the friars, see Lisa Noetzel, "Friar Francisco Pareja: Missionary and Linguist," *From La Florida to La California: Franciscan Evangelization in the Spanish Borderlands*, eds. Timothy J. Johnson and Gert Melville (Berkeley: The Academy of American Franciscan History, 2013), 206. In the second half of 2019, Timothy Johnson discovered an unknown catechism by Francisco Pareja housed at the Library of All Souls College in Oxford, England and published in Mexico in 1628. This is the seventh extant bilingual imprint in Timucua and Spanish co-authored by

pointed out, some of these bilingual texts rank among the most extensive and accomplished in their genre compared to those written in Mexico for evangelizing the larger and much wealthier Nahua populations.[2] Tragically, terribly, decimated by epidemics, colonial exploitation by the Spaniards and the ravages of commodified slavery by the English and their Indigenous allies, the missionized Indigenous peoples of Florida almost disappeared by 1763, when the Spaniards gave up Florida to the English in exchange for Cuba.[3]

There is an extensive colonial archive of administrative correspondence, charters, relations, and reports from missionaries, governors, and other royal functionaries about exchanges with the Timucua, and a general historiography of these missions is fairly well-known. But in contrast with central Mexico, the friars did not research Indigenous pre-contact practices in Florida producing works like Motolinía's *History of the Indians of New Spain*, the Dominican Diego Durán's *Historia de Indias*, the bilingual twelve-book *Florentine Codex* overviewed by Bernardino de Sahagún, Jerónimo de Mendieta's *Historia eclesiástica indiana*, or Juan de Torquemada's *Monarquía Indiana*, to mention a few well-known proto-ethnographical works by the missionaries. In Florida, besides a few official reports or *relaciones* by friars and bishops on

---

unacknowledged Timucua *atiqui* (linguist) and Pareja. The translation into English of the title of the catechism reads as "Part Four of the Catechism in the Timucua and Castilian Languages, which Treats the Manner of Listening to the Mass and its Ceremonies." For Johnson's reflections on his discovery, see Timothy J. Johnson, "What Dreams are Made of: The Rediscovered Catechism 'The Mass and its Ceremonies' of Friar Francisco Pareja," *St. Augustine Catholic*, July/August 2021, 18–20.

2. Timothy J. Johnson, "Fray Francisco de Pareja and the Cultures of Confession," in *Franciscans and American Indians in Pan-Borderlands Perspective: Adaptation, Negotiation and Resistance*, eds. Jeffrey M. Burns and Timothy J. Johnson (Oceanside, CA: The Academy of American Franciscan History, 2018), 133.

3. Almost disappeared, but not gone. After the destruction of San Luis de Talimali in 1704, refugees settled in Mobile Bay in Alabama with the French, and eventually in Louisiana, where communities of their descendants still live today. The Talimali Band Apalachee Indians of Louisiana is one such tribe. See Donald G. Hunter, "The Apalachee on Red River, 1763–1834: An Ethnohistory and Summary of Archaeological Testing at the Zimmerman Hill Site, Rapides Parish, Louisiana," *Louisiana Archaeology* 12 (1985): 7–127, and Michelle M. Pigott, "The Materiality of the Apalachee Diaspora: An Indigenous History of Contact and Colonialism in the Gulf South," *Southeastern Archaeology* (2022): 53–73. Another community of Apalachee emigrated with the Spaniards to Veracruz, Mexico, in 1763 and established a new community there called San Carlos de Chacalacas. The town changed its name to Úrsulo Galván in 1930, and Apalachee descendants may still be living there today. See John E. Worth, "Exploring an Eighteenth-Century Refugee Mission in West Florida: Archeological Investigation at Mission San Joseph de Escambe," *Unearthing the Missions of Spanish Florida*, eds. Rochelle Marrinan and Tanya Peres (Gainesville: University Press of Florida, 2021), 136.

Indigenous practices they witnessed at the missions, many pre-Contact traditions were recorded in bilingual catechisms and confessionals mostly with the objective of eradicating those practices considered incompatible with Christianity. In recent decades these bilingual texts co-produced by the Franciscan missionaries and Timucua intellectuals have begun to be read for the treasure trove of linguistic and ethnographical cultural insights they can offer. Indeed, in 1973 Jerald Milanich, William C. Sturtevant and Emilio F. Morán made a pioneering inroad into the exploration of Francisco de Pareja's 1613 *Confessionario* as a source for Timucua ethnography. They extracted from the text all those Timucua cultural practices the friars deemed "diabolic" or at least superstitious, and thus needed to be "confessed." This effort offered contemporary scholars new possibilities for inquiring into the supposedly controversial local cultural practices of the Timucua people.[4] However, because Timucua is a language that has not been spoken since the mid-eighteenth century, scholars have only been able to work with Spanish versions of the texts. But with recent breakthroughs by linguist-anthropologist George Aaron Broadwell, translations into English of the Timucua versions of these imprints are becoming available for the first time. The divergences between the Spanish and the Timucua versions that emerge when comparing them with one another offer possibilities to approach how the polyglot Timucua intellectuals or *Atiqui*, adapted, subverted, interpreted and/or misread the Spanish sources according to their own criteria, cultural understandings and advertence. Although through a glass darkly, the *atiqui*'s interventions in the texts offer new entry points to glimpse Timucua epistemologies and understandings of the world.[5] Moreover, many pages from extant imprints have no equivalents in Spanish.[6] It is likely that these pages were produced not by the friars, but by the Timucua intellectuals themselves. In this sense, as Alejandra Dubcovsky and George A. Broadwell have pointed out, the Timucua *atiqui* in these

4. See Jerald T. Milanich, William C. Sturtevant and Emilio F. Moran, *Francisco Pareja's 1613 Confessionario: A Documentary Source for Timucuan Ethnography* (Tallahassee: Division of Archives, History and Records Management, Florida Department of State, 1972).

5. For some salient studies in this direction see George Aaron Broadwell, "Shadow Authors: The Texts of the Earliest Indigenous Florida Writers," in *Franciscan and American Indians in Pan-Borderlands Perspective*, 139–52; Broadwell, "The Things They Formerly Worshipped: Timucua Christian Texts on Native Worship," *Facing Florida: Essays on Culture and Religion in Early Modern Southeastern America*, eds. Timothy J. Johnson and Jeffrey M. Burns (Oceanside, CA: The Academy of American Franciscan History, 2021), 51–62; Dubcovsky and Broadwell, "Writing Timucua," 2017.

6. Indeed, as Broadwell has pointed out in "The Things They Formerly Worshipped," in Francisco Pareja's *Cathecismo en Lengua Castellana y Timuquana of 1627*, 53, there are many brief parts in Spanish that are then elaborated extensively in Timucua.

imprints may very well be the first Native American *authors* in present-day United States.[7]

As is well known, Gregorio de Movilla was the second most important Franciscan author of record of Florida imprints, having co-written two of the ten extant works, and the last known to be published—the *Forma Breve de administrar los sacramentos a los indígenas*, and the translation into Timucua of the *Explicacion de la Doctrina que compuso el Cardenal Bellarmino, por mandado del Señor Papa Clemente*.[8] Both volumes were printed at the house of Juan Ruiz in Mexico City in 1635. Believing in the confessional need to standardize the explanations of the fundamental doctrines of Catholicism to strengthen and unify the Church's resistance against the "heretical" [read Protestant] challenges of the period, the Council of Trent published in 1566 the lengthy *Catechismus Romanus* or Roman Catechism for clergy and ministers. But this catechism was obviously beyond the grasp of the common people.[9] Therefore, Pope Clement VIII commissioned the renowned Italian Cardinal Bellarmine to write on the fundamental tenets of the Catholic faith in a more persuasive and accessible manner so that priests and preachers would "accommodate themselves to the capacity of their listeners" to reach wider audiences.[10] Following the pope's mandate, Bellarmine wrote two works that were approved in 1598. One of these was a short catechism or *Doctrina Breve* for children and for adults who had not learned the tenets of Christianity. The second one was an almost three times longer, comprising much more detailed catechism for preachers where all the fundamental dogmas of Christianity were discussed at length. Both catechisms were presented in dramatic form except that in the longer one, it is the learner who asks questions and receives carefully crafted and reasoned answers from the

7. See Dubcovsky and Broadwell, "Writing Timucua: Recovering and Interrogating Indigenous Authorship," for this argument.

8. The titles in English are *Brief Way of Administering the Sacraments to the Indians and Spaniards that Live Among Them* and the *Explication of the Doctrine Composed by Cardinal Bellarmine at the Behest of Pope Clement VIII*. The *Explicacion* also contains two additional catechisms, both in Timucua and Spanish, as well as twenty-six exempla also in Spanish and Timucua.

9. Antje Flüchter, "An Introduction," *Translating Catechisms, Translating Cultures: The Expansion of Catholicism in the Early Modern World*, eds. Antje Flüchter and Rouver Wirbser (Boston: Brill, 2017), 20.

10. Sebastian de Lirio, "Prologo a los curas," *Declaracion copiosa de la dotrina christiana, compuesta por orden del Beatissimo Padre Clemente 8 de felice memoria por el Padre Roberto Belarmino del Compañía de Iesus. . . . Con adiciones de exemplos al fin de los capítulos ſacados de graues autores por el Maeſtro Sebaſtian de Lirio, Catedratico de Prima de Griego, y Corrector de libros en la Vniversidad de Alcalà* (Madrid: Viuda de Alõſo Martin, 1615).Translation into English is mine.

teacher.[11] This was the dialogical catechetical format revitalized by none other than Martin Luther in 1526. [12] Both Bellarmine catechisms became instant international bestsellers. The longer one had many editions in Spanish, and the first may have been published in Lisbon in 1614. In addition, the Bellarmine was translated into Latin and at least twenty European languages,[13] as well as into Arabic, Armenian, Caldean, Syriac, and Greek.[14] Spanish missionaries and clerics translated the text into Pampangan (1621), Ilokano (1621),[15] and Quechua (1649), among other languages around the world. Both the long and short catechisms in Timucua appear in Movilla's volume of the *Explicacion de la doctrina*.

In its performance of Catholic Christocentric universality, Movilla's translation of Bellarmine's lengthy catechism covers the mandatory subjects Christians must know, such as the explanation of the Sign of the Holy Cross, an explication of the twelve articles of the Creed, the petitions of Our Father and the Hail Mary, the Ten Commandments, the Seven Sacraments, the Theological and Cardinal Virtues, and other fundamental dogmas of Catholic doctrine.[16] However, unlike

---

11. The text of the short catechism of the Bellarmine contained 96 questions asked by the teacher, while the longer one contained 273 questions with examples to clarify difficult doctrinal points. See Bernard L. Marthaler, *The Catechism Yesterday and Today: the Evolution of a Genre* (Collegeville, MN: The Liturgical Press, 1995), 50.

12. In the age of confessionalism in the sixteenth century, catechisms were assiduously written so that everybody, regardless of social group, gender, proper age or profession, would know the contours of their "denominational identity." Antje Flüchter, "Introduction," *Translating Catechisms, Translating Cultures: The Expansion of Catholicism in the Early Modern World*, eds. Antje Flüchter and Rouven Wirhser (Boston: Brill, 2017), 19. In his attempt to propagate the tenets of reformation, Luther reintroduced in 1526 the question-and-answer format in his small catechism for the people. This format became dominant among Protestants and Catholics alike since it was considered most fitting for the mental and intellectual level of the masses. See George Strauss, *Luther's House of Learning: Indoctrination of the Young in German Reformation* (Baltimore, MD: Johns Hopkins University Press, 1978).

13. Or twenty-two languages according to Peter Burke, if Piedmontese and Sicilian were to be included. Peter Burke, "Cultures of Translation in Early Modern Europe," in *Cultural Translation in Early Modern Europe*, eds. Peter Burk and R. Po-chia Hsia (Cambridge: Cambridge University Press, 2007), 17.

14. Joaquín Moles, "Introducción," in *Explicacion mas copiosa de la Doctrina Christiana Breve que de orden del Papa Clemente VIII compuso para los Niños y los adultos no instruidos en los Mysterios de nuestra Santa Fé Catholica . . . Roberto Bellarmino. . .* (Madrid: Pantaleon Aznar, 1777), 30. This was a new translation of the Bellarmine into Spanish. Translations into these diverse languages certainly evince the global reach of the Bellarmine.

15. Beningo Albarrán González,"La primera traducción de la *Doctrina Cristiana* del cardenal Belarmino al ilocano (Filipinas)," *Livius: Revista de estudios de traducción* 12 (1998): 9–20.

16. Movilla included at the end of the volume of the *Explicación* many of the exempla that Sebastián de Lirio had already added in the Madrid edition of 1615.

the reigning Jerónimo de Ripalda catechism in Mexico at the time with its three hundred plus questions answered in a couple of short, standardized sentences, Movilla's Timucua catechetical literature—as well as that by Pareja—is much longer and discursive, showing high levels of theological complexity, verbal richness, and thorough attention to detail.[17] Mark Christensen has argued that "the presentation of Christian doctrine betrays its audiences."[18] Indeed, the way the text speaks or globalizes its doctrinal message yields insights about how it is informed, shaped, and structured by the audience it addresses. This is the concept of the implied audience that can offer glimpses of an Indigenous perspective by way of the Timucua posited as communicative partners of the text.

With this notion in mind, I examine in this essay Movilla's 1635 prologue to the *Explicacion de la doctrina que compuso el Cardenal Bellarmino* and compare two passages from Spanish and the Timucua versions. In the prologue Movilla as author constructs Timucua audience for his Spanish readership through his claims—somewhat imprecise as we will see—regarding the audience's "capacities," knowledge, and expectations. Next, in examining and comparing the passages, I aim to show not only how "global" Christian doctrine was imparted to a Timucua audience, but I also attempt to focus on the role of the Indigenous interlocutors as *implied audience* of the text. Building on Wolfang Iser's concept of the implied reader, Wolf Schmid argues that this narratological category centers on "to whom the work is directed and whose linguistic codes, ideological norms, and aesthetic ideas must be taken into account if the work is to be understood."[19] The implied audience

17. Moreover, by the time Movilla's lengthy volume of the *Explicacion de la doctrina* was published for preaching to the Timucua, significantly shortened versions of the Ripalda catechism were produced in Mexico in 1634 and 1637, with only a couple dozen of his questions and answers. Bartolomé Castaño would steal the show of "little doctrines" in 1644 with his *Catecismo breve de lo que precisamente debe saber el cristiano*. Louise Burkhart has argued that the "little doctrine" or *doctrina pequeña* was a simplified catechetical format listing anywhere from 17 to 29 questions about basic doctrinal tenets all Christians had to know, along with short, scripted answers. The little doctrine format circulated in at least eleven Indigenous languages in Mexico. See Louise Burkhart, "The 'Little Doctrine' and Indigenous Catechesis in New Spain," *Hispanic American Historical Review* 94, no. 2 (2014): 167.

18. Mark Z. Christensen, *Translated Christianities: Nahua and Maya Religious Texts* (University Park: Pennsylvania State University Press, 2014), 11.

19. Wolf Schmid, "Implied Reader," *The Living Handbook of Narratology*, eds. Peter Huhn et al (Hamburg: Hamburg University, 2009), 161–73. See also related concepts such as the hypothetical or authorial audience by Peter J. Rabinowitz in "Truth in Fiction," *Critical Inquiry* (1977), 121–41; Wayne Booth's "postulated reader" in *The Rhetoric of Fiction* (Chicago: University of Chicago Press, 1983): 137–44; and Umberto Eco's "model reader" in *The Role of the Reader: Explorations of Semiotics of Texts* (Net Library, Inc.; Bloomington: Indiana University Press, 1994), 8–12. More recently Brian Richardson has given

is the range of possible active receiving subjects the author anticipates, hypothesizes, or foresees, and according to whom the message is fashioned so that (at least some) communicative success may be achieved. In the heightened persuasive context of catechetical dynamics, the competence and codes of the intended audience, whether literate or non-literate, must be especially considered if any understanding, desire for, or interest in things Christian is to be generated. Thus, in pursuing the category of the implied audience in the *Explicacion*, I can reasonably assume that Movilla had an actual, on-site empirical experience of the Timucua, and that by learning the language and promoting the translation and production of the text, as a missionary he wanted or at least hoped to establish effective acts of communication with his Indigenous audience. Therefore, by being attentive to the accuracy and subtleties of the language of the text, the complexity of the propositional contents, the demands of their decoding and the depth of their inferential cues, we will have another entry point to approach a Timucua perspective as they faced and interacted with the epistemic and socio-economic challenges posited by their others of Christianity and the stakes of early modern globalization brought about by their interference.

Of course, this entry point is through a hall of mirrors, darkly. In contrast with the Nahuas of central Mexico and except for two extant letters by Timucua chiefs, there are no extant records of Timucua direct testimonies of their experience or perspectives regarding Christianity, their own Indigenous culture on the ground or prior to Contact, and/or of the welcome or unwelcome presence of the missionaries in their communities. Most of what can be accessed regarding their voices and experience is mediated by texts the Timucua co-authored with the colonizers, by documents produced altogether by the Europeans, or by what the archaeological interpretations of their surviving material culture will tell. And yet, while we do not have enough evidence to reconstruct the differential dynamics between the anticipated and the actual, empirical Indigenous reception of the catechetical texts, this does not mean that they were radically incommensurable. It is useful to remember on this account Marco de Marinis's argument in the *Semiotics of Performance* that even though the audiences and interpretants posited by a performance text

a lively account of multiple implied audiences in a single text in "Singular Text, Multiple Implied Readers," *Style* 41, no. 3 (2007): 259–74. Although the notion of the implied reader has been usually theorized for works with aesthetic dimensions, varying levels of ambiguity and diverse positionalities of literate audiences, the notion is a fitting tool to work with catechetical texts. Because the communicational intent of (more or less) unequivocal, doctrinal messages is at their core, catechetical texts must arguably be especially sensitive to the skills and competences of their audiences, literate, illiterate, or non-literate, in order to maximize reception.

cannot be confused with the actual, empirical receptors, it is not unacceptable to assume that they are somehow related to each other.[20] Surely, the audience that the text foresees in order to produce the communicative act will never be equal to its empirical, flesh-and-blood actual audience. But this does not require that we presuppose an unbridgeable gap between the two. As suggested above, in the catechetical context communication of a specific set of beliefs to the audience is high priority.[21] Although not unthinkable, it is unlikely that the implied audience of a catechetical text would be totally alien to the competence or state of mind of the empirical, historical audience destined to process its messages.

The Prologue: Movilla's (Slanted) Construction of the Timucua Audience for a Spanish Readership

Beyond the sometimes endless and convoluted titles of doctrinal and catechetical works, and as has been recently argued by Lieve Behiels, in the prologues the authors express to their superiors and/or confreres their estimation of the situatedness of their partner audiences, whether Indigenous or non-indigenous, and how this inflects the style and even content of the work.[22] Indeed, Movilla addresses his rich prologue to the *Explicacion* to "religious, ministers and pastors, or parishioners of the small herds of the Lord."[23] He registers there etic epistemic information about the Timucua critical to their reception of the doctrine laid out by the Bellarmine. In a not atypical translational missionary move, Movilla alerts his Spanish readership that due to the differences in the Timucua language and especially to the fact that it did not have names that could signify "God, Divinity, the Angels, or spirits or any other supernatural things,"[24] it was necessary to use metaphors, comparisons, and linguistic roundabouts or periphrasis, and to leave aside some of Bellarmine's similes and examples.[25]

---

20. Marco de Marinis, *The Semiotics of Performance*, trans. Áine O'Healy (Bloomington and Indianapolis: Indiana University Press, 1993), 168.

21. See "Catechisms," *New Catholic Encyclopedia*, 2nd ed., vol. 3, "Gale, 2003," 239–46; *Gale In Context: U.S. History*, link.gale.com/apps/doc/CX3407702132/UHIC?u=miami_richter&sid=bookmark-UHIC&xid=4c42c3a1.

22. Lieve Behiels, "La traducción como alimento y otras enseñanzas: una exploración temática de los prólogos de textos doctrinales misioneros americanos," *Hermēneus* 20 (2018): 11–35.

23. Gregorio de Movilla, "Prólogo," *Explicación de la doctrina que compuso el Cardenal Belarmino*, ++ ij. Translation into English is mine.

24. Movilla, "Prologo," ++ ij.

25. This observation, or cautionary metatextual statement is also present in Fr. Francisco Pareja, who in the "Advertencia" of his catechism of 1627, educates readers regarding

Related to the absence of words in Timucua to name the supernatural, Movilla says he had to do an even more crucial adaptation than explaining it with tropes.[26] He calls his readers' attention to the fact that he did not follow Bellarmine's full explanation of the First Commandment because the Italian Cardinal talked about the many gods of the Gentiles, but that the Timucua "in these provinces" did not have idols nor had known what God was.[27] The assessment about ignorance of a monotheistic God "in the European sense"[28] coincides with René de Laudonnière's observation seventy-five years earlier in his *Historie Notable* that: "They [the Timucua] haue no knowledge of God, nor any religion, sauing what they see, as the Sunne and the Moone."[29] However, Movilla's statements are perplexing because by the time he co-authored the *Explicacion* with the *atiqui*, the coastal Mocama had been missionized since 1587, inland Timucua chiefdoms since 1608, and the Yustaga/Cotocochuni province since 1623 when Fray Alonso de Pesquera and Movilla himself negotiated the acceptance of friars with the cacique of the land.[30]

The issue of ancestor worship and idols is even more puzzling. According to his prologue, Movilla feared that with Bellarmine's explanation of the First Commandment, the Timucua would learn not only about the many gods of the Gentiles, but that these gods had also been adored.[31] Certainly, the Italian cardinal had written that the Gentiles had worshipped the sun, the moon, as

---

the untranslatability of some *frasis,* or ways of expression in Timucua. He adds however that despite the belief shared by many that this language is "barbaric," it is "very fecund" (Pareja, *Catecismo* 1627, np).

26. See Otto Zwartjes for an overview of early modern historiography of translation studies in the context of Spanish missionary practice in the New World, and for the translation strategies used by early modern missionaries. Indeed, Movilla represents himself as seeking his own creative solutions for the lack of Indigenous terms to represent Christian concepts. Otto Zwartjes, "Missionaries' Contribution to Translation Studies in the Spanish Colonial Period: The *Mise en page* of Translated Texts and Its Functions in Foreign Language Teaching," *Missionary Linguistics V: Translation Theories and Practices*, eds. Otto Zwartjes, Klaus Zimmerman, and Martina Schrader-Kniffki (John Benjamins Publishing, 2014), 8–9.

27. "Y como eftas Prouincias, ni teniã idolos, ni fabian que cofa fueffe Dios . . . querria que no fupiefen, ni oyefen que vbo, ay, ni puede hauer mas que vn folo Dios, en tres Personas. . . ," Movilla, "Prólogo," *Explicacion de la doctrina*, ++ij.

28. John H. Hann, *A History of the Timucua Indians and Missions* (Gainesville: University of Florida Press, 1996), 111.

29. René de Laudonniere, "Preface," *Three Voyages*, trans. Charles E. Bennett (Gainesville: University Presses of Florida, 1975), 12–13.

30. John E. Worth, *The Timucuan Chiefdoms of Spanish Florida* (Gainesville: University Press of Florida), 1:44–76.

31. ". . . en la explicaciõ del primer mandamiento del decálogo, no figo à Belarmino, por q trata de la multitud de Diofes de la Gentilidad, y como vbo quién los adorò," Movilla, "Prólogo," *Explicacion de la doctrina*, ++ij.

well as "some dead men."[32] But nothing of this was new for the Timucua. Although at the time Movilla writes, Timucua worship practices for the sun and moon to my knowledge had not been recorded beyond Laudonnière's references, their Indigenous elaborate funerary rites for deceased caciques in pre-contact times may be considered observances bordering on worship. Laudonnière himself describes in his *First Voyage* death rituals in which the whole village grieved and fasted for the cacique during three consecutive days and where certain women wailed for him in the morning, noon, and night for six months, among other acts of mourning.[33] Much closer to Movilla's time, Fray Alonso de Jesús mentions in his 1630 *Memorial* that the graves of caciques in La Florida were kept separate "and in the highest hills" and that children of commoners were buried with the cacique, upon which the parents gained elite status.[34] As Tamara Shircliff Spike has argued, the transformation of a deceased individual into a venerable ancestor was so central to Timucua cosmology that it was grafted into their very kinship terminology.[35]

Regarding the issue of idols, Fray Jerónimo de Oré mentions in his relation of 1617 that with the consent of the cacique of Timucua, Fray Martín Prieto had burned twelve images or "idols" in the town of San Martín, and six in each of four additional towns of the province.[36] But in the very same

32. Bellarmine's text reads as follows: "In the second part [of the First Commandment], God commands not to have anything that has been created as God. And in doing this sin the Gentiles, which previously not knowing the true God, they *had and worshipped as God several creatures like the sun or the moon, or some dead men*, in its own sin sorcerers and sorceresses, and all malefics, necromancers and diviners who give to the devil of hell, the honor that is given to God" (Bellarmine, *Doctrina Christiana*, 1614, ff. 82v–83r; unpublished translation into English by George Aaron Broadwell, emphasis is mine).

33. Laudonniere, *Three Voyages*, 15, "Preface," 15.

34. Fray Alonso de Jesús and John Hann, "1630 Memorial," 99.

35. Tamara Shircliff Spike, "Death and Death Ritual among the Timucua of Spanish Florida," in *From La Florida to La California: Franciscan Evangelization in the Spanish Borderlands*, eds. Timothy J. Johnson and Gert Melville (Berkeley, CA: The Academy of American Franciscan History, 2013), 201.

36. F. Luis Jerónimo de Oré, Raquel Chang-Rodríguez and Nancy Vogeley (eds. and trans.), *Account of the Martyrs in the Provinces of La Florida* (Albuquerque: University of New Mexico Press, 2017), 144. Fray Jerónimo de Oré had been commissioned to visit the Franciscan province of Santa Elena. He visited La Florida in 1614 and then again in 1616, after which he composed the *Account* most likely in 1617. As part of Oré's commission, the friar submitted a questionnaire to the *custodio* (superior of a religious province in formation), the *definidores* (friars who formed part of the internal governing body of the province), and other friars holding official appointments in the mission regarding the progress of their evangelization endeavors. Oré collected their responses as part of the material he put together for his account, as pointed out by Chang-Rodríguez, "Introduction," *Account*, 15–17, and more recently by Noble David Cook and Alexandra Parma Cook in

relation Oré quotes Fray Francisco Pareja as declaring that he had "not found any trace of idolatry, or witchcraft" among the Timucua.[37] Although the statuettes burned by Prieto may not have been considered enough to amount to organized "idolatrous" religious practices like those of the Mexica in Central Mexico, it is intriguing that Pareja (and years later, Movilla) fully ignored Fray Prieto's testimony as officially reported by Oré.[38] Moreover, in the Timucua sections with no Spanish equivalent in Pareja's 1627 bilingual catechism, the inscribed speaker rebukes the Indigenous narratees or inscribed audience in the text, stating that "the Timucua make their [own] lord, and every country and every town creates another god and believes in him. . ." and that "there are many Gods that exist in each village and on every side."[39] George A. Broadwell has also brought attention to the word *chapi*, which in most of Pareja's catechetical texts refers to objects that were worshipped, and how the voice also stood for "soul/spirit."[40] Broadwell suggests that such multiple

---

Luis Gerónimo de Oré: The World of and Andean Franciscan from the Frontiers to the Centers of Power (Baton Rouge: Louisana State University Press, 2023), 191–201.

37. Pareja's statement was an answer to the question on whether there were causes for denying the sacrament of Communion to the Timucua. See the statement in *Account*, 138.

38. For the complexity of the Mesoamerican Late Postclassic pantheon, the monumental *Florentine Codex* is instructive and may suffice as an example. The codex was produced in several stages in the *altepetl* or city-states of Tepepulco, Tenochtitlan, and Tlatelolco between 1547 and 1577. In the first and second books of this multi-authored work by Nahua informants and intellectuals, and by Franciscan Bernardino de Sahagún, there is extensive evidence of rich, elaborate pre-Contact calendrical rituals in every month of the Mesoamerican year, dedicated to the presiding deity or deities of the month, as well as of the buildings and temples dedicated to the gods, and detailed accounts of their refined insignia. For a good, recent volume on many aspects of the production and importance of this text as well as a solid bibliography, see *The Florentine Codex: An Encyclopedia of the Nahua World in Sixteenth-Century Mexico*, eds. Jeanette Favrot Peterson and Kevin Terraciano (Austin: University of Texas Press, 2019). There is little possibility that the Franciscans working in La Florida would have had no knowledge of some of the contents of this work related to Nahua pre-Contact beliefs, practices, and pantheon. This could explain why Pareja, who may have missionized in Mexico for sixteen years before coming to Florida, felt that the Timucua did not have a formalized pantheon and religious practices that hindered their capacity to receive the Eucharist.

39. Translation of the Timucua into English is by George Aaron Broadwell, "The Things They Formerly Worshipped: Timucua Christian Texts on Native Worship," *Facing Florida: Essays on Culture and Religion in Early Modern Southeastern America*, eds. Timothy J. Johnson and Jeffrey M. Burns (Oceanside, CA: The Academy of American Franciscan History, 2021), 56. The full title of the Pareja catechism in which the passages appear is *Catecismo en Lengua Timuquana y Castellana en el qual se instruyen y cathequizan los adultos infieles que an de ser Christianos. Y no sera menos util para los ya Christianos* (Mexico: Juan Ruiz, 1627), ff. 13r–15v.

40. Broadwell, "The Things They Formerly Worshipped," 60.

meanings could certainly jibe if one considers *chapi* as figures with "infused animating spirits."[41]

These inconsistencies intimate that neither Pareja nor Movilla paid enough attention to the Timucua sections of the former's bilingual catechisms of 1612 or 1627 where the *chapi* and the many gods in all villages were denounced.[42] It would seem that once Pareja dictated to the *atiqui* or gave them in writing what the latter should translate into Timucua, he never went back or looked in depth at the final product.[43] Another possibility is that Pareja and/or Movilla simply did not have enough competence in Timucua to understand the substantial amounts of writing that the *Atiqui* authored without Spanish equivalents.[44] Be that as it may, their construction of the Timucua as having no "idols" was inaccurate and paternalistic but more favorable for

41. Broadwall, "The Things They Formerly Worshipped," 61. Broadwell refers to the talking, animated "bionic Greek statues" in Greek classic art, as a belief having some parallels with the *chapi*. Interestingly, such ensouled statues were also alluded to in the passages from the Bellarmine that Movilla explicitly suppressed. Writes Bellarmine: "In the third part [of the First Commandment] God commands . . . that not only we should not have as God the things that He created . . . but that we must not fashion ourselves things to have and adore as God; sin that the Gentiles committed, who were so blind, that they made idols; that is, statues of gold, silver, wood or marble, and they persuaded themselves that those were gods; especially because the devils from hell sometimes got into them, and made them talk, move, and in this way they [the Gentiles] offered them [the statues] sacrifices and they worshipped them." Bellarmino, *Declaracion de la Doctrina Christiana* (Lisbon: Antonio Alvarez, 1614), ff. 83v–84r; translation into English is mine. Bellarmine seems to register here the controversial passages from the *Asclepius* attributed to Hermes Trismegistus, where the latter explains how Egyptian sages had built statues with special materials that would attract demons to inhabit them, and thus make the statues move and speak. The famous or infamous passages can be found in *Asclepius* 23 (80–81) and 38 (90–91). Quotations from the *Asclepius*—and their very harsh treatment as idolatrous—had first been known to the West in St. Augustine's *City of God*.

42. Broadwell, "Things They Formerly Worshipped," 56.

43. Christensen refers to James Lockhart's hypothesis regarding the Nahua evangelization theater, where the North American *nahuatlato* speculates that the Franciscans gave Nahua authors written or oral directives in Spanish to produce the plays in Nahuatl, and then never looked back at what the Indigenous writers had produced. Christensen then makes the point that the same thing may have happened with other texts that Indigenous intellectuals were charged to write in their language. Christensen, *Translated Christianities*, 10. This could be the case in the passages of the *Cathecismo* of 1627 that Broadwell discusses in his piece, "Things They Formerly Worshipped."

44. Dubcovsky and Broadwell argue from the linguistic evidence that Pareja had a "limited grasp of Timucua grammar." See their article "Writing Timucua," 424, and Broadwell, "Shadow Authors: The Texts of the Earliest Indigenous Florida Writer," in *Franciscan and American Indians in Pan-Borderlands Perspective*, 2018, 139–52. See also the chapter by Henning and Katenkamp in this volume, 43–64.

a Spanish readership since the Timucua were not represented as "transgressors" of the First Commandment. These inconsistencies may have significant implications regarding co-production practices of the bilingual catechetical texts in La Florida.

Two more caveats. The *Explicacion* of Bellarmine's *doctrina* is only in Timucua. Movilla explains in his prologue that to save printing costs, the source text in Spanish was not included because "everybody had the Bellarmine in Castilian." This paratextual statement would have most likely referred to readers who would be using the text to preach, but it could have also referred to Timucua bi- or multi-lingual intellectuals who spoke and/or read Spanish and acted as mediators between the friars and the community, just like the Nahuas did with the Franciscans in Mexico.[45] Indeed, Movilla acknowledges the presence of an *Atiqui* who had helped him fine-tune the Timucua *Explicacion*: "I translated (the Bellarmine), and finished putting it in order and polishing it with the atiqui, so that I could catechize with it, or somebody else if he so chose."[46] In the prologue then, Movilla founds the linguistic precision, cogency and flow of the text on the participation and competence of the Timucua mediator. And while it may be very difficult to assess the extent of the acknowledged intervention of the unnamed *Atiqui*, Movilla's statement warrants that he was present in the production of the text for its specific audience. This unnamed *Atiqui* was the competent, indispensable Indigenous agent who organized, refined, and enabled the text to speak in a style, tone and voice that a Timucua audience would consent to listen to, if only for a while.

The Implied Audience and First Article of the Creed in the Timucua *Explicacion de la doctrina*

Movilla and the *Atiqui*'s co-authorship allows us then a closer and more nuanced look at the posited transcultural competence of the implied Timucua audience in the *Explicacion*. For the text was fashioned not only according to what Movilla exogenously thought, believed, or imagined the Timucua would understand or find meaningful. The *Explicacion* was mediated by a Timucua intellectual who regardless of his elite status as a multicultural, polyglot literate subject, was without question much closer culturally and linguistically to the

45. Louise Burkhart argues that in *visitas* or communities in central Mexico that had no resident priests, children and adults were compelled to participate in weekly readings of catechetical texts led by the *fiscal*, "the indigenous church official who oversaw a large part of community religious life." Burkhart, *Little Doctrine*, 169.

46. "Traduxele [el Belarmino] y acabele de poner en orden, y limarle con el Atiqui, para Cathequiçar yo por el, y alguno otro si le pareſieſe," Movilla, "Prologo" ++r.

audience, literate or or non-literate, than Movilla. And although the unnamed *Atiqui* should not be readily allegorized as a disinterested, all-knowing representative of the Timucua community and of what it could or would understand, his acknowledged Indigenous intervention suggests a more accurate anticipation of what the Timucua audience could be expected to grasp, and how it could be more properly addressed to engage its attention.

I will examine a couple of passages from the *Explicacion* that deal with the first article of the Creed in which the concept of God as Creator is explained. As mentioned earlier, the Bellarmine is a dialogical text dramatizing a catechetical session between two characters: a subject of knowledge who is of course the priest, father or teacher, and an inquiring learner. Although the knowing subject always has the answer, in both the source text in Spanish and in the Timucua version the learner shows independence and initiative by constantly asking further questions or requesting clarifications about the issue at hand, until he or she is satisfied or moves on to another topic. While the student has declared she is strongly inclined to learn because she has heard that it is necessary to know Christian doctrine to be saved, she does not seem to be convinced only by the priest's authority, but also by the soundness, patient, or exalted elaborations of his answers. The character of the avid, tireless learner certainly serves as an ideal model for the implied audience of the text, Indigenous and non-Indigenous. But they are not mirror images because the communicative operation of the text does not depend on the implied audience's ability to pose all the questions that the inquisitive learner asks. To fulfill at least some of its communicative function, the text just requires that its implied audience remain interested in and attentive to the development of the catechetical dramatic performance between the characters of the priest and the student. The *Atiqui*'s job is to make linguistic and semantic choices for the implied Timucua audience that will reduce its distance with the empirical Indigenous audience outside the text—as much as possible.

After the priest has declared the full Creed to the learner, the latter requests a detailed explanation of each of its words in both the Spanish and the Timucua versions. In the Spanish source text, the learner wants to know what it means to believe in God.[47] The priest explains:

> It means that we must believe firmly that there is a God even though we don't see him with the eyes of our body, and that this God is one and alone, and that is why we say 'in God' and not 'in gods.'

---

47. Bellarmine, *Declaracion copiosa de la doctrina* (Lisbon: 1614), 9r. George A. Broadwell used the Lisbon edition of 1614 for the Spanish source text. I thank him for his generosity in sharing with me his unpublished translations into English of both the Spanish source text and the Timucua version.

The priest explains the meaning of believing in God as the cognitive certainty of His reality as a unique and only being, independently of all material evidence available to the senses. But the demand of the firmness of certainty would seem to entail a bodily experience of cognition, irrespective of the external world and its capacity to affect perception.

In the rendering of the Timucua text, the question in the source text is modified to inquire not after an experience or cognitive state of belief, but rather to the meaning of uttering the statement: "*What does it mean 'I believe in God'*"? Accordingly, the reply is:

> We do not see him (with) the eye of the body, but we say that there is one God, thinking 'God truly exists.'

That is, belief is explained as saying something contemporary or immediately after a thought. Although the body as a perceiving eye cannot see God, to believe in Him means to think or to have thought "He really exists" and then to say it. The experience of the certainty of a wholehearted conviction in the existence of God is not necessary to produce the utterance of the belief in his existence in the Timucua version. Only thought is required here. Such a subtle distinction could reflect the Atiqui's intervention for although we do not know what the powers of thought meant for the Timucua, the demands on the learner in the Timucua Bellarmine would seem to be easier to assent to. For even if she did not know or feel much about this one God that the friars were constantly referring to, she could agree on the possibility of thinking about the truth of his existence, and then saying it. This, of course, would not have been enough for some friars. For them, the attendant feeling produced by the certainty of belief would be missing.

A couple of questions down the road, the learner asks why it is said that God is omnipotent or all powerful. The priest in the source text responds as follows:

> Because he can do anything that he wants (which is what omnipotent means), and nothing can be difficult for him, and if you were to say to me that God cannot die or sin, and thus it seems that he cannot do all things, then I would say to you that the power to die or sin is not a power but impotence as when it is said of the bravest soldier that he can conquer all, and cannot be defeated by anyone; it does not defame his bravery to say that he cannot be defeated, because to be defeated is not a strength but a weakness.

The priest/teacher in the source text goes into a deep explanation defining the omnipotence of God. But then he anticipates the paradox of God's omnipotence with the impossibility of His perishing or sinning, explaining that dying or committing a sin is not an act of power, but a lack of it. However, while it could certainly be argued that dying should not be conceived as a power (unless by choice of suicide), sinning could be the consequence of an intentional, forceful act of the will. The subsequent analogy of the bravery of the all-conquering soldier whose courage is not diminished by the fact that he is unable to be defeated, is not very felicitous either. The Timucua version deletes the uneasy paradox and the less-than-convincing analogy altogether:

> Because whatever the lord wants, he [can] do, omnipotent the Lord God alone (?) [can] do this.

Due to Movilla's translation, the *Atiqui*'s intervention or both, the Timucua version hits the nail on its head by tersely defining the singular omnipotence of God as doing whatever he wants. The economy of the explanation in Timucua signals an accurate understanding of the core of the theological issue as it stays away from the flamboyant digressions of the source text.

The relentless learner in the Spanish version then asks for the meaning of "Creator," while in the Timucua text he asks after the meaning of the statement about the creator and Maker of all. The source text explains this as follows:

> It means that God has made things from nothing, and that only he can reduce these things back to nothing, and even though the angels, humans and the demons do and undo some things, they can't make these things but they need to make them out of some material, which already existed, and they can't unmake this material either, but they can transform it into other things. . . . Thus God alone is called and is creator because he alone does not need any material to make things.

To illustrate the unique powers (and demanding idea) of nothingness, both texts coincide in offering the example of how men bring houses into being, but to do so they must use things or materials that are at hand. The building materials in the source text are presented as stone, lime, and wood while in the Indigenous version they correspond to the familiar, essential ones of wood, mud, and palmetto with which the Timucua constructed their homes.[48] However, even though the Timucua version acknowledges the singular faculty of God to create things without materials, out of nothing and without reason (*maha ynetoro*), it probes further on God's will as the originating source of his creativity:

> So it is the Lord God (by?) wanting, long ago made the sky and the earth and all things out of nothing. If he wanted, he could make it finish and cease out of nothing. . . . They [angels, people and demons] cannot do

---

48. Broadwell makes this observation in his unpublished translation of the passage.

> it from nothing. God from his own will, without wood and without any other thing, made it only from his will.

This greater emphasis on will and want in the Timucua text may be significant. To fulfill its communicative potential and convey an idea of the very difficult, hardly conceivable creative omnipotence of the Christian God, the text must assume that its implied Timucua audience has an esteemed notion of the will as a positive, even engendering force that can make things happen. Otherwise, the statements insisting on its importance to portray the unique powers of this God would not be very compelling. The capacity of the Christian God to create from nothingness or without reason, *maha ynetoro*, is recognized in both the source text and the Timucua. But in the latter, *maha ynetoro* is subordinated to the idea of His powerful will as a more original, anterior source of creation. Of course, we do not have enough information to know how the empirical Timucua audience interpreted the notion of the will and its limits. But if only the theoretical notion of the Timucua as implied audience of the text offers the possibility of a philological and cultural lead that can be pursued. For it allows us to consider that the text intervened by the *Atiqui* anticipates that the Timucua audience is likely to be more drawn to decode the unique creative entity of the Christian God by underscoring the notion of an esteemed, forceful will and the overwhelming power of its want or desire With such a consideration, of course, we will delve deeper into the intricacies of Timucua-Spanish epistemic relations. But also, by way of this relational dynamics, we may be able to inch closer to glimpse a Timucua culturally situated construct of the will, to the possibilities and impossibilities of its powers, and to what this may tell us about Timucua notions of agency.

The semantic contents of the first article of the Creed in the *Explicacion de la doctrina* such as thought and the production of belief, the invisibility of the godly body, nothingness and its creative relation to the will and to the unique substance of the wanting powers of the Christian God, are complex, demanding, and challenging to audiences both Indigenous and non-Indigenous. I propose then that the *Explicacion* is implying a highly competent Indigenous audience, interested in actualizing the communicative codes of the text. Resistance to these codes never erupts in the source or the Timucua texts, but full consent to those codes is not always immediate or explicit. Whether fully convinced or not, after each explanation by the priest, the inquisitive or even relentless learner that serves as model for the implied audience and (hopefully) also for the empirical audience on the ground, moves on to her next question, showing initiative and sometimes a remarkably independent reasoning process.

There is very little information about how the actual *Explicacion* was delivered to the real Timucua audience, how the latter interpreted the text, or how they were interested, or simply uninterested in its contents. Scholars have posited that the monolingual version of the *Explicacion,* as well as the extant bilingual imprints evince a Timucua literate community.[49] The Timucua intellectuals or even the friars themselves most likely also performed out loud readings of the *Explicacion* for non-literate Timucua.[50] Be that as it may, the passages discussed are only two examples of differentials between the Spanish source text of the Bellarmine, and the Timucua version. There are passages in Timucua with no Spanish equivalent. As more of the Timucua text becomes available to contemporary readers, we will be able to conjecture how the long and extensive Bellarmine was adapted by Movilla and the *Atiqui* to make it as engaging as possible to its implied Timucua audience, and what these conjectures may tell us about the Timucua during the first decades of the seventeenth century, even if only through the dark mirror of their expected or wished for responses by the friar and the *Atiqui.* For now, I submit that the notion of the Timucua implied audience in the *Explicacion* evinces that it was constructed as wielding a comfortable competence to relate to intangible, or even abstruse concepts of divinity. Within the missionizing constraints of a universalist Christian discourse, the text of the *Explicacion* addresses the Timucua audience as subjects with robust agency and discernment, beyond what their construct in the prologue for the Spanish readership seems to anticipate. Of course, the agency, discernment and clarity of judgment shown by the learner that would serve as model both for the implied and empirical Timucua audiences of La Florida, ironically also always already entailed the possibility that those audiences would have the freedom to accept or not the expounded tenets of Christianity, according to interests other than what the friars had foreseen, anticipated, or hoped for.

---

49. See Johnson, "Francisco Pareja and the Cultures of Confession," 130–37, and Broadwell, "Shadow Authors," 152.

50. See note 45 on the Indigenous church officials or *fiscales* in Mexico as readers of catechetical texts for the non-literate Nahuas when friars or priests were unavailable.

CHAPTER SEVEN

Fish, Fowl, and Fruit: Foodways and the Franciscan Mission System of La Florida

LEE NEWSOM, *Flagler College/Pennsylvania State University*

The Franciscan mission system of Spanish La Florida was established under royal edict in conjunction with Spain's territorial expansion into North America, in this case, the greater southeastern region, in the wake of having successfully colonized portions of the Caribbean, Central, and South America. By all accounts, the Franciscan missions associated with this northern territory were pivotal to the success of Spanish colonization in the region, thus understanding the nature and operation of the missions, here with emphasis on foodways, is integral to an overall understanding of the Spanish colonial enterprise. Archaeobotanical and archaeozoological data derived from a series of La Florida's Franciscan missions form the basis of this essay.[1] The various plant and animal remains recovered and identified from the sites provide direct evidence of the types of mission food resources and related matters, augmented by relevant ethnohistoric documentary sources.

The Franciscan Order first took full charge of the missionization process in La Florida in 1572–1573.[2] Multiple missions were established over the

---

1. This is an abridged version of a lengthier piece on Spanish mission foodways, slated for separate publication.

2. Rochelle A. Marrinan and Tanya M. Peres, "Unearthing the Missions of Spanish Florida," in *Unearthing the Missions of Spanish Florida*, eds. Tanya M. Peres and Rochelle A. Marrinan (Gainesville: University of Florida Press, 2021), 7–8; Robert Allen Matter, "Missions in the Defense of Spanish Florida, 1566–1710," *Florida Historical Quarterly* 54, no. 1 (1975): 20; Zelia Sweett and Mary H. Sheppy, *The Spanish Missions of Florida* (Washington, DC: Work Projects Administration, 1940), 21–23; John E. Worth, "Catalysts of Assimilation: The Role of Franciscan Missionaries in the Colonial System of Spanish Florida," in *From La Florida to La California: Franciscan Evangelization in the Spanish Borderlands*, eds. Timothy J. Johnson and Gert Melville (Berkeley, CA: The Academy of American Franciscan History, 2013), 135–37.

course of the First Spanish Period (1565–1763). Two major towns or presidios and their garrisons were involved from the outset, specifically, St. Augustine (1565–) and Santa Elena (1566–1587), which were founded by Pedro Menéndez de Avilés in coastal Northeast Florida and South Carolina, respectively. These two settlements acted as the entry points for food provisions and other subsistence support for La Florida, interacting directly, however intermittently, with Spain and Havana, Cuba, the ultimate regional seat of power. The presidios in turn interacted and articulated with the original Franciscan missions in immediate proximity of the two settlements, eventually including additional later missions or *doctrinas* and their associated *visitas*, as these were established over time and in a mainly east to westward progression across northern Florida and southern Georgia (the so-called "mission chain").

In 1566, St. Augustine's Spanish colonists, including clergy, left Menéndez 's original encampment (1565–1566), known as the Fountain of Youth Park site, and relocated to nearby Anastasia Island. The Spanish settlement was moved back on shore in 1572, where St. Augustine is currently situated.[3] The mission enterprise was fully realized under the auspices of the Franciscan Order by 1573, ultimately with a return to the mainland in 1587, when the Mission Nombre de Dios/La Leche Shrine was established.[4] The Convento de San Francisco (or Convent of Saint Francis) (1588–1763) was St. Augustine's original Franciscan church and friary; it also served as the Order's primary administrative center in La Florida.

The success of the Franciscan missions, thus also of the Spanish colonial enterprise in La Florida, depended absolutely upon the cooperative relationships that the missionaries forged and promoted with local Native American peoples. Per Worth, "Into this scenario stepped the missionaries of the Franciscan Order, whose arrival during the 1570s and 1580s eventually provided a successful model for colonial expansion in Spanish Florida, resulting in the structural assimilation of literally dozens of Indigenous chiefdoms surrounding St. Augustine, providing access to both arable soils and experienced native farmers through the mechanism of the missions."[5] The Franciscan model

3. Kathleen A. Deagan, *Historical Archaeology at the Fountain of Youth Park (8-SJ-31), St. Augustine, Florida: 1934–2007,* Florida Museum of Natural History Miscellaneous Papers in Archaeology 62 (Gainesville: FLMNH, 2008a), 19–29; Kathleen A. Deagan, *Summary Report on Archaeology at 8SJ34, The Nombre de Dios/LaLeche Shrine Site, St. Augustine (1939–2009)*, Florida Museum of Natural History Miscellaneous Reports in Archaeology (Gainesville: FLMNH, 2011), 12–19.

4. Amy Bushnell, *The King's Coffer: Proprietors of the Spanish Florida Treasury, 1565–1702* (Gainesville: University Presses of Florida, 1981); Deagan, *Summary Report 8SJ34,* 19–20.

5. Worth, "Catalysts," 136–37, 283.

specifically entailed immersion within Native American communities, which was accomplished literally on the ground by placing the missions directly within Native American population centers, with emphasis on the larger towns and seats of Indigenous power and influence.[6] In this way the friars established immediate contact and gained some first-hand understanding of the Indigenous socio-political structure and food resources, among other things. All of this necessarily also rested upon the voluntary acceptance of the missions and missionaries by native political leaders, including to live among them within their communities.[7] Ultimately, this framework provided direct access to the Indigenous populace to effect cultural assimilation and conversion to the Catholic religious doctrine, as well as to the associated food resources and labor, bolstering the subsistence and survival of the missions. By extension, the Spanish garrisons and presidios achieved some access to local food resources, thus enhancing their food security, while the missions had the overt protection and other support of the military as required.[8]

The Indigenous people with whom the colonizers primarily interacted were the Timucua, who were centered in and around St. Augustine, including various subgroups or local polities situated farther to the north, south, and west; the Guale, who lived farther north, including but not limited to the Georgia coastal region, and the Apalachee, whose territories extended west from the Timucuan domain across the Florida panhandle and encompassed

---

6. Keith Ashley, "Grafting onto the Native Landscape: The Franciscan Mission System in Northeastern Florida," in *From La Florida to La California: Franciscan Evangelization in the Spanish Borderlands*, eds. Timothy J. Johnson and Gert Melville (Berkeley: The Academy of American Franciscan History, 2013), 151.

7. See Ashley, "Grafting," 151; Kathleen A. Deagan, "Spanish-Indian Interaction in Sixteenth-Century Florida and Hispaniola," in *Cultures in Contact: The Impact of European Contacts on Native American Cultural Institutions A.D. 1000–1800*, ed. William W. Fitzhugh (Washington, DC: Smithsonian Institution Press, 1985), 281–318; David Hurst Thomas, "War and Peace on the Franciscan Frontier," in *From La Florida to La California: Franciscan Evangelization in the Spanish Borderlands*, eds. Timothy J. Johnson and Gert Melville (Berkeley: The Academy of American Franciscan History, 2013), 105–30; Rochelle A. Marrinan, "The Lives of Friars in Apalachee Province," in *Unearthing the Missions of Spanish Florida*, eds. Tanya M. Peres and Rochelle A. Marrinan (Gainesville: University of Florida Press, 2021), 244–79; Worth, "Catalysts," 131–42; John E. Worth, "Missions and Colonialism: The View from Spanish Florida, 1513–1763," in *Methods, Mounds, and Missions: New Contributions to Florida Archaeology*, eds. Ann S. Cordell and Jeffrey M. Mitchem (Gainesville: University of Florida Press, 2021), 283–309; and cf. Rebecca Saunders, "Catholic Intrusions: Spanish Colonial Missionization of the Old World and the New, with an Emphasis on La Florida," in *Methods, Mounds, and Missions*, 310–36.

8. Worth, "Catalysts," 137–38; and see Worth, "Missions and Colonialism," 289–91; cf. Matter, "Missions," 22–25.

also portions of Georgia and Alabama. Prior to European arrival, these groups were variously sedentary or seasonally so, the latter pertaining especially to those living along the coasts. Foraging, hunting, and fishing, with emphasis on interior and coastal wetlands and near-shore marine environments was common to all these peoples and was conducted year-round. Maize-focused agriculture was well developed and especially important and productive in the Apalachee Province but some degree of plant management, including cultivation of maize and/or other cultigens, was also practiced variously by the other groups to greater or lesser extents, depending on cultural tradition and environmental circumstances.

The settlements of St. Augustine and Santa Elena, along with other early footholds in La Florida, began a process that led to the eventual elaboration and expansion of the Spanish mission system, as alluded above, particularly during the seventeenth century. Archaeological evidence from thirteen Franciscan missions and two related sites (Table 1 and citations therein) spanning the sixteenth through seventeenth centuries and variously situated within the Timucuan, Guale, the Apalachee provinces, reveals the types and nature of food resources and associated subsistence practices availed in support of the mission system. Introduced "Old World" (i.e., European, Eurasian, or African origins) plants and animals such as wheat (*Triticum* sp.), melon or cantaloupe (*Cucumis melo*), pig (*Sus scrofa*), and cow (*Bos taurus*), were present from the outset of the Spanish settlement and Franciscan missionization process, for example, at the Fountain of Youth Park and the Mission Nombre de Dios sites in St. Augustine. Cattle raising ultimately proved highly successful throughout much of the region and beef became the primary source of domestic animal protein for the Spanish residents of La Florida.[9] In contrast, sheep, thus mutton, as another traditional Iberian staple, proved unsuitable to the climatic conditions and was dropped from the suite of Eurasian domestic animals raised in La Florida.

Cattle production indeed served as a major means of support for the seventeenth-century Franciscan missions, as well as some private Spanish ranching enterprises in the Apalachee and western Timucuan provinces.[10] Pigs and chickens were also maintained and thrived in the new setting, evidently including at the various missions. The concerted presence of cows, pigs, and chickens effected some semblance of traditional Iberian animal

9. Elizabeth J. Reitz and Gregory A. Waselkov, "Vertebrate Use at Early Colonies on the Southeastern Coasts of Eastern North America," *Inteernational Journal of Historical Archaeology* 19 (2015): 26, https://doi.org/10.1007/s10761-014-0280-3.

10. Robert Allen Matter, "Economic Basis of the Seventeenth-Century Florida Missions," *Florida Historical Quarterly* 52, no. 1 (1973): 11–13; Reitz and Waselkov, "Vertebrate Use," 21–45.

Table 1. Archaeological Sites and Sources of Archaeobotanical and/or Zooarchaeological Evidence

Site	Date	Source
Fountain of Youth Park (8SJ31)	1565–1566	Newsom lab data; Orr and Colaninno 2008; Scarry 1989; Reitz and Scarry 1985
Mission Nombre de Dios (8SJ34)	1587–1793	Deagan 2011; Orr 2001; Reitz 1985, 1991; Ruhl 1993, 1995
San Juan del Puerto (8DU53)	1587–1702	Ashley 2013; Ashley and Douberly-Gorman 2021; Ruhl 1993
Convento de San Francisco	1588–1763	Reitz 1985; Reitz et al. 2010
Santa Catalina de Guale, St. Catherines Island, Georgia	1602–1702	Pavao-Zuckerman and Reitz 2011; Reitz et al. 2010; Ruhl 1990, 1993
Santa Catalina de Guale (8NA41), Amelia Island	1602–1702	Pavao-Zuckerman and Reitz 2011; Reitz et al. 2010; Ruhl 1990, 1993
Fig Springs (8CO1) (Mission San Martín de Ayacuto)	1608–1656	Newsom and Quitmyer 1991
O'Connell Mission Site (8LE157), Mission San Pedro y San Pablo de Patale	1633–1704	Blackmore 2000; Marrinan 2021; Peres 2021
Pine Tuft (8JE1), Mission San Juan de Aspalaga	1655–1704	Ruhl 1993; Scarry 1986, 1993
Hontoon Island (8VO202) (San Salvador de Mayaca)	1655–~1680	Newsom 1987; Wing 1987; Wing and McKean 1987
Mission San Luis de Talimali (8LE4)	1656–1704	Pavao-Zuckerman and Reitz 2011; Reitz 1993; Ruhl 1993; Scarry 1987, 1992, 1993
The Scott Miller Site (8JE2), Nuestra de la Purissima Senora Concepción de Ayubale	16??–1704?	Ruhl 1993; Scarry 1986, 1993
Riverbend (8VO2567)	17th century	Russo et al. 1989
Baptizing Spring (8SU65) (San Juan de Guacará or San Augustín de Urica)	17th century	Pavao-Zuckerman and Reitz 2011; Ruhl 1993
Indian Pond (8CO229) (Santa Cruz de Tarihica)	17th century	Ruhl 1992

husbandry practices at the missions and elsewhere in La Florida, particularly as regarded the later missions and their associated Native American communities. Moreover, ongoing production of meat, poultry, eggs, milk, butter, lard, tallow, skin, and hides allowed also for regular shipments of surplus food, finished products, and livestock from the missions to St. Augustine and even Havana.[11]

Notwithstanding all the above, the collective zooarchaeological evidence makes it abundantly clear that wild vertebrates, particularly fish, always dominated both secular Spanish and Franciscan diets throughout the First Spanish Period. Per Reitz et al., the Spanish modified and adapted by "incorporating much of the Native American coastal traditions."[12] Thus, while the Spanish colonists, if not also Franciscan clerics, had the means and potential to have deployed their own fishermen, and may frequently have done so, some rapid education drawing on Indigenous ecological knowledge and cooperation with native fishers is implied and was likely necessary.[13] Wild aquatic and wetland resources indeed were the mainstay of protein reliance at the Franciscan missions. This included a variety of fish, turtles, and waterfowl, as well as shellfish. Marine fish—especially the sea catfishes (Ariidae), mullet (*Mugil* spp.), and members of the drum family (Sciaenidae, e.g., black drum, red drum)—were among the most commonly utilized resources at the coastal missions. Deer (*Odocoileus virginianus*), several types of small mammals like raccoon (*Procyon lotor*), and gopher tortoise (*Gopherus polyphemus*), among others, were also relied upon, sometimes extensively so, as food resources at the various mission locations.

Aside from the abovementioned wheat and melon, additional "Old World" plant taxa were introduced over time, provided either directly from Spain or via the well-established Spanish colonial towns and missions of the greater New Spain, including those of the North American Southwest region. Common pea (*Pisum sativum*), chickpea (*Cicer arietinum*), watermelon (*Citrullus lanatus*), peach (*Prunus persica*), common fig (*Ficus carica*), and hazel-

11. Tanya M. Peres, "Feeding Families and Friars in Apalachee Province during the Mission Period," in *Unearthing the Missions of Spanish Florida*, 235–37; Marrinan, "Lives of Friars," 250–51; Elizabeth J. Reitz, et al., *Mission and Pueblo of Santa Catalina de Guale, St. Catherines Island, Georgia: A Comparative Zooarchaeological Analysis*, Anthropological Papers of the American Museum of Natural History (New York: AMNH, 2010), Number 91: 26–27; Jonathan Sheppard, "'With the Many Enemies that it has': The Collapse of Apalachee Province," in *Unearthing the Missions of Spanish Florida*, 308.

12. Reitz et al., *Mission and Pueblo*, 77.

13. See Reitz et al., *Mission and Pueblo*, 182–83; Elizabeth J. Reitz and Chester DePratter, "Indigenous American Fishing Traditions at the First Spanish Capital of La Florida: Santa Elena (1566–1587 CE), South Carolina, USA," *International Journal of Historical Archaeology* (2023): 1–2, 28, https://doi.org/10.1007/s10761-023-00723-5.

nut (*Corylus avellana*) are variously evinced among the mission sites, drawing from the archaeobotanical evidence. The presence of additional "Old World" exotics, such as varieties of citrus, are indicated at least by documentary sources.

Several exotic New World, that is, tropical American, crop staples, or cultivars were also translocated to La Florida in the context of Spanish settlement and the developing mission enterprise. This included butternut squash (*Cucurbita moschata*), chili pepper (*Capsicum annuum*), and new varieties of maize (*Zea mays*) from the Caribbean Islands or other circum-Caribbean locations. These plants were likely grown in La Florida's mission gardens variously in concert with the "Old World" domesticates and alongside traditional Southeastern Indigenous crops. The strongest evidence for the presence of introduced varieties of maize comes from the missions of Apalachee Province, where the new form(s) were grown in proximity or in association with Indigenous eastern complex maize. Archaeobotanical evidence for the native maize has proven ubiquitous among the mission sites analyzed. The Indigenous common bean (*Phaseolus vulgaris*), pumpkin/squash (*Cucurbita pepo*), sunflower (*Helianthus annuus*), and bottlegourd (*Lagenaria sicereria*) have also variously been recorded from La Florida mission contexts.

Aside from the plant taxa themselves, as a set of introduced American and traditional southeastern crops, evidence for cooperation with Native Americans may be inferred from maize kernels recovered from at least one of the sites that are indicative of the Indigenous preparation practice for hominy. Known in Spanish as *nixtamal*, this entails soaking and cooking dry kernels in an alkaline solution (water mixed with soda ash), to soften them prior to further processing or cooking.[14] Moreover, the collective archaeobotanical data demonstrate the presence at the missions of a variety of wild plant foods—for instance, persimmon (*Diospyros virginiana*), red mulberry, (*Morus rubra*), wild grape (*Vitis* spp.), oak (*Quercus* spp.), and hickory (*Carya* spp.)—that likewise suggest cooperation and/or access to traditional Indigenous knowledge concerning edible plant resources, including the means to prepare them for consumption. These add to the picture of locally sourced food items, encompassing fresh and/or dried fruit, vegetables (e.g., cabbage palm [*Sabal palmetto*] meristems or buds), nut flour, nut oil, and beverages.

The Franciscan missions assumed an increasingly greater role in the overarching Spanish colonial enterprise, including foodways, as the mission

14. Thomas P. Myers, "Hominy Technology and the Emergence of Mississippian Societies," in *Histories of Maize: Multidisciplinary Approaches to the Prehistory, Linguistics, Biogeography, Domestication, and Evolution of Maize*, eds. John E. Staller, Robert H. Tykot, and Bruce F. Benz (Burlington, MA: Elsevier, Inc., 2006), 511–20; Brian Stross, "Maize in Word and Image in Southeastern Mesoamerica," in *Histories of Maize:*, 582. And see Matter, "Economic Basis," 25.

system was solidified and expanded across the northern portion of the Florida peninsula. This pertains especially to the major missions, Santa Catalina de Guale on the east coast and San Luis de Talimali in the Florida panhandle, that is, the Apalachee region. Separately and together, the archaeological evidence for animal and plant reliance at the various locations provides insights into adaptive change in subsistence practices and associated foodways, including the idea of fusion or hybrid cuisines, as well as new or emergent control over subsistence resources. Flexible resource choice, management, and a situationally evolving agrobiodiversity are evident. Taken together, the details reflect on broader cultural adaptations and resilience on the part of Spanish colonists, including the clergy, and the several interacting Native American polities. The collective data reveal some aspects of the decision-making process that occurred at the Spanish settlements and missions, such as the exercise of food options and choices, as well as the unique multi-cultural dynamics that ensued under the circumstances, topics on which I briefly elaborate here. Some adaptative retention of traditional European food items and related practices is evident, particularly regarding introduced domesticated animals, which in some locations thrived, as noted earlier. Other traditional elements of the cuisine, especially plant foods, faded or were at least partially replaced by Indigenous homologs, for example, American maize for European grains (but see below). Ultimately, a unique blend or hybrid of European and Native American foodways and subsistence patterns occurred among both the Spanish colonists and Indigenous people alike, as Hurst Thomas, among others, has observed.[15]

The reviewed archaeological assemblages, both plant and animal, reveal important aspects of the dynamics associated with food resources, along with the exercise of options—food alternatives—particularly as concerned the missions. On the surface it seems readily apparent that Spanish colonial, including missionary, conceptions of what constitutes adequate food resources and what was deemed necessary or traditional as to basic foodways, was flexible or adaptable under the circumstances, fully amenable to change as the situation required. Thus, the broader substitutions of local marine faunal resources in place of those of the Iberian homeland, perhaps likewise small game for long familiar species like hares, were seemingly readily made and did not represent momentous changes, at least superficially. Nevertheless, while such changes did not necessarily equate with big conceptual, practical, or dietary shifts for the Spanish colonists, including clerics, other changes were not so easily made. For example, Eurasian livestock and their derivative products, such as meat, milk, and cheese, along with cooking in animal fats, were deeply integrated

15. Hurst Thomas, "War and Peace,"119.

aspects of the traditional cuisine, but sustained reliance on all such as this was complicated, at least initially.

Much discussion regarding Spanish La Florida centers on food choice, especially substitutions and particularly featuring sheep and wheat (see below). Sheep were disadvantaged from the start, thus largely discontinued among the live animals tended, as noted earlier.[16] Further reiterating, the absence of sheep, therefore mutton, meant that the colonizers were unable to maintain this aspect of their traditional Iberian food practices. In her discussion of "analogous foods," Peres suggested that deer meat may have directly substituted for traditional reliance on mutton.[17] Indeed, that venison was a restricted, high-status food in Spain, may not have mattered in colonial La Florida.[18] Nevertheless, Reitz et al. suggest that venison, along with chicken, may still have been viewed as a status marker among the clergy and others living in La Florida, regardless of their individual ethnic or cultural backgrounds.[19] Indeed, consumption of both appears to have been relatively greater at the Convento de San Francisco. Perhaps this (status foods) pertained also to the presence of black bear (*Ursus americanus*) and turkey (*Meleagris gallopavo*) there. Both animals were also identified from Santa Elena, the Governor's seat, and bear was identified at Santa Catalina (the Spanish Pueblo North).[20] As far as I am aware, black bear is recorded for no other Spanish colonial contexts, aside from the Berry Site (Juan Pardo expedition of 1566–1567) in North Carolina.[21] Among Southeastern Indigenous peoples, bear was traditionally considered a high-value food such that both the meat and fat were typically or largely reserved for dignitaries, special guests, celebratory meals, and feasting.[22] Perhaps the local Indigenous groups

---

16. See Reitz et al., *Mission and Pueblo*, 1–150.

17. Peres, "Feeding Families," 221.

18. Reitz et al., *Mission and Pueblo*, 24.

19. Reitz et al., *Mission and Pueblo*, 184; and see Kathleen A. Deagan, "Environmental Archaeology and Historical Archaeology," in *Case Studies in Environmental Archaeology, Second Edition*, eds. Elizabeth J. Reitz, C. Margaret Scarry, and Sylvia J. Scudder (New York: Springer Science + Business Media, LLC., 2008b), 21–42; and Elizabeth M. Scott, "Who Ate What? Archaeological Food Remains and Cultural Diversity," in *Case Studies in Environmental Archaeology*, eds. Elizabeth J. Reitz, Lee A. Newsom, and Sylvia J. Scudder (New York: Plenum Press, 1996), 339–56.

20. Reitz and DePratter, "Indigenous American Fishing," 20–21, 24; Reitz et al., *Mission and Pueblo*, 146.

21. Heather A. Lapham, "Fauna, Subsistence, and Survival at Fort San Juan," in *Fort San Juan and the Limits of Empire: Colonialism and Household Practice at the Berry Site*, eds. Robin A. Beck, Christopher B. Rodning, and David G. Moore (Gainesville: University Press of Florida, 2016), 271–302.

22. Lapham, "Fauna," 298.

similarly gifted bear meat (as well as the fat and skins) to the occupants of the early presidio and Convento, likewise the friars at Santa Catalina. The clergy at the Mission San Pedro y San Pablo de Patale (the O'Connell Mission site) also ate venison and turkey, as well as pork.[23] Turkey was recorded for sixteenth-century St. Augustine and Santa Elena but in limited numbers.[24]

The grain-related provisions sent at least to the early colonies at St. Augustine and Santa Elena, among others, commonly were in the form of hardtack, biscuits, and/or processed flour, but the presence of intact wheat grains at the Franciscan missions and elsewhere evinces that unprocessed grains were also shipped and moved to the various locations. The underlying thinking presumably was to refill and have convenient grain stores for eventual bread making, if not use of the grain as planting stock in support of local production. Nevertheless, native eastern complex maize has been suggested to have replaced Spanish reliance on European grains, particularly wheat. This is a reasonable assumption and may indeed have been the case, at least situationally. The primary reasoning underlying the suggestion of replacement rests on wheat's poor climatic fit and its generally minor presence among the sites, with typically a single or very few grains recorded. The Mission Santa Catalina de Guale and some of the Apalachee area missions, where the grains have been identified in relatively large numbers, are exceptions. Moreover, the collective evidence suggests that wheat was widely distributed across the region, thus was perhaps routinely available to the various missions. It may be that wheat's presence and enduring importance in La Florida have been misunderstood. Besides the early Menéndez contexts (Fountain of Youth Park and Santa Elena, along with Fort San Felipe), wheat has been identified from at least six of the sixteenth- and seventeenth-century missions, including both Santa Catalina locations.[25] Low numbers or nothing recorded from some of the sites might well be misleading, given attrition or loss through food preparation and consumption or taphonomic factors that adversely affected grain stores. All things considered, wheat alternatively could be construed as having been ubiquitously present, ignoring grain counts and placing the emphasis on the evidence for its temporal and spatial distribution across La Florida.

Wheat indeed was reportedly grown in St. Augustine and in the Apalachee Province during the First Spanish Period, and production seems to have been reasonably successful in the latter area, however sporadic or lim-

---

23. Marrinan, "Lives of Friars," 273; Peres, "Feeding Families," 233.

24. See Reitz and Scarry, *Reconstructing Historic Subsistence*, Appendix D.

25. Donna L. Ruhl, "Old Customs and Traditions in New Terrain: Sixteenth and Seventeenth Century Archaeobotanical Data from *La Florida*," in *Foraging and Farming in the Eastern Woodlands*, ed. C. Margaret Scarry (Gainesville: University Press of Florida, 1993), 255–83.

ited.[26] If not sourced from locally grown wheat as just suggested, then presumably most or all the archaeological occurrences of wheat grains found among the mission contexts originated as shipped seed stock. If not directly from Spain, this may have entailed seed sent from the Franciscan missions of the northwestern portion of New Spain, that is, the greater Southwest region.[27] The same likely pertained also to olives (olive oil), almonds, and wine grapes (wine), among others.[28] To this same point, Peres (citing Hann 1988) called attention to the fact that the wheat grown in the Apalachee Province originated from grain shipped from western New Spain.[29] Thus, the wheat found at least at the later sites could well have been sourced from the westernmost missions, which by the seventeenth century were highly successful in producing wheat and others of the introduced cereals, including barley, oats, rye, and flax.[30] *Wheat even displaced maize* as the primary crop in portions of these arid-lands regions.[31] The further implications are that wheat

---

26. Jerry Lee, "Imported Ceramics and Colonowares as a Reflection of Hispanic Lifestyle at San Luis de Talimali," in *Unearthing the Missions of Spanish Florida*, eds. Tanya M. Peres and Rochelle A. Marrinan (Gainesville: University of Florida Press, 2021), 170; Matter, "Economic Basis," 27; Peres, "Feeding Families," 223, 234; Ruhl, "Old Customs," 271–73; Donna L. Ruhl, "Oranges and Wheat: Spanish Attempts at Agriculture in La Florida," *Historical Archaeology* 31, no. 1 (1997): 42–44.

27. Karen R. Adams and Suzanne K. Fish, "Subsistence through Time in the Greater Southwest," in *Subsistence Economies of Indigenous North American Societies: A Handbook*, ed. Bruce D. Smith (Washington, DC: Smithsonian Institution Scholarly Press, 2011), 147–83; Neil H. Lopinot, "The Spanish Introduction of New Cultigens into the Greater Southwest," The *Missouri Archaeologist* 47 (1986): 61–84; Lee A. Newsom and D. Ann Trieu Gahr, "Fusion Gardens: Native North America and the Columbian Exchange," in *Subsistence Economies of Indigenous North American Societies: A Handbook*, ed. Bruce D. Smith (Washington, DC: Smithsonian Institution Scholarly Press, 2011), 557–76; and see William W. Dunmire, *Gardens of New Spain: How Mediterranean Plants and Foods Changed America* (Austin: University of Texas Press, 2004); and José Refugio de la Torre Curiel, "Talking to the Desert: Franciscan Explorations and Narratives of Eighteenth-Century Arizona," in *From La Florida to La California: Franciscan Evangelization in the Spanish Borderlands*," eds. Timothy J. Johnson and Gert Melville (Berkeley: The Academy of American Franciscan History, 2013), 297–321.

28. The western missions and associated Indigenous peoples also produced common pea, broad beans, chickpea, lentil, cowpea, peanut, carrot, radish, white potato, butternut squash, artichoke, melon/cantaloupe, watermelon, cucumber, cabbage, lettuce, onion, leek, garlic, anise, coriander, black pepper, chili pepper, mustard, mint, sugarcane, peaches, apricot, plum, apple, pear, quince, fig, mulberry, citrus varieties, pomegranate, pecan, and English walnut. Newsom and Trieu Gahr, "Fusion Gardens," 557–76.

29. Peres, "Feeding Families," 237.

30. Newsom and Trieu Gahr, "Fusion Gardens," 557–76.

31. Adams and Fish, "Subsistence," 161; Newsom and Trieu Gahr, "Fusion Gardens," 567.

grain stores for seventeenth-century La Florida were reasonably secure, with ongoing resupply from western New Spain, if not also from Europe, along with grain grown locally in Apalachee Province.

It seems clear that the idea that maize completely replaced and served instead of wheat in La Florida does not accurately or fully describe the situation on the ground. Wheat was present, if only at times in small quantities, throughout the period of Spanish settlement and the development of the mission system. There were undoubtedly instances when wheat was at least temporarily unavailable in some locations and at any given time, especially those missions and *visitas* that were farther removed from the presidios and major missions. Under those circumstances, whether of occasional or frequent occurrence, the daily breadstuffs consumed at the missions could have been made from maize flour or alternatively from other native flour sources. That the greatest quantities of archaeological wheat are associated with the church complexes of the Franciscan missions suggests that this grain was reserved as much as possible for use in celebration of the Eucharist, that is, as the sacramental bread, as others have suggested.[32] Moreover, use of other flour types for this purpose was prohibited by church doctrine and practice.[33] I add then too that it seems reasonable to assume as well that wheat was reserved for and constantly available, or nearly so, to the Convento de San Francisco, the Franciscan headquarters.

The Franciscan missions were directly involved in when, where, and how plant cultigens, including introduced taxa such as wheat, were produced and distributed across La Florida, especially as time progressed. The Franciscans' long-established traditions and innovations involving horticulture, viticulture, and arboriculture will have been central to this process, coupled with

32. Peres, "Feeding Families," 237; Ruhl, "Old Customs," 265; C. Margaret Scarry, "Plant Production and Procurement in Apalachee Province," in *The Spanish Missions of La Florida*, 368; and see Ruhl, "Oranges and Wheat," 42–43.

33. The sources and nature of the sacraments are codified under Church Canon Law, such that the host can only be made of wheat flour. Specifically, under Article 3, Canon 924, Section 1, "The most holy eucharistic sacrifice must be offered with bread and with wine in which a little water must be mixed." Under section 2 (emphasis added), "*The bread must be only wheat and recently made so that there is no danger of spoiling.*" Canon 926 specifies that per "ancient tradition" the sacramental bread is unleavened. Furthermore, regarding the wine per section 3, it ". . . must be natural from the fruit of the vine and not spoiled." I note also that under Canon 925 (emphasis added), *it is possible to hold the Eucharistic celebration when one or the other of the sacraments is unavailable*; thus, "Holy communion is to be given under the form of bread alone, or under both species according to the norm of the liturgical laws, or even under the form of wine alone in a case of necessity." Vatican, New Code of Canon Law (1983), Article 3, Canon 924, §§ 1–3, https://www.vatican.va/archive/cod-iuris-canonici/cic_index_en.html.

their intimate familiarity and management of numerous homeland heirloom cultivars and landraces.[34] It is therefore reasonable to assume that mission gardening and related matters were well developed in the context of La Florida's missions, at least by the seventeenth century. Furthermore, the success of the Franciscans was facilitated by the Order's advocation of an open and inclusive approach with the Indigenous peoples. In many instances, though not all, this translated into situationally flexible and generally productive relationships with the local inhabitants with whom the friars lived and closely interacted. Most or all staple crop production involving native cultigens was certainly done by the local Indigenous populations in support of their entire communities, including both resident missionaries and the Native American inhabitants, many of whom had accepted Catholicism. And it will have been the associated Indigenous knowledge, for example, regarding the nixtamalization process for the preparation of maize, recalling my earlier mention of hominy (which not only facilitates food processing but significantly enhances nutritional value, e.g., avoidance of the disease pellagra) that made these foods accessible. The newly introduced neotropical races of maize were almost certainly first grown and experimented with by experienced Native American farmers and their maize fields became the laboratories in which new hybrid races of maize emerged and were reproduced. In addition, much or all the hunted, fished, and gathered foods will have been provided by Native Americans, and from the very beginning. Thus, these three aspects—wild faunal and plant resources, cultivated plant staples—of mission-related subsistence practices and foodways necessarily retained a decidedly native character, with emphasis on local and traditional food sources, as specified above.

The ubiquitous presence among the mission contexts of maize demonstrates its continued central importance. Eventually hybridization and introgression between the native and exotic maize races occurred, as just alluded, drawing especially from the archaeobotanical data from San Luis de Talimali and others of the Apalachee missions.[35] Over and above all as just related, the Spanish missions, perhaps almost immediately but certainly by the peak of missionization, pushed or were charged to intensify staple crop produc-

34. See Dunmire, *Gardens of New Spain*; Newsom and Trieu Gahr, "Fusion Gardens," 566–69.

35. C. Margaret Scarry, "A Preliminary Examination of Plant Remains," in *Archaeology at San Luis: Broad-Scale Testing, 1984–1985*," ed. Gary Shapiro (Tallahassee: Florida Bureau of Archaeological Research, 1987), 249–56; C. Margaret Scarry, "Plant Remains from the San Luis Council House and Convento," in *Archaeology at San Luis: The Apalachee Council House*, eds. G. Shapiro and B. McEwan (Tallahassee: Florida Bureau of Archaeological Research, 1992), Appendix 6.

tion, largely in response to the needs and dictates of the garrisons and presidios.[36] Worth describes how the mission system as a whole was mobilized to support the presidio in St. Augustine, providing not only Indigenous labor but prodigious quantities of maize, to wit: ". . . annual production of more than a million pounds of corn in fields around St. Augustine by the mid-seventeenth century along with the annual transport of an additional 125,000 lbs. of surplus corn produced in the mission provinces themselves."[37] By this time maize and perhaps other produce from the Apalachee Province, along with livestock and related products, as noted earlier, was also being shipped to Havana, effectively bringing things full circle.[38] This mandated maize/crop production will also have been realized or carried out by Native American agriculturists associated or interacting with the separate mission provinces. Nevertheless, this presumably also entailed some direction or refocusing by the Franciscans. In other words, beyond native leaders simply calling in more resources via their personal influence and social networks and/or causing more unit-area of ground to be cultivated, it is quite plausible or even predictable that intensification of crop production entailed considerable modification of traditional Native American agricultural management practices under the influence of the clerics. That is, I posit that a transformation of subsistence production occurred, one which was more in line with traditional European concepts and practices. This hypothetically included dispensing with the traditional and comparatively low intensity cultivation practice in which maize, beans, and squash were grown together as an inter-mixed crop, in favor of new mission-influenced agricultural plots or so-called "religious fields."[39] These were likely to have been devoted exclusively to intensified maize production involving monocropping and shortened rotations to ensure more than one crop annually, along with the incorporation of more productive hybrid races of maize. This very likely also included soil amendment using manure collected from the Eurasian animals associated with the mission settlements, especially in the Timucuan and Guale provinces. It is probably no coincidence that most of the evidence for the presence of hybrid forms of maize is associated with the Apalachee mission province, not to mention the

---

36. Hurst Thomas, "War and Peace," 119–20; Donna L. Ruhl, "Spanish Mission Paleoethnobotany and Culture Change: A Survey of the Archaeobotanical Data and Some Speculations on Aboriginal and Spanish Agrarian Interactions in La Florida," in *Columbian Consequences: Archaeological and Historical Perspectives on the Spanish Borderlands East,* vol. 2, ed. David H. Thomas (Washington, DC: Smithsonian Institution Press, 1990), 562; and see Peres, "Feeding Families," 237; and Marrinan, "Lives of Friars," 255.

37. Worth, "Missions and Colonialism," 292.

38. See Peres, "Feeding Families," 237.

39. Matter, "Economic Basis," 37; Peres, "Feeding Families," 224.

efforts and apparent success there with growing wheat, all as described above. To that last point, adding wheat to the crop inventory represents an additional form of agricultural intensification. This too was cultivated mainly by Native Americans, and just as I suggested for the (hypothetically) reorganized maize production, will have necessitated some direction from the Franciscans, the exotic grass and its cultivation being completely unfamiliar to the Apalachee and others.

Similarly, cattle, pigs, and chickens ultimately were raised by Apalachee, Guale, and Timucuan people under the purview of the Franciscan missionaries.[40] At least initially, this will also have entailed some direction regarding long-established European animal husbandry practices.[41] All of this—intensified crop production involving at least maize and wheat, along with animal husbandry—was carried out mainly or exclusively in support of the missions (food provisions), as well as to provide for the presidios and beyond.[42] Certainly, a fusion of Native American and Iberian subsistence practices is implied by all the above; however, collectively this represents a marked departure from traditional Native American practice. One outcome was that it created a situation wherein the Spanish could maintain some reliance on their familiar Eurasian animal protein sources and derivative products, if not also wheat. The other was greater volumes of food supplied to the presidios and beyond in fulfillment of the increased demand. Otherwise, Native American foodways, with emphasis on the traditional staples, fishing, and so on, are likely to have remained largely unchanged.

Mission homegardens existed as another aspect of the newly emergent subsistence patterns and a venue where introduced and native plants were simultaneously cultivated. As Scarry noted concerning the Spanish secular populations of St. Augustine and Apalachee (a comment that I thus extend also to the missionary population), "the mainstays of the diet were Indigenous crops, but 'Old World' plants grown in kitchen gardens gave the diet a superficially Iberian character."[43] My above point about the perpetuation of key Iberian resources is mirrored here. The gardens may have been tended by Franciscan clerics, but they seem also to have been the purview of local Native Americans, perhaps working alongside the missionaries and in concert with management of their own traditional homegardens. It seems reasonable to assume that the introduced neotropical butternut squash and lima bean may have been incorporated as part of the traditional practice of

40. Peres, "Feeding Families," 227.

41. Reitz and DePratter, "Indigenous American Fishing," 28.

42. Peres, "Feeding Families," 223, 227.

43. Scarry, "Plant Production," 369.

growing native squashes (pumpkins, squashes, and ornamental gourds) and common beans together with eastern complex maize (i.e., the so-called maize-beans-squash agriculture), at least when and where traditional crop production was conducted. Others of the introduced plant taxa such as the chili peppers, melons, watermelons, and peach, if not also citrus, among others, such as tobacco, were almost certainly also cultivated in both mission and Native American home gardens (also those of the Spanish pueblos).[44] Watermelon and peach indeed were widely accepted by Native Americans and were successfully reproduced throughout La Florida and farther distant. This is probably true also of others of the introduced taxa for which the evidence is more limited.

One potential gap in terms of preserving, achieving, or fully realizing something of an "Iberian character" aspect to the cuisine on the part of the Spanish colonizers and missionaries, would have been the inability to grow the European wine grape in La Florida, thus precluding routine access to the wine, aside from its inclusion in shipped provisions. Wine was customary and important as both a daily beverage and as a fundamental element of the Eucharistic rite. While the Indigenous yaupon (*Ilex vomitoria*) tea could have been adopted as a daily beverage, it would have been absolutely precluded as a substitute for the latter purpose, again, according to Church doctrine (see footnote 33). This has led to the suggestion that Franciscan clerics undertook viticulture in La Florida to address the problem, experimenting with native grape species, of which there are several. A historic report of possible vineyards at Santa Elena, along with the archaeological discovery there of possible arbor trenches, provide some support.[45] Matter specified that "cultivated grapes" were among the crops introduced by the Franciscans to enhance "Indian farming."[46] Moreover, according to Dunmire, Spanish and English colonists living along the east coast produced wine from native grapes by the late 1500s.[47] Experimental archaeology involving hybridization and vine grafting of the European grape and at least two native Florida species has also occurred.[48] And native grapes support a thriving wine industry in the region today. Elsewhere in New Spain with the appropriate climatic conditions, Franciscan mission viticulture availing nursery stock from European wine grape

44. See Dunmire, *Gardens of New Spain,* 292–93; Matter, "Economic Basis," 37; Peres, "Feeding Families," 222–23.

45. Ruhl, "Old Customs," 265–66.

46. Matter, "Economic Basis," 24.

47. Dunmire, *Gardens of New Spain,* 286.

48. Francisco Watlington-Linares, "The First American Wine," *Eastern Grape Grower and Winery News* 10–11 (1983): 50–52; Francisco Watlington-Linares, "Adaptive Viticulture in the Caribbean Basin" (PhD diss., University of Florida, 1990).

cultivars was quite successful.[49] To reiterate, this was another potential source of wine, as well as grapes and grape vine cuttings, regarding La Florida.

The presence of the ultimate hybrid or fused foodways traditions that we now associate with the Franciscan mission enterprise and generally extend also to Spanish La Florida is a fascinating topic to consider. It is important that we never fail to recognize that this phenomenon always hinged closely upon complex and sometimes difficult interactions between the Franciscans and the several groups of Indigenous people with whom they lived and interacted. Per Hurst Thomas, "negotiations and flexibility involved in running a Franciscan mission in La Florida. . ." were inherent to the process.[50] This cultural dynamic minimally included the sharing of ideas and food sourced from multiple geographic regions, but also involved conveyance of traditional ecological and agricultural knowledge, equipment, labor, and key elements of the agricultural base, such as climatically adapted maize and wheat cultivars, among others, on the part of both Spanish and Native Americans working in close cooperation, one way or another.

ACKNOWLEDGMENTS

Much of the data that form the basis of this essay represent the original research of several individuals, including specialists, whose work I gratefully acknowledge. Any errors of fact are my own. I am deeply grateful to Dr. Kathleen Deagan for pointing me to a variety of relevant sources and materials, as well as providing productive comments on draft versions. I would also like to express my gratitude to Dr. Timothy Johnson for having invited me to participate in the original conference, ultimately this edited volume. I also gratefully acknowledge The Nombre de Dios/LaLeche Shrine and the Catholic Diocese of St. Augustine for their support of our past and ongoing archaeological research at Nombre de Dios, as well as the conferences and publications.

---

49. Dunmire, *Gardens of New Spain,* 286; Newsom and Trieu Gahr, "Fusion Gardens," 567.

50. Hurst Thomas, "War and Peace," 120.

Section Two

CHAPTER EIGHT

Learned Friars Who Rejected Study? Learning and Education among the First Generations of Franciscans in the Americas

FRANCISCO JAVIER ROJO-ALIQUE, *Instituto Teológico de Murcia OFM*

INTRODUCTION

For some time now, scholars had observed that, for a better understanding of the work of evangelization in the Americas, we need to deepen our knowledge of the theological, anthropological, and spiritual background of the missionaries coming from the "Old World."[1] This paper attempts to contribute in this regard by offering an overview of the subject of learning and education among the first generations of Franciscan evangelizers who traveled to the "New World" from Spain in the first half of the sixteenth century. At that time, the Order of Friars Minor was the largest religious institute in the Roman Catholic Church. This may therefore help to explain why nearly 50 percent of the religious present in the "New World" in the 1500s were Franciscans.[2] Moreover, the Friars Minor had a long missionary tradition, dating back to their origins in the thirteenth century.[3]

---

1. Melquíades Andrés Martín, "Filosofía y espiritualidad de los primeros españoles en Iberoamérica," *Revista de estudios extremeños* 48, no. 2 (1992): 455. Mónica Ruiz Bañuls, "El franciscanismo en el contexto evangelizador novohispano: raíces del mensaje misional," *Sémata, Ciencias Sociais e Humanidades* 26 (2014): 494, https://revistas.usc.gal/index.php/semata/article/view/1905.

2. Pedro Borges, ed., *Historia de la Iglesia en Hispanoamérica y Filipinas (siglos XV–XIX)*, Vol. 1: *Aspectos generales* (Madrid: Biblioteca de Autores Cristianos, 1992), 440.

3. James Muldoon, "Franciscan Friars," in *Trade, Travel and Exploration in the Middle Ages: An Encyclopedia*, eds. John Block Friedman and Kristen Mossler Figg (New York: Routledge, 2000), 198–200.

The vast majority of the Franciscan evangelizers in the Americas were members of the Observant branch of the Order. During the fifteenth century these friars had undertaken missionary work in the Iberian colonies in the Canary Islands, the African coast, and in the Kingdom of Granada, recently conquered by the Catholic monarchs. In these territories, the friars employed styles and methods of evangelization similar to those later used in America.[4] Understandably then, the Spanish rulers considered the reformed Friars Minor among the most capable people to preach the Gospel to the natives of the recently discovered "New World."[5] On their part, the Observant Franciscans enthusiastically faced the challenge of engaging in the missionary endeavor, as soon as the first news of Columbus' expedition arrived in Europe.[6]

But furthermore, the popes and the Spanish monarchs requested that the evangelizers dispatched to the "New World" should be "learned" people. This could pose a problem to recruit Observant Friars Minor as missionaries, as many of them, especially those who belonged to the strictest reform movements of their Order, were reluctant to study, and considered that learning in an organized manner was inimical to the core Franciscan values of humility and simplicity. However, it did not seem difficult to recruit Friars Minor who were Observant and proficient in theology or canon law at the same time. In a paradoxical way, contemporary documents and chronicles evidence that, in fact, many of the Franciscan missionaries in the Americas, even those who came from communities of the strictest Observance, were "learned" friars.

Trying to shed some light on this paradox, in this essay I will first introduce the different attitudes of Spanish reformed Franciscans towards the pursuit of studies in the fifteenth and early sixteenth centuries. Then, I will describe the ways in which the Spanish Observant friars accessed learning during the aforesaid period when they gradually developed their own network of schools and curriculum of studies. Finally, I will briefly highlight how Fran-

4. Francisco Javier Rojo-Alique, "The Old and New Worlds of Spanish Observant Preaching," in *Preaching and New Worlds: Sermons as Mirrors of Realms Near and Far*, eds. Timothy J. Johnson, Katherine Wrisley Shelby, and John D. Young (New York and London: Routledge, 2019), 268–70; Andrés de Guadalupe, *Historia de la Santa Provincia de los Ángeles de la Regvlar Observancia y Orden de Nvestro Seráfico Padre San Francisco* (Madrid: Mateo Fernández, 1652), 211–12. Antonio Rubial García, *La hermana pobreza: El franciscanismo de la Edad Media a la evangelización novohispana* (Mexico City: Universidad Autónoma Nacional de México, 1996), 53–54.

5. Steven E. Turley, *Franciscan Spirituality and Mission in New Spain, 1524–1599: Conflict Beneath the Sycamore Tree (Luke 19, 1–10)* (London: Routledge, 2014), 8; Rubial, *La hermana pobreza*, 54–55, 94–95.

6. Rojo-Alique, "The Old and New Worlds," 270–71, Grado Giovanni Merlo, *En el nombre de Francisco de Asís. Historia de los Hermanos Menores y del franciscanismo hasta los comienzos del siglo XVI* (Oñati: Arantzazu, 2005), 494.

ciscan evangelizers put into practice their academic knowledge and skills in missionary pastoral work in the "New World."

ATTITUDES TOWARDS LEARNING OF THE SPANISH REFORMED FRANCISCAN GROUPS IN THE FIFTEENTH AND SIXTEENTH CENTURIES

In the fifteenth and sixteenth centuries, two quite distinct, and in some way opposite currents coexisted within the Spanish Franciscan reform movement: while some groups of Observant friars wished to return to canonical norms, other communities pursued a lifestyle that lay outside and beyond the official canon.[7] This division between "moderate" and "strict" Franciscan positions on observance was reflected in their different attitudes towards learning and the pursuit of studies.

Opposition to the Pursuit of Studies and Academic Careers in Strict Observant Communities

At its beginnings, anti-intellectualism was one of the main features of the Franciscan Observant movement. Like their spiritual forerunners, many of the early observant groups followed an eremitical style of life, and were opposed to learning, because they considered that the pursuit of studies and academic careers threatened the Franciscan ideals of poverty and humility. This does not mean that the early generations of reformed Friars Minor were necessarily ignorant or poorly educated. Many of the outstanding figures among them were literate people, acquainted with patristic, monastic, and mendicant spiritual classics, and they were able to present and defend their position in debates and polemical writings in a brilliant and eloquent manner.[8] This can be explained in part by the fact that the Observant lifestyle was found to be very appealing to mature and often well-trained friars, who had received their education in Conventual Franciscan *studia*, or in universities before they joined the reformed communities.[9] A good number of them were disenchanted with their

7. Duncan Nimmo, *Reform and Division in the Medieval Franciscan Order: From Saint Francis to the Foundation of the Capuchins*, 2nd ed. (Rome: Capuchin Historical Institute, 1995), 500.

8. Bert Roest, *A History of Franciscan Education, c. 1210–1517* (Leiden: Brill, 2000), 156; Roest, "*Sub humilitatis titulo Sacra Scientiam abhorrentes*: Franciscan Observants and the Quest for Education," in *Rules and Observance. Devising Forms of Communal Life*, eds. Mirko Breitenstein, Julia Burkhardt, Stefan Burkhardt, and Jens Röhrkasten (Berlin-Münster: LIT Verlag, 2014), 80–82, 104.

9. Yet in the first half of the sixteenth century, the Spanish Observant Province of Los Angeles, which emerged from the Franciscan reformed group initiated by Friar Juan de Guadalupe, did not open any study house of their own because some the friars who took

studies, and considered that the pursuit of knowledge for its own sake could not lead to sainthood. Maybe without being conscious of it, the Observant friars were then in some way heirs and participants in the controversy between scholasticism and mystical theology originated around 1100, which was poignantly exacerbated in the fifteenth and sixteenth centuries.[10]

In the Iberian Peninsula the best example of this attitude towards learning can be found in the Villacrecian congregation, a small group of eremitical communities initiated by Friar Pedro de Villacreces in Castile at the beginning of the fifteenth century.[11] In the 1450s Friar Lope de Salazar y Salinas, one of Friar Pedro's disciples, was the author of a series of normative and apologetic writings.[12] These texts allow us to approach the congregation views on learning and study in some detail, and can also help to understand the attitude of the Spanish reformed Franciscans towards the study of systematic theology.[13] Friar Lope details that Villacreces, who had received a solid theological education in Toulouse, Paris, and Salamanca, had warned his disciples of the danger that the pursuit of studies could entail to Franciscan life. Friar Pedro did not reject the study of theology as such, but only the study of theology considered as a merely speculative science, according to nominalist principles. As many other Observant friars, he believed that the affective path was a much more successful way to gain access to God than the "cold" rational theological thought of that time.[14]

---

the habit in that province held degrees from Salamanca, Alcalá de Henares and Seville: "Por el largo espacio de ochenta y tres años estuuo la santa Prouincia de los Angeles sin estudios de Artes, y Theologia: por dos razones, la primera atendiendo al espiritu de nuestro Padre san Francisco [...]. La segunda razón, que tuuo la Prouincia para no tener estudios, fue, porque la diuina prouidencia la dio varones doctos, graduados en las Vniversidades de Salamanca, Alcalá, y Seuilla, que tomaron en ella el habito, y profesaron [...] y algunos Religiosos, que iban al Colegio de S. Pedro y S. Pablo de Alcalà para estudiar." See Guadalupe, *Historia de la Santa Provincia de los Ángeles*, 489.

10. Roest, *A History*, 158–59; Melquiades Andrés, *La teología española en el siglo XVI* (Madrid: Biblioteca de Autores Cristianos, 1976), 1: 95.

11. A good description of the Villacrecian movement in English can be found in Nimmo, *Reform and Division*, 500–15.

12. These writings were published by Fidel de Lejarza and Ángel Uribe, *Las reformas en los siglos XIV y XV*, Monographic issue of *Archivo Ibero-Americano* 17, nos. 65–68 (1957): 661–945.

13. Roest, "Sub humilitatis," 106; Andrés, *La teología*, 93–94.

14. Andrés, *La teología*, 93–95. "E ésta fue la opinión del beato e buen Maestro Fray Pedro de Villacreces [...]: 'Rescibí en Salamanca grado de Maestro, que no merezco; empero, más aprendí en la cella llorando en tiniebra, que en Salamanca, o Tolosa, e en París estudiando a la candela'. [...] E más decía. 'Más quisiera ser una vejezuela simple con caridad de amor de Dios e del prójimo, que saber la teología de San Agustín o del Doctor Sutil Escoto'. E por tanto, el primer estudio que él enseñaba a sus discípulos era el llorar e

With these principles in mind, the Villacrecians developed a structured program of studies for their congregation, which deliberately excluded the study of grammar, philosophy, and law. Novices received a thorough immersion in the Franciscan Rule, the Rule for hermits written by Saint Francis, and a selection of spiritual readings. Those cleric friars destined to preach, read and hear confessions, were trained in practical theology, and studied the sacred scripture with the help of Nicolas de Lyre's commentaries. They were also instructed in doctrine and moral theology making use of handbooks for confessors, brief compendia of dogmatic theology, especially the *Compendium theologiae veritatis* by the Dominican theologian Hugh Ripelin of Strasbourg, and manuals for preaching and for the administration of the sacraments.[15] In addition, the Villacrecian friars cultivated the study of pious and affective theology in a remarkable way. Friar Lope affirmed that they were "very literate" in the spiritual writings of the founders of different religious orders, predominantly those of Saint Francis and his companions, Clare of Assisi, Anthony of Padua, Bonaventure, as well as other works written by recognized patristic and spiritual authors, such as Cassian, Climacus, Saint Bernard of Clairvaux, or Saint Augustine.[16] In summary, the disciples of Pedro de Villacreces considered essential for their education the same corpus of devotional and spiritual texts that was significant among early Franciscan Observants and other non-Franciscan religious reformers throughout Europe, who required less-technical and formative readings than those used in schools.[17]

We could then infer that the normative writings of Lope de Salazar y Salinas show us, in general terms, the educational principles that were probably adopted in the radical eremitical Franciscan Observant communities. But, as Bert Roest points out, some aspects of the Villacrecian organization appear to have been rather unusual. Keeping this in mind, it is also true that many other eremitical Observant groups from the fifteenth and sixteenth centuries shared the same rejection of existing forms of higher education, even within a specific context of religious literacy. In the Iberian Peninsula, these initiatives included the congregation of Juan de la Puebla and Juan de Guadalupe, where penitential practices, prayer, and contemplation were preferred to study.[18]

---

aborrescer el estudio de las letras." Lope de Salazar, *Segundas Satisfacciones,* arts. 2–3, in Lejarza and Uribe, *Las reformas*, 862–63.

15. Salazar, *Segundas Satisfacciones*, 864. Roest, "Sub humilitatis," 100–104; Roest, *A History*, 167. Andrés, *La teología*, 94.

16. Pedro de Villacreces, *Memoriale Religionis*, 12, 14–15; Lejarza and Uribe, *Las reformas*, 711, 713, 723–24; Salazar, *Segundas Satisfacciones*, 865.

17. Andrés, *La teología*, 94; Roest, "Sub humilitatis," 103.

18. Roest, "Sub humilitatis," 104, 106. For example, Friar Juan de la Puebla considered that contemplation and religious life were the best ways to reach the knowledge of

In 1519, the followers of Juan de Guadalupe were incorporated into the Franciscan Observant Province of San Gabriel, where the Discalced reform of Saint Pedro de Alcantara had its origin. Most of the Friars Minor who arrived in America in the first half of the sixteenth century came precisely from the province of San Gabriel, and also from that of La Concepción, which had absorbed the Villacrecian communities.[19] Not surprisingly then, we can find echoes of the early-Observant attitude of distrust of learning among the first generations of Franciscan missionaries in the "New World." For example, Martin de Valencia, a friar from the province of San Gabriel who led the expedition sent to start the evangelization of Mexico, rebuked those learned friars who were only devoted to "human" study, without pursuing the knowledge of devotion, oratory, and contemplation, because Friar Martin was well aware "that human wisdom inflates and leads to pride, and the spirit is what gives life and the source of charity."[20]

Evolution of Attitude towards Study among Moderate Observants

As we have just seen, at the dawn of the sixteenth-century distrust of learning still lingered among the Observant Franciscans, including those who undertook missionary work in the Americas.[21] But even though they

God, in a practical more than speculative path: "De aqui passaua al conocimiento de Dios, dandole esta contemplacion ancho campo, para amarle, y agradecerle el beneficio singular de haberle traido a la Religion [...]. Y como la Religion es la escuela de todas las virtudes, en ella aprendia, como las habia de exercitar. Practicaualas, llenando mas el alma de ellas, que tenida de noticias el entendimiento. Esta ciencia de seruir a Dios es mas practica que especulatiua. Esse sabe mas que obra mas." Guadalupe, *Historia de la Santa Provincia de los Ángeles*, 19.

19. Rubial, *La hermana pobreza*, 66.

20. "Una vez platicando con otros Religiosos letrados y predicadores, [friar Martín] preguntó de una questión, que más fue por vía de rreprehensión charitativa que por querer saber la verdad, y dixo: 'El predicador ha de ser espiritual y letrado, pero ya que estas dos cossas no tenga ¿quál es más neçesario para aprovechar en la predicación? ¿ser letrado y no espiritual, o spiritual y no letrado?' [...] Entonzes el varón de Dios hablo spiritualmente aprovechando su rrespuesta, y dixo en pocas palabras ex abundantia cordis una doctrina consolatoria a los presentes simples rreligiossos que la oyeroon, y rreprehensiva con charidad a los letrados que solamente se dan al estudio humano, no procurando el estudio de la devoción, oratoria y contemplaçión, porque sabía el varón de Dios que la sabiduría humana infla e induze a la sobervia, y el espíritu es el que vivifica y de do procede la caridad que ediffica y aprovecha al próximo." Fr. Francisco Jiménez, *Jhesus, Maria, Franciscus: Vita fratris Martini de Valentia*, ed., in Rubial, *La hermana pobreza*, 227–28.

21. Manuel Lázaro Pulido, "*Scholastica colonialis.* El contexto curricular de los misioneros franciscanos extremeños," *Caurensia* 6 (2011): 161, https://doi.org/10.17398/rc.v6i0.

claimed to be simple and unlettered men, most of the Friars Minor who labored in the "New World" at that time were proficient in theology or canon law.[22]

In fact, we must keep in mind that the Observant movement was not uniform, and that disposition towards the pursuit of studies had evolved among the Franciscan Observants from the first half of the fifteenth century. A good number of Observant friars of the second generation, such as Bernardino da Siena, considered it necessary to embrace the urban apostolate again, a decision that implied an evolution of their reform ideals. The emphasis of Observant Franciscan life was then put on procuring the conversion of society through effective performance of pastoral tasks, especially preaching. And study was considered essential again because only well-prepared preachers could carry out their ministry in an effective and doctrinally sound way. As a result of this, from around 1450 onwards the friars of the regular Observance *sub vicariis* began to organize study houses of their own, where the students would be educated with a proper curriculum of liberal arts, canon law, and moral theology. Keeping distant from the emphasis on refined terminist logic, philosophy, and speculative theology that was given in the schools of the Conventuals, the Observants focused more on practical readings, suitable to provide an instrumental basis for pastoral work.[23]

At the end of the fifteenth century, for the most part Observant Franciscans still did not pursue higher academic degrees. But, at the same time, the progress of the Observant *studia* network was facilitated to a great extent by the entry of learned scholars into the Observant movement and by the takeover of Conventual friaries with existing study houses, some of which were in close relationship with local universities. These developments gradually had an effect on the nature and the scope of theological studies among the Observants *sub vicariis*, and on their position towards degrees. The necessary pursuit of higher education led the Observants *sub vicariis* to reestablish direct links between their own study programs and the degree courses in the universities, and even to return to attend lessons in the *studia generalia*.[24]

---

22. This is pointed out by the Franciscan chronicler Jeronimo de Mendieta, who remarks, "aunque por su humildad y propio menosprecio [these friars] holgaban de ser tenidos por simples y sin letras, todos ellos habían oído, unos el derecho canónico, y otros la sagrada teología. Y así el ministro general fray Francisco de los Ángeles, en la Obediencia que dio a los doce, intitula a los más de ellos predicadores doctos." Jerónimo de Mendieta, *Historia eclesiástica Indiana* 3.36 (quoted by Rubial, *La hermana pobreza,* 147).

23. Roest, "Sub humilitatis," 82–86, 105.

24. Roest, *A History,* 165–67; Bert Roest, *Franciscan Learning, Preaching and Mission c. 1220–1650:* Cum Scientia Sit Donum Dei, Armatura ad Defendendam Sanctam Fidem Catholicam. . . (Leiden: Brill, 2015), 144–45.

The general tendency towards the acceptance of studies among the Franciscan Observants became very clear in the first decades of the sixteenth century, and had as a consequence a substantial impact on the creation of significant libraries in their friaries during the early modern period. Their collections were specialized in moral theology, sermon collections, and *praedicabilia*.[25]

We can observe a similar evolution in the Iberian Peninsula, especially among the Franciscans who belonged to the moderate Observance *sub vicariis* faction. In the first decades of the fifteenth century, the communities of prominent friaries such as Oviedo and Valladolid had refused, out of humility, to accept the title and status of Master.[26] But, notwithstanding this, as in other regions of Europe, the Observant friars became gradually aware of the need of learning for an efficacious apostolate. For this reason, they committed themselves to the study of practical theology, more appropriate for pastoral work than the academic theology of that time. In 1451, the statutes of the Ultramontane General Chapter of Barcelona stated the establishment of one or more study houses in each Observant vicariate, where friars could be instructed "*in primitivis scientiis et in sacra theologia*."[27] Attempts were soon made to implement these regulations. In 1456, the Archbishop of Toledo erected the Franciscan Observant friary of Santa María de Jesús in Alcalá de Henares, where he established three chairs of liberal arts, several other sciences and sacred doctrine.[28] Ten years later, the Provincial Observant Congregation of Santiago set forth that all young friars should receive lessons, even if they could not be exempted from choir.[29]

But the most important school of the Observance in the Hispanic Kingdoms was located in San Francisco of Salamanca. In that friary, the Conventuals had maintained a *studium generale* and developed links with the nearby university, which was the most prominent institution for higher education in the Kingdom of Castile. In 1443, the Observant faction of the Order took

---

25. Roest, *A History*, 212–13.

26. Nimmo, *Reform and Division* 497. Francisco Javier Fernández Conde, "La Orden franciscana en Asturias: orígenes y primera época," *Boletín del Instituto de Estudios Asturianos* 43, no. 130 (1989): 406–07; Francisco Javier Rojo Alique, "El convento de San Francisco de Valladolid en la Edad Media (h. 1220–1518) III: Vida en el convento y proyección social," *Archivo Ibero-Americano* 66, no. 255 (2006): 465.

27. Roest, *A History*, 165; Isaac Vázquez Janeiro, *En busca de un nombre para el traductor del Carro de las Donas de F. Eximénez* (Madrid: Consejo Superior de Investigaciones Científicas, 1981), 25.

28. Pedro de Salazar, *Coronica y historia de la fundacion y progresso de la provincia de Castilla de la orden del bienauenturado padre san Francisco* (Madrid: en la Imprenta Real, 1612), 162, https://bibliotecadigital.jcyl.es/es/consulta/registro.do?id=131.

29. Isaac Vázquez Janeiro, "San Bernardino de Sena y España. Notas para una historia de la predicación popular en la Castilla del siglo XV," *Antonianum* 55 (1980): 706–07.

control of San Francisco and its *studium*. Some years later, the Franciscan school in Salamanca was reestablished and linked again to the university, and became a significant study center.[30] Though they kept themselves distant from academic degrees, it seems that the Observants still pursued scholastic learning in the theology faculty of the nearby university.[31] In fact, in 1505 a group of friars turned up at Salamanca, to inform them that the Franciscan general Egidio Delfini and provincial ministers had recently forbidden the presence in the University of any Friars Minor, from whichever branch of the Order. Apparently, the ban did not have much effect, maybe because Egidio Delfini was soon removed from his office.[32] In addition, a document dated in 1475 mentions the existence in San Francisco de Salamanca of a library, whose collection was supplemented five years later by the bequest of local bishop Gonzalo de Vivero, who donated most of the volumes from his personal library to the Franciscan friary.[33]

In the early 1500s, the Archbishop of Toledo Francisco Jiménez de Cisneros, an Observant Franciscan himself and a great promotor of the regular Observance *sub vicariis* in the kingdoms of Castile and Aragon, initiated a project to establish centers for the study of theology and humanism, and developed new degree programs to restore the study of theology and the formation of priests. To that end, Cisneros planned to create two universities, the first of which should have been founded in Seville. To begin with, the Archbishop tried to institute a school in the local Convent of Santa Clara for the Andalusian Observant Franciscans. This project could not be completed because of the opposition of the friars, and especially of the lay people who held the property of the Conventual community. Soon thereafter, in 1502 Cisneros gained the Catholic monarchs' support for the erection of a *studium generale* in the great friary of San Francisco of Seville. This new university would have been open not only to the members of any religious order, but to the secular clergy and the laity as well. But, once again, this plan did not come to fruition, due to the local authorities' lack of interest. In the friary of San Francisco, the archbishop could only establish a Franciscan school, which flourished in the years that followed.[34]

Cisneros was much more successful in his attempt to transform the existing schools of Alcalá de Henares into the *Universitas Complutensis*, which

30. Manuel de Castro, *San Francisco de Salamanca y su* studium generale (Santiago de Compostela, 1998), 76–77; Lázaro, "*Scholastica*," 163.

31. Castro, *San Francisco de Salamanca*, 43, 65–66.

32. José García Oro, *El cardenal Cisneros: Vida y empresas* (Madrid: Biblioteca de Autores Cristianos, 1993), 2: 177.

33. Castro, *San Francisco de Salamanca*, 72–74.

34. Andrés, *La teología*, 102; García Oro, *El cardenal Cisneros,* 2: 237–38.

established chairs in logic, rhetoric, philosophy, Greek, Hebrew, canon law, and separate chairs for Scotist, Thomist, and Nominalist theology.[35] The Complutensian University can be therefore considered as an extension of the Franciscan archbishop's program of religious reform and his quest for a better-educated clergy. The new University of Alcalá became an open space where the spirit of reform was reflected in a learning stance based on the revitalization of the studies of arts and theology, which took their inspiration from humanist principles.[36]

Archbishop Cisneros therefore belonged to that group of reformed Franciscans of his time who believed that there was no conflict between the pursuit of academic degrees and living an Observant life.[37] This belief led him in 1508 to institute the College of San Pedro y San Pablo, a school next to the University of Alcalá for twelve Observant Franciscan students, who could attend classes and obtain degrees in theology from the Complutensian University.[38] As in so many other things, Cisneros was ahead of his time in this regard. His fully modern conception of Franciscan higher education was well received among the friars of the Castilian Observant provinces. But, on the other hand, the superiors from other Spanish Observant provinces still maintained their traditional attitude of distrust towards university life and the pursuit of academic degrees. In the General Chapter held in Burgos in 1523, where the Spanish Fr. Francisco de los Ángeles Quiñones was elected minister general of the Order, the Observant Franciscans resigned their chairs in *studia generalia*. In such an atmosphere, between 1515 and 1525 Franciscan masters ceased teaching at the University of Alcalá. As late as 1532, the statutes of the Ultramontane Chapter of Toulouse absolutely prohibited the pursuit of academic degrees. But it must be said that this decree was not fully implemented and was overturned in 1541. At the same time, the General Chapter of 1523 had also established the creation of provincial study houses for the training of young friars in theology and other sciences necessary to carry out their ministry.[39] In Spain, like in other regions of Europe, it seems

35. Roest, "*Sub humilitatis*," 94–95. A detailed description of the origins of the Complutensian University can be found in García Oro, *El cardenal Cisneros*, 2: 233–501.

36. Erika Rummel, *Jimenez de Cisneros: On the Threshold of Spain's Golden Age* (Tempe: Arizona Center for Medieval and Renaissance Studies, 1999), 54; Ramón González Navarro, "La Universidad de Alcalá de Henares en los comienzos del siglo XVI," in *L'Université en Espagne et en Amérique Latine du Moyen Âge à nos jours, I. Structures et acteurs*, eds. Jean-René Aymes, Ève-Marie Fell, and Jean-Louis Guerena (Tours: Presses universitaires François-Rabelais, 1991), 23–42, https://doi.org/10.4000/books.pufr.5837.

37. Roest, "*Sub humilitatis*," 95.

38. Roest, *A History*, 167–68.

39. Andrés, *La teología*, 97–98; Castro, *San Francisco de Salamanca*, 82–83.

that the position of the Franciscan Observants towards university degrees and the embrace of scholastic learning remained ambivalent until well into the sixteenth century.[40]

Despite their opposition to the pursuit of academic careers, and even though education was reduced to a bare minimum in the eremitical and discalced communities, the Observant Franciscans maintained their commitment to study. To such extent that, according to the statistics, in the sixteenth century there were about 7,500 educated friars in the Spanish Franciscan provinces. Thereby, the Observants could provide a significant number of intellectually trained people, who could assume a leading cultural role not only in the Iberian Peninsula, but especially in the "New World," where the school formation received by the Franciscans had a great influence on their missionary and pastoral work.[41]

Moreover, we have evidence of Observant Franciscans who held degrees from prominent universities and, in one way or another, contributed to the early evangelization of the Americas. For example, Friar Juan de Tecto (Johann Dekkers), Friar Jean Focher, and Friar Juan de Gaona, who worked as missionaries in New Spain, had taken their doctorates in Paris, while Friar Peter of Ghent had been educated at Leuven. For their part, the superior of the group of the "Twelve Apostles" of Mexico, Friar Diego de Almonte, Friar Bernardino de Sahagún,[42] Friar Antonio Ortiz,[43] and Friar Alonso Herrera had pursued studies in Salamanca.[44]

In the "New World," the Franciscans also started building their own academic network from an early date.[45] In 1535, there was already a *studium* at the friary of San Francisco of Mexico City, which had among its first students the linguist Friar Alonso de Molina, Friar Diego de Olarte, a former companion of Cortés who later became provincial minister in 1564, and Friar Diego Valadés, who wrote *Rhetorica Christiana*, the first book by an author from New Spain printed in Europe.[46]

---

40. Roest, "*Sub humilitatis*," 105.

41. Lázaro, "*Scholastica*," 161–62.

42. Lázaro, "*Scholastica*," 158; Rubial, *La hermana pobreza*, 98, 147.

43. Friar Antonio Ortiz had pursued studies in law and sacred scripture in Salamanca before he joined the Franciscan Order. See Salazar, *Coronica*, 112.

44. Ángela Perea López, "Alonso Herrera," in *Real Academia de la Historia, Diccionario Biográfico electrónico* (https://dbe.rah.es/biografias/51295/alonso-herrera).

45. Cristóbal Colón himself had a project to establish a first theological school in La Española, where four proficient masters in theology ("quatro buenos maestros en Santa Theologia") would teach spiritual doctrine. García Oro, *El cardenal Cisneros*, 2: 601.

46. Francisco Morales, OFM, "Sacerdocio y orden franciscana entre los naturales del valle de Puebla-Tlaxcala," *Dimensión Antropológica* 22, no. 65 (2015): 206.

Curriculum of Studies of the Franciscan Missionaries and Its Implementation in the "New World"

As we have just seen, it took the Franciscans of the Observance a long time to develop their own school network with a set curriculum of studies. But this fact did not imply that they did not have access to learning, or that they lacked religious instruction altogether.[47] As far as we know, the Observant friars who were part of the first generations of missionaries in the Americas were theologically educated to some extent. They did not receive specific formation regarding missionary or pastoral work. Their studies were rather grounded in the scholastic philosophical and theological methodology, using concepts from Greek and Roman philosophy. As noted above, some of these friars had also pursued studies in universities such as Salamanca, where they could get acquainted with humanist thought as well. The intellectual context of education that the Spanish Observant Franciscans received in the first decades of the sixteenth century was, in summary, quite eclectic.[48]

The intellectual training of the Franciscan friars who traveled to the Americas was structured according to two interconnected factors: the person who studied and the level of studies. To begin with, lay brothers followed a formation program different from the clerical friars who would be ordained priests. The members of this latter group who were deemed proficient enough pursued higher education. Among the Franciscan missionaries present in the "New World," thus, there were lay and clerical friars alike, who had received different types of education and training, which enabled them to develop their skills in a wide variety of tasks.[49]

In any case, until the sixteenth century learning within the Franciscan Order was characterized, as expected, by a progressive understanding of theology. Once they had completed their novitiate, the friars were instructed in grammar and the introductory disciplines of the liberal arts. Then, after a thorough examination, they received a three-year course on philosophy. Finally, after due examination, the most proficient students were sent to pursue higher studies in moral or doctrinal theology. Moral theology schools were intended to train future preachers and confessors, whereas doctrinal theology schools received students for the lectorate and higher degrees. Former students from these higher education centers usually held positions of responsibility in the Order.[50]

47. Roest, *A History*, 158.
48. Lázaro, "*Scholastica*," 160.
49. Lázaro, "*Scholastica*," 162.
50. Lázaro, "*Scholastica*," 162.

The Observant Franciscans gradually developed their own network of provincial schools of grammar, philosophy and theology. In the first half of the sixteenth century, several General Chapters of the Order established that logic and metaphysics should be taught in philosophy schools. For the teaching of philosophy and theology, lectors of these *studia* had to rely on the Franciscan and the Church's intellectual traditions. For this reason, at least until the sixteenth century the standard textbook was the *Liber Sententiarum* of Peter Lombard, which was studied with the help of the *Summa* of the Franciscan master Alexander of Hales. To study the Sentences of Lombard, Franciscan students could also use the commentaries written by other Franciscan authorities, such as François de Meyronnes, Richard of Mediavilla, and especially Bonaventure.[51] From the beginnings of the fourteenth century onwards, the works of John Duns Scotus had gradually replaced the teaching of Alexander of Hales and Bonaventure in the degree programs of the most prominent *studia generalia* of the Order, especially that in Paris.[52]

Teachings of Franciscan theological authorities, such as Alexander of Hales, Bonaventure, and notably Scotus, were very influential as a source of inspiration of many Franciscan authors. But that should not make us think of the existence of a Franciscan school, in the strict sense of the word, during the late medieval period. There certainly existed some tendencies of "school formation" within the Order of Friars Minor, even though they were probably less pronounced than was thought by modern scholars.[53] It is probably more precise to speak of a Franciscan intellectual milieu, where many friars shared a comparable, but not always identical, theological sensibility. Minorite theologians, inspired by their own interpretation of the Franciscan experience, could thus adopt radically different positions in their philosophical and theological works.[54]

From the early sixteenth century, a keen interest in Scotism emerged among the Observant Franciscans, especially after they took control of Paris and other *studia generalia* and they considered it necessary to position the Franciscan intellectual tradition against other religious orders. In 1500, the teachings of John Duns Scotus were officially adopted as the school doctrine to be taught at the higher theological centers of the Order.[55] In Spain the adoption of Scotus's theology was not something completely new, since the *studium* of San Francisco of Salamanca had a chair of Scotism since the

51. Lázaro, "*Scholastica*," 163–64; Roest, *A History*, 194.

52. Roest, *Franciscan Learning*, 116–17.

53. Roest, *A History*, 195. For an in-depth analysis of the subject, see 172–96; Roest, *Franciscan Learning*, 116.

54. Roest, *A History*, 190, 193; Andrés, *La teología*, 106.

55. Roest, *Franciscan Learning*, 185.

1400s.[56] But the Spanish Observants increasingly began to propagate the doctrine of the Subtle Doctor after establishing the Complutensian University. In Alcalá de Henares, a chair on Scotism was added to the traditional chairs in Thomism and Nominalism, and the *Reportata* was adopted as the textbook for learning Franciscan theology of the Subtle Doctor. After some decades of decline, possibly due to lack of interest or capacity among the masters who taught Scotism in Alcalá and Salamanca,[57] from the 1540s teaching of Scotist theology was increasingly propagated throughout the Franciscan *studia* in the Iberian Peninsula. It should be noted as well that Duns Scotus exerted a significant influence on ascetic works written by Observant authors throughout the sixteenth century.[58]

Notwithstanding the acceptance of Scotism as official theological doctrine, many Franciscan Observants still preferred Bonaventure's teachings, which were considered less complicated for their use at lower and intermediate level schools, and more appropriate for pastoral and edificatory purposes as well.[59] Bonaventure was especially appreciated by those Franciscan authors who had sympathies for a more affective theology, which was developed not at the higher centers of learning, but in a "para-academic" environment. In this wider area of theological and religious education, many teachings of Bonaventure exerted a crucial influence on the religious attitudes of late medieval Western Europe.[60] This can help to explain why in the 1500s Bonaventure remained a reference theologian for the Spanish Observant and Discalced Franciscans.[61] Even in those communities more resistant to scholastic formation and in recollection houses the friars still received some instruction in Latin, the Franciscan Rule, and the basics of doctrinal, moral, and mystic theology, using Bonaventurian works as primary texts.[62]

As Manuel Lázaro Pulido points out, the treatises on spiritual and mystical theology written by Bonaventure became "the uncontested reference works

56. Manuel Lázaro Pulido, "La tradición franciscana, lugar de construcción de las bases filosóficas en la península ibérica," *Carthaginensia* 26 (2010): 281.

57. García Oro, *El cardenal Cisneros,* 2: 436–37; Isaac Vázquez, "La enseñanza de la doctrina de Escoto en las universidades españolas," *Verdad y Vida* 19 (1961): 370–71.

58. Lázaro, "*Scholastica*," 164; García Oro, *El cardenal Cisneros,* 2: 435–37; Rummel, *Jimenez de Cisneros*, 56; Andrés, *La teología*, 107–108.

59. Roest, *Franciscan Learning,* 185; Roest, *A History*, 118.

60. Roest, *A History*, 195–96; Lázaro, "*Scholastica*," 165.

61. Lázaro, "La tradición franciscana," 286.

62. For example, as we know from a contemporary account, even in a small friary like that of Jarandilla, a hermitage that belonged to the San Gabriel province of the Franciscan strict observance, in the sixteenth century there was "lección de theología moral y mística y de explicación de Regla" (Lázaro, "*Scholastica*," 165–66).

for the Franciscan search of God through prayer."[63] To this contributed the fact that some spiritual treatises by or attributed to the Seraphic Doctor were printed before 1500 in Spain,[64] and his complete works were available in the Iberian Peninsula during the first half of the sixteenth century.[65] Thus libraries of many Spanish Observant houses, even the smallest ones, used to have in their collections volumes of the Bonaventurian treatises.[66] These works provided fundamental elements to the mystical literature that were developed by the Spanish Franciscan authors of the sixteenth century, such as self-knowledge or the personal conversion process, the following of Christ, and the self-transformation in God.[67] Not surprisingly then, Bonaventurian theological and mystical works were soon present and circulated in the "New World": as early as 1502, a copy of the *Doctrina cordis de Sant Buenaventura en romance* was part of a book collection brought by Franciscan missionaries to La Española.[68] Some commentaries on Bonaventure's *Speculum disciplinae ad novitios*, a treatise widely used in the formation of the Friars Minor, were written in New Spain during colonial times. And his *Teología Mística* was first printed in Mexico in 1549 by the Dominicans, which indicates the broad circulation of this work not only among the Franciscans, but among other religious and any other people who wished to devote themselves to the spiritual life.[69]

Summarizing, the first generations of Observant Franciscan missionaries in the "New World," to a greater or lesser extent, had an education in liberal arts, grammar, and at least a certain knowledge of doctrinal, mystical, and

63. "[Buenaventura se convirtió en] el referente incuestionable de la búsqueda franciscana de Dios desde la oración." Lázaro, "*Scholastica*," 165.

64. Pseudo-Bonaventure's *Meditationes vitae Jesu Christi* was edited in Barcelona in 1493, and in the Abbey of Montserrat six years later. Catalan and Castilian versions of this work were published in the first decades of the sixteenth century. A first Castilian translation of Bonaventure's *Soliloquium* was sent to press in Seville in 1497. His *Regula novitiorum* was also printed in Seville in 1497 (Atanasio López, "San Buenaventura en la bibliografía española," *Archivo Ibero-Americano* 8, no. 16 (1921): 345–49, 355–56, 359–61.

65. Jessica A. Boon, *The Mystical Science of the Soul: Medieval Cognition in Bernardino de Laredo's Recollection Method* (Toronto-Buffalo-London: University of Toronto Press, 2012), 231, note 56.

66. Bonaventure's works were present, for example, in the library collections of most of the friaries belonging to the strict Observance Province of Los Ángeles. Lázaro, "*Scholastica*," 165–66.

67. Lázaro, "La tradición franciscana," 288.

68. Mariano Errasti, *América Franciscana. I.—Evangelizadores e indigenistas del siglo XVI* (Santiago de Chile: CEFEPAL, 1986), 39; García Oro, *El cardenal Cisneros*, 2: 635.

69. Francisco Morales, "New World Colonial Franciscan Mystical Practice," in *A New Companion to Hispanic Mysticism*, ed. Hilaire Kallendorf (Leiden: Brill, 2010), 93–94. https://doi.org/10.1163/ej.9789004183506.i-518.18.

moral theology that relied on the teachings of the great Franciscan masters, such as Alexander of Hales, John Duns Scotus and, above all, Bonaventure. But when these friars arrived in the Americas, they were compelled to put into practice the scholastic education that they had received in Europe in a completely new context, in which scholarship had to be the handmaiden of pastoral care. Hence the challenges of missionary work led them to adopt more practical and pastorally oriented forms of theological thought, eventually open to some elements of the humanist and scientific approach.[70]

At an early stage, colonial scholasticism did not develop in a university environment, but in activities such as the learning and study of Indigenous languages and cultures. The geographical and cultural distance between European missionaries and Amerindians was extraordinary. From their arrival to the Americas, the friars were aware that communicating the Gospel and the principles of Catholic faith across language barriers posed the greatest intellectual challenge of their encounter with the local native people. Moreover, evangelizers had to make the Christian message accessible to people who belonged to a pagan world, a cultural context unknown to them before, where misinterpretation of the truths of faith was more than probable.[71]

To overcome these challenges, sixteenth-century missionaries became "the prototype ethnographers of the modern era." In fact, as Nancy Farriss points out, "the evangelization of America has been deemed an impressive feat of applied anthropology and applied linguistics."[72] In this task, the friars labored hand in hand with skilled Indigenous collaborators in the creation of a new language, which adapted the terminology of the local vernacular to adequately transmit and explain the Christian doctrine. Soon after arriving in Mexico, the Franciscans established schools to provide young natives with a basic education, essential for further evangelization. Their students quickly learned Spanish and served as interpreters for the friars in their missionary campaigns. At the same time, they helped the European evangelizers to learn Nahuatl themselves.[73]

Soon thereafter, in 1536 the Friars Minor established the Colegio de Santa Cruz de Tlatelolco, where native students, most of them the sons of Nahua leaders, were to receive an elite education in Spanish and Latin grammar, rhetoric, philosophy, logic, and possibly theology. Among its faculty members were such prominent figures as Friar Andrés de Olmos, Friar Juan de Gaona, or Friar Bernardino de Sahagún, and other Franciscans who held

---

70. Lázaro, "*Scholastica*," 156.

71. Nancy Farriss, *Tongues of Fire: Language and Evangelization in Colonial Mexico* (Oxford and New York: Oxford University Press, 2018), 3, 6, 198–99.

72. Farriss, *Tongues of Fire*, 202.

73. Farriss, *Tongues of Fire*, 6, 37, 204.

degrees from the best universities in Europe and had a strong humanist background as well.[74] The Colegio de Tlatelolco was immediately an academic success, as it trained "a generation of superbly trained scholars renowned for their Classical learning and translation skills."[75] The Franciscans assigned a key role to their trilingual students and former students, who helped them not only in translation work, but also in the creation of dictionaries, grammars, catechisms, and devotional literature written in the Amerindian languages. Even more, Santa Cruz alumni were authors or co-authors of treatises on topics as diverse as preaching, ethnography, law, poetry, or natural sciences.[76] Considering all these facts, we can realize again that a significant group of Observant Franciscan missionaries were highly literate people, with a thorough scholastic education, but who had to apply their knowledge from a much more down-to-earth approach, in a completely new context where the missionary effort implied practical and pastoral theological approaches more than theoretical reflection, in order to provide an answer to the major challenge posed for evangelization in the "New World."[77]

CONCLUSIONS

From the very beginning of the evangelization of the Americas, contemporary documents and chronicles refer to the first Franciscan missionaries who labored there as "*sabidos y letrados*," even though the vast majority belonged to the Observant fold of their Order and were resistant to studies.

To understand this apparent paradox, it must be noted that the representation of Franciscan Observants as "ignorants" and totally opposed to learning is misleading. Even though they considered that the pursuit of degrees posed a threat to the Franciscan ideals of poverty and humility, the reformed Franciscans did not necessarily reject the study of practical and spiritual theology, and considered it very important that reformed friars could read a corpus of devotional and spiritual texts. In this way, they followed the teachings of Saint Francis, who was of the opinion that learning was necessary among the friars, but it should remain subordinate to the ideals of simplicity and poverty of the

74. Francisco Morales, "Tlatelololco y el diálogo intercultural," in *El Colegio de Tlatelolco; Síntesis de historias, lenguajes y culturas*, eds. Esther Hernández and Pilar Máynez (México City: Editorial Grupo Destiempos, 2016), 66–71.

75. Farriss, *Tongues of Fire*, 143.

76. Farriss, *Tongues of Fire*, 206; Aysha Pollnitz, "Old Words and the New World: Liberal Education and the Franciscans in New Spain, 1536–1601," *Transactions of the Royal Historical Society* 27 (2017): 124, https://doi.org/10.1017/S0080440117000068; José Rubén Romero Galván, "El colegio de Tlatelololco, universo de encuentros culturales," in *El Colegio de Tlatelolco: Síntesis de historias, lenguajes y culturas*, 20–24.

77. Lázaro, "*Scholastica*," 157.

Minorite life.[78] Besides, from the early 1400s study was again deemed essential by many friars of the Observance for an effective and doctrinally sound performance of preaching and pastoral tasks. As a result of this, the friars of the moderate Observant fold established their own academic network where the students would be educated within a proper curriculum of liberal arts, canon law and moral theology.

In fact, a significant group of friars belonging to this movement who served as missionaries in the Americas were highly literate people, with a thorough scholastic education. At the same time, their education in Observant houses of study provided them with a practical approach, in which academic learning had to be the handmaiden of pastoral work. This helped them to face the major challenges posed by the evangelization of the "New World," where the missionary effort implied practical theological methods more than theoretical reflection. This approach favored an exchange with local people and cultures, as a consequence of which emerged a totally new Mexican form of Christianity and culture that has survived to the present.[79]

In this manner, Franciscan Observant missionaries in the Americas demonstrated with their lives and work that the pursuit of learning was compatible with Saint Francis' ideals of poverty and humility. The case of Friar Toribio Motolinia, who was described by Friar Bernardino de Sahagún as a "very good friend of holy poverty, most humble and devoted man, and a proficient learned person"[80] was not, then, exceptional.

78. Roest, *Franciscan Learning*, 16.

79. Farriss, *Tongues of Fire*, 7

80. "[V]arón muy amigo de la santa pobreza, muy humilde y muy devoto y competentemente letrado." Quoted by Errasti, *América Franciscana*, 242.

Chapter Nine

Geographia sacra mexicana: *Franciscan Imaginings of World and Space in Sixteenth-Century Mexico*

Jennifer Scheper Hughes, *University of California, Riverside*

An eighteenth-century oil painting housed at Mexico's Museo Nacional del Virreinato shows St. Francis contemplating a crucifix. Francis raises his bare foot, marked by luminous, red stigmata, to steady a small, dark orb: a globe[1] (Figure 1). Even given his authoritative stance, the saint's unshod foot speaks to his poverty and humility, and his countenance, eyes cast downward, is characteristically modest. The earth rests securely under the sublime perfection of Franciscan dominion. We perceive that the ordered and idealized spherical world of nascent modernity is not just a European or Christian object but, more specifically, a Franciscan one.

This essay begins with a small set of artworks from the seventeenth and eighteenth centuries depicting Franciscan engagement with the globe, created in the context of Spanish American evangelization.[2] I refract these visual images through Mexican historical materials to draw out complex, ambivalent, and contested Catholic understandings of the global in the centuries of Spanish imperial rule in the Americas. Franciscan perceptions of the world as a coherent, Catholic territoriality were destabilized by their experience in the

---

1. The original provenance of this work is the church of San Francisco Mazapa (near Teotihuacan). Courtesy of El Instituto Nacional de Antropología e Historia de México: https://mediateca.inah.gob.mx/islandora_74/islandora/object/pintura%3A2305.

2. This chapter is an expansion upon the 2023 Tibesar Lecture that I presented at the Franciscan IV Conference: Landscapes and Languages at Flagler College St. Augustine, Florida. Support for further research and analysis was provided by way of my appointment as Yang Scholar of World Christianity at Harvard Divinity School 2024-5, culminating in the 2025 Hackett Lecture at Harvard's Center for the Study of Religion. Material from this chapter is scheduled to appear in the Spring/Summer 2026 issue of the *Harvard Divinity Bulletin*. Thanks also to Jalane Schmidt (UVA) and also to UC Riverside's Latino and Latin American Research Center writing group.

Figure 1. St. Francis's dominion over the earth. Oil on canvas, 52.7 × 36 cm. Courtesy of El Instituto Nacional de Antropología e Historia de México.

American continent. Their feet-on-the-ground confrontation with the so-called "New World" both stirred and frustrated Franciscan desires for an intelligible and ordered globe under their jurisdiction. Here, I develop these observations, drawing out questions related to evolving Franciscan perceptions of the global horizon of Catholicism. Some of the questions suggested by these visual materials are of a theological nature: for example, what is the relationship of the emerging geographical earthly corpus, the early modern globe, to the body of Christ? The larger historical context of these centuries is defined by the relational asymmetry of Spanish and Indigenous worlds under violent Spanish invasion and centuries of European imperial rule. This asymmetry is reproduced in territorial modes. Therefore, I necessarily consider how Indigenous Catholic ordering of geo-religious space contested and constrained the realization of Franciscan global territorializations in Mexico.

The Mexican image of Francis that opens this chapter originally hung in the colonial Franciscan monastery "*convento*" church, Francisco de Asís de Mazapa. The mission-convento rests in the shadow of the sacred Mesoamerican city of Teotihuacán, which has stood as imposing, monumental ruins since a millennium before the Spanish invasion. For more than two centuries the painting remained barely two kilometers from the historic Pyramid of the Sun and the Avenue of the Dead. Its original context of meaning was the evangelization of the Native people of Mexico. The church boasts other colonial artworks of Francis—including a fresco of the reception of his stigmata.

The visual depiction of a world that has submitted to Francis' rule may seem discordant. Wasn't the saint's renunciation of the material world definitive and final? He is meant to refuse the world, not lay claim to it. A Spanish painting with a similar motif speaks to this contradiction. A rendering of St. Francis from c.1668, by the Baroque painter Bartolomé Esteban Murillo, shows the saint in a mutual embrace with Christ on the cross. As he leans toward Christ, Francis pushes away a dark orb with his uncovered foot, symbolizing his rejection of the material world. His body turns away from the spurned globe and toward Christ. The difference in gesture in the two works, one in which the earthly sphere is thrust away and the other in which it is steadied and drawn near, is starkly evident. To embrace Christ, one must reject the world. In the context of New World evangelization, Francis' Old-World apprehensions about the dangers of earthly power and influence seem to have been at least partially reconciled with his pious humility and devotional poverty.

Medieval historian Julie McClure has taught us much about Franciscan perceptions of the world including their global perspective and purposes. The Franciscans "were not merely mendicant monks wandering the world in poverty, but missionaries who also wanted to convert the world to their vision of Holy Poverty." McClure argues that the Franciscans stood in a "dialectical" rather than symbiotic relationship with the "global spread of money and markets," even as they engaged unequally with Indigenous people, and ultimately became imbricated with the history of empire.[3] In their utopian imaginings, the entire globe would be subject not just to the Church, but to the rule of Francis.

Three additional early modern artworks reiterate the theme of Franciscan dominion over the globe. Two of these appear in a seventeenth-century printed history of the order focused on the "New World," authored by an anonymous Franciscan priest from Brussels. Another related image, more publicly accessible, is a tiled panel on the exterior of San Lorenzo church in Valencia, Spain. Considered together, these illustrations from disparate parts of the world reveal complex Franciscan imaginings of earth, geography, and place. The works in question reflect what might be termed a Franciscan *geographia sacra*. In its original iteration, "geographia sacra" referred to the scholarly study of biblical geographies. Indeed, in the seventeenth century Franciscans worked to map the Holy Land.[4] But in these centuries geographia sacra also

3. Julia McClure, "The Globalisation of Franciscan Poverty," *Journal of World History* 30, no. 3 (2019): 335–62, 337.

4. Marianne P. Ritsema Van Eck, *The Holy Land in Observant Franciscan Texts (c. 1480–1650): Theology, Travel, and Territoriality*, vol. 17 (Leiden: Brill, 2019), and Marianne Ritsema van Eck, "Mapping Imagined Territory: Quaresmio's Chorographia and Later Franciscan Holy Land Maps," in *Constructing and Representing Territory in Late Medieval and Early Modern Europe*, eds. Mario Damen and Kim Overlaet (Amsterdam: Amsterdam University Press, 2021), 326.

referred to the monastic orders' efforts to "portray their global reach."[5] It is on the latter meaning that our attentions rest.

Drawing on significant colonial Mexican sources, both Spanish and Indigenous, I show how Franciscan projections of the world as a constant, cosmic orb under their spiritual, geo-religious, jurisdiction were fraught and frustrated by Spanish American realities.

Seraphic Atlantic, Heavenly Globe: Franciscans Wresting the Earth

A striking, "two worlds" Franciscan image appears in the 1652 *Abrégé des fruits acquis par l'ordre des Frères-Mineurs es quattres parties de l'univers, nommément la conversion du Nouveau-Monde, recueilli par un Père cordelier en Bruxelles* [Summary of the fruits acquired by the Orders of the Friars Minor in the four parts of the universe, namely the conversion of the New World].[6] A richly metaphorical woodblock illustration serves as the frontispiece of the chapter dedicated to the evangelization of Mexico. On the bottom right, three Franciscan brothers kneel to contemplate a large, geographical globe with three continents demarcated and named: Africa, Europe, Asia (Figure 2). The friar nearest to the foreground gestures to the African continent with his left hand and to Asia with his right. A second friar clasps his palms, gazing down at the globe in reverent admiration, while a third motions to St. Francis who stands apart, on the left side of the image. Francis spreads his arms to draw the viewer's attention to a second orb, born aloft by two cherubim. This second globe, here represented as a heavenly donation to the Franciscan order, contains the American continent. The caption reads, "*S. Francisco Atlanti Seraphico. Unus non sufficit orbis*": "Seraphic Atlantic. One world is not enough." Franciscan territorial ambitions are thus rendered comparable to those of Alexander the Great, to whom the famous phrase is originally (but not verifiably) attributed: one world to conquer is not sufficient. Some may be surprised to find the Franciscans expressing what seems to be such raw, imperial desire. The phrase "one world is not enough" lent its potency to many iterations of global imperialism: King Phillip II, who reigned over the Spanish empire during the crucial period from 1556 to his death in 1598, adopted the phrase to capture his wide-ranging,

5. Zur Shalev, "Early Modern *geographia sacra* in the Context of Early Modern Scholarship," in Kevin Killeen, Helen Smith, and Rachel Willie, eds., *The Oxford Handbook of the Bible in Early Modern England, c. 1530–1700* (2015; online ed. Oxford Academic, 12 November 2015).

6. I am grateful to Timothy Johnson for directing me to this image. Père cordelier en Bruxelles, Un. A. du texte. (1652). *Abrégé des fruits acquis par l'ordre des Frères-Mineurs es quattres parties de l'univers, nommément la conversion du Nouveau-Monde, recueilli par un Père cordelier en Bruxelles* (Brussels: F. Vivien), 132.

Figure 2. Sublime Atlantic, two worlds of the Franciscans. Abbregé universelle, Chez Francois Vivien, 1652, Societe de geographie, Paris.

colonial ambitions. In the Catholic context, the motto is more commonly associated with the Jesuits. Just a decade prior to the Franciscan image under discussion, it is inscribed below an illustration from the weighty Jesuit volume *Imago primi saeculi* (1640).[7] Today, it appears, in the titles of contemporary studies of the Jesuits, including the introductory essay to the *Oxford Handbook of the Jesuits* (2017). In adopting the familiar saying as their own, the Franciscans surely meant to rival these other imperial ventures with a more perfect and sublime dominion. They identified themselves as the Seraphic Order. The phrase "Atlanti Seraphico" that appears below the two worlds image refers not just to the transcendent, awe-inspiring revelation of a "new world," but avows that the Atlantic world belongs, definitively, to the Franciscans.

7. "Introduction: Is One World Enough for the Jesuits?," in *The Oxford Handbook of the Jesuits*, Oxford Handbooks (2019; online edition, Oxford Academic, 6 November 2017), https://doi.org/10.1093/oxfordhb/9780190639631.002. 0006, accessed 14 September 2024. https://academic.oup.com/edited-volume/34656/chapter/ 295286206. For another example, Moya, José Luis Betrán Maya, "Unus Non Sufficit Orbis: La Literatura Misional Jesuita Del Nuevo Mundo," *Historia Social* no. 65 (2009): 167–85, http://www.jstor.org/stable/40658065.

The Sublime Atlantic print captures a moment of terrestrial disruption. What is the place of this new continent, this new hemisphere, in relation to the known world? Here, and in some other visual materials from these centuries, the American continent appears not just as a "new world" but in fact as a second globe.[8] The earthly orb that rests on the ground, surrounded by the three friars, is the one that Francis himself would have known in his own time: the world as it was, before the "discovery," the revelation, of vast American continents erupted to challenge European comprehension. The artist invents an anachronistic moment, the collapse of almost three centuries of time. Francis, who died in 1226, is projected into the future, to the moment of European discovery. It is simultaneously the moment of donation—the heavens have bestowed the Americas upon the Franciscan order, transferred to their care and spiritual administration. But now they are meant to care for not just one world, but two?

Historians and geographers have explored how this hemispheric revelation unsettled early modern European understandings of a stable and comprehensible globe. From the dawn of the sixteenth century, the world was ever more vast and ever more accessible: both expanding and contracting simultaneously. In her monograph *Worldmakers*, literary critic Ayesha Ramachandran probes the sense of disruption and epistemological crisis that resulted from the "increasing emphasis on worldly plurality, contingency, and the limitations of human perception and knowledge" in the sixteenth and seventeenth centuries. She follows transformations in European understandings of the "world" with attention to the "conceptual, imaginative, and metaphysical challenges posed by the task of envisioning an abstract totality."[9] The discovery of the Americas simultaneously inspired and troubled the unifying construct of the "world" as a coherent theological totality, the ultimate aspiration of the project of European Christian empire. Changes in European ideas of place, globe, and earth were similarly felt by the Franciscans who lived out some of these novel spatial realities in New Spain.

As we contemplate the woodblock print from various angles, it is evident that the Franciscans are not of the world, but rather outside of it: regarding, observing, and directing. They are leviathans, as large as a galaxy, and the earth is small and compliant in their hands. Julie McClure writes of the Franciscan "earthrise" perspective in the early modern period in which the Franciscan view

8. This is the case, for example, in the Jesuit image from the *Imago primi saeculi* discussed above.

9. Ayesha Ramachandran, *The Worldmakers: Global Imagining in Early Modern Europe* (Chicago: University of Chicago Press, 2019), 6–7. "One of the signs of change is lexical; the words used to designate 'world' in both classical and vernacular languages undergo significant reconfiguration over the sixteenth and seventeenth centuries" (10).

of the earth is characterized by remove: "Elevated by poverty and raised by a zeal for souls, the Franciscans invented a location from which they were looking back and seeing the world as a whole from afar."[10] And so it appears here. The friars seem to be studying the globe, making sense of it from their "earthrise" perspective. Interestingly, the friars' globe seems to be about the same size proportionally of those crafted by the Flemish cartographer, Gerardus Mercator. Over the better part of the sixteenth century, Mercator's workshop produced hundreds of globes reflecting not just centuries of accrued cartographic knowledge, but also drawing on the latest scientific methods and discoveries.[11] They were meant to be studied, to be used much as the Franciscans seem to be doing here. Timothy Johnson has argued that place is central to the Franciscan ethos and episteme from the thirteenth century. Writing about the medieval, Franciscan priest Roger Bacon, Johnson notes his insistence on the need to "develop a true perspective of the world accompanied by reasoned understanding of where a person is situated in relationship to the physical world, and thus to the heavenly spheres and God."[12] In the sixteenth and seventeenth centuries, and beyond, the Franciscans were striving for understanding of the earthly globe and their place on it. This striving to comprehend the new global reality is evident, for example, in the publication of the exhaustive thirty-five volume, "cosmographic" chronicle of the order, *Orbis Seraphicus*, by the Franciscan Domenico de Gubernatis in the 1680s. This work catalogues the Franciscans' global expansion across their Seraphic world.[13]

---

10. Julia McClure, "Earthrise: The Franciscan Story," *The Medieval History Journal* 20, no. 1 (2017): 89–117, 98.

11. Notably, Mercator's globes came in paired sets, one terrestrial and one celestial. The only extant set in North America is housed at Harvard University's Pusey Library.

12. Timothy Johnson, "Place, Analogy, and Transcendence: Bonaventure and Bacon on the Franciscan Relationship to the World," in Gert Melville, Bernd Schneidmüller, Stefan Weinfurter, eds., *Innovationen durch Deuten und Gestalten: Klöster im Mittelalter zwischen Jenseits und Welt* (Regensburg: Schnell and Steiner, 2014), 89. Bacon writes, "Since then the knowledge of place in the world is of maximum utility, therefore there must be a different description of them, for the things of this world cannot be known except through the knowledge of the places in which they are contained. Place is the principle of the generation of things. . ." (quoted by Johnson, 89).

13. Dominicus de Gubernatis, et al., *Orbis seraphicvs. Historia de tribvs ordinibvs a seraphico patriarcha S. Francisco institvtis, deque eorum progressibus, & honoribus per quatuor mundi partes, scilicet Evropam, Asiam, Aphricam, & Americam, in obsequium Iesv Christi, & ecclesiae romanae, atque in fidei catholicae defensionem, & dilatationem reportatis* (typis S. Caballi, 1682). The title translates as: "Orbis seraphicvs: The history of the tribes founded by the seraphic patriarch S. Francis, and of their progress and honors throughout the four parts of the world, namely, Europe, Asia, Africa, and America, in obedience to Jesus Christ, and the Roman church, and in the defense and expansion of the Catholic faith."

Figure 3. Winged Francis subdues a sublime globe. San Lorenzo church, Valencia, Spain. Photograph courtesy of Jalane Schmidt, 2024.

In searching out the theological and cosmological meanings of the Franciscan globe motif, I move from the Brussels print to explore another, subsequent iteration. A tiled panel on the exterior of San Lorenzo church in Valencia, Spain contemplates the same themes. Here we encounter another evocative image of Seraphic dominion over the globe (Figure 3). In the image, St. Francis seizes the earth, shown as a *globus cruciger*, an orb beneath a cross, representing Christ's rule over the world. Four continents are named, corresponding to the four cardinal directions. The image is replete with objects of obscure symbolic meaning. At the center, the winged saint tethers and steadies the globe with his rope-like cincture: a knotted Franciscan cord. From heaven, Christ utters his promise to the mendicants: his earthly donation. The Latin scroll at the top reads, "I give this land to you and your seed after you," citing Genesis chapter fourteen. Christ's wounds are mirrored in Francis' stigmata. The wings may be a simpler reference to Seraphic nomenclature, but in the colonial Andes, the Cuzco school developed an artistic tradition of Francis shown floating with angel's wings: "Francis in the sky."[14] Culminating in the

14. See the review essay, Diana Roberts, "Francis in the Sky" *Anales Del Instituto de Investigaciones Estéticas*, 1:113 (2018): 199–215. I am grateful to Charlene Villaseñor Black

work of seventeenth-century native artist, Basilio de Santa Cruz Pumacallao, the Cuzco tradition of a soaring saint Francis seems have made it back to Europe. Perhaps the winged saint in the Valencia example speaks further to the American territorialization of Franciscan global authority.

There has been a church at the San Lorenzo location since the thirteenth century. The structure was built over a destroyed mosque: a token of the Reconquista. However little remains of the original beyond an archeological site: the church itself has risen and fallen many times since. It was only at the beginning of the twentieth century that the Franciscans, who had long been in Valencia, claimed San Lorenzo as theirs. Art historian Alberto Ferrer Orts explains that at that time the existing church was reconditioned under Franciscan direction, including alterations to the façade.[15] The San Lorenzo panel appears to be a mid-twentieth century recreation or evocation of Franciscan artworks typical of Valencia in the eighteenth century.[16] There is some chance that it is an older artwork that was moved from another location in Valencia and reinstalled at San Lorenzo, but more research would be required to make this determination. Thus, a centuries old motif of Franciscan dominion reasserts itself in the modern imagination: more than two million tourists visit the city each year.

A final related image warrants consideration. Returning to the seventeenth-century, Franciscan chronicle from Brussels, the title page of the volume features another figurative image of the globus cruciger (Figure 4). But here, strikingly, the world is also conflated with Christ's body. His crucified hands and feet project out from the world, and the circle is surmounted by a crown of thorns. This globus cruciger as body of Christ, is ensconced and encircled by the identifying cord of the Friars Minor. Indeed, the cord extends and circles around the entire image, functioning as a defining frame. Here again we find a representation of the globe that is disciplined by Franciscan rule.

The illustration conflates Christ's body with Francis (known as the alter Christus, the "living icon of Christ") with the corpus of the earth. The terrestrial globe is the body of Christ. Previously, I have considered the idea of the colony in relation to Christ's mystical body. In the context of Catholic

---

for her consultation on this image. https://doi.org/10.22201/iie.18703062e.2018.113.2661.

15. Albert Ferrer Orts, "La iglesia y el convento de San Lorenzo (Valencia), antigua sede de la provincia franciscana de San José de Valencia, Aragón y Baleares," *Hispania sacra* 68, no. 138 (2016): 491–501, 495.

16. Ferrer Ortis, from the University of Valencia, affirms the panel's likely twentieth-century provenance, and suggests that it must have been installed after the Civil War because it shows little sign of damage. Personal communication, September 2024.

Figure 4. Sublime globe as Body of Christ. Abbregé universelle. Chez Francois Vivien, 1652, Societe de geographie Paris.

empire in New Spain, the colony was reimagined as the *corpus mysticum*, a potent ordering narrative capable of interpreting the place of millions of presumed Christian Indigenous subjects and their occupied territories within the expanding body of the universal Church. The colonial corpus mysticum became sacralized: a living thing, enfleshed and incarnate. Here the earth itself, as an object of Christian rule and evangelization, is superinscribed upon, conflated with, Christ's mystical body: the two are co-identified as territorial and theological jurisdictions. Christ's own body was given to the service of European Christian empire building.[17]

Readers familiar with the history of the church in Latin America will surely recognize the resonance of these corded, bounded worlds with the missionary practice of *congregación*, of forced resettlement of Indigenous people into European-style towns and cities, typically under the watchful guardianship of

17. See Jennifer Scheper Hughes, "The Colony as the Mystical Body of Christ: Theopolitical Embodiment in Mexico," *Social Analysis* 64, no. 4 (2020): 21–41.

monastic orders. That is to say that there were almost always real-world applications for these highly abstract theologies. Historian Daniel Nemser has linked *congregación* to colonial processes of racialization, calling it "a pastoral technology par excellence."[18] Closely related to this is the strategy of "*reducción*," a spatial ordering more common in Jesuit territories. Following the logic of these visual sources, to be *congregado* was to be under the foot of Francis, to be enclosed within his cincture. Timothy Johnson has linked the "reduction of souls" in Florida among the Timucuan to the "sacramental imperative." Congregation facilitated unhindered access to the sacraments. In Florida the reduction of Indigenous people for purposes of Christian civilization (of "*policía cristiana*") is fundamentally about "ordered living" and specifically the "ordering of spatial relationships."[19]

In each of these four visual representations, the Christian earth is a well-ordered orb, governed by divine structure, and under the custody of the Franciscan order. In his extensive study of spheres, German philosopher Peter Sloterdijk writes, "the orb is a held-holding body of order." The perfect orb is "the ontology of the finished world."[20] He goes on to observe that to grasp the orb is "being in praise."[21] Perhaps our Valencia Francis extends his tether in praise of the globe? This idea is closely related to emerging early modern ideals of united global humanity, such as was espoused by the Spanish Dominican thinkers Bartolomé de las Casas and Francisco de Vitoria. For them, "all the nations and the peoples of the globe belong to one world community."[22] But at the same time these idealized visual materials speak to territorial disruption and reveal a sense of apprehension. There is something unsettled in the Franciscan wresting. Why should they need to so vigorously, even anxiously, reiterate their earthly authority? Perhaps the Mexican image that opens this study, Francis steadying the orb with his foot, serves as a case in point. By the time of this work's creation, the Franciscans had largely lost their bid for privileged spiritual jurisdiction in Mexico, not least of all at the hands of

18. Daniel Nemser, *Infrastructures of Race: Concentration and Biopolitics in Colonial Mexico* (Austin: University of Texas Press, 2017), 88.

19. Timothy Johnson, "Are They Damned? Timucuans, Theology, and the Necessity of the Sacraments," in Jeffrey M. Burns and Timothy J. Johnson, eds. *Facing Florida: Essays on Culture and Religion in Early Modern Southeastern America* (Oceanside, CA: Academy of American Franciscan History, 2021).

20. Peter Sloterdijk, *Globes: Macrospherology* (South Pasadena, CA: Semiotext(e), 2014), 33, 39.

21. Sloterdijk, *Globes*, 37.

22. John Leddy Phelan, *The Millennial Kingdom of the Franciscans in the New World: A Study of the Writings of Gerónimo de Mendieta (1525–1604)* (Berkeley and Los Angeles: University of California Press, 1956), 6. Phelan is writing of Vitoria here, but the same is true for Las Casas.

secularizing bishops. We turn, now, to observe how these idealized visions succumb to colonial Mexican realities.

Sahagún's Lament: How to Grieve a Disordered World

The idealized visions of Franciscan global territorializations discussed above were often frustrated by New World realities on the ground. That mendicant utopian aspirations for evangelization of the continent remained unfulfilled is not a new observation for the study of Catholic origins in Mexico. Almost sixty years ago, John Leddy Phelan wrote precisely about the failed millennial hopes of the Franciscan order. Within a half century of their arrival, missionary hopes were already dissolving into apocalyptic despair. Phelan goes even further, labeling the Franciscan vision for a future Indigenous Catholic republic a "stillborn" dream.[23] But hope and despair are both transitory states: they ebb and flow and bleed into each other, and surely, they sometimes existed simultaneously in this difficult and complicated landscape. And who is to say when a dream is truly dead?

In c.1576, the eminent Franciscan theologian, Bernardino de Sahagún lamented that the vision of a sublime, Christian globe was being thwarted by two great forces: the tenacity of Indigenous religion, on the one hand, and the reality of Indigenous demographic cataclysm, what the Spanish termed "*mortandad*," on the other. I refer here to the friar's primordial text, his masterwork: *La historia general de las cosas de la nueva españa* (*General History of the Things of New Spain*), a multi-volume compendium of Nahua history and culture, almost a half century in the making. Across several pages, spanning three subsections, Sahagún probes the dissonance between an idealized vision of the global Church and lament for its weakened condition in Mexico, contradicting Catholicism's global expansion. Reading these pages, with their urgency, their grief, and their immediacy, is a jarring textual encounter.

I return to these startling pages of the *Historia general* as would an exegete, to uncover and contemplate their many layers of meaning. Indeed, art historian Diana Magaloni Kerpel (who has done a great deal to make the *Historia general* accessible), writes that the complexity of this work is deserving of profound and attentive study. . . ."[24] I draw out Sahagun's anguish for an altered globe and distorted earth. The passages in question appear in the

23. Phelan, *Millennial Kingdom*, 69.

24. Diana Magaloni-Kerpel,"Painting a New Era: Conquest, Prophecy, and the World to Come," in Rebecca Brienen and Margaret Jackson, eds., *Invasion and Transformation: Interdisciplinary Perspectives on the Conquest of Mexico* (Denver: University Press of Colorado, 2008), 125–49, 126.

penultimate volume, Book XI, dedicated to "earthly things." "Paragraphs" (really, they are chapters) six, seven, and eight schematize the nature and types of mountains, stones, and roads in Nahua culture, respectively. Among the range of objects examined in this section are medicinal plants, stones and shells of precious value, red cochineal dye, and even the smoking volcano, Popocatepetl. Sahagún's translation of these paragraphs diverges almost completely from the original Nahuatl, so much so that one might speak of these sections as a separate sort of treatise, missive, or epistle. Until recently his digression has not been readily available for study.[25]

Sahagún's reflections on the global pasts, present, and future of the church is textually situated within sections of the *Historia general* dedicated to Mexico's physical, geological setting. They were largely, if not entirely, written in the midst of a deadly *cocoliztli* outbreak which took some two million lives.[26] Recalling here Johnson's assertion about the importance of place for the Friars Minor, it makes sense that Sahagún's global reflections in this text are so clearly emplaced within the physical geography of Mexico. His depiction of the shrinking global horizon of the Church is nestled within descriptions of the topographic contours of the Mexican land. Here the Franciscan wrestles with the Church's emplacement, and the contradiction between the world as it should be and the world as it is.

Sahagun describes the first obstacle to the Franciscan global vision in paragraphs six and seven. In paragraph six, on the right side of the page, Nahua experts elaborate the many kinds of peaks, hills, valleys and slopes that define Mexican lands. But in the left column, Sahagún worries over sacred sites and mountains still regarded by Indigenous communities as the seat of divinity. The Nahua original of paragraph seven catalogues different stones and rocks and their uses. But, instead of translating, Sahagún bemoans the persistence of "idolatry" among Indigenous Mexican Catholics, using the trope of stones to reflect on worship of "idols." The faith, he argues, has been received only shallowly in these lands.[27] The geological and geographic reality of Mexico remains steeped in Indigenous religion, and resistance to Christianity, after fifty years of evangelization.

---

25. This material was only made more broadly available with publication of a high-resolution digital version of the codex by the Medicea Laurenziana library in Florence, Italy. Most recently the Getty has published a version that includes translations of the complete work. https://florentinecodex.getty.edu/.

26. Jennifer Scheper Hughes, *The Church of the Dead: The Epidemic of 1576 and the Birth of Christianity in the Americas* (New York: New York University Press, 2021).

27. 236r–236v. "Bien creo que hay otros muchos lugares en estas Indias donde paliadamente se hace reverencia y ofrenda a los ídolos con disimulación de las fiestas que la iglesia celebra a Dios y a sus sanctos, lo cual sería bien investigase para que la pobre gente fuese desengañada del engaño que agora parece."

In the eighth paragraph, Sahagún transitions abruptly to recall the Church militant as it traversed, even circumnavigated, the earth. It is an idealized vision of a Catholic globe. He writes, "It is evident to all that the Church militant began in the kingdom of Palestine and from there it sojourned (*caminó*) to various parts of the world (*mundo*): to the east, and to the west, and to the north, and to the south."[28] The four cardinal directions correspond to the four continents that have been the focus of Christian evangelization (Africa, Asia, Europe, and the Americas). Sahagun's appeal to mundo is purposeful in its evocation of symmetry and perfection. Notably, "world" proliferates as a term of art in sixteenth-century European texts.[29]

What is the world that Sahagún imagines here, from the sanctuary of the workshop atelier where he worked side by side with Nahua experts and co-authors? First and foremost, mundo, the earthly realm, is the field of the church militant. The idea of the Church militant defines the world as the site of a cosmic battle against sin, the stage for the conversion of souls, and for the global expansion of Christianity. (Conversely, the "Church triumphant" pertains to the realm of heaven.) The Christian world represents a new level of divine perfection: sublimely ordered Christian space. Sahagún is writing around the time of the publication of the Dutch cartographer Zacharias Heyns' *Le miroir du monde* (1579), an abbreviated atlas, the frontispiece of which depicts the globe "as the face of the deity."[30] In that image, the perfection of the world as orb, its sublime dimension and symmetry, mirrors not just the body of Christ, but the face of God.

Sahagún quickly surrenders this transcendent theological vision to one that is more pained and difficult. In these pages, he draws a visual picture, a disharmonious mental map, of a flawed world that is resistant to the itinerant, pilgrim Church:

---

28. 237v. "A todos es noto que la yglesia militante, comenco en el reyno de Palestina: y de alli camino por diversas partes de mundo, hazia el oriente, y hazia el occidente, y hazia el norte, y hazia el medio dia." https://florentinecodex.getty.edu/book/11/folio/237v?spTexts=&nhTexts=.

29. Ayesha Ramachandran traces the "the verbal omnipresence of 'the world,'" in many texts of this century, tracing its transformation: "One of the signs of change is lexical; the words used to designate 'world' in both classical and vernacular languages undergo significant reconfiguration over the sixteenth and seventeenth centuries. Derived from two related but distinct classical concepts—the oikoumene or orbis terrarium (the circle of lands) and the kosmos or mundus (the 'world' or more amply, universe)—the words for 'world' in most European vernaculars (world, welt, monde, mondo, mundo) begin to combine both meanings into a single term in the early modern period." Ramachandran, *The Worldmakers*, 10.

30. Ramachandran, *The Worldmakers*, 7.

> From Palestine (. . .) the church went to Asia, although there it no longer exists and all that (is to be found there now) are Turks and moors. The church also went to Africa, where there are no longer any Christians. It went to Germany, where there remains nothing but heretics. It went to Europe, where the majority (today) do not obey the church. (237v)

The greatest dissonance arises in the failure of the Church to take root in Mexico, on which Franciscan millennial hopes rested.[31]

It is at this point that the Franciscan identifies the second major threat to the evangelization of New Spain. He grieves the devastating consequences of the *cocoliztli* epidemic as it rages around him. Because the destruction of Native communities is so complete, he reasons, the Church has come "to the end of its road" in the Americas.[32] Incongruously, the promise of worldwide Christian evangelization is, in his estimation, at the point of collapse. The Franciscan hope for a Catholic globe has failed. If the globe is the face of the deity (as Heyns depicts), then by extension we might even conclude that in this moment the demographic cataclysm distorts the face of God. In the recent *mortandad*, the church in America faltered and its future is no longer in Mexico or Peru (the two epicenters of Christian evangelization in the hemisphere).

Abandoning the idea of an unflawed Catholic world, Sahagún shifts to speak instead of "lands" (*tierras*). Mexico, he writes, ". . . is a sterile *land* and difficult to cultivate and there the Catholic faith has very weak roots." Land is a more ambiguous term than world. In the context of European thought lands have less authority, they are less fundamentally ordered, and they are perhaps more available for the projection of emotion, for loss, for grief. Thus, for Sahagún, the perfection of the globe surrenders to the imperfection of the land.

After nearly fifty years of evangelizing ministry in Mexico, the mortandad signaled for Sahagún the shortening (even closing) of the Catholic horizon in the Americas. The Americas have been rendered a sort of ghost continent, reduced to a pass through. If the Church has a future, he writes, it is in the east, "in the kingdom of China." Marred by *mortandad*, Sahagún's Catholic globe contracts and falters even as it had seemed to be expanding toward perfection.

ORBIS TERRARUM: INDIGENOUS WORLD MAPS AND THE BODY OF CHRIST

While the Franciscans dreamed of the perfect orb of a Seraphic world, Indigenous Mexican Catholic communities asserted their own territorial vision of a sublime world, powerful enough to rival European imaginings. In their

31. See Phelan's discussion of hope and despair in *The Millennial Kingdom*.
32. https://florentinecodex.getty.edu/book/11/folio/237v?spTexts=&nhTexts=.

vision, ancestral lands remained intact, but were now reimagined as Indigenous Catholic territorialities, under their jurisdiction and governance.[33] Of particular interest for this study are circular or globe-like maps of Indigenous provenance from the second half of the sixteenth century. Two of these are of particular relevance here, the circular maps of Amoltepec and its sister community, Teozacoalco, both painted in 1580, in the aftermath of the cocoliztli outbreak described above.[34] These Indigenous-authored maps form part of the *Relaciones geográficas*, commissioned by King Phillip II as part of a comprehensive survey of New Spain. Both are currently housed at the Benson library at UT Austin. I interpret these as Catholic world maps, analogous to the European visual representations of the globe considered here. While they pertain to local, bounded, territories, they are, in fact, idealized representations of emplaced world views and the projection of globally imagined sacred histories.

The Teozacoalco map is the largest, and the most complex among the most well-studied maps in this collection[35] (Figure 5). The Mixtec community of Teozacoalco represents itself here as a blue-green cosmic orb. Fourteen churches, nestled within circular body of the community, are bound together in hallowed relation. Forty-six toponymic boundary markers defend, enfold, and encircle the ancestral territory, projecting it into the future. Through the emplacement of churches on Indigenous territory, the map affixes Catholicism onto local cartographies. In its mystical, globe-like self-understanding, the community of Teozacoalco projected itself onto a Mixtec-Christian plane. Here is the Mexican corpus mysticum: the shared body of Indigenous Catholic corporate belonging.

Art historian Amara Solari has identified a colonial Maya map from the Yucatán that suggests the superimposition of Christ's wounded body, pierced with arrows, over Indigenous territory, his limbs oriented to the cardinal directions reflecting "a Maya conception of landscape being created from the very materiality of a sacrificed deity."[36] That is to say that Indigenous Catholics in Mexico sometimes also imagined the conflation of the earth, their world and territories, with the body of Christ. Some contemporary Maya communities speak of "the world as a maize field tended by Jesus."[37] The Catholic Teoza-

---

33. This is an argument that I make at length in the fourth and final chapter of *Church of the Dead: The Epidemic of 1576 and the Birth of Christianity in the Americas.*

34. The map of Tabasco in this collection, dating to 1579, is another example.

35. This discussion of the Teozacoalco map draws on my prior analysis in *Church of the Dead*, 138–39, ff.

36. Amara L. Solari, *Maya Ideologies of the Sacred: The Transfiguration of Space in Colonial Yucatan* (Austin: University of Texas Press, 2013).

37. Karl Taube, "Ancient and contemporary Maya Conceptions about Field and Forest" in *Lowland Maya Area: Three Millennia at the Human-Wildland Interface*, eds. Scott Fedick, Michael Allen, Juan Jiménez-Osornio, and A. Gomez-Pompa (London: Routledge, 2003), 462.

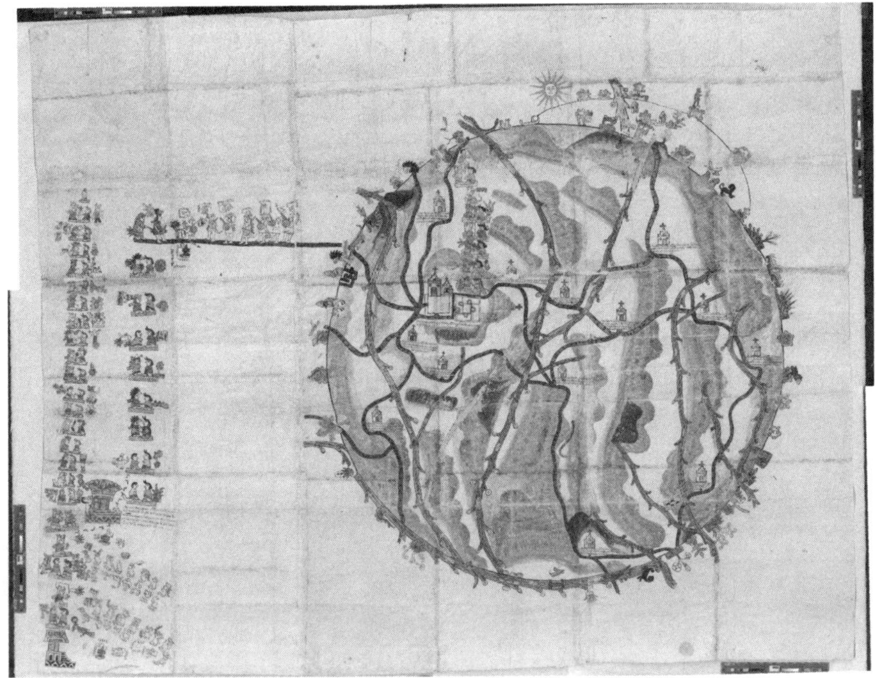

Figure 5. Teozacoalco world map, 1580, Oaxaca, Mexico. LLILAS Benson Latin American Studies and the Collections, University of Texas at Austin.

coalcan vision of Mexican sacred territory contests the Orbis Seraphicus and defies its application in colonial congregación in favor of Indigenous Catholic emplacements that affirmed local authority over the Church and its practices.

A second example, from Amoltepec, a minor Mixtec settlement within Teozacoalco's network, reiterates the circular form (Figure 6).[38] The ancestral geographic border of the community of Amoltepec is defined by the nineteen glyphic toponyms (recognizable, named locations). The sacred matrix that sustains and anchors the community is the carefully drawn mission church, the hill, and the Native temple figure left of center within the circle. A seated pair of *principales* rule over the community. Here we are meant to understand that the Church, as a physical structure, a cultural institution, and a global order, is contained within Indigenous territory.

Returning to Solari's work, she has studied the unusual circular form of some early colonial maps, beginning her analysis with the Maya Land Treaty

38. https://collections.lib.utexas.edu/catalog/utblac:e1372d7e-40f1-47b5-90b4-cb9568457187.

Figure 6. Painting of Amoltepec, 1580, Oaxaca, Mexico, 81 × 92 cm. LLILAS Benson Latin American Studies and the Collections, University of Texas at Austin. Photo by author.

Map of Gaspar Antonio Chi (1557), narrating local history. These round maps are an Indigenous innovation of the early colonial period, Solari explains, but she does not find evidence that the circular shape is influenced by European cartographic techniques for representing the known world. Rather, "this compositional form is . . . derived from pre-Columbian spatial conceptions, which understood space, and particularly one's home territory, in circular terms."[39] Solari persuasively links the round maps to pre-Invasion calendrical and other cultural understandings of space and time. Yet, I do not find that the pre-Hispanic worldviews manifest in these ringed maps to be necessarily exclusive of other meanings and referents. It seems likely that Mexican communities within the reach of Franciscans would have comprehended the importance of the divine globe for the Spanish evangelizers, and perhaps would have come into contact with images representing the sacred,

39. Amara L. Solari, "Circles of Creation: The Invention of Maya Cartography in Early Colonial Yucatán," *The Art Bulletin* (New York, NY) 92, no. 3 (2010): 154–68, 154.

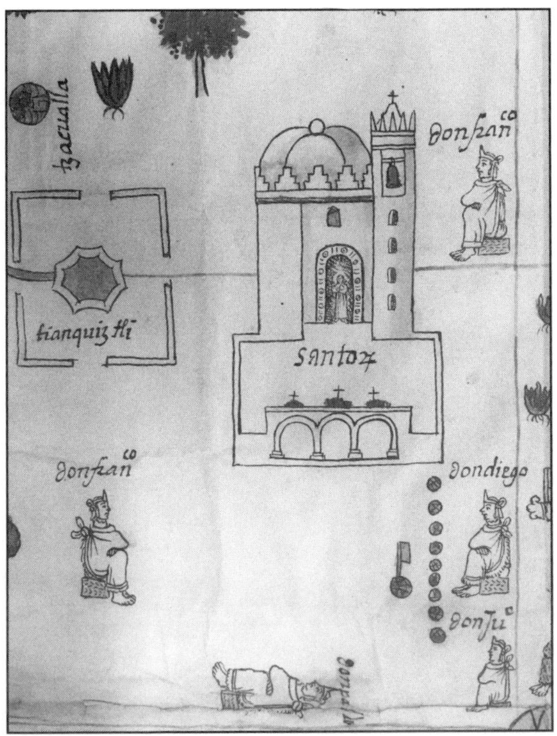

Figure 7. Painting of Cempoala, 1580, 83 × 66 cm. LLILAS Benson Latin American Studies and the Collections, University of Texas at Austin. Photo by author.

earthly orb. Whether explicitly or implicitly, these maps contest European Catholic global territorialities.

One more map merits consideration here: the territorial map of the Indigenous pueblo of Cempoala (Hidalgo, Mexico), also painted in 1580. While not round in shape, it does sprawl out in a circular orientation, and certainly can be read as an Indigenous reckoning with Franciscan theological emplacement in Mexico. Like the other two discussed here, it is a counter-map that asserts local Indigenous territorialities, local ways of ordering and organizing sacred and political space, over and against Spanish ecclesial ones.

The portion of the map in question occupies about one eighth of the total cartograph (Figure 7). It depicts the Franciscan monastery compound of Cempoala with its church and walled atrium. No fewer than five lords, or principales, sit in vigil and oversight over the central church. They have attributes of nobility and are individually named. The principales are seated in the traditional Mesoamerican posture of political authority and rule.

Figure 8. Painting of Cempoala, 1580, detail. 83 × 66 cm. LLILAS Benson Latin American Studies and the Collections, University of Texas at Austin. Photo by author.

Although the church is the largest human-made structure featured on the map, the Indigenous landscape, with its key geological and topographic features, dwarfs and overshadows the church structure. The map is replete with Mesoamerican symbolism and referents: glyphic toponyms, waterways, mountains, and other geographic markers define the space and even the original temple is present. Together these mark Cempoala as Indigenous, not Spanish, territory. Perhaps the work of California Indian scholars studying the history of the missions pertains here. Tsim Schneider et al. write, "Franciscan fathers aspired to hold (and often claimed to hold) unquestioned power over California Indians, but the missions they founded were pockets of colonial ambition appearing relatively briefly within the longer duration and geographies of ancient national territories."[40]

40. Tsim D. Schneider, et al., "Scaling Invisible Walls: Reasserting Indigenous Persistence in Mission-Era California," *The Public Historian* vol. 42, no. 4 (2020): 97–120, 101. See also Nathan P. Acebo, "Survivance Storytelling in Archaeology," *The Routledge Handbook of the Archaeology of Indigenous-Colonial Interaction in the Americas* (Routledge, 2021), 468–85.

The Cempoala map includes an unusual representation of a Franciscan friar. Spanish persons rarely if ever are featured on the Indigenous mapas (Figure 8). While the governing pricipales rule over the Franciscan monastery of Cempoala, the diminutive friar hovers in shadows in the doorway of the church. Perhaps 5 mm in height, he is extraordinarily small—a fraction of the size of the lords of Cempoala. Examining the map in person, one puzzles at the technique required to render such a minute yet detailed figure, holding a sacred book and grasping a cross raised aloft. Distinct from Spanish Franciscan self-representations, this friar is limited in his domain, constrained—*congregado* and *reducido*, one could say. Domesticated and in his proper place, he is limited and constrained in his sphere of action and influence. Cloistered, it seems he dare not exit nor take action outside of the confines of the church. The diminutive Cempoalan Franciscan, whose spatial domain of authority is highly circumscribed, stands in stark contrast to the larger than life images of Francis and the Friars Minor that open this study.

Conclusions

Here I have probed the history of the Church at a critical juncture when its global horizon and Mexican placemaking were challenged by lived realities in New Spain. Franciscan desires to project their rule over a coherent, transcendent globe were disrupted by epidemic cataclysm. I have also considered how Indigenous Catholic intentions for the ordering of geo-religious space further impeded the realization of Franciscan global territorializations in Mexico.

Chapter Ten

The Space between Franciscans and Nahuas: Representations of Sixteenth-Century Mexico's Landscape

Jennifer R. Saracino, *University of Arizona*

When the first Franciscans arrived on the soil of Mexico-Tenochtitlan, the famed capital city of the Aztec Empire that anchors the foundations of present-day Mexico City, they encountered a native population that had long called the lands their home. The Indigenous population they met comprised many diverse ethnic groups, but at the time of Cortés's invasion, the Mexica ruled the Aztec Empire (as part of the Triple Alliance) in the central basin.[1] The Mexica and their counterparts held deep-seated cosmological beliefs in a pantheon of deities whom they believed to govern the natural forces of the world around them.[2] These supernatural beings governed the outcomes of everyday activities, as well as agricultural seasons, the prosperity of crops, and ultimately, the survival of humanity. These numinous beings were associated with features of the natural landscape, and correspondingly, the Indigenous population, particularly the leaders of the Aztec Empire, constructed elaborate ritual complexes replete with

1. "Aztec" is a common term used to refer to the Indigenous population that lived in the central Valley of Mexico at the time of Spanish conquest, but it is imprecise. The ethnic group that controlled the so-called Aztec Empire at the time of conquest was known as the Mexica who spoke the Indigenous language Nahuatl. Because Nahuatl was the most widely spoken language of the basin, after the Spanish invasion, the native population are largely referred to as the Nahua, which is the term I will use throughout this essay.

2. For more in-depth studies and accounts of Aztec (and Mesoamerican) religion, see Michael E. Smith, "Creation, Sacrifice, and the Gods," in *The Aztecs* (Oxford: Blackwell Publishers, 1996), 204–43; David Carrasco, *Religions of Mesoamerica* (Waveland Press, 2014); and Miguel León Portilla, *Aztec Thought and Culture: A Study of the Ancient Nahuatl Mind* (Norman: University of Oklahoma Press, 1990).

temples, plazas, and other structures around which they could focus the community's religious activities. As the Aztec Empire grew in strength, Mexica rulers increasingly tied their cosmological beliefs and ritual to the interests of the state and empire.[3] Thus, the landscape that the Franciscans infiltrated in New Spain was imbued with the cosmological beliefs of the native population, both inherent in its natural form as well as in the many temples and structures built by the Mexica and others.

In thinking about the ways in which the landscape of Indigenous Mexico was transformed, it is crucial to investigate the spatial practices of the various constituencies of the early colonial population—both its settlers and its native communities. For the Franciscans, or the Order of Friars Minor, the transfiguration of space was a fundamental aspect of their original vow to uphold their evangelical mission to spread Christianity throughout the entirety of the known world. They sought to Christianize the Indigenous landscape, transfiguring sacred space from one devoted to pre-Hispanic deities to one fully dedicated to Christ. As scholars Santa Arias and Mariselle Meléndez have proposed, when we think about the transformation of colonial Mexico, we must consider the "geographic and spatial imaginations" of those involved.[4] In my consideration of the Franciscans' methods, the framing questions for this essay are (1) what constituted their geographical and spatial imagination and (2) how did they attempt to impose these ideologies upon the native Nahua population? How did the Nahua respond to and perceive these transformations themselves?

In this essay, I analyze representations of space, articulated by both Franciscan and Nahua authors, to understand how the Franciscans brought both their preconceived notions and observations to compete with the perceptions and practices of the Nahua who continued to occupy and use these spaces. This essay offers an analysis of passages from Fray Toribio de Motolinía's *Historia de los indios de la Nueva España* and engravings from Diego de Valadés's *Rhetorica Christiana* in comparison to the Uppsala Map, a map of Mexico-Tenochtitlan authored by Nahua converts likely under Franciscan supervision circa 1541.[5] The aim of this comparative analysis is to offer the reader a sense

3. Smith, *The Aztecs*, 204.

4. Santa Arias and Mariselle Meléndez, "Space and the Rhetorics of Power in Colonial Spanish America: An Introduction," in *Mapping Colonial Spanish America: Places and Commonplaces of Identity, Culture, and Experienced*, eds. Santa Arias and Mariselle Meléndez (Lewisburg: Bucknell University Press; London: Associated University Presses, 2002), 13. In the introduction to their volume discussing the geographical and spatial imagination, Arias and Meléndez cite Edward Soja's *Postmodern Geographies: The Reassertion of Space in Critical Social Theory* (London: New York: Verso, 1989).

5. The Uppsala Map is a shorthand title I will use henceforth, but the map has no official title. The nickname comes from the city in Sweden where the map is held today.

of how Franciscans' attempts to Christianize and shape human-environmental interactions were confronted by the perceptions and actions of the native people they encountered. As we will see, the perception of the landscape authored by Nahua artists in the Uppsala Map of Mexico-Tenochtitlan presents an alternative to the idealized views offered in the writings of Fray Toribio de Motolinía and in the engravings by Fray Diego de Valadés.[6]

Many scholars have devoted their energies towards carefully delineating exactly how sacred space was forged and transfigured in early colonial Mexico City. Foundational voices in the field of art history include George Kubler and John McAndrew, who authored meticulous studies of monastic architectural forms in New Spain. These authors analyzed the architectural innovations of Mexican monastic complexes that included a large outdoor patio or *atrio* as well as an open chapel, a freestanding, unroofed apsidal structure that could accommodate the presence of hundreds of native neophytes for the purposes of proselytization.[7] In more recent decades, invaluable additions to this scholarship have been made by scholars who have aimed to foreground Indigenous agency in the forging of sacred space in colonial New Spain. Art historians have taken renewed interest in the architecture of monastic complexes and attempted to delineate the spiritual metaphors and cosmological symbolisms that both missionaries and the Indigenous population inflected upon these monastic spaces.[8] In addition, Barbara Mundy has challenged the idea that Spanish conquistadors erased the Indigenous presence of pre-Hispanic Tenochtitlan by focusing on the multitude of ways in which Nahuas contributed to the urban identity and fabric of colonial Mexico City.[9] This essay endeavors to complement these many superb and exhaustive studies by juxtaposing two well-known, Franciscan-authored representations with one authored by Indigenous artists, to observe and dwell in spaces of overlap, liminality, or disjuncture between them.

---

6. I would like to express my sincere gratitude to Savannah Esquivel who provided many thoughtful insights as I worked through the ideas presented in this essay.

7. George Kubler, *Mexican Architecture of the Sixteenth Century* (New Haven: Yale University, 1948); John McAndrew, *The Open-air Churches of Sixteenth-century Mexico: Atrios, Posas, Open Chapels, and Other Studies* (Cambridge, MA: Harvard University Press, 1965).

8. Jeanette Favrot Peterson, *The Paradise Garden Murals of Malinalco: Utopia and Empire in Sixteenth-century Mexico* (Austin: University of Texas Press, 1993); Samuel Y. Edgerton, *Theaters of Conversion: Religious Architecture and Indian Artisans in Colonial Mexico* (University of New Mexico Press, 2001). Amara Solari devoted her book to an investigation of the contribution of Maya people and worldviews to the transfiguration of sacred space at the Franciscan convent at Itzmal. Amara Solari, *Maya Ideologies of the Sacred: The Transfiguration of Space in Colonial Yucatan* (Austin: University of Texas Press, 2013).

9. Barbara E. Mundy, *The Death of Aztec Tenochtitlan, the Life of Mexico City* (Austin: University of Texas Press, 2015).

Throughout their evangelization mission in post-conquest Mexico, the Franciscans sought to understand, represent, and ultimately control the configuration of New Spain's landscape. This took the form of physical interventions—including the construction of churches, monasteries, and schools—as well as actions such as the instruction and conversion of the Nahua. As will be discussed in this essay, we can glimpse what the initial Franciscans were thinking through the writings of Fray Toribio de Motolinía, one of the original twelve Franciscan friars sent to New Spain who arrived in 1524. However, the Franciscans often faced opposition from multiple sources in their efforts to build a successful evangelization campaign, including secular authorities, other colonial administrators, and *encomenderos* who felt as if the Franciscans were overstepping their legal authority.[10]

The challenges the Franciscans faced highlight the contentions among the various officials and administrators of New Spain as well as those between colonists and the Indigenous population who already inhabited these lands. Spatial theorists have long discussed how space is socially constructed.[11] For example, social theorist Henri Lefebvre has employed the term "representational spaces," which, as Barbara E. Mundy has explained, might be thought of as features of the built environment or "lived spaces."[12] Lefebvre's idea of "representational spaces" illuminates the notion that

---

10. In the colonial *encomienda* system of the Spanish Atlantic world, Spanish *encomenderos* could collect tribute and services from Indigenous subjects if they promised also to provide for their spiritual welfare. For more, see Lesley Byrd Simpson, *The Encomienda in New Spain: The Beginning of Spanish Mexico* (Berkeley: University of California Press, 1982); Elizabeth Andros Foster, "Life and Works of Fray Toribio Motolinía" in Motolinía's *History of the Indians of New Spain*, ed. and trans. Elizabeth Andros Foster (Berkeley: The Cortés Society, 1950), 3.

11. Santa Arias and Mariselle Meléndez, "Space and the Rhetorics of Power in Colonial Spanish America: An Introduction," in *Mapping Colonial Spanish America: Places and Commonplaces of Identity, Culture, and Experienced*, eds. Santa Arias and Mariselle Meléndez (Lewisburg: Bucknell University Press; London: Associated University Presses, 2002), 14. Additionally, the authors cite Michel Foucault and his concept of "heterotopias, that is, the idea that sites or locales are fundamentally "not superimposable" because they live "within a set of relations." The notion of *heterotopia* is particularly helpful in thinking about the ways in which the Franciscans' idealized notion of a Christianized landscape could not simply overlay or erase Indigenous notions of sacrality that the landscape already possessed. Foucault, "Of Other Spaces," Diacritics 16:1 (1986): 22–27.

12. As summarized by Barbara Mundy, Lefebre's idea of "representational spaces" is in addition to both "representations of space" as well as "spatial practice." Lefebvre argues that "representational spaces", or the built environment, cannot be treated separately from "representations of space" that inform and inflect upon one's experience of a place (that is, the spatial practices enacted within a lived environment. Mundy, *The Death of Aztec Tenochtitlan, the Life of Mexico City*, 11–12.

spaces are not only physically constructed, but they are naturally imbued with "ideologically coded, and culturally specific, ideas about space" by those who have designed and continue to use them.[13] The spatial practices enacted within and around a site continue to shape its meaning throughout time. Because of the diversity of people who use a particular space and inflect it with their own culturally specific ideas, there exists contested or multivalent meaning within the social construction of space. One monastery or area of physical land can become a site of ongoing negotiation and contestation. The meaning of space, particularly in a fraught colonial landscape, is in a continual state of becoming as part of the actions, or set of spatial practices, that transpire there.

REPRESENTATIONS OF THE FRANCISCAN CHURCH AND MONASTIC COMPLEX IN THE FRIARS' ACCOUNTS

In some regards, the transfiguration of the physical and spiritual landscape of New Spain began in the Franciscans' minds before they even left European soil. The Franciscans who would go to New Spain maintained an "apocalyptic interpretation of history," meaning that they firmly held that once all people of the world were known and identified, the Second Coming of Christ would be nigh.[14] Because of this millenialist belief, the Order sought to evangelize as many people as possible. In 1524, twelve Franciscans arrived in New Spain, purposefully replicating the apostolic mission of Christ and his twelve disciples. The organization of this highly symbolic mission built on the idea that St. Francis himself served as a model of Christ and his disciples were meant to spread the word of Christianity on earth.

The writings of Fray Toribio de Motolinía, one of the original twelve Franciscans to travel to New Spain together, compiled a detailed account of the Franciscans' evangelical mission in New Spain. It was penned within the initial decades after the Spanish invasion, providing evidence of their early tactics as well as an extensive description of his perception of the Indigenous inhabitants, their history, their customs, and landscape.[15] The introductory letter in Motolinía's account mentions that he was writing in

---

13. Mundy, *The Death of Aztec Tenochtitlan, the Life of Mexico City*, 12.

14. Georges Baudot, *Utopia and History in Mexico: The First Chroniclers of Mexican Civilization (1520–1569)* (Denver: University Press of Colorado, 1995), 80.

15. Formerly Fray Toribio de Benavente, he selected the name "Motolinía" for himself after claiming that the Nahua used this word (meaning "poor") to refer to his destitute appearance when he walked by. He declared it his name in honor of the Franciscan vow of poverty and the first Nahuatl word he ever learned. Toribio de Motolinía, *Motolinía's History of the Indians of New Spain*, trans. and ed. Elizabeth Andros Foster, "Life and Works of Fray Toribio Motolinía," 2.

1541, and it seems that he was working on his history as early as 1536.[16] As one of the original twelve Franciscans, his account offers one of the most invaluable records of the Franciscans' initial strategies and engagements on New Spanish soil.

The Franciscans were highly mindful of their spatial strategy in their attempts to achieve a fully Christianized New Spain. As part of the evangelization of the Indigenous inhabitants, the Franciscans believed it to be of paramount importance to construct churches as the foci of their Christianization efforts. As Motolinía wrote:

> The friars also endeavored to have churches built everywhere, and now in almost every province which has a monastery there are churches dedicated to the twelve apostles, especially to Saint Peter and Saint Paul, who, besides the churches named for them, have their images painted on every altarpiece everywhere.[17]

As Motolinía's description attests, the Franciscan evangelization mission in New Spain necessitated ample construction of churches and, eventually, monastic complexes. Few architectural plans came from Europe to New Spain before 1550 and perhaps none before 1540. The first friars thus based their monastery plans on memory, and these early models served as a template for subsequent complexes of the sixteenth century.[18]

Due to several new and unprecedented challenges, these monastic complexes incorporated many architectural features with scant precedent in Europe. The Franciscans adapted the architectural plans of their monasteries in New Spain out of a need to accommodate large Indigenous congregations and construct monasteries as quickly and efficiently as possible. A typical monastic complex might include the following features: a single-nave church, an open-air chapel, an atrium, and cloister where the Franciscans lived on the premises. The new monastic complexes accommodated hundreds of Nahuas.

The convent of San Francisco in Mexico-Tenochtitlan incorporated one of the first open-air chapels into its design, reflecting the desire to accommodate growing crowds of Indigenous Christian converts.[19] In Europe, this architectural feature was nonexistent. Open-air chapels in New Spain, although largely varied and idiosyncratic, generally extended into a large courtyard or *atrio* (atrium), a chapel in which to celebrate the Mass or witness

---

16. Foster, "Life and Works of Fray Toribio Motolinía," 14.

17. Motolinía, *Motolinía's History of the Indians of New Spain*, 48.

18. John McAndrew, *The Open-Air Churches of Sixteenth-Century Mexico: Atrios, Posas, Open Chapels, and other studies* (Cambridge: Harvard University Press, 1965), 128.

19. McAndrew, *The Open-air Churches of Sixteenth-century Mexico: Atrios, Posas, Open Chapels, and Other Studies*, 340.

Figure 1. Diego Valadés, The Monastery of San Francisco from *Rhetórica Christiana*. Perugia: Petramiacobum Petrutium, 1579. Courtesy of the John Carter Brown Library.

Christian liturgy, secondary chapels or *posas,* and a large cross near the center of the atrio.[20]

The outdoor atrio, and its fundamental role in the evangelization of the Nahua, has become a well-known feature of the monastic complex through ample scholarship on a canonical image found in Franciscan friar Diego de Valadés's *Rhetorica Christiana*.[21] Valadés was born in Mexico in 1533, and he published this important account of the Franciscans' evangelization campaign in the Americas in Perugia, Italy in 1579.[22] Valadés's account included twenty-seven copperplate engravings that illustrated the Franciscans' evangelization tactics, philosophy, and early modern theory on the art of memory. Valadés's work reflects the profound influence of his humanist education, referring to Classical authors such as Plato and Aristotle in his written Latin prose, and he looked to other European prints as source and inspiration for many of his engravings.

20. McAndrew, *The Open-air Churches of Sixteenth-century Mexico: Atrios, Posas, Open Chapels, and Other Studies*, 314.

21. For a recent interpretation and contextualization of this image, see Mundy, "Forgetting Tenochtitlan," in *The Death of Aztec Tenochtitlan, the Life of Mexico City*, 114–27.

22. There is some debate as to whether his mother might have been Indigenous; thus, he is often described as the first mestizo person to join the Franciscan order.

In what is likely the most well-known engraving from Valadés's work, the representation of the idealized mission takes place within the atrio commonly found in many Franciscan monastic complexes throughout New Spain (Figure 1). Four posa chapels are situated within the frame at each corner of the page. The interior space is framed by a set of walls whose shape is echoed by an orderly, double row of conventionalized bell-shaped trees within. At the center of the page, the Franciscans, identifiable by their tonsures and plain robes, carry the symbolic church on their backs, a metaphor for their apostolic mission to transplant Christianity on New Spanish soil and re-establish the Church anew. They are led by St. Francis himself on the far right, carrying a small crucifix in his left hand and gazing upwards towards the heavens.

The Holy Spirit, in the form of the dove, radiates from within the two central pillars of the church. Dotted lines extend outward from this site to guide the viewer's attention to the surrounding vignettes that illustrate different aspects of the Franciscans' evangelization program. For example, in the bottom center of the atrio, a scene of baptism takes place and clockwise to the right, the friars administer the sacraments of marriage. Directly above this scene, the Nahua are being taught how to write their names. In the upper right and left, we can see the central role images played in the friars' instructional methods. In the upper right, the creation of the world is taught, while, in the upper left corner, Pedro de Gante, a foundational Franciscan friar and mentor to Valadés, uses pictographic imagery to communicate with the Indigenous students. Thus, the First Holy Roman Church (as referenced in the Latin text beneath the friars "Primi Santae Romane") is configured as the foundational model for the establishment of the Church in New Spain, a spiritual anchor for all the friars' subsequent evangelization tactics. The orderly architecture of the atrios complex figures prominently into the image, governing the activities that transpire within. As we can see, the friars' instruction of the sacramental rites was equally important to the evangelical mission, and it all takes place seamlessly within this architectural space.

Notably, scenes from the pre-Hispanic Mexican landscape are also included within the collection of copperplate engravings in the *Rhetorica Christiana*. In one engraving intended to represent pre-conquest Mexico, Valadés depicted a large platform pyramid topped with a free-standing open-air chapel (Figure 2). This architectural feature is a notable post-Conquest architectural innovation, indicating the invented and imagined character of Valadés's representation (it is worth reiterating that Valadés was born in 1533, and thus, would never have beheld a pre-Conquest religious ritual). In the central scene on the temple platform, natives adorned with feathered headdresses (a popular iconographic trope used in early modern European prints for depictions of Indigenous peoples) are seated, surveying the heart sacrifice that takes place within the open-air chapel. A central figure standing above

Figure 2. Diego Valadés, "Mexico City," 1579, copperplate engraving. In *Rhetorica Christiana ad concionandi et orandi usum accommodate* [...] *ex Indorum maximè deprompta sunt historiis* (Perugia: Petrus Jacobus Petrutius, 1579). Courtesy of the John Carter Brown Library.

the sacrificial victim offers the heart to the idol, rendered as a Greco-Roman style human figure on a pedestal (complete with contrapposto). In front of the temple, several groups of native inhabitants dance around drummers.

The centrality of the church to the Franciscan mission is made abundantly clear through the juxtaposition of these engravings, that is, the pre-Hispanic sacrifice scene and the idealized atrio. The colonnaded portico of the primitive church containing the Holy Spirit stands in stark opposition to the heart sacrifice and idol worship atop the platform pyramid in the other image. Valadés's dancing Indigenous people contrast sharply with the orderly groups of Nahua students gathered at the feet of various Franciscans. The rectilinear form of the atrio provides structure and order to the composition, analogizing the process of civilization (here implicitly tied to an increasingly orderly society) that is implied by the Franciscans' instruction. In contrast, in the depiction of the pre-Hispanic scene, Valadés manipulated the perspective of the image, so that the entirety of the landscape is tilted up towards the viewer. In this way, the viewer can peruse the landscape around the temple, in which various Indigenous inhabitants are engaged in mundane quotidian tasks, seemingly unaware of the sacrificial ceremonies taking place in the central temple. The dynamic diagonals of the landscape guide the viewer's eye throughout, providing a stark visual contrast to the orderly structure of the idealized atrio engraving. They also carry the viewer's gaze away from the spiritual landscape of pre-conquest Mexico depicted in the center and towards scenes and images that are indicative of the economic potential of the land's natural resources and Indigenous laborers.

The Representation of New Spain's Economic Potential in the Friars' Accounts

In the sacrifice scene, the landscape surrounding the temple communicates an idyllic and pastoral representation of everyday life in contrast to the ritual violence depicted at center. Valadés's representational aims change in the depicted surroundings. He instead seeks to capture the economically productive aspects of the daily life of the Indigenous people. This image highlights the ways in which the native inhabitants steward the landscape and successfully harvest its natural resources. In the upper portion of the image, Indigenous inhabitants perched on rafts extend a large net into the lake to catch fish. In the middle-left portion of the composition, a woman grinds corn on a *metate* while the women around her prepare tortillas. Towards the bottom of the image, people harvest maguey and cacao or tap trees for sap. These vignettes communicate what European audiences may perceive as positive and salvageable aspects of Indigenous ways of life, meaning, these activities might help sustain colonial populations on a practical level as well as yield economic profit for colonizers if the natives can be successfully converted.

Throughout the *Rhetorica Christiana*, Valadés's prints have a clearly intended didactic tone. In many of the images, he used a labeling system to help the viewer decipher the composition. In the idealized atrio scene, each vignette is accompanied by a letter of the Roman alphabet. In the sacrifice engraving, he labeled a variety of native tree species at the bottom of the page. The viewer can see maguey, cacao, and pineapple among other species. These labels help advertise the land's natural resources. And yet, on a more sinister level, this didacticism lends this imagined landscape a pretense of authenticity.

A similar sort of attention on New Spain's economic potential can be gleaned from Motolinía's account as well. In the third part of *Historia de los Indios de la Nueva España*, at least six chapters are devoted entirely to a discussion of the agricultural riches, natural resources, and the existing Indigenous economy of New Spain. In chapter six, he comments on the abundance of merchants and craftspeople, livestock, and the "crowds of Indians come into the city laden with supplies and tributes."[23] In terms of plant species,

23. Motolinía, *Motolinía's History of the Indians of New Spain*, 204.

Motolinía describes blackberry bushes, wild grapevines, and cacao.[24] He also notes Malabar pepper, cinnamon, and liquidambar trees. His description of liquidambar trees, also depicted on Valadés's image of a pre-Hispanic native village, illuminates the possibilities of their use:

> The sap that is drawn from them is called by the Spaniards liquidambar; it is sweet-smelling, has medicinal virtues, and is highly valued among the Indians. The Indians of New Spain mix it with its own bark to solidify it, for they do not want it liquid, and make it into cakes which they wrap in big leaves. They use it for perfume and also to cure certain diseases.[25]

Motolinía's attention to the medicinal or healing aspects of particular plants anticipated the friars' more sustained efforts to systematize native plants and healing knowledge in the form of longer encyclopedic projects like the Badianus Herbal, a compendium of native plants and their healing remedies, compiled by native physician Martín de la Cruz and Nahua translator Juan Badiano, at the Colegio de Santa Cruz in 1552. It also predates the creation of the *Historia general de las cosas de la Nueva España* (widely known as the Florentine Codex), compiled by Fray Bernardino de Sahagún and a team of Nahua collaborators, artists, and scribes from approximately 1555–1577.[26]

Motolinía also not so subtly vaunts the integral role of the Franciscans in ensuring that the natural landscape can produce optimally. For example, in chapter eight, he wrote:

> The Friars Minor . . . taught many people how to graft, which is the reason why there are today many very good orchards. There will be many more, for the Spaniards, seeing that the land produces a hundredfold what they plant, are doing a great deal of planting and grafting good fruit and valuable trees.[27]

He also described how, if the Franciscans and the Christianized Nahua can continue to steward in the landscape according to Motolinía's prescrip-

---

24. Motolinía, *Motolinía's History of the Indians of New Spain*, 217.

25. Motolinía, *Motolinía's History of the Indians of New Spain*, 218.

26. The Colegio de Santa Cruz was a Franciscan-run institution for higher education established by Juan de Zumárraga, Antonio de Mendoza, and Sebastián de Fuenleal in 1536. Both the Badianus Herbal and the *Historia general de las cosas de la Nueva España* were made in the orbit of the Colegio, its instructors, and its alumni. For more on the Badianus manuscript, see Emily W. Emmart Trueblood, *The Badianus Manuscript (Codex Barberini, Latin 241) Vatican Library; An Aztec Herbal of 1552* (Baltimore: Johns Hopkins Press, 1940); for more on the *Historia General de las Cosas de la Nueva España* (widely known as the Florentine Codex for its present location in Florence, Italy), see Jeanette Favrot Peterson and Kevin Terraciano, *The Florentine Codex* (Austin: University of Texas Press, 2019).

27. Motolinía, *Motolinía's History of the Indians of New Spain*, 219.

tions, then the economic potential of New Spain will surpass the agricultural productivity of Spain. He wrote in chapter 18:

> In the city of Los Angeles some Spanish citizens have five or six thousand feet of mulberry groves, wherefore such quantities of silk will be produced here that it will be one of the rich things in the world and this will come to be the center of the silk industry; for there are many plantations of mulberries, and with what is planted and raised in many other parts of New Spain, within a few years more silk will be raised in this country than in all Christendom.[28]

As these passages reveal, in addition to his appreciation of the abundance New Spain has to offer, Motolinía's account is also highly aspirational. He envisioned a hybridized landscape that produced both native crops and plants in abundance as well as varieties of commodities he knew well from Spain. Motolinía's aspirational vision and Diego Valadés's idealized and invented landscapes of New Spain contrast with a third representation, that produced by Christianized Nahuas in the Uppsala Map of Mexico-Tenochtitlan, which offers an important counterpoint from the perspective of those who actively lived on and worked the land.

A Representation of New Spain according to Nahua Artists

Dated to roughly 1540–1555, the Uppsala Map of Mexico-Tenochtitlan was painted by Nahua artists just a couple decades after the Spanish Conquest (Figure 3).[29] In fact, it is the only known painted representation of Mexico-Tenochtitlan, Tlatelolco, and its surrounding basin to come from the sixteenth century. It was likely created at the Colegio de Santa Cruz, an institution of higher education established exclusively for sons of Nahua elites in 1536 by Antonio de Mendoza, Sebastián Fuenleal, and the Franciscan bishop Juan de Zumárraga. The scale of the Colegio has been enlarged in comparison to all the other buildings present on the urban plan. The Uppsala Map, as a singular representation of the landscape of the Valley of Mexico, provides an important counterpoint to the descriptions of Motolinía and the representations of Valadés.

First, in the Uppsala Map, the ubiquity of the Christian church is notable. There are approximately sixty churches depicted in the landscape outside of Mexico-Tenochtitlan. They all take the form of a schematized tri-

---

28. Motolinía, *Motolinía's History of the Indians of New Spain*, 268.

29. Jennifer Saracino and Barbara E. Mundy, "Dating the Mapa Uppsala of Mexico-Tenochtitlan," *Imago Mundi* 73, no. 1 (2021): 2–15.

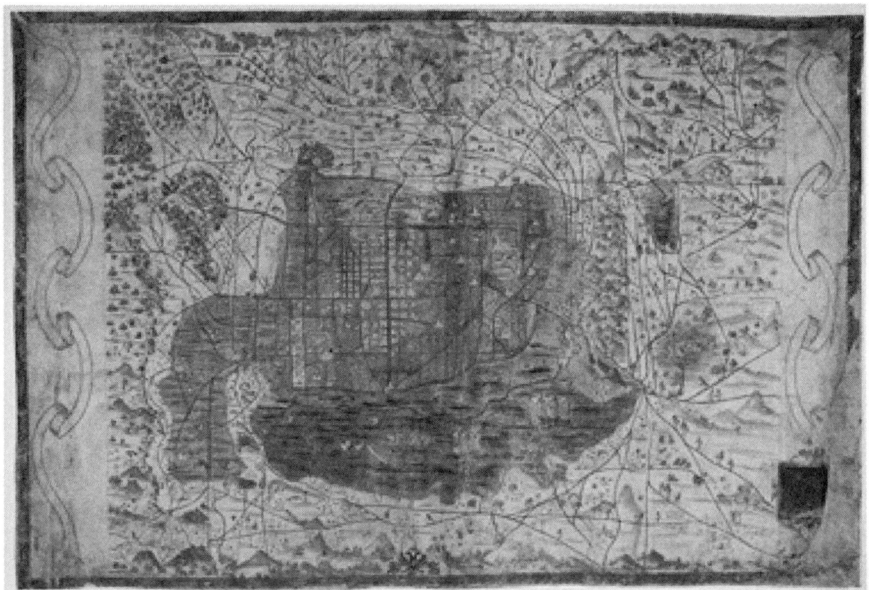

Figure 3. Map of Mexico-Tenochtitlan and the basin of Mexico, c. 1540, ink on parchment. Uppsala University Library, Uppsala, Sweden.

partite structure. A spire crowns the middle section, while two smaller buildings flank the central nave. Oftentimes, the church is accompanied by a large cross nearby. The cross may be alluding to the atrio space referenced in Valadés's idealized atrio image, or it may simply be a large cross erected in the vicinity of the church.

If we juxtapose the representation of the churches in the Uppsala Map with those described textually in Motolinía and then visually in Valadés, the church constitutes a central aspect of the Franciscans' evangelizing mission in all three representations. However, they play a slightly different role in all three. In Valadés's representation, the church fundamentally anchors and frames the most essential activities that transpired between the Franciscans and the Nahua. We do not see what happens outside of the ritual complex the way that we do with Valadés's invented representation of pre-Conquest Indigenous lands in the sacrifice-themed engraving. Motolinía discusses the importance of church construction as a first step in the Franciscans' evangelizing mission, however, the schematization and standardization of all the churches throughout the landscape homogenizes them. None stand out as being more obviously decorated or adorned than another.

In the Uppsala Map, it is the way the church stands within the community in relation to its surrounding structures and activities that is the most striking.

Figure 4. Church of Santa Maria de la Victoria accompanied by tecpan from a map of Mexico-Tenochtitlan (detail), c. 1540, ink on parchment, Uppsala University Library, Sweden.

The churches in each represented community often stand alongside other discrete entities—a Nahua *tecpan*, or council house, a Central Mexican place glyph, and diminutive square houses. In effect, the church constitutes part of the identity of many communities; however, it is not necessarily the only structure that identifies the community as the representations of Motolinía or Valadés might suggest. For example, in the upper left portion of the map, the artists have rendered the church of Santa María de la Victoria (Figure 4). Diagonally to the upper right of the church, an enormous cross is elevated upon a stepped platform. Diagonally to the lower right of the church, the artists rendered a tecpan at roughly the same scale as the community church. A tecpan before Spanish Conquest served as a kind of seignorial palace. In the early colonial period, it continued to serve as a site of importance, and in the Uppsala Map, it is likely signifying the local Indigenous *cabildo*, or town

30. Susan Toby Evans, "The Aztec Palace under Spanish Rule: Disk Motifs in the Mapa de México de 1550 (Uppsala Map or Mapa de Santa Cruz)," in *The Postclassic to Spanish-Era Transition in Mesoamerica: Archaeological Perspectives* (Albuquerque: University of New Mexico Press, 2005), 13–34.

Figure 5. Hospital-pueblo of Santa Fe from a map of Mexico-Tenochtitlan (detail), c. 1540, ink on parchment, Uppsala University Library, Sweden.

hall.[30] Many of the settlements throughout the Uppsala Map that possess a church also have a tecpan in their vicinity, identifiable by their flat roofs and their lintels inscribed with concentric circles. The concentric circle lintel is likely another continuity with pre-Hispanic convention, as jade disks were often used in pictographic convention to denote sites of importance or authority.[31] Thus, in the Uppsala Map, unlike Motolinía's or Valadés's descriptions, we see the coexistence of the Catholic Church with the Indigenous cabildo as sites of community importance.

Another distinguishing feature of the Uppsala Map is the majority Nahua inhabitants interacting with the landscape in such a way as to suggest the rich breadth and variety of daily life for early colonial Mexican society. Valadés's idealized atrio image shows a variety of activities (all having to do with learning the sacraments of the Church) taking place within the monastic complex. However, in the Uppsala Map, there is only one depiction of what appears to be Indigenous converts huddled within a community. In the upper left corner of the map, a label identifies Santa Fe, marking the *hospital-pueblo* established by Vasco de Quiroga in 1532. Still, however, it is not clear whether these

31. Evans, "The Aztec Palace under Spanish Rule," 19–20.

Nahua people are learning about the sacraments as they are depicted in Valadés's idealized atrio. Instead, this group appears to be partaking in a communal meal (Figure 5).

As mentioned earlier, Motolinía devoted chapter eight of the third treatise to describe mulberry trees, blackberry bushes, and grapevines. He also described cacao, malabar, cinnamon, and liquidambar trees, which are also visually described in Valadés's image of the sacrificial scene. In the Uppsala Map, there is no indication of any of this sort of vegetation, or the practice of tree grafting, which Motolinía described as something the Friars Minor taught the local population.[32] While cacao and liquidambar are rendered in Valadés's image, the Nahua artists focus more on representations of nopal cactus and maguey. They also render some practices rooted in traditional Nahua customs such as catching waterfowl using nets and stakes planted in the swampy marsh. At the northeastern corner of Lake Texcoco (the lake's lower right in the map), a Nahua person harvests salt from the shores. Motolinía's account emphasizes the potential of the imported European crops while the representations of the Nahua in the Uppsala Map seem to focus more on pre-conquest Nahua traditions of harvesting and gathering.

The Uppsala Map and Motolinía's descriptions do align in one manner though. The representations of the Nahua inhabitants in the Uppsala Map appear to reaffirm Motolinía's description of the landscape in chapter six of book three more than in any other chapter. For example, of all the Nahua inhabitants depicted on the map, merchants or burden-carriers far outnumber any other activity. Motolinía noted how many native people came into the city "laden with supplies and tributes" and arrived via boats or *canoas*.[33] Motolinía also noted the presence of European-introduced livestock. In the Uppsala Map, just west of the island of Tenochtitlan (located towards the top of the map), we see at least three Nahua people shepherding a variety of livestock (Figure 6). Three shepherds oversee their respective flocks. In the upper left, the animals bear horns, identifying them as cattle. The lower group in the trio appears to have a dog assisting in the shepherding of the flocks.

The Liminality Between Nahua and European Representations of New Spain's Lived Spaces

In considering the ways in which the representation of New Spain's landscape differs among Fray Toribio de Motolinía, Fray Diego Valadés, and the Nahua artists of the Uppsala Map, it is critical to consider the intended audiences of each author (or group of artists). Motolinía, as one of the founda-

32. Motolinía, *Motolinía's History of the Indians of New Spain*, 219.
33. Motolinía, *Motolinía's History of the Indians of New Spain*, 204.

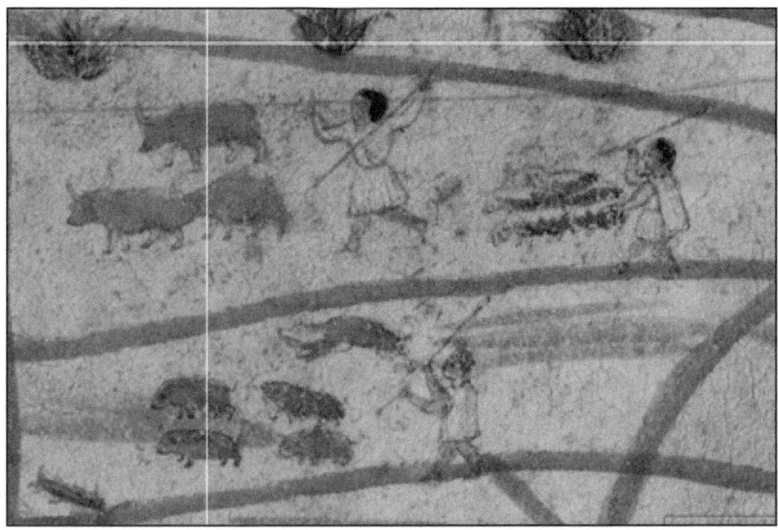

Figure 6. Nahua shepherding European-introduced livestock from a map of Mexico-Tenochtitlan (detail), c. 1540, ink on parchment, Uppsala University Library, Sweden.

tional twelve Franciscans, sought to write an authoritative and comprehensive history of the Franciscans' evangelization efforts. Diego Valadés had similar goals; however, having already relocated to Italy, he likely knew that his description would be successfully published and distributed among expressly European audiences. Both authors intended their works for European audiences, although Motolinía's account was not published in full until the nineteenth century.[34] Valadés also had the opportunity to create images to accompany the text, and thus, these images add another layer of information to his narrative. The Uppsala Map differs markedly from these Franciscan sources because it documents the changing landscape from the perspective of Christianized Nahua artists. Because any documentation pertaining to the commission, creation, or dissemination of the map is as-of-yet undiscovered, we can only piece together the mystery of the map's patronage and circulation through iconographic clues on the map itself.

In the lower right-hand corner of the map, a decorative cartouche dedicates the map to Charles V, then king of Spain and Holy Roman Emperor,

34. The complete text was published with the title *Historia de los Indios de la Nueva España* by Joaquín García Icazbalceta in the first volume of his *Colección de Documentos para la Historia de México.* Toribio de Motolinía, *Motolinía's History of the Indians of New Spain*, 20.

from Alonso de Santa Cruz, the king's royal cosmographer who likely acquired the map and then dedicated it to the king. The fact that the dedication appears to overlay the decorative ribbon border on the right side of the map indicates that Alonso de Santa Cruz likely acquired this map secondarily.[35] Even if Charles V was the final recipient of this map, the enlargement of the Colegio de Santa Cruz on the right side of the island city suggests that this map might have been commissioned either by Franciscan patrons, or perhaps, benefactors of the Colegio.[36]

The representations of New Spain's landscape analyzed in this essay range in the aspects of the landscape each author or set of authors wished to emphasize. Motolínia described the natural resources and topography of New Spain with great enthusiasm, and he also made sure to discuss the potential of imported European goods and crops. Diego Valadés included representations of plant species described in Motolinía's account as well as plant species native to Mexico. However, the completely invented nature of his sacrifice image throws the objectivity of his depictions into doubt. The Nahua artists of the Uppsala Map offer a critical counterpoint to both Franciscan-authored representations. Although no map is inherently objective, the Uppsala Map provides an alternative perception of the landscape, its natural resources, and the human-landscape interactions of the basin—not only from a Nahua point of view, but also from the perspective of those living in New Spain at the time of the map's creation. We might compare these circumstances to the moment in which Valadés created his images. In 1579, he had been living in Italy for seven years. Thus, in some ways, Valadés's images are not only based on idealization and appropriation of European templates but also on his slightly-more-distant memories of living in New Spain.

In this essay, I wanted to compare three different perspectives of the landscape of New Spain to offer a new consideration of the transfiguration of the Nahua landscape after Spanish conquest. Although we can never arrive at a completely unified vision of what that landscape looked like, or even what its colonial population originally sought to make it, the triangulation of its varied

---

35. This hypothesis was mentioned by Manuel Toussaint in Toussaint, Federico Gómez de Orozco, Justino Fernández, *Planos de la Ciudad de México, Siglos XVI Y XVII: Estudio Histórico, Urbanístico y Bibliográfico* (México: Universidad Nacional Autónoma De México, 1938; 1990).

36. The enlargement of the monastery of Santiago Tlatelolco and the Colegio de Santa Cruz has been discussed in each of these analyses: Sigvald Linné, *El Valle Y La Ciudad De México En 1550: Relación histórica fundada sobre un mapa geográfico, que se conserva en la biblioteca de la Universidad de Uppsala, Suecia* (Stockholm, Sweden: Statens Etnografiska Museum, n.s., no. 9. [Esselte], 1948), 201; Donald Robertson, *Mexican Manuscript Painting of the Early Colonial Period: The Metropolitan Schools* (Norman: University of Oklahoma Press, 1994), 159.

sixteenth-century representations allows us to come closer to the concept of Lefebvre's triad of spatial production. The experiences of these spaces were overlaid with diverse spatial practices, and thus, these spaces' meaning was ultimately contingent on the various actors who participated in its making. Additionally, considering Lefebvre's idea that representations of space also influenced "representational spaces," or the built environment, the analysis of these three representations together allows us to gain a better sense of how the diverse community of New Spain imposed their heterogeneous conceptions on the transforming landscape. By comparing their various representations, we can begin to grasp the complex, charged, and continually shifting construction of space in colonial New Spain. We can never quite arrive at the inherent truth value of Motolinía, Valadés, or the Nahua authors of the Uppsala Map; however, by comparing all three, we can see their points of overlap, agreement, and difference. It is somewhere within these liminal spaces that we might understand how New Spain was constituted and what it meant to each of these authors.

Chapter Eleven

Origins of the Stations of the Cross in Early Colonial Mexico

John F. Schwaller, *University at Albany (SUNY)*

In 1680 a remarkable book appeared from the press of Francisco Rodriguez Lupercio.[1] It was a handbook to allow the faithful reader to pray the Stations of the Cross. The devotion had been spreading in the Church for some two centuries, largely at the hand of members of the Franciscan Order. What was curious about this version was that it was written in Nahuatl, the language of the Mexica, known to many as the Aztecs. It was written, more accurately translated, by the Franciscan missionary Fr. Agustín de Vetancurt, and only exists today in a manuscript copy made by a Native of north-central Mexico some two decades later. The history of this little book and of the spread of the devotion to colonial Mexico opens a unique view into the world of faith, evangelization, and religion.

The devotion of the Stations of the Cross creates a spiritual space that links participants across time and space with the final hours of Jesus Christ. Because it focuses on Jesus's walk from the seat of the Roman government in Jerusalem to his crucifixion and entombment, practitioners feel the devotion must be an ancient remnant of the early Church. Indeed, the first serious scholarship on the devotion looked to the Holy Land for the roots of the practice. Certainly, Christian pilgrims to Jerusalem across the ages have been attracted to the sites associated with Jesus's ministry on earth. But the best evidence that has been uncovered points to the devotion having a European origin. Rather than being as ancient as Christianity itself, the preponderance of evidence points to the devotion coming into its present form in the fourteenth or even fifteenth century. Moreover, the Stations of the Cross is merely one of many different devotions that emerged in the period, as sensibilities

1. This is a heavily condensed version of the early history of the Stations of the Cross in colonial Mexico, much of which appeared in John F. Schwaller, *The Stations of the Cross in Colonial Mexico: Via crucis en mexicano by Fray Agustin de Vetancurt, and the Spread of a Devotion* (Norman: University of Oklahoma Press, 2022).

regarding prayer and secular participation in spiritual acts became more inclusive. Even with a burgeoning interest in participatory and stational devotions, it still took until the early eighteenth century for the Stations of the Cross to receive papal sanction and endorsement.

It is a surprise, then, that the devotion already had multitudes of adherents in sixteenth- and seventeenth-century Mexico. The celebration expanded beyond a few churches or convents as it flowed out to the streets and roads of the city. In addition, permanent chapels were erected to link Franciscan churches with *humilladeros* on the edge of town. The devotion attracted so many adherents that the Franciscans used it as a tool for the further evangelization of the Natives. As a result, a small handbook to the devotion, written in Nahuatl for that Native market, was printed toward the end of the seventeenth century, a full fifty years before the pope recognized the devotion.

The popularity of the Stations of the Cross emerged as a result of several trends in Western Christianity. Central was the fascination with the holy places of Jerusalem. This then was added to the medieval Church's focus on the suffering of Jesus during his final hours. Those two trends intermingled with innovations in spiritual disciplines of the *devotio moderna*, whose practices included silent prayer and the contemplation of religious themes, such as the lives of the saints and Christ's Passion. Adherents of the *devotio moderna* were most common in the Lowlands, from whence the practices spread throughout Europe. In the early Church, silent prayer was an accepted form of devotion but not universally practiced. In the Middle Ages silent prayer took hold as a widespread practice with the rise of monastic orders whose members took vows of silence.[2] With tacit Church approval, the faithful would practice silent prayer and meditation in daily devotions. Beginning with various changes as early as the thirteenth century, but developing more fully in the fourteenth, a new set of religious practices evolved. While silent prayer and meditation continued to be important spiritual components, this passive, interior form of prayer gave way to a more physical style in which movement of the body assisted in creating the spiritual experience. The faithful would stand, kneel, sit, and walk about as dictated by specific prayers or meditations. This physical involvement allowed devotees, no matter where they found themselves, to imagine that they were at the holy sites and create a mental itinerary. By the fourteenth century, some Christians who wanted to immerse themselves even more in the life of Christ found that images from the events of the Passion assisted them in their prayer life. Others imagined walking alongside Jesus as he moved toward his crucifixion. These trends, then, linked to create the devotion that we now know as the Stations of the Cross.

---

2. Pieter W. Van der Horst, "Silent Prayer in Antiquity," *Numen* 41 (1994): 20–21.

In medieval times, roadside crosses, *humilladeros*, were erected to denote the edges of cities. These came to be symbols of Golgotha, the site of Jesus's crucifixion. In the Low Countries and on the Iberian Peninsula, in particular, people also built churches, chapels, and palaces in imitation of the holy sites in Jerusalem. These functioned as late medieval tourist attractions, allowing the faithful opportunities to see what those holy places might look like without having to undertake the arduous and dangerous journey. These structures easily became stand-ins for the actual biblical sites. Christians could then use the chapels, crosses, and palaces as focal points for their celebration of the Stations, moving through the streets as they prayed and sang. At this time, other traditions involving religious processions in towns and cities marked the important events of the Church year. Weekly or monthly processions for the Stations, usually on Fridays, fit easily into the ritual calendar.

The Franciscan friars came to play an important role in the development and spread of the Stations of the Cross, although they were not the only religious order involved. Although the Franciscan Order was not even founded until the thirteenth century, from the time of its founding, it became involved in several of the threads that came together to create the devotion of the Stations of the Cross. In particular, the friars eventually became an official Roman Catholic presence in Jerusalem.

By the time Saint Francis began his ministry in the early thirteenth century, Jerusalem had undergone various political changes. Importantly, Francis desired to preach the Gospel to the Muslims there. After several failed attempts, he reached the Holy City in 1219–1220. Thereafter Franciscans established themselves in several places in the Holy Land, but in 1291 the friars were expelled and took up exile on the island of Cyprus. Pope John XXII granted the Dominicans authority to establish houses in Syria, keeping a fair distance from any previously developed Franciscan convents. Then, in 1322, the King of Aragón requested that the sultan in Damascus allow some Catholic friars or monks to take control of the Church of the Holy Sepulcher. The members of Catholic religious orders would serve alongside the Orthodox priests already there. It looked like these Catholic religious would be Dominicans, but at the last minute their mission ended. Instead, Franciscan friars arrived by 1327, seemingly acting on permission gained by Aragón.

Within a few years, the Franciscans had also acquired the site where Christ was supposed to have celebrated the Last Supper, known as the Cenacle House. This building had previously been under the control of Augustinians but had been abandoned before the Franciscans began their work. Franciscan presence in the Holy Land was confirmed in 1342 when Pope Clement VI gave authority for the creation of the Franciscan Custody of the Holy Land under a special minister provincial in the order. As a result, these Franciscans became known as the Guardians of Mount Zion in Jerusalem. By the mid-fourteenth century, the Franciscans had begun to perform rites at two other important sites in the Holy Land, including the Church of the Nativity in Bethlehem and the Tomb of the Virgin Mary in the Kidron Valley, over which they had been granted control by local ecclesiastical authorities, political authorities in both the Middle East and Europe, and the papacy. This gave the Franciscans a unique and important place among religious orders of the Catholic Church, having been entrusted with so many of the places that were specifically mentioned in the Bible and infused with such sanctity. The Franciscans, as late as the latter part of the fifteenth century, extolled the spiritual benefits of visiting the holy places. In about 1485, Francesco Suriano, a Franciscan, wrote a Treatise on the Holy Land, ostensibly to an Italian nun, noting, "Those things which touched Christ only for a while were strongly imbued with His virtue and grace. . . . Because of that the [Holy Land's] trees, woods, vegetables, grass, bread, water, stones, and everything else there is holy, and filled with virtue." Thus, the Franciscans established themselves as an order having close ties to the Holy Land, building on Francis's own mission. Franciscan devotional practices developed at about the same time as the flourishing of the *devotio moderna*, such as their early adoption of apostolic poverty, renunciation of the world, and imitation of Christ. Francis preached that the Gospel was to be exemplified in the lives of the friars.

As it developed in Western Europe, the Stations of the Cross as a devotion came to exist in three separate modalities. The words of the prayers and meditations lie at the heart of the devotion. These were recorded in books so that they could be invoked at any time. But from the very beginning, alongside the words were images. Sometimes there were plaques, paintings, sculptures, bas-reliefs, or even chapels created not just to evoke a visual response in the faithful but also to transport them mentally to the Holy Land and into the steps of Jesus's Passion.

The Stations of the Cross was not the only devotion to be developed during this period of fervor and experimentation in the Church. Many of the competing devotions secured small numbers of ardent followers. Several emerged as Christians embraced the many elements of the Passion.[3] The variety among them is somewhat confusing. Some devotions focus on Jesus's falls throughout the Passion narrative, not just the specific falls along the route to

3. Herbert Thurston, *The Stations of the Cross* (London: Burns & Gates, 1914), 62–75; Amédée de Zedelgem, "Aperçu historique sur le devotion au chemin de la croix," *Collectanea franciscana* 19 (1948–49): 72–76. Zedelgem devotes many pages to exploring all the different types of assemblages such as the seven falls, the seven sorrows, the seven paths, and more: 72–96. "Devotions," *Catholic Encyclopedia*, New Advent, http://www.newadvent.org/ cathen/12275b.htm.

Calvary. Two forms within this genre became fairly widespread: the Three Falls, which are included in the Stations of the Cross, and the Seven Falls, covering events beyond the route of the Passion. In a genre that may have influenced the Stations of the Cross, a devotion known as the Nine Leadings, or Nine Movements, also had a wide popularity in the fourteenth and fifteenth centuries. It is a crucial element in the development of the Stations because it incorporates movement into the devotion itself and focuses on moving from one place to another. In this, it differs significantly from the Falls and the Stations themselves in that they have specific moments as their focus: the moment when Jesus took up his cross or when he met the women of Jerusalem. In the devotion of the Nine Leadings, the movements are less tied to a specific instance or place.[4] For example, the first Leading calls on the penitent to consider Christ's movement from the Garden of Gethsemane to the house of Annas. The Leadings focus on moments when Christ was taken from one point to another.

Another very popular devotion was the Seven Sorrows of Mary. Unlike the other stational devotions that focus on events around Jesus's Passion, this devotion runs the gamut of Mary's life and experiences, beginning with the circumcision of Jesus as an infant and culminating in his crucifixion. Nonetheless, as with the other devotions, the Sorrows of Mary also became associated with a set of sculptural pieces that evoke the emotions of the specific moments commemorated in the devotion. Parallel to the development of the Seven Sorrows was a devotion dedicated to commemorating the Seven Joys of Mary. A form of this devotion using the Rosary is known as the Franciscan Crown. In that variant, the Rosary contains seven groups of ten beads for which the practitioner remembers each of the joys and says a set of prayers, such as the Lord's Prayer and the Hail Mary.[5]

One genre of devotions that played directly into some versions of the Stations of the Cross focused on the Wounds of Christ and the Effusions of Christ's Blood. The Five Wounds of Christ, a popular devotion in the fourteenth century, focuses on the wounds to Jesus's hands, feet, and side incurred during the Passion. In contrast to the Five Wounds, the devotions of the Effusions consider all the blood that Jesus shed in his Passion, from his scourging, to the imposition of the crown of thorns, to cuts incurred along the road to Calvary, to his final crucifixion. As with the other devotions studied here, several variants were based on different numbers of effusions from seven to fifteen and beyond.[6]

---

4. Mitzi Kirkland-Ives, "Alternate Routes: Variation in Early Modern Stational Devotions," *Viator* 40 (2009): 261–62.

5. "Franciscan Crown," *Catholic Encyclopedia*, New Advent, http://www.newadvent.org/cathen/04540a.htm.

6. Kirkland-Ives, "Alternate Routes," 265–66.

The devotion of the Stations of the Cross was imported into Spain from the Lowlands along with other practices associated with the *devotio moderna*. The earliest known devotionals in Spanish containing the prayers and meditations for the fourteen stations are reported to have been published in 1625. While the Franciscans were not the sole originators of the Stations of the Cross, in Spain the devotion became associated with the order, and in particular with Third Order Franciscans. In various kingdoms of Spain, Third Order Franciscans had either built or taken control of structures associated with the celebration of the events of Holy Week. Later, the devotion gained wide popularity and renown due to the efforts of an Italian Franciscan, Saint Leonard of Port Maurice (1676–1751), who is credited with building more than 570 Stations of the Cross throughout the Italian peninsula.

Christian worship in Spain became the model for worship in newly settled areas in the New World. It was perfectly natural for the Spanish to bring all the trappings that had developed on the Iberian Peninsula. Processions and stational devotions, including the Stations of the Cross, were part of the Spanish liturgical and devotional repertoire. In Mexico, in particular, the Spanish encountered a Native religion that also valued public displays in processions and stational devotions. Thus, these practices provided the missionaries with a means of introducing the new religion to the Natives. But clearly, large numbers of Spaniards were already practicing the devotion of the Stations of the Cross, since chapels dedicated to that devotion were erected within a few decades of the Spanish invasion.

The seventeenth century witnessed the full flowering of the Stations of the Cross as a popular and widely practiced devotion. This period when the Catholic Church came to grips with reforms that had been proposed by various critics inside and outside the Church is called the Catholic Reformation. The period also coincided with a movement in the arts that came to be known as the Baroque. In the Baroque, artistic sensibilities appreciated complexity over simplicity, the hidden over the obvious. The devotion of the Stations of the Cross is a Baroque devotion. It is not merely a set of prayers. There are actions that accompany the prayers. The practitioner is required to walk from station to station, frequently engaged in prayer or song, kneeling and standing. Each station is also multilayered in that a bas-relief, painting, or sculpture illustrates the essential features of that station. Thus, the devotion exists as prayers, actions, works of art, and frequently songs all at once. In its complexity, the Stations of the Cross is a supremely Baroque practice. The Stations of the Cross is also a supreme example of the Catholic Reformation. If the Protestant Reformation tended to make spirituality more internal and personal, devotions like the Stations of the Cross utilize the external and collective. While the devotion can certainly be followed in private and in silence, it became an important tool that the Catholic Church could use to organize popular celebrations not only in churches and cloisters but also through the streets.

The Mexica (Aztecs) had their own religious processions that constituted integral parts of their annual round of festivals. Religious processions played an important role in several months of the Mexica solar year, the *xiuhpohualli*.[7] The solar calendar contained eighteen months of twenty days each, plus five unnamed days, the *nemontemi*. During the months of Toxcatl and Panquetzaliztli there were processions that made a specific series of stops at important places on the island of Tenochtitlán-Tlatelolco, the ancient site of Mexico City, as well as in other parts of the Central Basin, where the city is located. In addition to these two important processions, many of the monthly festivals included processions within the sacred precinct of Tenochtitlán in which young people paraded from one place to another and priests conducted processions from temple to temple. During several months, lines of priests, sacrificial victims, and the general populace might process from one place to another for a specific ceremony or ritual, frequently dancing as they went along. For example, in the month of Tepeilhuitl, five women representing mountains were carried by other women and paraded in a procession. The route was not stipulated, merely that they all must arrive at the Templo Mayor, the main temple in the center of Mexico-Tenochtitlán, and then were sacrificed to the god of rain, Tlaloc.[8]

After the Spanish invasion of 1519, and the defeat of the Mexica by the alliance of Spaniards and other Native groups, the Franciscan missionaries arrived in 1524. Their first concern was to communicate with the Natives and to begin evangelization. While the missionaries attempted to avoid confusion of Christianity with pre-contact religions, the use of certain practices from the old religion allowed for an easier transition into the new faith. Processions and devotions like the Stations of the Cross were important pieces in this process.[9] The missionaries also needed to begin the construction of churches for the celebration of the Eucharist. The architecture of the early missionary churches included the features of an enclosed patio, known as an atrium (*atrio*), and small chapels placed around its perimeter, usually in the corners,

7. While many books and authors refer to the residents of central Mexico in pre-Hispanic times as the Aztecs, that is not a name that they commonly used for themselves. In general, they used the name Mexica. In this essay, I will follow that convention. When discussing all the Native groups who also spoke the Aztec language, Nahuatl, I will refer to the larger group as the Nahua.

8. Bernardino de Sahagún, *Florentine Codex*, 13 vols., eds. and trans. Arthur J. O. Anderson and Charles Dibble (University of Utah Press, 1950–82), 2:133. The *Florentine Codex* was a twelve-volume compilation of Mexica history and traditions collected by a Spanish friar, Bernardino de Sahagún, written in Nahuatl and Spanish.

9. John McAndrew, *The Open-Air Churches of Sixteenth-Century Mexico* (Harvard University Press, 1965), 216–17; Kirkland-Ives, "Alternate Routes," 266.

called *posas* because of their resemblance to covered wells. The assembly of structures provided the early missionaries with a place to conduct most of the essential business of evangelization until such a time when a church and other permanent structures could be erected.[10]

The procession seems to have been both a missionary technique and a ritual understood and embraced by the Natives. Writing about the very earliest years of the colony, the friar known as Motolinía, Fr. Toribio de Benavente, noted that by about 1528, seven years after the conquest, the Natives of Texcoco organized a religious procession to beseech God to relieve their suffering caused by flooding that year.[11] The friar also described the processions of the Natives during the commemoration of Holy Thursday and Good Friday. These were penitential acts in which the Natives used so-called disciplines (ropes embedded with pieces of metal) to scourge themselves. Otherwise, the processions seem to have resembled the processions found in many Spanish cities during Holy Week: penitents walking defined routes, carrying lighted candles, crosses, and scourges. While in procession, the penitents would recite a set of prayers and sing songs appropriate to the day.[12] The devotion they recited in all likelihood contained elements that would later be associated with the Stations of the Cross.

As the Spanish population of New Spain grew with new arrivals from Europe, they brought many local religious practices from Europe with them. One of these seems to have been the devotion of the Stations of the Cross. Processions on certain holy days clearly played an important role in the spiritual life of early colonial New Spain.[13] Others occurred with special intentions to relieve droughts or stop floods and pestilence and at other times while seeking divine intervention. Relics of saints and important religious images were similarly paraded in the streets for a variety of purposes. Indeed, processions were so important and integral to the full religious experience that one of the very first books published in Mexico was a short treatise by Dionisio Richel, a Carthusian monk, on the manner in which to hold processions.[14]

---

10. Diego Valadés, *Rhetorica cristiana* (Apud Petrumiacobum Petrutium, 1579), ff. 210–14.

11. Motolinía [Toribio de Benavente], *Memoriales o Libro de las cosas de la Nueva España*, ed. Edmundo O'Gorman (Mexico City: Universidad Nacional Autónoma de México, 1971), 119.

12. Motolinía, *Memoriales*, 93–94.

13. Johnathan Truitt, *Sustaining the Divine in Mexico Tenochtitlan: Nahuas and Catholicism, 1523–1700* (Norman: University of Oklahoma Press, 2018), 162–63, provides a table showing all the regularly scheduled processions in Mexico City in this period.

14. Dionisio Richel, *Este es un cōpēdio breue que tracta de la manera de como se hā de hazer las p[ro]cessions* (Cromberger, 1544).

Writing in the late sixteenth century, the chronicler of the Dominican Order, Fr. Agustín de Dávila Padilla, recorded processions during Holy Week, on Good Friday in particular. What is important about this account is that he refers to some of the stops along the route as "stations." The specific procession that he describes began at the Dominican church. From there the participants proceeded to the cathedral, three blocks south. The procession then went all the way to the edge of town, three blocks west, to where the main Franciscan church was located. From the Franciscan church, the Dominican procession then went to the convent of Nuestra Señora de la Concepción, three blocks to the north and a bit to the east. After that stop, the Dominicans returned to their home church, three blocks back to the east. Theirs was a clockwise procession.[15]

In New Spain there is some evidence that the devotion of the Stations of the Cross formed an important part of religious life in the colony by the late sixteenth and early seventeenth centuries, becoming widespread much earlier than it did in Europe. In 1612, the *actas de cabildo* (minutes of the municipal council) of Mexico City mention a procession, perhaps related to the Stations of the Cross that departed from the Franciscan convent on the edge of the center city and then passed out of the populated area to the west, along the road that went to Tacuba, to a *humilladero*. The procession and its route came to the attention of the city fathers because of flooding along the road. A few months later, the aldermen discussed a request to help improve the *humilladero*.[16] In 1616, the archbishop, don Juan Pérez de la Serna, reported a ritual similar to the Stations of the Cross processing from the Franciscan monastery along a road he called Armargura (Bitterness), of a distance and length similar to the route taken by Christ in his Passion.[17] In all likelihood, this is the same procession and route as the other, with the street named Armargura being the road to Tacuba, which is the modern-day Avenida Juárez. Between 1611 and 1612, it seems that chapels were built along the road from San Francisco to the edge of town and the *humilladero*. In 1616, the Franciscans received approval for an indulgence to be granted to individuals who prayed the whole devotion.[18] Taken as a whole, there is clear evi-

15. Juan de Dávila Padilla, *Historia de la fundación y discurso de la Provincia de Santiago de Mexico de la Orden de Predicadores* (Ivan de Meerbecque, 1625), 565–68.

16. Alena Robin, *Las capillas del Vía crucis de la ciudad de México: Arte, patrocinio, y sacralización* (Mexico City: Universidad Nacional Autónoma de México, 2014), 42–43.

17. Alena Robin, *Las capillas del Vía crucis de la Ciudad de México: Arte, patrocinio, y sacralización del espacio* (Mexico City: Universidad Nacional de México, 2014), 43–44.

18. Juan B. Iguiniz, *Breve historia de la tercera orden Franciscana en la Provincia del Santo Evangelio de Mexico desde sus orígenes hasta nuestros dias* (Mexico City: Ed. Patria, 1951), 89–90.

dence that there was a formally established route for the Stations of the Cross in Mexico City. The procession began in the Church of Saint Francis, passed along the south side of the municipal park known as the Alameda, and then went west to the *humilladero* located on the western edge of the city.

By the early seventeenth century, the devotion of the Stations of the Cross had become more firmly established as a unique ritual, one particularly associated with the Third Order Franciscans. The Third Order had been officially founded in Mexico in 1614 at a meeting of the provincial leadership. In colonial Mexico, the Third Order existed as a hybrid between a traditional religious sodality, or confraternity, and a religious order itself. Members seldom became friars or nuns. They were expected to comply with the spirit of the Franciscan Rule, but without taking the necessary vows of celibacy, poverty, and obedience. Nonetheless, many chose to dress in the habit of the order and follow the precepts of the order as best they could.[19] The account books of the Third Order Franciscans in Mexico City indicate that they annually spent varying amounts on the preparations for and execution of the Stations of the Cross. The expenditures occurred between January and May, peaking in March and April, since Easter is a moveable feast, it wanders through the calendar from late March to late April. Unfortunately, the records are incomplete, so it is difficult to determine when the practice began after the order's founding in 1614. Nonetheless, it is clear that the ceremony became an important ritual for the capital in the early to mid-seventeenth century.[20]

In early colonial Mexico, the Stations of the Cross and other devotions were important tools in the spread of Christianity. They allowed the faithful to participate as individuals in a mass of others. As a missionary tool, it must have provided a comfortable way in which to become familiar with Christianity. The Mexica, prior to the arrival of the Spanish, also used processions and stational devotions to create a sense of collective identity in the worship of the divinities.

The printing press was established in New Spain in 1536. It took nearly a century, however, for the first guides to the devotion of the Stations of the Cross to be printed. In New Spain, from the late seventeenth century through the eighteenth century, at least twenty-eight different titles featured stational religious devotions. Many of these were principally for use during Holy Week but could be adapted for many other occasions. Quite a few were so popular that they went through multiple printings. For example, one popular title, *Practica para andar las estaciones de la Semana Santa*, was published four

---

19. Brian Belanger, "Between the Cloister and the World: The Franciscan Third Order of Colonial Querétaro," *The Americas* 49 (1992): 157–59. In modern times, some Third Order Franciscans profess vows and at times ordained deacons and priests.

20. Robin, *Las capillas del Vía crucis*, 49–50.

times in Mexico City between 1720 and 1826. In fact, there seem to have been two books circulating with the same title, since the 1754 edition is very different from the 1758 edition. This illustrates some of the variations that one finds in these devotional books.

As noted, a significant number of spiritual handbooks followed devotions other than the Stations of the Cross. One of the popular books was a European devotion devoted to the Five Wounds of Christ, which competed with the Stations in the early development of stational devotions. The theme of the Five Wounds was particularly important in Mexico among Franciscans. Although the province of the Franciscan Order that encompassed all central New Spain was called the Holy Gospel Province (Santo Evangelio), the crest that the order used was one depicting the five wounds of Christ: the nail wounds on his hands and feet and the spear wound in his side. The five wounds were particularly meaningful to the Franciscans because Saint Francis had a divine vision while on a retreat in the hills of central Italy, at a place called Mount Alverno. There he saw the vision of a seraph hovering in the sky. At that moment, Francis was inflicted with the wounds of Christ, called the stigmata. Among the many different stational devotions that appeared in eighteenth-century Mexico is an anonymous pamphlet titled *Salutacion a las Sacratissimas* [sic.] *cinco Llagas de Christo* (Greeting to the Most Sacred Five Wounds of Christ), which appeared in 1777. In this devotion the faithful person is to perform the Act of Contrition,[21] and then have a meditation and prayer for each of the five wounds: left foot, right foot, left hand, right hand, and side.[22]

The popularity of these guides to various devotions of Christ's Passion was impressive. One of the most widely embraced was the version published under the title *Manual de exercicios para los desagravios de Christo*, ostensibly by Francisco de Soria, a Franciscan friar. Although Soria appears as the author, the title page lists Fr. Diego de Oviedo, whose role is not explained and who dedicates the work to the Third Order of Saint Francis. One of the editions has the note that it was originally licensed for publication in Madrid in 1705 by the press of Antonio Gonzalez de Reyes.[23] Soria's little guide was reprinted in New Spain at least twenty-seven times between 1686 and 1793, just over a century. Scholars also know of editions that appeared in Mexico City (twenty), Puebla (six), and Guatemala (one). The prayers, meditations, and other devotions prescribed

21. An Act of Contrition is a common prayer that may take many different forms. The basic outline of the prayer is to acknowledge that a person has sinned, to be truly sorry for the sins, and to offer a sincere desire to not sin again.

22. *Salutacion a las Sacratissimas cinco Llagas de Christo nuestro redentor, para alcanzar una feliz y santa Muerte* (D. Felipe de Zuñiga y Ontiveros, 1777).

23. *Soria, Manual de exercicios para los desagravios de Christo nuestro señor* (Herederos del Lic. D. Joseph de Jauregui, 1778), title page.

by Soria were intended to unite the penitent with the image of Jesus known as Santo Cristo de los Desagravios (Holy Christ of Redress).[24]

In several of the editions, the final twenty pages consist of a set of meditations and prayers for the celebration of the Stations of the Cross featuring the traditional fourteen stations. Upon closer analysis there are at least two different versions of the prayers and meditations for the Stations of the Cross appended to the Soria *Manual de exercicios*. The simpler version is attributed to Fr. Antonio de la Anunciación and carries the title of "Luz para saber andar la Via Sacra."[25] In yet other editions of the Soria *Manual*, a slightly different devotional of the Stations of the Cross appears for which no clear attribution is provided. Rather, the text explains, "Other authors, Holy Fathers, Supreme Pontiffs, can see the well-reasoned, in the Via Crucis published in Rome, in the year 1702, which was in our convent of Aracoeli, and in the very learned, cautious, and most devout writing about the Via Sacra or Via Crucis, also published in Rome by our very reverend Father Fray Miguel Angel Candia, in 1703."[26] The Aracoeli church is known as Saint Mary of the Altar of Heaven.[27]

---

24. *Desagravios* is a difficult word to translate, some authors use "atonement" or "reparations." It means "to erase or repair an offense to one's honor or fame resulting in complete satisfaction." Taylor, "An 'Evolved' Devotional Book," 69, translates it as "atonement." But theologically, "atonement" refers to Christ having suffered to erase the sins of humanity. The term "desagravio" in this context is the action of humans providing redress for the abuses caused to Jesus. Others have suggested "reparation" or "redress," which are closer to the meaning. Berdette, "Reparations for Christ Our Lord: Devotional Literature, Penitential Rituals, and Sacred Imagery in Colonial Mexico City," in *Sensuous Suffering: Pain in the Early Modern Visual Art of Europe and the Americas*, eds. Lauren Kilroy-Ewbank and Heather Graham (Leiden: Brill, 2018), 358. Some editions, such as the 1810 in Mexico, attribute authorship to Fr. Fernando Martagon, of the Propaganda Fide College, Biblioteca Nacional de México, Obras Antiguas, Raras, RSM 1810 M4MAR. That edition does not have the Stations of the Cross appended to it.

25. Soria, *Manual de exercicios*. Little is known of Anunciación. In all likelihood he was a Franciscan from Cadiz. A reader in theology, he also published a book in Cadiz in 1669 that argued in favor of receiving communion daily: *Tratado de la communion quotidiana* (Juan Lorenzo Machado, 1669).

26. "Otros muchos Authores, Santos Padres, Summos Pontifices, podrâ veer el curioso, en la Via Crucis impressa en Roma, el año de 1702, el cual se anda en nuestro Convento de Aracoeli, y en la doctissima, curiosa, y devotissima Escritura de la Via Sacra, o Via Crucis, impressa tambien en Roma por nuestro muy Reverendo Padre Fray Miguel Angel Candia, el año de 1703." The word *curioso* was used twice, and in this period would be a false cognate of "curious." It means, "cautious," "well reasoned," or "neat." Soria, *Manual de exercicios*, 86.

27. Located on the Campidoglio, it is reached through a long staircase of 124 steps. In the late thirteenth century, it was assigned to the Franciscans. It is one of the titular

These two guides to the devotion of the Stations of the Cross are very similar in that they have the traditional ordering: each station corresponds to the events that eventually became canonical, and each of the devotionals features the same fourteen stations in exactly the same order. While the meditations and prayers are similar, they are not copies of each other. Thus, there are two versions: one that we might call the Anunciación version and the other, which might be called the Candia version. But what is most confusing is that both appear as appendices or additions to the Soria *Manual de exercicios*.

Into this complicated world of popular devotions, and rival practices, the Franciscan Fr. Augustin de Vetancurt opted to take one of the versions of the devotional written in Spanish and translate it into Nahuatl. While Vetancurt was probably bilingual in Nahuatl from childhood, he also had cause to call on Native informants and assistants. There is evidence that one of Vetancurt's Native assistants, don Manuel de los Santos Salazar, went on to become a priest himself and continued his labors in the field of Nahuatl. Vetancurt served on the board of examiners when don Manuel sought entry into the priesthood. Later don Manuel recalled fondly that Vetancurt had introduced him to the works of Fr. Juan de Torquemada and don Carlos de Sigüenza y Góngora.[28] Vetancurt noted that among his other publications was "The Via crucis [Way of the Cross] in Nahuatl, published two times, both by Francisco Rodríguez Lupercio." Nevertheless, none of the scholars who study the history of printing in colonial Mexico has been able to find a copy. The work was popular. According to Vetancurt, it was published twice before 1700. Some of the guides to early printing have descriptions of the book—for example, that it consisted of eleven leaves, some twenty-two pages, and was approximately the size of many other devotional manuals already seen.

Within the manuscript collection of the Academy of American Franciscan History, there is a piece titled "To Know How to Walk the Stations of the Cross and the Indulgences That One Gains Following It, translated by the Reverend Father Fr. Agu[stín] de Vetancurt."[29] The title page carries a date

basilicas of the city, meaning that it is recognized as one of the historic parishes to which cardinals are assigned by the pope. It is the official church of the City Council of Rome.

28. Camilla Townsend, *Annals of Native America: How the Nahuas of Colonial Mexico Kept Their History Alive* (Oxford: Oxford University Press, 2017), 202–203, 206–207.

29. "Para saber andar las estaciones de la via sacra y las yndulgencias que ganan Vitando [*sic*] la traducido en lengua mexicana por el R. P. Fr_ Augn de Vetacurt." *Vitando* means "avoiding," but that does not fit here. It might be a contraction of *visitando*, which would mean more like "visiting" or "following." The original Spanish version used the word *visitando*.

of 1680. Certainly, the theme of the work and the date it carries correspond to what little we know about the via crucis mentioned by Vetancurt himself. Upon further examination, the manuscript dates from 1738 and was copied by Matheo de San Juan Chicahuastla. Based on this limited information, it is fair to conclude that the manuscript held by the academy is in fact a manuscript copy of the published edition of the Vetancurt work.

The Catholic Reformation and the Baroque were both ways that Europeans influenced the populations of colonial Mexico. What is most remarkable about the Vetancurt translation of the *Via crucis* is that it bridges European and Native cultures. While on the one hand, as a Christian devotion, the book was clearly of European origin. But at the same time, it was popular enough in colonial Mexico to warrant two editions. It stands as a unique example of a work written with Native readers in mind. Many manuals and handbooks that allowed parish priests to operate in a Nahuatl-speaking parish were bilingual, offering prayers and responses in both Spanish and Nahuatl. This work, however, was written completely in Nahuatl. Unlike many books intended for use by parish priests, which were written in a two-column format (Nahuatl and Spanish) this work only was written in Nahuatl. In this regard, it fits into a thread of works that had disappeared more than thirty years earlier: recreational works written for a Nahuatl readership. The Vetancurt *Via crucis* is actually precocious in that the Nahuatl version of that devotion appeared well before the devotion itself gained widespread support in the larger population. Clearly, there were adherents in the cities, as is evidenced by the construction of chapels dedicated to the devotion in Mexico City and Puebla, but it was not until the early eighteenth century that the pope authorized and regularized the devotion.

CHAPTER TWELVE

Missions and Kivas—A Symbol of Coexistence of Old and New Religious Cultures in the Southwest Borderlands?

HELMUT FLACHENECKER, *University of Wuerzburg*

CULTURAL–RELIGIOUS LANDSCAPES

Nearly every natural environment is continually modified by human interactions over time. During this never-ending process, cultural landscapes develop and are modified, reflecting the interdependency of humankind and nature. Innovative and adequate skills create specific local environments. Humans transform nature to survive, and in doing so develop countless scales of social, political, and religious ways of being.

This process also includes the shaping of nature in a religious way, as in creating sacred spaces, shrines, and places of worship. Among features reflective of Christianity are churches, crosses, bells, and wayside shrines, such as those seen in the historical Catholic parts of Europe in early modern Times.[1]

During the process of Christian evangelization, in our case the Spanish mission in New Mexico, two very different systems of religious landscapes entered into a dramatic conflict. This is demonstrated by two kinds of religious monuments—on one side kivas, circular pits representing sacred places and used as ceremonial chambers, operating as religious and social gathering places for the ancestral Pueblo people, and on the other, the strongly contrasting Franciscan missions, mainly in New Mexico, but also, as a comparative point, in Florida. In some places, kivas and mission churches existed side by side.

---

1. Helmut Flachenecker, "The Christian Landscape in Southern Germany in the Aftermath of the Reformation: Religious Separation as a Source of Regional Identity," in *Regional History as Cultural Identity*, eds. Kenneth J. Bindas and Fabrizio Ricciardelli (Rome: Viella, 2017) 151–65.

Kivas—Sacred places

Timothy Johnson has pointed out that liturgical texts are performative, such as a sacred "play" acted by priests, monks, and laity. They recite the words of God while processing, playing music, and involving the surrounded architecture.[2] Time and place interact, becoming a vivid sacred space. The interaction could differ, depending on the occasion. Johnson's observations, especially noting his Franciscan examples, are not limited to Christian locations, but also include, in a way, religious buildings of the Native Americans such as kivas where Puebloans performed religious ceremonies.[3] In particular, kivas were the center of religious ceremonies such as the Serpent Cult or the Undying Fire.[4] Performative religious acts could combine native beliefs with the "new" Christian ones.

"Kiva" is a word of the Hopi language; the Spanish word "estufa" means "a warm or steamed room." These rooms were mostly built underground and might be developed from former pit houses. The function of these buildings varied from a social gathering room either for special families or the whole community to a ceremonial place, and in this function, kivas acted as sacred places.[5]

The difficulties of determining a room as a kiva in pre-Columbian times by archaeological evidence are described by Watson Smith. Not every kiva was circular; some were rectangular or D-shaped and not clearly differentiated from other rooms. Rarely are there clear indications of uniformity in kiva architecture. Often it is only the differentiation of a particular room from others that reveals the kiva.[6]

Kiva pits had roofs of timber covered with cedar strips and clay. In the center of the roof there was generally a rectangular entrance, with a ladder passing through the sacred smoke rising from a fire on the pit floor. Behind the fire

---

2. Timothy J. Johnson, "The "Prayed Francis" and the Liturgical Experience of the Minor Brothers," in *The Prayed Francis: Liturgical Vitae and Franciscan Identity in the Thirteenth Century*, eds. Marco Bartoli, Jacques Dalarun, Timothy J. Johnson, and Filippo Sedda. (St. Bonaventure: Franciscan Institute Publications, 2019), 19–50.

3. Florence C. Lister, "Aztec West's Great Kiva" in *Aztec, Salmon, and the Puebloan Heartland in the Thirteenth Century*, eds. Paul F. Reed and Gary M. Brown (Albuquerque; University of New Mexico Press, 2018), 45–52.

4. Alfred Vincent Kidder, *Pecos, New Mexico: Archaeological Notes* (Andover: Philips Academy, 1958), 227–41.

5. Watson Smith. *When is a Kiva" And other Questions About Southwestern Archaeology*, ed. Raymond Thompson (Tucson: The University of Arizona Press, 1990), 55-57 [Introduction to a paper from Smith by the editor]. Also Stephen Plog, *Ancient Peoples of the American Southwest* (London: Thames & Hudson, 2008), 18–22.

6. Smith, "When is a Kiva? in *When Is a Kiva?*, 59–75, see 66–71; Smith, "D-Shaped Features, in *When Is a Kiva?*, 77–90. —Rectangular kiva with a small antechamber see Plog, *Ancient Peoples*, 20.

a small hole symbolized a spiritual passageway for a person's soul to enter and exit at birth and death while symbolizing the way of the ancestral pueblo people from the underworld to the "new" world on the surface. The kiva's sometimes cribbed roof may symbolize the sky above the "new" world. Some of the kiva's walls were decorated with symbols, such as in the Lowry Ruins, Colorado.[7]

Unfortunately, very little is visible today. Only older pictures give a thorough impression of the geometrical symbols. Such painted kivas, few in number, are mostly dated to the fourteenth and early fifteenth century.[8] The Franciscan friar Francisco Atanasio Dominguez gave a similar description in his report about the missions in New Mexico in 1776. He called the kivas *estufas*: "Some of them are underground, and others are above ground with walls like a little house, and of them all, some are round while others are rectangular. But the entrance is always through a *coi*, or trap door on the roof. . . . These *estufas* are the chapter, or council, rooms and the Indians meet in them, sometimes to discuss matters of their government for the coming year, their planting, arrangements for work to be done, or to elect new community officials, or to rehearse their dances, or sometimes for other things."[9] It was no coincidence that the Franciscan emphasized the social functions of a kiva to be more or less religious. The reference to the dances shows that Dominguez knew about the religious functions of a kiva, which he viewed as community rooms and places of idolatry. While assessments by the Franciscans differed at times,[10] Puebloan societies understood that organization of a Hopi kiva was based on "clan or maternal descent," and by other groups on "paternal descent or marital connection."[11] They could be used as places of teaching or for diverse events celebrated in a community center.

There are smaller "private" kivas in a pueblo for clans (families), but there is also at least one for the wider community. One such example is the great kiva of the Aztec Ruins in New Mexico found in the center of the "western great house," which was finished in 1125 CE and reconstructed in 1934 (Figure 1). Scholars have debated at length the purposes of this room, where

7. Adrian S. White and David A. Breternitz, *Stabilization of Lowry Ruins* (Boulder: Bureau of Land Management, 1976). For images of Kiva B, see 22, 107, 125.

8. Plog, *Ancient Peoples*, 128–29, 164–65.

9. *The Missions of New Mexico, 1776. A description by Fray Francisco Atanasio Dominguez with other contemporary documents*, trans. and annotations Eleanor B. Adams and Fray Angelico Chavez (Albuquerque: The University of New Mexico Press, 1956), 256. See also footnote 49.

10. James E. Ivey, "Convento Kivas in the Missions of New Mexico," *New Mexico Historical Review* 73:2 (1998): 121–52, here 143.

11. Elsie Clews Parsons, *Pueblo Indian Religion*, vol. 1 (Chicago: Chicago University Press, 1939), 141.

Figure 1. Aztec Ruins—Great Kiva. Photo by author.

four pillars hold an enormous ceiling. This biggest kiva in the Aztec Ruins is 48 feet at its widest point. It was the gathering point for "ceremonies, feasting, trade, and social interaction."[12] Greater kivas have also been excavated in the Great Chaco pueblos and other places.[13]

Of the many kivas in the Southwest, two others must be mentioned. One is Pueblo Bonito in Chaco Canyon in New Mexico, the largest house of ancestral Puebloans. It was built between 850 and 1200 CE and contains two major and approximately 30 smaller kivas.[14] The bigger ones were for community gatherings and the smaller ones appear to be family or "clan kivas."[15] The unusual "cribbed roofs" found on great kivas in the Chaco area (Figure 2), are estimated to have required 30 people for 100 days (10 hours a day) to build such a roof.[16]

---

12. Gary M. Brown, "The Greatest Houses at Aztec, Built to Last," in "Aztec West's Great Kiva" in *Aztec, Salmon, and the Puebloan Heartland in the Thirteenth Century*, 31–44.

13. Alfred Vincent Kidder, *An Introduction to the Study of Southwestern Archaeology* (New Haven: Yale University Press, 1966), 171–72. In Northern San Juan County, a "unit-type dwelling" with a house, kiva, and burial ground was excavated, 207–11.

14. Brian Fagan, *Chaco Canyon: Archaeologists Explore the Lives of an Ancient Society* (Oxford: Oxford University Press, 2005) and *Pueblo Bonito* (Tucson: Western National Parks Association, 1980).

15. Bainbridge Bunting, *Early Architecture in New Mexico* (Albuquerque: University of New Mexico Press, 1976), 22–23.

16. Plog, *Ancient Peoples*, 102, 105–107 (quote on 105).

Figure 2. Chaco Canyon—Pueblo Bonito. Photo by author.

Cliff Palace in Mesa Verde, Colorado also contains kivas built by the Ancestral Puebloans between 1190 and 1260 CE (Figure 3). For an estimated 150 rooms there existed 23 kivas. All mentioned examples were abandoned by the time the Spanish arrived. Thus far, the most northern kivas have been excavated in the Lowry Ruins and in Chimney Rock, both in Colorado. These pueblos were mostly deserted for diverse reasons before the Spaniards arrived.

KIVAS AND FRANCISCAN MISSIONS IN NEW MEXICO

Pecos

Pecos Pueblo (Figure 4) was the easternmost Pueblo village at the edge of the Rio Grande Valley. It protected the area against the sometimes-hostile Indigenous people of the Plains. A Franciscan mission was built in 1617/1618 a short distance from the pueblo; this could be interpreted as "neutral zone" between the old Indigenous and new Christian cultures.[17] In the 1620s the Franciscan destroyed "idols" there, made of stone, clay, or wood, hardly an act of understanding or "inculturation."[18] Idolatry was generally deemed as a common sin of Indigenous societies from a Christian perspective. But under what circumstances was the destruction possible and practicable? Every time? The Franciscans

17. John L. Kessell, *Kiva, Cross, and Crown: The Pecos Indians and New Mexico 1540–1840* (Albuquerque: University of New Mexico Press, 1987), 104–105, 113.

18. Kessell, *Kiva, Cross, and Crown*, 110–11.

Figure 3. Mesa Verde—Cliff Palace. Photo by author.

had no overall strategy, and they were very cautious, especially during the early days of their mission work. A new head of a friary could act more tolerantly towards Indigenous culture, favoring a more complex inculturation.[19]

Another observation might clarify the situation: Even when Franciscans attempted to suppress the old rituals, they continued to be driven by the still influential "priests of the idols," as Spanish documents described them.[20] Evangelization is not a straightforward, one-sided process. After the first introduction of new beliefs, forms of the old and new religion existed in parallel; even the Spanish settlers were sometimes open-minded towards some Indigenous rituals ("powders and herbs"), which were useful in healing.[21] In brief, Franciscan attitudes were also changed by contact with the native ways of life; they often showed an interest in the old religious habits as well and some friars realized that evangelization should not go hand in hand with the brutal destruction of Indigenouse sacred places and religious images.[22] The Dominican monk and bishop Bartholomé de las Casas had already described the impossible connection of brutal conquest with "happy" converted natives.[23]

---

19. Kessell, *Kiva, Cross, and Crown*, 121; Ivey, "Convento Kivas," 129.

20. Kessell, *Kiva, Cross, and Crown*, 132.

21. Kessell, *Kiva, Cross, and Crown*, 152–53.

22. Ivey, "Convento Kivas," 127–29.

23. Bartolomé de las Casas, *Brevísima Relación de la Destrucción de las Indias* (finished 1542, published 1552). His example is the conversion of the native people in Hispanola.

Figure 4. Pecos Pueblo—Franciscan Mission and Kiva. Photo by author.

The second church in Pecos, built in 1625, was the biggest mission-church north of Mexico City: it was a monumental landmark meant to demonstrate the victory of Christianity. As with every church in New Mexico in these times it was built by men and women of the native community.[24] Its size was intended to impress the Pecos and all who visited the place, including the Apaches or Comanches from the Great Plains who came annually to Pecos for trading. Its architecture created a building never before seen by Indigenous people. The church with its white-plastered wall "must have seemed at most [as] a wonder."[25]

As mentioned, there were kivas not only in the Pecos pueblo.[26] One was also in the area of the *convento*, perhaps coexisting with the friary. Ivey

24. Mariah Wade, "The Missionary Predicament: Conversion Practices in Texas, New Mexico, and the Californias," in *From La Florida to La California. Franciscan Evangelization in the Spanish Borderlands*, eds. by Timothy J. Johnson and Gert Melville (Berkeley: The Academy of American Franciscan History, 2013), 285–96, here 287 and Annie Lux, *Historic New Mexico Churches* (Salt Lake City: Gibbs Smith Publisher, 2007), 34–35.

25. Kessell, *Kiva, Cross, and Crown*, 124–29.

26. Archaeological research at the kiva by Alfred Vincent Kidder took place in the 1920s: Alfred Vincent Kidder, *Pecos, New Mexico: Archaeological Notes*, 29–42, 143–219, 227–41. For the history of Pecos after 1776, see John L. Kessell, *The Missions of New Mexico Since 1776* (Albuquerque: University of New Mexico Press, 1980), 223–32.

described it as a "convento kiva."[27] Does this local religious landscape have specific factors? The kiva focused on here was on the south side of the convent cloister. According to the National Park Service at Pecos, it was built not long after the first church was erected in 1617. The possible reason is the source of much discussion. One explanation is that the pueblo people themselves built the kiva in veneration of the new Christian beliefs in the late seventh century, but this does not fit according to archaeologists, since this kiva is older. It is more likely that the Franciscans themselves built it in the 1620s to 1640s.[28] Their aim could have been to attract the new Christians with the help of a newly erected sacred place, a kiva. This was a long time practice to show that an inculturation of Christianity in sacred spaces of the former religion might be possible and welcomed, despite the differing value systems. Inculturation stands for a presentation, an adaption of Christian teachings in a non-Christian environment. So, there is no "pure" form of Christian cult; it changes according to the people targeted for conversion.[29] Kivas stand for a "useful conversion architecture."[30] Again, the Franciscans could only proceed very cautiously at the beginning of their missionary efforts, as already mentioned. This is probably also the reason why the mission complex was developed very slowly.[31]

In any case, the Franciscans replicated the religious elements of the kiva in Pecos Pueblo according to the visual appearance of sacred 'Puebloan' architecture. This attempt at inculturation reflected the long-standing Christian practice of evangelization within the context of material sites familiar to Indigenous peoples.[32] The hope was that the two groups would come together, "sometimes in a spirit of cooperation, sometimes in an atmosphere of coercion and conflict" in these common areas.[33] So, Spanish ceremonies,

---

27. Ivey, "Convento Kivas," 139, 145–46.

28. *Pecos. National Historical Park* (Western National Parks Association:, 2009). See also *Pecos Ruins: Geology, Archaeology, History and Prehistory*, ed. David Grant Noble (Santa Fe: Ancient City Press, 1993); *Ancient Ruins and Rock Art of the Southwest*, ed. David Grant Noble (New York: Taylor Trade Publishing, 2015), 217–20 (The kiva is not mentioned!), Ivy, *Convento Kivas*, 140.

29. *Inkulturation zwischen Tradition und Modernität. Kontext—Begriffe—Modelle*, ed. Fritz Frei (Freiburg: Universitätsverlag, 2000) and Peter Schneiller, *A Handbook on Inculturation* (New York: Paulist Press, 1990).

30. Ivey, "Convento Kivas," 121–22. Also, James E. Ivey, *In the Midst of Loneliness: The Architectural History of the Salinas Missions* (Santa Fe: Southwest Cultural Resources Center, 1998, 1991), 420.

31. Levine, *Our Prayers*, 17.

32. Néstor Medina, *Christianity, Empire and the Spirit. (Re)Configuring and Mission in World Christianity* (Leiden: Brill, 2018).

33. Noble, *Ancient Ruins and Rock Art*, 204.

even though they were different from those of the Indigenous people, included Indigenous elements: Puebloans celebrated kachina dances on church grounds on special Christian feast days and held kiva ceremonies. The intended results were "Christian and traditional rites" could have a peaceful coexistence, tolerated by the 'wise' Franciscan friars.[34]

The Franciscans' considerations of missionary tasks in early modern Times had its roots in the thirteenth century. In particular, the works of the acclaimed theologian, Bonaventure, played an important role. Conversion and penance were key concerns. The Franciscan concept of proselytizing is based on eschatological ideas of renewal.[35] Another historical root is based in the experiences of converting the Moors on the Iberian Peninsula. In the face of a presumably "dying and evil world," all people should have the chance to renew their Christian life or experience faith in Jesus Christ. The ideal image of the Christian community, the original apostolic community in Jerusalem, should be revived. The main task of the brothers should be, according to Bonaventure, to combine contemplation and mission. But there was a further consideration favored by the Dominicans. This concerned promoting a reasonable way of convincing unbelievers, with the help of a dialogue between, and a combination of spiritual elements from differing religions, making it easier for converts to accept the new faith and live it consciously. There is also a particular Spanish focus: reflecting the unification of Spain under Queen Isabella and King Ferdinand, to be Spanish meant to be a Christian. Thus, Spanish colonial expansion implied an extension of Christianity, and missionizing was inevitable. Its authors were mostly Franciscans.[36] For them it was clear: Indigenous peoples were human beings with souls and the right to life and freedom. That said, the different languages and cultures of the New World represented a crucial challenge for the missionaries.[37]

In this context there was an interpretative change regarding the Kiva, from devilish structure that must be immediately destroyed to sacred space, which should perhaps remain within an intercultural context. There was a strong indication that the Indigenous peoples had a "fundamental capacity

34. Robert C. Galgano, *Feast of Souls, Indians and Spaniards in the Seventeenth-century Missions of Florida and New Mexico* (Albuquerque: University of New Mexico Press, 2005), 75.

35. E. Randolph Daniel, *The Franciscan Concept of Mission in the High Middle Ages*, (Lexington: The University Press of Kentucky, 1975), 26–36, see 30: "In other words, the friars were to be both contemplatives and missionaries, striving for union with God and inspiring others to seek to reform themselves to the model of the evangelical life."

36. Edwin Edward Sylvest, *Motifs of Franciscan Mission Theory in Sixteenth Century New Spain Province of the Holy Gospel* (Washington: Academy of American Franciscan History, 1975), 4.

37. Sylvest, *Motifs*, 42–44, 87–88.

for God," even they chose the devil's side.[38] They could achieve redemption and Christian living, if they are willing to convert. All these considerations would explain the absence of evidence for the complete ruination of kivas in the Pecos Pueblo. Inculturation and peaceful coexistence of kiva and church seems conceivable within a relatively peaceful mission process, though it remains unclear under what conditions this could have taken place.

However, all these considerations are upended if the kiva near the convent is not as old as our first information indicates. Using archaeological evidence, Alden C. Hayes has argued in his book, *The Four Churches of Pecos*, that the kiva south of the convent was built during the 1680 revolt. The Indigenous people destroyed the church and convent building, and, as a sign of the "victory" of the traditional faith, they built this kiva in what had been the sacred area of the friary.[39] Archaeological research also shows that of the ten kivas in the pueblo, five were used as places of trash collection, three others lost their roofs, and only two continued in use over the centuries.[40] Whether the latter indicate inculturation is unclear from the archaeological evidence. Archaeological reports simply did not discuss this matter.

The archaeologist Alfred Vincent Kidder has admitted that dating of sherds in the backfill of the former kivas was not given particular attention. He regretted that he never emphasized this question during his excavation campaign.[41] Thus, it is very unclear when the kivas were filled—1617/1618, after 1680, or another date? Ivey pointed out recently that already existing archaeological evidence has to be reconsidered; for him the bricks and mortars found were made between 1620 and 1640, not later.[42]

Destruction of kivas happened before the arrival of the Franciscans, and, especially in New Mexico, during the Revolt of 1680, but also before.[43] Another crucial question is why some kivas were destroyed, and some were not. The old believers with their priests, even during the times of oppression, never yielded. Moreover, a permanent misunderstanding between the two sides was ongoing.

Another social problem worsened when the natives divided themselves into Christians and non-Christians. However, for example after the Revolt,

---

38. Sylvest, *Motifs*, 46–48.

39. Alden C. Hayes, *The Four Churches of Pecos* (Albuquerque: University of New Mexico Press, 1974), 32–33. Following this argumentation Kessell, *Kiva, Cross, and Crown*, 238–39.

40. Kidder, *Pecos*, 236–40.

41. Kidder, *Pecos*, 237.

42. Ivey, "Convento Kivas," 139.

43. Kidder, *Pecos*, 238. Also, Michael V. Wilcox, *The Pueblo Revolts and the Mythology of Conquest: An Indigenous Archaeology of Contact* (Berkeley: University of California Press, 2009).

there was a "leeway" which "should be allowed converted Indians" to live their faith.[44] Consequently rivalry existed not only between Spaniards and the Indigenous people, but also within the Puebloans between Christians and Non-Christians. Thus, the uprising in New Mexico seemed to be foiled by native Christians in some regards.[45] As a result, the Franciscans had to deal with at least two groups of believers and therefrom resulting divisions between families. In the 1640s and 1650s they lost control over the pueblos, especially Jemez. When Governor Trevino (1675–1677) gave the order to destroy kivas, what were his intentions? Was it an attempt to regain the authority over the pueblos the missionaries had already lost? Or was it a signal of a restored relationship between the Spanish administration and the missionaries?[46] This relationship was complicated, too. There are no hints that the governor's order was ever carried out.

DESTRUCTION OF KIVAS

Incidentally, these disputes continued into the eighteenth century. While Governor Mogollón ordered the destruction of the kivas, Governor Juan de Tafoya allowed the active kivas to remain open under the condition that the natives would provide him with more deerskins.[47] On the other hand, the Franciscans could not prevent the "scalp dance" in which not only the kivas played a role, but also the missionary church itself. The Natives "go to the church as if to give thanks. This lasts about as long as three Credos," as Francisco Atanasio Dominguez remarked in 1776. And "so the fathers are unable to abolish this custom and many others."[48] The influence of the friars on local customs remained limited. They had to accept compromises to be able to work as missionaries at all. For the Puebloans the connection of church and kiva seemed to be less problematic than for the Franciscans.

There were always times of changes and of mutual rejection. The revolt in New Mexico is a striking example of this. As soon as the rebellious Puebloan people drove out the Spaniards and murdered the missionaries, the churches were destroyed, the bells removed.[49] Christian names were banned,

---

44. Kidder, *Pecos*, 239.

45. Wilcox, *Pueblo Revolt*, 143.

46. Wilcox, *Pueblo Revolt*, 143.

47. Kessell, *Missions of New Mexico*, 258, n. 27.

48. Kessell, *Missions of New Mexico*, 257–58.

49. Bells and bell towers were also new buildings under a Christian auspice. They were a sign of Spanish supremacy, both politically and religiously, all in all a symbol of Spanish presence in the regions. Bells could be used as a form of peaceful interactions between Spaniards and natives. It is unclear, how bells "signaled colonial identities and social roles." Kristin Dutcher Mann, "Defining Time and Space. Franciscans and Bells in

and Christian marriages declared null and void.[50] As an immediate reaction, new kivas were built.[51] This shows that the ancient Indian priest caste was still functioning. The Spaniards therefore spoke of "conspiracies of sorcerers."[52] Even before the revolt, the missionaries had not succeeded in suppressing the Indian religion. At least, this is the story told by Native eyewitnesses who were interviewed by the Spaniards after suppression of the uprising. Since the statements are very similar, they probably truthfully reflect the reaction of the leaders of the uprising at the time.

In essence, the Spaniards proceeded in the same way during the reconquest, albeit in the opposite direction: the kivas, as a symbol of the "diabolical" religion of the natives, were now destroyed and Christianity was newly established in Puebloan sacred places. According to a governor's order in December 1681, the Spanish troops "shall set fire to the estufas, which are refuges of the devil, houses of idolatry, rape, and obscenity."[53] In a letter by an eyewitness, every estufa or kiva, "which is the house of idolatry where the said Indians practice their superstitions and abuses, and inside it were found many idols, masks, and figures of the devil, with herbs, feathers, and many other idolatrous objects, all of which were burned publicly."[54] The general visitator, fray Francisco de Ayeta, made a small ceremony: he went

---

Northern New Spain," in *The Franciscans in Colonial Mexico*, eds. Thomas M. Cohen, Jay T. Harrison, and David Rex Galindo (Norman: University of Oklahoma Press, and Oceanside, CA: The Academy of Franciscan History, 2021), 259–85, quote 265.

The Indigenous people were, nevertheless, interested in bells and learnt, how to cast a bell. Bell towers thus became a Christian landmark, documenting sacred places as well as the 'tonal' dominance of the new religion in time and space. Every mission had one. See the report of friar Francisco Atanasio Dominguez (1740 in Mexico City—before 1805) for the missions in New Mexico from 1776 for Jemez ("a small adobe belfry containing two small cracked bells," "two small bronze bells") and Pecos ("two small towers with a small bell donated by the King," "two small bronze bells" by the high-altar): *The Missions of New Mexico, 1776.* A description by Fray Francisco Atanasio Dominguez with other contemporary documents, 177, 209–20.

50. *Revolt of the Pueblo Indians of New Mexico and Otermín's attempted Reconquest*, ed. Charles Wilson Hackett (Albuquerque: University of New Mexico Press, 1942), 215: ". . . they [the Indian rebels] should burn all the images and temples, rosaries and crosses, and that all the people should discard the names given them in holy baptism and call themselves whatever they liked. They should leave the wives whom they had taken in holy matrimony and take any one whom they might wish, . . ." Also, 239–40.

51. *Revolt of the Pueblo Indians*, 240: The rebels "ordered all the estufas erected, which are their houses of idolatry, and danced throughout the kingdom the dance of the cazina, making many masks for it in the image of the devil." Also, 251.

52. *Revolt of the Pueblo Indians*, 245.

53. *Revolt of the Pueblo Indians*, 216.

54. *Revolt of the Pueblo Indians*, 228. A similar description of a kiva is found on 231.

into the kiva, recited a short prayer ("Praised be the most holy sacrament"), and set it on fire.[55] In the pueblo of Puaray the Spaniards found "two new estufas," built by the "apostate rebels against the royal crown of his Majesty."[56]

In their reconquest campaign, the Spanish realized that not all natives voluntarily joined the rebellion,[57] indicating that the people of the pueblos were not of one mind in their actions. Although it is not explicitly stated in the letters and interviews, there may have been Christianized Puebloans behind the opposition to the resistance who wanted to hold on to the new faith. Sometimes, "the God-fearing Christians among the rebellious apostates" were mentioned in Spanish sources.[58] In both cases, the missionary church and the kiva played a decisive role, but in no case was mutual respect for the religions or even tolerance to be found in these times of crisis.

And there is another, more scientific perspective as well: The narrative background to a lot of archaeological research tends towards a black-and-white scheme, intolerant Spaniards on one side, helpless Indigenous peoples on the other. This narrative derives from an Anglophile perspective known as the "black legend" and does not seem to represent the situation in the Spanish borderlands.[59] Methods of missionary activity always adapt more often on the ground than normative ideas of a rigid system suggest, while the response of Indigenous peoples veers between "resistance and accommodation."[60] Accommodation could mean acculturation only in peaceful acceptance.

COMPARISON WITH OTHER MISSIONS IN NEW MEXICO

Comparative examples with Pecos Pueblo could be the Salinas Pueblo with the mission San Bonaventura de las Humanas and San Ysidro (Gran Quivira), where a *convento* was built in 1630, located between the church and the chief house of the pueblo. Gran Quivira had at least eleven kivas.[61] One of them, the so-called "Kiva D," was excavated by Gordon Vivian. It was situated

55. *Revolt of the Pueblo Indians*, 229, also 250.

56. *Revolt of the Pueblo Indians*, 230, 233, 244.

57. *Revolt of the Pueblo Indians*, 233, 246.

58. *Revolt of the Pueblo Indians*, 249.

59. Julián Juderías, *La Leyenda Negra [1914]* (Salamanca: Junta de Castilla y León, 2003).

60. Wilcox, *Pueblo Revolt*, 17–18.

61. Alden C. Hayes, "The excavation of Mound 7, Gran Quivira," manuscript, Washington D.C., Office of Archeology, 1970, 188–89. *Excavation of Mound 7. Gran Quivira National Monument / New Mexico*, eds. Alden C. Hayes, Jon Nathan Young, A.H. Young (Washington, D.C.: U.S. Government Printing Office, 1981) 31, 50–61.

between "House A" and the chapel of San Isidoro. He suggested, without further evidence, that the Spaniard "may have" destroyed this kiva.[62]

Another kiva was also built in the garth or garden at the neighboring Salinas mission San Gregorio de Abó (erected c. 1626, abandoned in 1672/1675, *before* the revolt), "during the building of the church." The archaeologist who worked there suggested that it was used as "a disposal pit" for kitchen garbage.[63] A convent garth is surrounded by the cloister symbolizing the Garden of Paradise and representing a preferred place of monastic retreat. From a European perspective it seems strange to have a garbage place in the center of a cloister, a sacred, enclosed place set apart from the world, and sometimes used as a burial place for monks. And there is (normally) no kitchen in a cloister area.[64] Even in the sixteenth or seventeenth century there was no change in this kind of monastical landscape. We do not have written sources about this kiva close to the church, but an inculturation-process could be worth considering instead. For example, the kiva was built at the same time as the Franciscan mission. The situation at Pecos Pueblo comes to mind; perhaps San Gregorio de Abó was also a "convent kiva," which played an important role in the coexistence of the friars and Puebloans.[65] Both pueblos, San Gregorio and Pecos, were also situated in the transition zone, where natives from the Great Plains came in contact with the Puebloans. Perhaps the clash between the different religious beliefs of Native groups with a nomadic or sedentary way of life, and a Christian mission was another reason why the Franciscans built a kiva on the ground of their friary; perhaps it was an attempt at inculturation.

It is possible that the San Gregorio de Abó kiva's fate was akin to the situation found in the mission of Nuestra Señora de la Concepción at Quarai. The kiva seems to be older than the mission. Presumably as a sign of the superiority of Christianity, the Spaniards built a mission church and friary over the kiva there, which was back-filled.[66] Likewise at the church of San Bernardo de Aguatubi in Northeastern Arizona as the main altar was built over a sand-filled kiva, which still retained its roof and much wall plaster.[67] The situation

62. Gordon Vivian, *Excavations in a 17th-century Jumano Pueblo. Gran Quivira*, Archeological Research Series no. 8 (National Park Service, 1961), 51–59, quote 53.

63. Joseph H. Toulouse, *The Mission of San Gregorio de Abo. A Report on the Excavation and Repair of a Seventeenth-Century New Mexico Mission*, Monographs of the School of American Research 13 (Albuquerque: University of New Mexico Press, 1949), 11.

64. Ivey, "Convento Kivas," 135.

65. Ivey, "Convento Kivas," 139,145–46.

66. "Kivas Found at Quarai Monastery," *El Palacio* 40, nos. 22–24 (1957): 122.

67. *Franciscan Awatovi: The Excavation and Conjectural Reconstruction of a 17th-Century Spanish Mission Establishment at a Hopi Indian Town in Northeastern Arizona*, eds. Ross Gordon Montgomery, Watson Smith John Otis Brew., Harvard University vol.

in Awatovi is interesting because it was the only place in the Hopi region that advocated a return of the Franciscans after the revolt. This was violently prevented by the other Hopi.[68] And it was precisely at this place that the Franciscans were supposed to have succeeded in using violence by the previous destruction of the kiva.

The Franciscans seemed to demonstrate with this gesture the superposition surrounding a pagan ceremonial chamber, but is this interpretation resilient? This stratagem was a course of action but was not unique to Franciscans and New Mexico, but very common in medieval Europe. So, the kiva in a cloister such as in San Gregorio de Abó could also be interpreted this way. It shows the predominance of Christianity over religious rituals of the Natives. This kind of a Christian landscapes symbolizes "victory over Satanic forces."[69] But there is, according to new sources, another interpretation possible, as Robert C. Galgano pointed out. He writes: "As the ministers supervised the building of the church complexes, they permitted local natives to excavate large kivas in the patios of the conventos. Each was carefully centered in the courtyard and was in use until the 1660s."[70] Rarely can such interpretations be more contradictory to the earlier ones. Galgano based his estimation on the archaeological research of Ivey, concluding that the Franciscans were in charge of the "convento kivas" in the Salinas as in Pecos and other places. Ivey rejected the idea of Toulouse, that these kivas in the convento areas show a "superstition" of the Christian faith.[71] Also Watson Smith, even referring Montgomery's thesis, did not argue for a kiva's destruction, but was more convinced by the Franciscans' idea "to supplant the kivas as foci for religious observances . . . and thereby their new sanctuary with the old."[72]

The last group of Pecos people were transferred to Jemez in 1838.[73] The Franciscan mission there is on the far edge of the village where kivas are found in the shadow of the Franciscan friary and its church. On the other side of the road lies the Via Coeli monastery built in 1947, whose white-col-

---

XXXVI Peabody Museum (Cambridge: Harvard University Printing Office, 1949), 64–65, 134–36.

68. Smith, *When is a Kiva?*, 91–93 [Introduction to a paper from Smith by the editor].

69. *Franciscan Awatovi* 134, also 265–72; Montgomery calls it a "superposition" (see *Franciscan Awatovi*, 265–72); Ivey, "Convento Kivas," 132.

70. Galgano, *Feast of Souls*, 73.

71. Ivey, "Convento Kivas," 135–40. Also, Don Hanlon, "Spanish Mission Church in Central New Mexico. A Study in Architectural Morphology," in *Anthropologica*, 34 (1992): 203–29, here 214.

72. Smith, "Room 788" in *When is a Kiva?*, 107.

73. In detail see Levine, *Our prayers*, 23–31; for the decrease in the population of Pecos from 2000 in 1622 to 18 in 1838 see 41–71.

ored walls offers a sharp contrast to the red stone dominating the landscape. Its name is Via Coeli and was owned by the 'Servants of the Paracletes' (erected 1947), the nowadays parish church is dedicated to 'Our Lady of the Assumption.'

The Jemez mission has an interesting history in the seventeenth century, but information is very sparse.[74] The numbers of Franciscan missionaries and lay brothers were low, so it is uncertain how deep the process of proselytization could have been rooted in the minds of the Indigenous population. Also, the interests of the governor and the Franciscan brothers differed again. For the governor, evangelization was not at the top of his priorities. He and all Spanish settlers "benefited from the *encomienda* and *repartamiento* labor systems."[75] So, Governor Juan de Eulate, for example, adopted a more liberal policy towards Indigenous rituals.[76] Governor López de Mendizábal also allowed the practice of the old traditions, in exchange for greater labor extractions, as already mentioned.[77] The parallel existence of church and kiva may reflect this trend though it was not practiced by all governors. Some of them ordered the destruction of kivas and prohibited the old ceremonies. But were they successful?

Behind this, struggles between the civil administration and the ecclesiastical authorities became visible. The Franciscans could only interpret such behavior of the local authorities as an attack on their mission efforts. On the other hand, the number of monks and lay brothers was very small, so it was very difficult for them to get their issues heard in relation to all Indigenous people. The written sources give no clear picture of the interaction between the few Franciscans and large numbers of Puebloans. There are indications that the old dances and ceremonies were celebrated outside the pueblos somewhere in the landscape, so the Franciscans may have had little clue about these events. The missionaries could not teach complex theological issues, mainly because the native languages lacked words to adequately explain the Christian fundamentals.[78] Thus, baptism was often celebrated with a clear misunderstanding that baptism and old beliefs could be reconciled. Most of the Indigenous people remained "autonomous" in their reli-

---

74. France V. Scholes, "Notes on the Jemez Missions in the Seventeenth Century," *El Palacio* 44 (1938): 61–71, 93–102.

75. Wade, "Missionary Predicament," 287.

76. Scholes, "Jemez Missions," 68: Eulate had "great favor to 'idolaters' who wanted to continue the practice of the old religious customs."

77. Wilcox, *The Pueblo Revolts*, 241.

78. See an example with the Nahuas in Mexico: Louise M. Burkhart, *The Slippery Earth: Nahua-Christian Moral Dialogue in Sixteenth-Century Mexico* (Tuscon: University of Arizona Press, 1989).

gious beliefs and social networks. Spanish control in New Mexico was much weaker than in California or Texas.[79]

The missionaries had to deal with many diverse problems in isolation. The individual missionary had to make specific decisions based on the situation he encountered. He also had to survive in strange and sometimes hostile surroundings at pueblos or rural sites. Friars never would have survived—in New Mexico as in Florida—without the sustenance of the natives.[80] This may be one of the main reasons why some kivas survived. The Franciscans had to acknowledge that despite their missionary efforts, the Puebloans continued to practice their old rituals in secret, mostly outside of the pueblo and therefore almost invisible to the friars. This resistance remained tenacious, as the natives acted ostensibly faithful to all Christian ideals.[81]

Despite all the uncertainties of written and archaeological sources, it appears that some Indigenous people accepted the new religion. Their numbers will always be unknown, and the figures conveyed by the Franciscans to Spain and Mexico are certainly too high. Moreover, the Indigenous people were no longer united. The old narrative of church representing Spaniards and kiva equal to the old native religion breaks down by considering that Indigenous people, at least in part, were already Christianized and from the 1640s they warned the Spaniards of uprisings by their countrymen.[82] The remaining kivas could be a "bridge" for Catholic Natives. This was perhaps an attempt to reduce tensions between Christian and non-Christian Indigenous people.

EPILOGUE—A MODERN ADAPTION OF OLD FORMS IN A NEW LOOK

The syncretism of Indigenous religions and Christianity continues to the present day. As early as the eighteenth century, religious images from the Zuni religion in combination with Christian statues can be found in their churches. Since the Zuni already had their kivas painted, they continued this tradition in the Christian nave. Thus, in a sense, the place of Christian worship changed into a kiva and vice versa. The permanence of the old local culture in its sacred

79. Wade, "Missionary Predicament," 289.

80. Galgano, *Feast of Souls*, 2: Circa 1700 there were estimated 1,400 Spaniards in Florida and 3,000 in New Mexico.

81. Galgano, *Feast of Souls*, 154.

82. Wilcox, *The Pueblo Revolt*, 134–43. For the history of Jemez after 1776 see Kessell. *The Missions of New Mexico*, 181–86.

Figure 5. Santa Maria de la Vid Abbey in Albuquerque. Photo: With the generous permission from the Norbertine Community of New Mexico, Joseph Sandoval, director of communications.

place was thus ensured, and the church transformed itself as an "icon of local culture."[83]

By the way, when the inhabitants of some Pueblos in New Mexico celebrate the feast of their patron saints in the present, there is mostly a combination of Christian mass and old ritual dances in front of the church.[84] For example to maintain the present identity of the dispersed Pecos, the feast day of Nuestra Señora de los Angeles is held annually in the ruins of the mission church in Pecos.[85] Sacred places were designed by performative acts, combining both religions. So, Timothy Johnson's concept of sacred places defined by liturgies, works until today.

Therefore, the churches have to be attractive for liturgical acts of both religions: the natives changed the appearance of the churches, and the Franciscan builders accommodated them. The church buildings in New Mexico,

---

83. Kevin S. Blake, Jeffrey S. Smith, "Pueblo Mission Churches as Symbols of Performance and Identity," in *The Geographical Review* 90 (2000): 359–80 see 360 [quote], 366, 372, 374.

84. Charles M. Carillo, *Saints of the Pueblos* (Albuquerque, LPD Press, 2004), 6.

85. Levine, *Our Prayers*,125–30. Another example from the early twentieth century, see Parsons, *Pueblo Indian Religion*, 847–48.

as a result, developed a particular "hybrid building type" that also incorporated forms of the kivas. For example, both sacred spaces had little natural light, thus documenting the faith's connection to the earth. There was—mostly—no spatial separation between the sanctuary and the nave. Both kiva and church described a unified space, behind which was the "concept of a compact, unitary design for sacred spaces."[86] The church construction reflects the religious needs of the Puebloans.

Even today, such connections between the different religious forms can be found. So, this paper closes with a modern combination of kiva and church: the new church of the Premonstratensian (Norbertine) monastery in Albuquerque, dedicated to Saint Norbert of Xanten, is built in the form of a kiva. It is a symbolic unification of both religions and a sign of tolerance in the present.

86. Hanlon, "Spanish Mission Church," 213, 227.

Chapter Thirteen

The Spanish Clarist Abbess Mother Luisa de la Ascensión (1565–1636): Her Religious Activities and Franciscan Missionary Network

Jane D. Tar, *University of Saint Thomas (Saint Paul)*

In the early seventeenth century Franciscan missionaries traveled to Carrión de los Condes on the pilgrimage route of the Camino de Santiago in Northern Spain to seek the counsel of the Clarist abbess, Luisa de la Ascensión at the Convent of Santa Clara.[1] An authoritative woman spiritual leader in the tradition of the late medieval "living saint," Luisa de la Ascensión not only took a keen interest in, but also contributed to the advancement of Franciscan devotional and evangelical endeavors. The first half of this essay focuses on Luisa de la Ascensión's ecstatic spirituality, her religious activism, and the formation of her widespread cult. The second provides a reconstruction of Luisa de la Ascensión's missionary network bringing to light testimony located in the order's chronicles and other sources concerning the nun's interactions with Franciscans about to embark on missions for the first time or veterans returning from them. The great value missionaries placed on Luisa de la Ascensión's advice, prophecy, intercessory prayers, and devotional objects attests to the nun's recognized contemporary spiritual leadership against the backdrop of the order's historical encouragement and promotion of its women religious as evangelists and prophets.[2]

---

1. By convent tradition, Santa Clara in Carrión was founded by two disciples of Saint Clare of Assisi from the Convent of San Damiano while on the Camino de Santiago in 1231 to earn the indulgences of the Jubilee Year of 1232; see Patrocinio García Barriúso, *La Monja de Carrión: Sor Luisa de la Ascensión Colmenares y Cabezón: Aportación documental para una biografía* (Madrid: Ediciones Monte Casino, 1986), 41.

2. To be sure, Luisa de la Ascensión was not the only nun with missionary interests and connections. For others, see Magnus Lundberg, *Contemplative Women and Salvation in Colonial Spanish America and the Philippines* (Uppsala: Swedish Institute of Mission Research,

Luisa de la Ascensión's Spirituality, Activities, and Influence[3]

From the permeable cloister of the Convent of Santa Clara in Carrión de los Condes, the reputation Mother Luisa de la Ascensión gained in the early decades of the seventeenth century for heroic virtue led to an acclaim that extended far beyond the geographical boundaries of the Iberian Peninsula.[4] In his annals of the order, the Irish Franciscan, Luke Wadding, depicted Luisa de la Ascensión as a global living saint, beloved "in Spain, foreign countries and throughout the Indies."[5] In truth, the abbess's performative spirituality, consisting of raptures that overtook her at the sound of the church organ after having received the Eucharist, reminiscent genealogically of her late medieval and sixteenth-century charismatic women forbears, attracted all manner of visitors to Carrión eager to witness Mother Luisa ecstatic, her face far more youthful than her years, her body light (Figure 1).[6] Domingo de Aspe, Luisa de la Ascensión's Franciscan confessor and the author of a hagiography of the nun at the height of her fame in the 1630s, describes how "everyday—sometimes a hundred and forty people—from every kind of nation, and of every sort, quality, and rank" would congregate before dawn at the door of the Santa Clara church to await her celestial transformation during Mass.[7]

2015), and Sarah E. Owens, *Nuns Navigating the Spanish Empire* (Albuquerque: University of New Mexico Press, 2017). On the famous bilocations of the Franciscan Conceptionist abbess, María de Ágreda, a younger contemporary of Luisa de la Ascensión, and her writings concerning them, see Anna M. Nogar, *Quill and Cross in the Borderlands: Sor María de Ágreda and the Lady in Blue* (Notre Dame: Notre Dame University Press, 2018), 7–39.

3. In adopting women's religious activities as a category of analysis, I am indebted to Lise Lehtsalu, Sarah Moran, and Silvia Evangelisti, "Introduction: Perspectives on Women's Religious Activities in Early Modern Europe and the Americas," *Journal of Early Modern History* 22, 1–2 (2018): 1–7.

4. I take the term, "permeable cloister," from Elizabeth Lehfeldt, *Religious Women in Golden Age Spain: The Permeable Cloister* (Aldershot, UK: Ashgate Publishing, 2005).

5. See Hipólito Barriguín Fernández, ed. *Fray Francisco Calderón: Primera parte de la crónica de la Santa Provincia de la Inmaculada* (Concepción, Valladolid: Diputación de Valladolid, 2008), 289–90, for the Wadding quote. All translations are my own, unless otherwise specified.

6. Regarding Castilian living saints including Franciscan nuns and *beatas* prior to Teresa of Ávila, see Pablo Acosta-García and Rebeca Sanmartín-Bastida, "Digital Visionary Women: Introducing the *Catalogue of Living Saints*," *The Journal of Medieval Iberian Studies* 14 (2022): 55–68, https://doi.org/10.1080/17546559.2021.1980897.

7. Domingo de Aspe, *Tercera parte de la vida de Soror Luisa de la Ascensión* (Archivo Histórica Nacional de España, Inquisición, Legajo 3709, Caja 1), 151v.

Figure 1. Portrait of Mother Luisa de la Ascensión, Museum of Santa Clara, Carrión de los Condes, Spain.

Just as important to transnational pilgrims and Franciscans who made the trip to Carrión were Luisa de la Ascensión's material religious objects that she asked God to bless from a hermitage in her convent's garden. These encouraged devotion to Luisa de la Ascensión's principal counter-reformational causes—the defense of the Eucharist, the Holy Trinity, and above all, the Virgin Mary's Immaculate Conception. Moreover, they reportedly worked miracles. Those fortunate enough to obtain an audience with the Nun of Carrión might receive one from her own hand.[8] If not, penitents could create their own contact relics by touching those they brought with them easily purchased at shops selling them in the town to an original Mother Luisa cross and two rosary beads located at the convent's turn; or they might receive from the Santa Clara sisters crosses or rosary beads that the women touched to Luisa de la Ascensión's head while she was enraptured during Mass.[9]

---

8. For example, in 1633, five English Franciscans traveling from Douai to the order's general chapter in Toledo, spent two days in Carrión. At the end of their visit, Luisa de la Ascensión presented each one of them in person with one of her original crosses; see the travel journal by the English friar, Francis Bell (British Library, Sloane MS 1570), 24v.

9. Pedro de Balbas, *Memorial informativo en defensa de Sor Luisa de la Ascensión* (Madrid: Diego Díaz de la Carrera, 1643), 82v–83r. At their convent turn the Discalced

Like the Santa Clara nuns, Luisa de la Ascensión's brother, Francisco Colmenares, employed at the royal court in Madrid as a *guardadamas*, was also a purveyor of her devotional items—but he dealt with the holy mother's most prized relics. In this way, Juan de Santander, a Franciscan commissary general of the Indies (1626–1630), came by one of the rare full-sized crosses that the ascetic "crucified abbess" used to reenact the Passion of Christ during Lent.[10]

In addition to her raptures and relics, Luisa de la Ascensión regularly shared with devotees her illuminated knowledge, divinely granted. Word had it from reliable Franciscan sources that she could disclose the secret names of guardian angels or confirm the release of souls from purgatory.[11]

In 1616, Luisa de la Ascensión founded a religious confraternity devoted to the defense of Mary's Immaculate Conception that quickly enrolled many members of the laity and professed religious, excepting Dominicans who did not support the doctrine.[12] Antonio Daza, a general chronicler of the order, hagiographer of Mother Juana de la Cruz, one of Luisa de la Ascensión's spiritual directors and her collaborator, devotes a chapter in his Immaculist opus, *Libro de la Puríssima Concepción*, to publicizing the confraternity whose membership he claims to have soared to 80,000 individuals, including Philip III of Spain and his family, leading aristocrats and religious figures of the day.[13] Published in three editions in the 1620s, copies of Daza's book crossed the

---

Carmelite nuns of Villanueva de la Jara similarly had ready an image or figure of Baby Jesus in a box (perhaps given to its *tornera*, Ana de San Agustín, by Teresa of Ávila herself) to which one-contact relics could have been made not only to promote alms giving but also devotion. See Elizabeth A. Lehfeldt, "Baby Jesus in a Box: Commerce and Enclosure in an Early Modern Convent," *Mapping Gendered Routes and Spaces in the Early Modern World*, ed. Merry E. Weisner-Hanks (Farnham: Ashgate, 2015), 203–11.

10. Patrocinio García Barriúso, *La Monja de Carrión*, 274; for an extended account of the nun's imitation of the Passion of Christ that appeared in print during her lifetime, see 176. Regarding the spiritual exercise's iconographical representations through the centuries, see Cristina Gónzalez, "Beyond the Bride of Christ: The Crucified Abbess in Mexico and Spain," *The Art Bulletin* 99, 4 (2018): 102–32.

11. For example, Luisa de la Ascensión had informed Sebastián Salazar, a provincial of the order, and guardian of Segovia, of his own guardian angel's name; after his death, Mother Luisa received illumination that Salazar's soul had spent only five hours in Purgatory; see Bell (British Library, Sloane MS *1570*), 26r.

12. On the Immaculate Conception in early modern Spanish contexts, see Rosilie Hernández, *Immaculate Conceptions: The Power of the Religious Imagination in Early Modern* Spain (Toronto: University of Toronto Press, 2019).

13. Antonio Daza, *Libro de la Puríssima Concepción* (Madrid: Viuda de Luis Sánchez, 1628), 66r–87r. In a document dated 1625, Luisa de la Ascención's brother, Francisco Colmenares, stated that the confraternity had by then enrolled 140,000 members; see García Barriúso, *La Monja de Carrión*, 159.

Atlantic thus contributing to contemporary knowledge in New Spain of Luisa de la Ascensión and her good works.[14]

In 1617, the Mercedarian friar, Alonso Remón, likened Luisa de la Ascensión's renown as a spiritual counselor in Spain at the time to that of a sixteenth-century Franciscan Conceptionist visionary nun predecessor, Isabel de la Natividad, a "great servant of God" who frequently drew members of the laity to her Convent of Nuestra Señora de la Concepción in Mexico City (the first women's convent founded in New Spain), among them the wife of a viceroy, to discuss the state of their souls.[15] In a *Memorial* of 1636 written jointly in Luisa de la Ascensión's defense, the Franciscan officials, Pedro de Urbina (then the order's commissary general), and Joseph Vázquez (a theologian from Salamanca and former member of King Philip III of Spain's delegation to Rome in defense of the Immaculate Conception in the 1610s) went further, emphasizing the universal credit accorded her counsel. Indeed, they declare hyperbolically, so many European grandees had requested Luisa de la Ascensión's guidance over the decades "whether in writing or in person" that there is "hardly anyone to be found among them who has not done so."[16]

Not surprisingly, given Luisa de la Ascensión's religious affiliation, Franciscan friars looked to her for guidance too, much like the friar disciples or spiritual sons who gathered around the Italian tertiaries, Angela of Foligno and Margaret of Cortona, centuries before or more recently in Spain, the Franciscan third-order abbess Mother Juana de la Cruz of Cubas (1481–1534) whose cult Luisa de la Ascensión promoted and whose distribution of divinely blessed objects she emulated.[17] The "Saint of Burgos," Joan de

14. The National Library of Mexico holds three copies of Daza's edition of 1628 that came from various religious houses.

15. Alonso Remón, *Vida y muerte del siervo de Dios Don Fernando de Cordova y Bocanegra, y el libro de las colaciones y doctrinas espirituales que hizo y recopiló en el tiempo de su penitencia el año de 1588* (Madrid: Luis Sánchez, 1617), 6r–7v. Isabel de la Natividad's life of "prodigious sanctity," manifested itself, like Mother Luisa's, in constant raptures and ecstasies. On the convent's early history, see María Concepción Amerlinck, "Algunas noticias sobre objetos de plata en la Igelsia de la Concepción de México," *El jardín de las Hésperides: Estudios sobre la plata en Iberoamérica, siglos XVI al XX*, ed. Nuria Salazar Simarro et al. (León: INAH, Coordinación Nacional de Monumentos Históricos, Universidad de León, 2020), 237.

16. See Pedro de Urbino and José Vázquez (*BNE MS 6188, Notas al Memorial que el Santo Officio supremo dio para calificar las obras y virtudes de Sor Luisa de la Ascensión*), 262.

17. See Ronald E. Surtz, *The Guitar of God: Gender, Power, and Authority in the Visionary World of Mother Juana de la Cruz (1481–1534)* (Philadelphia: University of Pennsylvania Press, 1990). In view of the contemporary scarcity of and demand for the divinely blessed rosary beads of Mother Juana de la Cruz, Luisa de la Ascensión began the practice of taking devotional items to her private retreat in the convent gardens in imitation of Mother Juana where she asked God to bless them. The Convent of Santa Clara in Carrión

Tejada, for example, went to Carrión once or twice a year over a twenty-year period, staying for two weeks at a time so that he could discuss his spirit at length with Mother Luisa from which he always departed much consoled.[18]

Minister generals of the order likewise went to Carrión, in part because Mother Luisa's sanctity merited it, beginning with Juan Hierro (1612–1613) who took away with him as a relic one of her heavy penitential chains.[19] Antonio de Trejo (vicar general, 1613–1618) visited Luisa de la Ascensión, exchanged letters with her, and possessed the rosary that she claimed she had miraculously transported (via the phenomenon of bilocation) in 1614 to the tomb of Saint Francis in Assisi.[20] Benigno de Genova (1618–1625) paid her a visit in 1620 and again in 1621, the same year as the order's general chapter in Segovia.[21] Genova probably discussed with her a contentious topic at the time: the Discalced Franciscan friars' desire for greater authority and autonomy, threatening a division in the first order.[22] During one of the visits, Genova presented Luisa de la Ascensión with an image or sculpture of *Nuestra Señora de la Consolación y Guía* from the Indies that then worked "many miracles" in its new home.[23] Like Trejo, he was a member of the nun's Conceptionist confraternity. In a letter of 26 December 1626, Luisa de la Ascensión reported to her sister how Bernardino de Senna (1625–1631) had been to see her, staying in Carrión for three days.[24] Reminiscent of medieval Marian miracles on the sea, she supposedly once saved him from a sinking ship in the Mediterranean when as "her prelate" he had called on her.[25] In 1633, the English friar Francis Bell reported that during his visit to Mother Luisa in

possesses a seventeenth-century portrait of Mother Juana likely commissioned by Mother Luisa. Moreover, the convent would undoubtedly have possessed a copy of Mother Juana's hagiography by Antonio Daza.

18. Ignacio Omaechevarría, "Un plantel de seráfica santidad en las afueras de Burgos: San Esteban de los Olmos (1458–1836), Conclusión," *Archivo-Iberomericano* (1957): 574.

19. *Relación de la causa de Soror Luisa de la Ascensión*, 63v.

20. García Barriúso, *La Monja de Carrión*, 275.

21. García Barriúso, *La Monja de Carrión*, 104.

22. For example, the Discalced Franciscan guardian of the Convent in San Gil in Madrid, Luis de San Juan Evangelista, consulted Luisa de la Ascensión in writing concerning the matter, wanting to know God's will; see Garciía Barriúso, *La Monja de Carrión*, 112–14. Although Pope Gregory (1621–1623) approved, Luisa de la Ascensión advised against such a division in the order.

23. See the printed text without author, publisher, or year: Biblioteca Nacional de España, *Relación de la causa de Soror Luisa de la Ascensión, monia del Convento de Santa Clara de Carrión* (signatura 2/4228), 109r.

24. García Barriúso, *La Monja de Carrión*, 108.

25. *Relación de la causa de Soror Luisa de la Ascensión*, 119r.

route to the general chapter of Toledo, she urged him and his traveling companions to pray for the election of an Italian candidate for the generalship, Giovanni Battista de Campania (1633–1639), a "capable and zealous friar," subsequently elected at the chapter.[26]

Luisa de la Ascensión and Franciscan Missionaries

Franciscan missionaries, like Bell, martyred in England in 1643 during its civil war, also formed part of Luisa de la Ascensión's extensive religious network. The first visit of a missionary friar to Luisa de la Ascensión may have been that of Juan de Santa Marta in 1606 of the Spanish Franciscan province of Santiago. According to the Discalced Franciscan chronicler, Domingo Martínez, Santa Marta, a native of Barcelona and a talented musician, found himself questioning the direction of his religious vocation.[27] Should he continue to devote himself to the contemplative life or heed Juan Pobre de Zamora's recruitment call to join a contingent of some thirty friars, headed by Juan de los Mártires, scheduled to depart later that year for the far-off mission fields of the Philippines and Japan? Afflicted by doubts, the young friar requested permission from his provincial to travel in the latter's company to Carrión so that Luisa de la Ascensión might furnish him with insight regarding the momentous and life-altering decision that he must make. Luisa de la Ascensión's answer for Santa Marta—that God intended him to go on the mission, even though that might entail his death, provided him with the illumination that he needed. Hagiographies by two of Luisa de la Ascensión's confessors, Antonio Daza and Domingo de Aspe, later claimed that Luisa de la Ascensión had experienced a bilocation to Nagasaki in August 1618 during which she was able to witness Santa Marta's martyrdom and comfort him during the ordeal.[28]

According to the Discalced Franciscan chronicler Martínez, Luisa de la Ascensión confirmed for an anonymous friar who had traveled to see her in 1619 that it was God's will that he too should go on the Pacific mission. As it happened, not long after the friar's transoceanic embarkation, a terrible storm overcame the Spanish fleet. Commending himself to Luisa de la Ascensión's protection, he reported that she appeared supernaturally to him on his ship's quarterdeck, safeguarding all those aboard from the fate of some 1,500 individuals who perished in the tempest, among them the mission's

---

26. Bell (British Library, *Sloane MS 1570*), 21r.

27. Domingo Martínez, *Compendio histórico de la apostólica provincial San Gregorio de Philipinas de religiosos menores descalzos de N.P. San Francisco* (Madrid: Imprenta de la viuda de Manuel Fernández, 1756), 182.

28. García Barriúso, *La Monja de Carrión*, 91.

organizer, the Disclaced Franciscan custos of the Philippines, Fernando Moraga.[29] Luisa de la Ascensión's miraculous rescues were also reported by mariners in the Indies.[30] Perhaps this is why a ship built in the vicinity of Acaponeta, Mexico on its Pacific coast was named after her. Between 1632 and 1636, the frigate, *Madre Luisa de la Ascensión*, made several voyages of exploration along the Baja Californian coast, naming islands, one of them after the Conception, a toponymic transformation of the landscape. Had Luisa de la Ascensión known of it, one suspects that she would have wholeheartedly approved given her activism in defense of the Immaculate Conception doctrine.[31]

Not all members of Luisa de la Ascensión's missionary network were male religious. In the summer of 1620, the Poor Clare abbess, Jerónima de la Asunción of Toledo, and seven companions, including two nuns from Mother Juana de la Cruz's convent in Cubas, left Spain to undertake the first foundation of a convent in the Philippines under the First Rule of Saint Clare of Assisi.[32] At Mother Jerónima's behest, one of the nuns, Ana de Cristo, composed an account of their journey. Ana de Cristo records that prior to their departure from Seville, it had been made known to Mother Jerónima, their "captain," that the nuns would be accompanied mystically on their voyage for God's glory, by Saint Clare of Assisi, Saint Teresa of Ávila, and the [saint] of Carrión.[33] When they reached Mexico City, the nuns learned that Luisa de la Ascensión had already appeared in the viceregal capital via a vision, perhaps a bilocation, to a member of the city's Con-

---

29. Martínez Domingo, *Compendio histórico*, 153.

30. For her maritime interventions in the Indies, see Pedro Balbas, *Relación de la causa de Soror Luisa de la Ascensión*, 153r.

31. Regarding the frigate, Madre Luisa de la Ascensión, see Miguel León-Portilla, *La California Mexicana: Ensayos acerca de su historia* (Universidad Nacional Autónoma de México, Universidad Nacional Autónima de Baja California: Mexico City, 2000), 151–88.

32. Jerónima de la Asunción uses the term, "First Rule" of Saint Clare; see Pedro Ruano Santa Teresa, *La V.M. Sor Jerónima de la Asunción: Fundadora del Monasterio de Santa Clara de Manila y la primera mujer misionera en Filipinas* (Madrid: J. Vicente, 1993), 117. The "First Rule" followed by the nuns in Manila probably was an adaption by Saint Colette of France of Saint Clare's unmitigated rule (stipulating that her community live by alms alone). The Colettine reform and its rule were first introduced in Spain in the fifteenth century with the foundation of the reformed Discalced Convent of Santa Clara in Gandía. Other foundations followed, including the Convent of the Descalzas Reales in Madrid in the sixteenth century; see Ignacio Omaechervarría, *Las clarisas a través de los siglos* (Madrid: Editorial Cisneros, 1972), 101.

33. Sor Ana de Cristo, *Historia de nuestra santa madre Jerónima de la Asunción*, 1623–1629 (Toledo: Archivo del Monasterio de Santa Isabel de los Reyes), 83v. I thank Sarah Owens for providing me with this reference from Ana de Cristo's manuscript.

vent of Santa Clara, Mother Leonor de los Ángeles, a *mulata* esteemed for her sanctity.[34]

During their stay in Mexico City, Mother Jerónima and the nuns received several letters from Luisa de la Ascensión in support of their mission.[35] In one of them, Mother Luisa prophesied that their Manila foundation would result in "boundless glory for my sweet Jesus." To quote Sarah Owens, "Sor Luisa's words must have provided tremendous encouragement to the small group of founders, especially because the most difficult part of their journey still lay ahead of them."[36] As an abbess who had attempted the controversial reform of her own Clarist convent in the 1610s, Luisa de la Ascensión fully supported Jerónima de la Asunción's effort to implement the First Rule of Saint Clare in Manila, stipulating that the community be supported by alms alone. In one of the letters Luisa de la Ascensión sent to Mexico, she advised Mother Jéromina to "persevere with the First Rule and not to admit any mitigation of it."[37] In 1623, when a Franciscan prelate attempted to do just that, the indomitable Mother Jerónima persisted, writing to Philip IV of Spain to protest, citing the words of the "holy Mother Luisa de Carrión" in her defense.[38] It is possible that at some point Jerónima de la Asunción would have written to Luisa de la Ascensión in reply. If so, hers, like many other "letters and relations that came from the Indies" would have been read aloud by the Carrión nuns in their convent refectory, the community saying prayers for their sisters in Manila.[39]

Yet another Franciscan destined for the Pacific missions and devoted to Luisa de la Ascensión, was Antonio de Santa María from the town of San Millán, along the Camino of Santiago, east of Carrión. Professing as a Discalced Franciscan in Salamanca, he went on to serve first in the Philippines, then as confessor to the Franciscan nuns of Macao, including the visionary nun founder, Magdalena de la Cruz, from Mother Juana de la Cruz's convent of Cubas, who had accompanied Jerónima de la Asunción to Manila. Santa María was later appointed the order's prefect of China. In 1669, he died in Canton, according to his Discalced Franciscan hagiographer, holding on tightly to one of Luisa de la Ascensión's

34. Sarah E. Owens, "Crossing Mexico (1620–1621): Franciscan Nuns and Their Journey to the Philippines," *The Americas* 72, 4 (2015): 602.

35. Owens, "Crossing Mexico," 592–93.

36. Owens, "Crossing Mexico," 602.

37. For a transcription of her letter to Philip IV, see Pedro Ruano Santa Teresa, *La V.M. Sor Jerónima de la Asunción: Fundadora del Monasterio de Santa Clara de Manila y la primera mujer misionera en Filipinas* (Madrid: J. Vicente, 1993), 115–17.

38. For an account of the conflict between Jerónima de la Asunción and her Franciscan superior written by her confessor, see Ginés de Quesada, OFM, *Exemplo de todas las virtudes de la venerable madre Geronyma de la Assumpcion* (Madrid: Antonio Marin, 1717), 295–325.

39. *Relación de la causa de Soror Luisa de la Ascensión*, 149v, 160r.

images of Christ Crucified that "he always carried with him," possibly an engraving from Flanders that she sometimes handed out to the faithful.[40]

Further evidence of Luisa de la Ascensión's missionary network also comes from one of the membership books of the her Immaculist religious confraternity, preserved at the National Library of Spain.[41] On 9 June 1618, some thirty officials and other religious from the Indies present at the order's general chapter in Salamanca enrolled in it.[42] Of interest among the signatures are those of the linguists, Luis Gerónimo de Oré (born in Peru, commissioner of the Province of Santa Elena in Florida, appointed shortly after the general chapter bishop of Chile) and Agustín de Cevallos (who spoke several Indigenous languages and was active in Costa Rica).[43] The Spanish missionary nun founders of the Convent of Santa Clara in Manila were also members of the confraternity, recording their signatures along with their conventual sisters in Cubas and Toledo shortly before leaving for the Philippines, additional confirmation of the sisterhood of solidarity that existed between them, Luisa de la Ascensión and the Santa Clara Carrión community.

Another notable missionary who joined the confraternity at the order's general chapter of 1618 was Isidro Ordóñez.[44] Best known as the controversial friar on the New Mexico mission who in the early 1610s had jailed and excommunicated its governor, Juan de Peralta, in part for his starvation of its Indigenous peoples, Ordóñez was called back to Mexico City and reprimanded by the Mexican Inquisition for having overstepped his authority in 1617.[45] Ordóñez soon left for Spain and the general chapter of 1618, evidently residing there until his return to Mexico in 1626.[46] In a letter Luisa de

---

40. Juan de San Antonio, *Franciscanos Descalzos en Castilla: La Vieja Chronica de la Santa Provincia de San Pablo* (Salamanca: Imprenta de la Santa Cruz), 280.

41. BNE MS 8540, *Firmas de los miembros de los conventos y monasterios pertenecientes a la Hermandad.*

42. BNE MS 8540, *Firmas de los miembros*, 74v.

43. Regarding Oré, see Alexandra Parma Cook and Noble David Cook, *Luis Gerónimo de Oré: The World of an Andean Franciscan from the Frontiers to the Centers of Power* (Baton Rouge: Louisiana State University, 2024).

44. Regarding Ordóñez's years in New Mexico during the Oñate and Peralta governorships, see France V. Scholes and Lansing B. Bloom, "Friar Personnel and Missionary Chronology, 1598–1629, I," *New Mexico Historical Review* 19:4 (1944): 319–36.

45. On Ordóñez and the controversy, see M. Hidalgo Strolle, M. and J.H. Polt, ed., Fray Francisco Pérez Huerta, Report on the Conflict Between Pedro de Peralta, Governor of New Mexico, and Fray Isidro Ordóñez, Franciscan Commissary, 1617 (UC Berkeley: Research Center for Romance Studies, 2013). Retrieved from https://escholarship.org/uc/item/6gv962r9.

46. In June 1626 in Seville, both Ordóñez and his associate, Francisco de Guerra (a veteran of the Guatemalan mission), offered testimony on behalf of Ordóñez's servant,

la Ascensión sent to her brother in Madrid on 5 May 1626, she refers to alms received from Isidro Ordóñez, perhaps donated for prayers on his behalf or in exchange for some of her devotional items like the portrait or cross carried by the friars to the New Mexican missions in 1629 as related by the New Mexican custos, Alonso de Benavides in 1630.[47]

It is unknown whether Ordóñez ever visited the nun, but one of his associates, Pedro de Guerra, a member of the Guatemalan mission since 1593, did make the trip. In 1625, Guerra, having represented his province at the general chapter of 1625 in Rome, traveled to Carrión to ask Luisa de la Ascensión whether she thought he should retire to a contemplative life in his Franciscan home province of Santiago in Northern Spain or return to the mission.[48] Her response to Guerra, according to his chronicler's reconstruction of their conversation, was that he was still needed in Guatemala (where there was a shortage of priests) to defend its Indigenous people (the "poor Indians") and to instruct them in the Christian faith to ensure their salvation. Guerra went back to Guatemala where while serving as its provincial he died in 1648.

To return to Mother Luisa's confraternity book at the BNE: a perusal of its folio pages reveals that most signatures among the 10,000 or so included dates from between 1616 and the early 1620s. However, two missionaries enrolled later, on 9 November 1630, likely in Madrid at the Monastery of San Francisco el Grande. The first, Juan Ortiz Nieto, a creole born in the New Kingdom of Granada or Colombia, placed his signature at the bottom of the folio page containing those of the officials of Indies present at the general chapter of 1618, declaring that "I sign with all my heart and will here." The second friar and the Portuguese New Mexican custos, Alonso de Benavides, signed elsewhere in the confraternity book because he clearly would have needed more space to write the longer oath below:

Philippe de Meneses, who had accompanied Ordóñez to Spain from Mexico and wanted to return with him there. See Archivo General de Indias, Isidro Ordóñez, Contratación, 5395, N. 12, 1r–3r.

47. See Jesús Rebollo Prieto, Jesús, "Las escritoras de Castilla y León (1400–1800): Ensayo bibliográfico (PhD diss., Universidad Nacional de Educación a Distancia [Madrid], 2006), 304.

48. Francisco Francisco Vázquez, *Crónica de la Provincia del Santísimo Nombre de Jesús de Guatemala de la Orden de N. Seráfico Padre San Francisco en el Reino de la Nueva España*, vol. III, ed. Lázaro Lamadrid (Guatemala: Centro América, 1940), 100–102. Regarding the vocational conflicts veteran friars experienced in determining whether to continue to serve as missionaries in the field or return to their contemplative conventual lives (which Guerra's case illustrates), see Steven E. Turley, *Franciscan Spirituality and Mission in New Spain, 1524–1599: Conflict Under the Sycamore Tree (Luke 19: 1–10)*, (Farnham: Ashgate, 2014), 160–61.

> On behalf of all the conversions and provinces of New Mexico where our Seraphic religion has planted our holy Catholic faith, and has taught and preached the Immaculate Conception of Our Lady, the Virgin Mary, I again, Fray Alonso de Benavides, custodian of that province in my name and in its, promise the same defense of the Most Holy Virgin to whose mystery I dedicate those conversions, towns and churches; and on behalf of all the religious and on behalf of all the secular Spaniards, and all the Indians of those provinces I swear, promise, and sign on 9 November 1630, Fray Alonso de Benavides.[49]

Significantly, in Benavides's *Memorial* addressed to Philip IV of Spain on the spiritual and temporal treasures of New Mexico, published in Madrid on his arrival in 1630, Mother Luisa of Carrión and her devotional objects had featured prominently. As Benavides relates, in the late 1620s Franciscans had carried with them on the New Mexican mission one of Luisa de la Ascensión's crosses, which a friar had placed on the eyes of a Indigenous Moqui (Hopi) boy who had been blind from birth, miraculously giving him sight, resulting in the conversion of 10,000 Moquis.[50] Benavides also describes how the Xumano Indigenous people, who claimed to have been visited many times by a mysterious woman evangelist urging them to convert to Christianity, were shown Luisa de la Ascensión's portrait and asked if she were the woman in question. The Xumanos told them that although the woman preacher was dressed like Luisa de la Ascensión, she was younger and more beautiful. As is well known, Benavides later identified María de Ágreda as the evangelist in a letter to Mexican friars published in Madrid in 1631.[51] Nonetheless, subsequent European editions of Benavides's 1630 *Memorial*, published in French, Dutch, German, and Latin in the early 1630s, all included forewords to the reader identifying Luisa de la Ascensión as the nun evangelist appearing to the Xumanos. Behind these editions most probably, was Luisa de la Ascensión's indefatigable promoter and former confessor, Pedro de Castro, appointed by Philip IV in 1625 as the new confessor to the governess of the Spanish Netherlands, daughter of Philip II of Spain, Isabel Clara Eugenia. But Luisa de la Ascensión's confessor in Carrión, Domingo de Aspe, also took issue with Benavides's letter of 1631, published in Madrid, *Tanto se saco*, which had identified María de

49. Biblioteca Nacional de España MS 8540, 213v.

50. Alonso de Benavides, *Memorial que fray Juan de Santander, Comisario General de Indias, presenta a la Magestad Católica* (Madrid: Imprenta Real, 1630), 36–39.

51. See the Benavides letter of 1631, titled "Tanto que se saco," in Frederick Webb Hodge, George P. Hammond, Agapito Rey, eds., *Fray Alonso de Benavides' Revised Memorial of 1634* (Albuquerque: University of New Mexico Press, 1945), 135–43.

Ágreda as the nun preacher. A copy having come into his hands, he wrote to Benavides to complain in 1632.[52] Undoubtedly that is why in a subsequent *Memorial of 1634* (which remained in manuscript form) Benavides makes sure to mollify the supporters of Mother Luisa as the nun preacher by recounting the testimony of another missionary, Martín de Arvide, whom Benavides had sent to convert the Apaches in western New Mexico. In the 1634 *Memorial* Benavides writes that Arvide had informed him personally that he knew that Mother Luisa de la Ascensión had been transported many times to preach the Catholic faith to the Apaches and that they knew her by her name.[53] In his 1634 *Memorial*, Benavides also identifies the friar who had restored the sight of a Moqui boy as Francisco de Porras, adding that he used the "original" cross (meaning that it had come from Luisa de la Ascensión herself), "whenever he preached."[54] Importantly, Benavides also discloses that Juan de Santander, the Commissary General of the Indies in 1630, and a great devotee of Luisa de la Ascensión (who maintained that she had been the nun preacher who had appeared to the Xumanos) had gone to Carrión to investigate the matter. There he met with Domingo de Aspe, Luisa de la Ascensión's confessor, who showed him the hagiography of his confessant he had written, which included accounts of her bilocations that Santander copied and on his return to Madrid, showed to Benavides.[55]

If Luisa de la Ascensión and her relics were assisting the friars' conversions in the Indies, in a reversal, a friar returning from the Indies once helped Luisa de la Ascensión in a conversion closer to home. According to testimony of Philip IV of Spain's secretary, Don Sebastián de Contreras, around the year of 1634, he went to see Luisa de la Ascensión, taking with him a slave, who spoke to her and received one of her crosses, who then and there

52. Domingo de Aspe, Carta al P. Alonso de Benavides, custodio de las Indias, Carrión, 28 de agosto de 1632, Archivo Histórico Nacional de España, Inquisición, Leg. 3706, caja 1, 108. To bolster his case for the sanctity of Luisa de la Ascensión, Aspe mentions that María de Ágreda approved of her spirit and she, along with the Clarist nun Juana Rodríguez of Burgos, communicated orally and in writing with Mother Luisa via their confessors; Aspe, Tercera parte de la vida de Soror Luisa de la Ascensión, AHN, Inq. Leg. 3709, 55v. On the circulation of Benavides's 1631 letter in manuscript form in Spanish Franciscan circles at the time, see Nogar, *Quill and Cross in the Borderlands*, 36.

53. Frederick Webb Hodge, George P. Hammond, and Agapito Rey, eds., *Fray Alonso de Benavides' Revised Memorial of 1634* (Albuquerque: University of New Mexico Press, 1945), 79.

54. Webb Hodge, et al., eds., *Fray Alonso de Benavides' Revised Memorial of 1634*, 75–77.

55. Nogar, *Quill and Cross in the Borderlands*, 27.

decided to accept the Christian faith. On their return to Madrid, the custos of Florida, Alonso de Jesús, provided the new Christian with the catechetical instruction that he needed.[56] While in Spain, Alonso de Jesús also recruited friars to serve on the Florida mission departing in 1635. Maynard Geiger's biographical dictionary of the Floridian friars reveals that several missionaries that Alonso de Jesús recruited for the 1635 mission belonged to the same Spanish Franciscan province of La Concepción as Luisa de la Ascensión, attesting to the nexus between the local and the global.[57] To cite an earlier example, Gregorio de Movilla, definitor of the Province of Santa Elena in 1621, was himself born in Carrión de los Condes, later professing in the Concepción convent of Calahorra. Did friars on the Florida mission visit Carrión? If they did not, they would have had ample opportunities to acquire the nun's devotional items inundating Spain in the 1620s and 1630s, perhaps taking them to Florida.

Finally, not all missionaries who visited Mother Luisa were Spanish. During his meeting with Mother Luisa in 1633, the English friar Francis Bell, made sure to ask her whether he ought to obey his superiors and go on the mission in England or Scotland as his superiors were intending, or remain on the continent. Bell reports that she told him that he should obey his superiors since they knew what was best for the "health of his soul and God's glory." In January 1635, the Italian Jesuit, Marcello Mastrilli, later martyred in Nagasaki, Japan, in 1637, sent a letter from Madrid to a fellow Jesuit in Naples in which he stated his intention to go to Carrión, especially to see the "great servant of God."[58]

Conclusion

In Peter Burke's seminal essay, "How to Become a Counter-Reformation Saint," he singles out Luisa de la Ascensión as a nun who in virtue of her name recognition, good works and miracles was on a fast track to become one had it not been for her shocking inquisitorial trial, beginning in spring 1635.[59] The Inquisition's case against Luisa de la Ascensión, brought about to a great extent because she was being treated as though she were already

56. García Barriúso, *La Monja de Carrión*, 481.

57. Maynard Geiger, "Biographical Dictionary of the Franciscans in Spanish Florida and Cuba (1528–1841)," *Franciscan Studies* 21 (1940): V–140.

58. See his letter reproduced in Gio Battista Mastrilli, *Compendio della Vita, e Morte del P. Marcello Mastrilli* (Naples: Luc'Antonio di Fusco, 1671), 156–57.

59. Peter Burke, "How to Become a Counter-Reformation Saint," *The Counter-Reformation: The Essential Readings*, ed. David M. Luedke (Hoboken: Wiley-Blackwell, 1999), 134.

canonized, involved numerous charges of false sanctity, the unauthorized nature of indulgences said to have been granted her relics, as well as the unauthorized status of her Immaculist confraternity.[60]

To the amazement of many, on orders from Madrid, in the spring of 1635, during Holy Week, the elderly Luisa de la Ascensión was transported to Valladolid and housed in a convent of Augustinian Recollect nuns where she was subjected to daily interrogations by an inquisitor sent from Madrid that summer. Franciscans were barred from seeing her. However, after the departure of the Madrid inquisitor, other religious were granted permission to visit her. For example, Francisco de los Santos records in a general chronicle of the Hieronymite order that the Spanish prior, Domingo de Villaescusa, sent a monk to see Luisa de la Ascensión in Valladolid to tell her that he was praying for her because he knew that her prayers had helped so many others. In turn, Luisa de la Ascensión told the monk to tell Villaescusa that she would do the same for him; and she requested that when he became a bishop to remember her. Shortly thereafter, Philip IV appointed Villaescusa bishop of Chiapas, and later bishop of the Yucatán, confirming Luisa de la Ascensión's prescience for the Hieronymites.[61]

In 1637, while Luisa de la Ascensión's trial was still underway, the Inquisition issued an edict censoring all material objects relating to Luisa de la Ascensión in Spain and the Spanish Empire.[62] Referenced in the ban were all crosses, images of Christ and the Baby Jesus, engravings, illuminated parchments, signatures, portraits, engravings, rosary beads, and any relations concerning their privileges and graces, and all publications and manuscripts of Luisa de la Ascensión's life or relations referring to her. According to Carolina Yeveth Aguilar García, on 7 November 1637, a copy of the edict was hung from the principal door of the church of the royal mines of Taxco, Mexico.[63] No doubt, the Madre Luisa de la Ascen-

60. Politics also were involved: Mother Luisa, along with Antonio Daza, and the provincial of the Concepción, Alonso del Prado (later a commissary general of the Indies), were also repeatedly questioned by inquisitors about any revelations she had made concerning a very great person of the realm; see Carta del inquisidor, Juan Dionisio Portacarrero, 31 marzo 1636, AHN Inq. Leg. 3704, caja 3, 113r–114r.

61. Francisco de los Santos, *Quarta parte de la Historia de la orden de San Jerónimo* (Madrid: Bernardo de Diego, 1680), 475.

62. For a copy of the edict printed in Mexico City, see "Inquisición de México, 1637, July 10, Edict banning devotional objects, images, texts, etc. connected to Luisa de la Ascensión" (The University of Notre Dame Inquisition Archives, Inquistio-230).

63. Carolyn Yeveth Aguilar García, "Entre la verdad y la mentira: Control y censura inquisitorial en torno a las reliquias en la Nueva España, *Letras Históricas* 7 (Otoño 2012–invierno 2013): 23.

sión silver mine, registered in 1635 in Nuevo León, Mexico, had its name changed.[64]

Although thousands of material items relating to Luisa de la Ascensión in Spain and its colonies were turned over to inquisitors following the published edict, not all of Luisa de la Ascensión's devotees complied or complied immediately with it. The archbishop of La Plata, Francisco de Borja, for example, refused outright on two occasions to turn over his Mother Luisa rosary beads to inquisitors; they only obtained them after his death in 1643.[65] Others, like the widow of a Franciscan syndic in Zacatecas, Mexico, handed in her rosary beads but kept hidden in her desk another valuable relic.[66] Inquisitors deemed prophecies concerning Mother Luisa equally problematic. In 1653, Juan de Osuna, a secular official from Mérida, in the Western highlands of Venezuela, was transported to the Tribunal of the Holy Office in Cartagena, charged with sorcery for claiming that a treasure located in the nearby sierra could be used to defeat the Ottoman Empire, elevate Mary's Immaculate Conception to church dogma, and achieve the canonization of Luisa de la Ascensión.[67]

In 1648, years after her death in Valladolid, Luisa de la Ascensión was finally absolved of all charges, thanks to her able Franciscan defenders.[68] In 1655, the Franciscan minister general, Pedro Manero, secured permission from the Inquisition to return Mother Luisa's body to Carrión, albeit in secrecy, without any fanfare.[69] Despite the stipulation, when news reached Mexico City, a gazette reported that all Franciscan convents in the viceregal capital celebrated the event, friars and nuns ringing their church bells and singing the "Te Deum Laudamus."[70]

Even so, the inquisitorial ban issued in 1637 in Spain and the Indies on Luisa de la Ascensión relics remained in place; in 1668 and again in 1678 the

---

64. Regarding Francisco Bravo de Lagunas's registration of the mine, Madre Luisa de la Ascensión, on 20 August 1635; see Israel Cavazos Garza, *La Virgen del Roble: Historia de una tradición regiomontana* (Monterrey: Impresora del Norte, S.A., 1959), 28.

65. Paulino Casteñeda Delgado and Pilar Hernández Aparicio, *La Inquisición de Lima*, vol. 2 (Madrid: Editorial Demos, 1995), 519.

66. José Arlegui, *Crónica de la Provincia de N.S.P.S. Francisco de Zacatecas* (Mexico City: Por cumplido, Calle de los Rebeldes 2, 1851), 354–55.

67. Anna María Splendiani, José Enrique Sánchez Bohórquez, Emma Ceclia Luque de Salazar, *Cincuenta años de inquisición en el Tribunal de Cartagena de* Indias*: 1610–1660* vol. 3 (Santafé de Bogotá: Centro Editorial Javeriano, CEJA, 1997), 383–84.

68. On Luisa de la Ascensión's trial, see García Barriúso, *La Monja de Carrión*, 275–508.

69. García Barriúso, *La Monja de Carrión*, 505.

70. Francisco García Figueroa, ed. *Documentos para la historia de Méjico*, vol. 1 (Mexico: Imprenta de Juan de Navarro, 1853), 309.

Roman Congregation of Indulgences officially condemned them too.[71] By the end of the seventeenth century, the weight of these prohibitions had effectively consigned the once global living saint to a historical oblivion from which she has only recently reemerged.[72] This essay has sought to recover the figure of Luisa de la Ascensión as a strong and influential spiritual leader of the Franciscan order in the tradition of the "living saint," whose wide religious network included its missionaries, and whose religious activities had an impact on them. As is clear from the evidence presented, missionaries valued Luisa de la Ascensión's spiritual counsel and they used her devotional items as supports in their evangelical work. Just as importantly, the intercessory prayers Mother Luisa said for the missionaries must have strengthened their faith as they preached, taught, and ministered to new converts to Catholicism across the early modern world.[73]

---

71. Henry Charles Lea, *A History of the Inquisition in Spain*, vol. IV (New York: The MacMillan Company, 1907), 36–39.

72. In addition to García Barriúso's lengthy, essential biographical study, *La Monja de Carrión* (1986), see a recent discussion of the nun by Carlos Eire, *They Flew: A History of the Impossible* (New Haven and London: Yale University Press, 2023), 280–88. According to Eire: "In essence, Luisa has been absolved but relegated to oblivion and denied any veneration as a saint," 288.

73. My thanks to Timothy Johnson for organizing this conference and to Flagler College for hosting it.

Chapter 14

Early Modern Global Stagings of Sor María de Jesús de Ágreda and La mística ciudad de dios

Anna M. Nogar, *University of New Mexico*

Contemporary approaches to early modern communities of reading enrich and broaden our understanding of the seventeenth century Conceptionist nun, mystic, and abbess Sor María de Jesús de Ágreda. While many studies of Sor María and her foundational Marian work *La mística ciudad de dios* center on her biography or on close readings (theological and literary) of the text,[1] a more expansive approach that considers questions of audience and readership illuminates her extraordinary arc of influence. It also sheds light on the facets of her writing and biography that achieved lasting resonance from the late seventeenth century on, a prominence brought about by their publication, reading, and interpretation around the globe.

To this end, this essay focuses on the worldwide circulation of Sor María's writing in text, approached through analyses of two different groups of documents and their implied audiences. First, I examine a published eighteenth-century play, a *comedia de santos*, about Sor María and consider how her saint's life (*vita*) and *La mística ciudad de dios* are presented in it.[2] This reading

1. Anna M. Nogar, *Quill and Cross in the Borderlands: Sor María de Ágreda and the Lady in Blue, 1628 to the Present* (Notre Dame: University of Notre Dame Press, 2018) and Rosilie Hernánedez, *Immaculate Conceptions* (Toronto: University of Toronto Press, 2019).

2. As I explain in *Quill and Cross in the Borderlands*, Sor María's vita was the primary public-facing source for information about her multifaceted life. Published many times both as the preface to *La mística ciudad de dios* (referred to in the text as the *Prólogo galeato*) and as a separate document (the *Relación de la vida de la Venerable Madre Sor María de Jesús*), the text could be found in collections throughout Spain and New Spain (Nogar *Quill and Cross*, 38–39, 89–102). For the original texts, see Joseph Ximénez Samaniego, *Relación de la vida de la venerable Madre Sor María de Jesús de Ágreda* (Madrid: Imprenta de la Causa de la Venerable Madre, 1727) and María de Jesús de Ágreda and Joseph Ximénez Samaniego, *Mystica ciudad de Dios, milagro de su omnipotencia, y abismo de la gracia: historia divina, y vida de la Virgen Madre de Dios, reyna, y señora nuestra* (Madrid: Imprenta

illuminates how promotion of Sor María's case for sainthood emphasized specific aspects of her biography and *La mística ciudad de dios* for the public using a form designed for exhibiting saintly lives. Second, I analyze devotional literature produced in eighteenth-century Mexico and South India that advanced beliefs and practices relating to St. Joseph derived from *La mística ciudad de dios.* These devotional texts excerpted portions of *La mística ciudad de dios* that presented St. Joseph's biography and compiled, published, and translated these into prayerful praxis, establishing Sor María's contribution to global Josephine beliefs and popular practices.

TRANSLATING TEXT TO STAGE
La coronista más grande de la más sagrada historia Sor María de Jesús de Ágreda

Published in Madrid in 1736, the *comedia de santos* (or play) entitled *La coronista más grande de la más sagrada historia. Sor María de Jesús de Ágreda*[3] has received scant critical attention. The play's author, Manuel Francisco de Armesto, was a member of the Spanish court as well as the "Secretario del Secreto de la Santa Inquisición"[4] though further details regarding the author are sparse. Released in two parts, *La coronista más grande* was printed and sold by the Librería de Joseph de Cueñas, one of the presses that published texts generated by the Imprenta de la Causa de la Venerable Sor María de Jesus de Ágreda, the press charged with promoting Sor María's candidacy for sainthood throughout the eighteenth century.[5] The Cueñas storefront was located on Madrid's Plazuela de los Herradores, its location indicated for the play's potential readers by the *Gaceta de Madrid*, which announced the publications of Part One and Part Two of the play in its January 31, 1736, and October 9th, 1736, editions, respectively.[6]

---

de la Causa de la Venerable Madre, 1720). The author of Sor María's vita, Joseph Ximénez Samaniego, OFM, knew Sor María during her life and served as the Minister General of the Franciscan Order in Spain. In that position, he advanced the reading of Sor María's work and her case for canonization after her death: P. Víctor Añíbarro. "El P. José Ximénez Samaniego, Ministro General O.F.M. y Obispo de Plascencia (Conclusión)," *Archivo Ibero-Americano* (July–September 1944): 353–88.

3. Manuel Francisco de Armesto y Castro, *La coronista más grande de la más sagrada historia. Sor María de Jesús de Ágreda* (Madrid: En la Imprenta de Alfonso de Mora, 1736). On the contemporary study of the text, see Nogar, *Quill and Cross in the Borderlands,* 83–84.

4. Ivy Lilian McClelland, *Ideological Hesitancy in Spain, 1700–1750* (Liverpool: Liverpool University Press, 1991), 130.

5. Nogar, *Quill and Cross in the Borderlands,* 74–79.

6. Nogar, *Quill and Cross in the Borderlands,* 83.

Figure 1. Sor María de Jesús de Ágreda, writing *La mística ciudad de dios*. Artist unknown. Museo del Virreinato, Tepozotlán. Image courtesy of Cristina Cruz González.

If the eighty-seven-page play was performed, its production was not recorded in the *Gaceta de Madrid*, nor in similar outlets. Given the complexity of the elaborate sets or *tramoya* described within the play, and the difficulty of their implementation, the play may never have been staged. This would not have been unusual for a comedia de santos, a genre which Golden Age theater scholar Thomas Case notes "never seem to have been staged and seldom are read as literary material."[7] In the absence of contemporaneous commentary on the play, we might consider instead the messages about Sor María and her writing the work conveyed for its intended audiences, keeping in mind the early eighteenth century campaign to see her writing circulated and her canonization advanced, spearheaded by Spanish Franciscans.[8] Antonio Téllez de Azevedo offered the play its approbation, confirming that Armesto had met expectations for structure and content in a dramatic work, succeeding in "([balancing] the extremes, that, while observing the exact Rules, he has managed with notable approval of the Learned to relate to the general amusement of the ignorant, earning from all the greatest

7. Thomas E. Case, "Understanding Lope de Vega's 'Comedia de santos.'" *Hispanófila* 125 (January 1999): 11.

8. Nogar, *Quill and Cross in the Borderlands*, 67–76.

appreciation)"[9] The play's doctrinal aim is reiterated through Azevedo's affirmation that the work did not relate "any such element in opposition to our Holy Faith and good practices" (Aprobación),[10] even as it connected with the popular audiences to which it was directed.

The parameters of the comedia de santos genre shaped the content of *La coronista más grande*. This genre sought to display the virtuous aspects of a saint or holy person's life, often with didactic as well as spiritual ends. The central characters in a comedia de santos were either canonized saints or figures of popular religious devotion;[11] the latter was Sor María's case.[12] Aesthetic rules for comedias de santos were less proscribed than those of other dramatic forms of the time, and a similarly diversity of names was applied to the genre. In the seventeenth century, they were referred to as "comedia divina," "de santidad," "a lo de divino," or de "apariencia y tramoyas."[13] All the elements suggested by such terms figure into *La coronista más grande*, whose focus on the saintly aspects of Sor María's life, as well as on the exegetical and theological ideas presented in *La mística ciudad de dios*, is relayed within a plot that advances thanks to the conventions of the comedia. These conventions include a *capa y espada* storyline; the intervention of a humorous character (the *gracioso*); and the interjection of elaborate, symbolic stage structures (*tramoya*) deployed in concert with the play's exposition of its spiritual messages. The play includes other elements common to the comedia de santos, among them: the periodic appearance of the antagonistic Devil; the locating of action within a specific historical framework (which in this case includes King Felipe IV's 1643 visit to Ágreda); and advancing doctrine pronounced by the Council of Trent, specifically devotion to the saints and to the Virgin Mary.

The play's six acts, or *jornadas*, are split evenly between Part I and Part II. Each jornada involves three intersecting movements: 1) the capa y espada plot, which provides the play's dramatic momentum; 2) biographical elements of Sor María's life deriving from her vita; and 3) the staging of specific episodes from the lives of the Virgin Mary and Jesus as rendered in *La mística ciudad de dios*. Each movement of this complex intermingling provides a new vantage point from which audiences could understand Sor María as a religious

9. "Balancear de suerte los extremos, que ceñido a las precisas Reglas, ha conseguido, con la principal aceptación de los Doctores, enlazar la común diversión de los ignorante, mereciéndose de todos el mayor aprecio." McClelland, *Ideological Hesitancy in Spain, 1700–1750*, 132.

10. "Cosa alguna que se oponga a nuestra Santa Fe y buenas costumbres," "Aprobación," Armesto, *Coronista*, trans. Anna M. Nogar.

11. Case, "Understanding Lope de Vega's 'Comedia de santos,'"19.

12. Sor María de Ágreda's canonization case was closed in 1773 by Clement XIV without resolution, It was reopened in 2018. See Nogar *Quill and Cross in the Borderlands*, 59.

13. Case, "Understanding Lope de Vega's 'Comedia de santos,'"16.

authorial figure. The capa y espada movement takes place in the town of Ágreda and in Sor María's convent. It is comprised of a love story and escapade featuring Sor María's real paternal uncle Médel Coronel,[14] his (fictional) love interest Doña Clara, a gracioso named Celio, and various authority figures from the town of Ágreda. In the complicated plot course characteristic of a comedia, Médel is separated from his love, sent away to battle. Although the battle is unnamed, it references seventeenth century conflicts at the Spanish border with Cataluña that occurred during Sor María's life. Various jealousies and misunderstandings are happily (and predictably) resolved, and the Sor María character is portrayed as wise counsel and judge throughout.

The second movement presents biographical elements from Sor María's life drawn directly from her saintly biography. Both as the prologue to *La mística ciudad de dios* and as a separate publication, the *Relación de la Vida de la Venerable Madre María de Jesús de Ágreda*,[15] her vita achieved a wide readership.[16] The play represents major and minor elements of Sor María's biography. One of the play's main characters, Sor María's sister by birth, Sor Gerónima, did in reality live with Sor María in the family home-turned-convent, as the vita documents and the play indicates. King Felipe IV, Sor María's long-time correspondent, makes an important cameo appearance in the play's second part. Other elements of Sor María's vita pepper the dialogue between characters or emerge as exposition within the play. In Part One, Jornada Two,[17] a special *tramoya* (that is, a dramatic, mechanical scene device) is employed to explain how, by being declared the Virgin Mary's *vicaria*, an ill, underage Sor María becomes the abbess of her convent, a key moment of her *vita*.

The play's third movement stages episodes of *La mística ciudad de dios* as individual tramoya that abruptly punctuate the play's action. On example of this occurs in Part One, Jornada One[18] when the capa y espada plot is interrupted via an interjection during which the Virgin Mary's Immaculate Conception and birth by Saint Anne are described, and the Virgin Mary offers

14. Sor María's character cursorily acknowledges that she is related to Médel quite far along in the play.

15. Nogar *Quill and Cross in the Borderlands*, 75–76.

16. In preparing this article, I consulted a 1727 edition of the *Relación* published by the Imprenta de la Causa de la Venerable Madre, held at the Newberry Library. The inscription on the title page of the book provided an intriguing insight into its source: "Del convento de Mercenderos de Fuentes," perhaps referring to a community of Discalced Mercederians in the Spanish town of Fuentes de Andalucía (https://www.newadvent.org/cathen/10197b.htm). The text's marginalia suggest a readership for Sor María's biography that extended well beyond Franciscan communities.

17. Armesto, *Coronista*, 20–21.

18. Armesto, *Coronista*, 14–15.

divine benediction for Sor María's composition of *La mística ciudad de dios*. This divine sanctioning extends over Sor María and her Marian oeuvre and is reiterated throughout the play.

Each jornada of *La coronista más grande* include all three of these movements: the capa y espada plot, Sor María's biography, and specific theological/exegetical ideas from *La mística ciudad de dios*. Taken as a whole, therefore, the play teaches audiences about Sor María as a candidate for beatification by performing key passages of her vita and emphasizing important features of her best-known work. In doing so, it illuminates our present-day understanding of what her 18th-century advocates viewed as the most salient and doctrinally singificant facets of her beatification case.

The play opens with an earthquake and the entrance of the Devil on a dragon; he states his opposition to the Virgin Mary's holiness, comparing her to a long line of female heroes from the Old Testament (Esther, Rachel and Judith) and establishing the Virgin's role in quashing his ruses.[19] His monologue continues, providing a comprehensive history of the Coronel family, including the conversion of their home into a convent. This portion acts, in effect, as a dramatization of the árboles genealógicos of the Coronel family created in Spain and abroad which drew from Sor María's biography.[20] The nun's mystical spiritual travels are referenced in Part One, Jornada Three,[21] and ideas regarding her celestial voyages (as in her attributed work, *Mapa de las orbes celestiales*) as well her bilocation to New Mexico are addressed.[22] The rumors of bilocation summon a visit from Felipe IV (Part Two, Jornada One) and her subsequent long exchange of letters with the king is discussed.[23] Also in Part Two, Jornada One, a particularly distinctive detail of the vita is enacted: Sor María is joined in her writing by St. Inés and St. Ursula, who support her as she works.[24] Sor María is shown throughout the play "as if she is writing,"[25] as she completes *La mística ciudad de dios*[26] and receives divine approbation for what she writes.[27] Not all features of Sor María's biography as described in her vita are included in the play, nor have I here described every instance of them. However, these representative exam-

19. Armesto, *Coronista*, 40–43.

20. See Anna M. Nogar,. "Genealogías hagiográficas y viajes coloniales: Sor María de Ágreda en las Filipinas." *Revista de Soria* 89 (Summer 2015): 151–59.

21. Armesto, *Coronista*, 40–43.

22. Armesto, *Coronista*, 46–47.

23. Armesto, *Coronista*, 50.

24. Armesto, *Coronista*, 65–66. References Ximénez Samaniego, *Relación*, 171.

25. "Como que está escribiendo." Armesto, *Coronista*, 84.

26. Armesto, *Coronista*, 78.

27. Armesto, *Coronista*, 84–86.

ples suggest that the play provided a detailed and accessible abridgement of Sor María's vita.

La coronista más grande accomplished similar expository ends with the dramatization of specific sections of *La mística ciudad de dios*. In Part One, their presentation is formulaic: each exegetic segment within the jornada is prefaced by the character Sor María writing what will be acted out, as detailed in the stage directions: "The Scene opens and we see Sor María, as if in her cell, writing down what is portrayed [in the tramoya]."[28] Then, the staging shifts dramatically to an elaborate tramoya (for example, the descent of the Archangel Gabriel), which enacts the section of *La mística ciudad de dios* that Sor María is shown to be writing.[29] Once the exposition of the theological/exegetical concept concludes, the tramoya is hidden away and the play's capa y espada action continues. This engineered representation serves the dual purposes of emphasizing Sor María's authorship of *La mística ciudad de dios* and bringing to light particular ideas she detailed in it. Each Jornada depicts a specific concept from *La mística ciudad de dios*: Part One, Jornada One presents the Immaculate Conception theology[30]; Part One, Jornada Two, the Annunciation[31]; and Part One, Jornada Three, the Nativity.[32] One could read the selection of episodes as representative of key elements of *La mística ciudad de dios* that Sor María's promoters wished to circulate.

Although Part Two also stages exegetic scenes taken from *La mística ciudad de dios*, it does not follow Part One's blueprint for their presentation. In Part Two, Jornada One, Sor María is attended by two angels as she writes of Christ's circumcision, including a discussion between the Virgin Mary and God the Father regarding its necessity.[33] In Part Two, Jornada Two, Christ's crucifixion is tenderly and heartbreakingly presaged in a tramoya that lifts several characters off the stage.[34] In the same act, the Adoration of the Magi is depicted in a separate set change, with the Virgin Mary admonishing Sor María to note the details of the vision.[35] The final act (Part Two, Jornada Three) includes two different scenes of approbation for Sor María's writing of *La mística ciudad de dios*, each presented with its own tramoya. The first depicts Anna the Prophetess and Simeon the High Priest offering their bless-

---

28. "Abre el foro, y se verá a Sor María como en su Celda, escribiendo lo que representa." Armesto, *Coronista*, 13.
29. Armesto, *Coronista*, 28–29.
30. Armesto, *Coronista*, 14–16.
31. Armesto, *Coronista*, 28–31.
32. Armesto, *Coronista*, 34–36.
33. Armesto, *Coronista*, 51–76.
34. Armesto, *Coronista*, 65–66.
35. Armesto, *Coronista*, 72–75.

ings over Sor María and her completed work about the Virgin,[36] with Anna saying "Receive, beloved daughter of my love, congratulations."[37] As the play's secular capa y espada plot is resolved, the last tramoya descends, with the virtues of Faith, Hope and Charity alternately exhorting and praising Sor María and her work as the Virgin and Christ take leave.[38]

Although I was unable to locate these last two concepts explicitly expressed in *La mística ciudad de dios*, they are staged in the exact manner as the other exegetic episodes that interpret the text: prefaced by a staging of Sor María writing, a short introduction of the concept that she writes about, and the descent of a special tramoya illustrating the idea. This leads me to conclude that the two episodes are likely present in *La mística ciudad de* dios. Even if they are not, the sensibility of divine approbation for Sor María's authorship of the Virgin Mary's autobiography they convey certainly is. These two instances reinforce that message for the audience.[39]

Perhaps unsurprisingly given the many layers the play interweaves, twentieth-century Golden Age theater critique found the amalgamation of elements in *La coronista más grande* dizzying: "*La coronista más grande*. . . , in its would-be picturesqueness, encloses a series of sermonettes delivered at strategic intervals by Sor María on the life of the Virgin, and set into a sensational love-story with as many trimmings illustrative magic and marvel as any drama could physically accommodate. The bid for spectator's attention and emotional cooperation determines every dramatic mood and verbal sound."[40] In the twenty-first century, building upon more recent scholarship on Sor María, the play might better be understood considering the 18th-century global distribution and interpretation of her writing urged on by contemporaneous beatification efforts.[41]

---

36. Armesto, *Coronista*, 78–79.

37. "Recibe, amada hija mía de mi amor la enhorabuena." Armesto, *Coronista*, 79.

38. Armesto, *Coronista*, 84–87.

39. Neither concept is explicitly depicted in the *Relación*, although the sense of divine approval for her authorship of *La mística ciudad de dios* is.

40. McClelland, *Ideological Hesitancy*, 130. The confusion regarding interpretation of *La coronista más grande* might result from a lack of familiarity with how its source material, *La mística ciudad de dios* and the *Relación*, represents figures such as the Virgin Mary, Jesus and Sor María herself. Regardless, the literary summary provided by I.L. McClelland in 1991 is hardly flattering: "This thoroughly inartistic play is nevertheless vivid in color and stimulating in its popular emotion. The episodes and fulsome sentimentality would certainly infect a vulgo-audience, including vulgo-clergy, with theatrical interpretations of reality. . . . For the instruction of the masses it seemed to preserve and so, in the absence of genius, to exaggerate familiar forms of public address, and to opposed innovations advocated by those who put more emphasis on plain reason than on imaginative feeling." McClelland, *Ideological Hesitancy*, 132.

41. Nogar *Quill and Cross in the Borderlands*, chps. 3–4.

The concepts derived from *La mística ciudad de dios* that the play portrays echoed across the globe. Mexican art historian Francisco de la Maza notes that several New Spanish representations of the Virgin Mary and Saint Joseph reproduce details specific to Sor María's writing, including paintings of Saint Joseph wearing a gold reliquary around his neck that contained the Christ child's foreskin, alluding to the rite of circumcision depicted in the play.[42] Two works of New Spanish art represent scenes of the Nativity paralleling that in *La coronista más grande*; José Rodríguez Carneros's *La adoración de los pastores* (1725) and sMiguel de Cabrera's *Adoración* (n.d.).[43] The Carneros piece includes figures St. Ana, St. Joachim, Elizabeth and Zacharias, and the Archangels Michael and Gabriel, as well as shepherds. This collection of figures is detailed in the Nativity described in *La mística ciudad de dios*. While *La coronista más grande* is unlikely the direct source for these and other interpretations, the play seems to signal which biographical, apocryphal, and theological concepts relating to *La mística ciudad de dios* and to Sor María herself were popularized through canonization efforts and the ongoing reading of her writing around the world.

La mística ciudad de dios and Devotion to St. Joseph

Current studies examining Sor María de Ágreda's writing invoke reconsideration of her erudite legacy, and invite the examination of under-explored topics arising from it. Recent research into her correspondence examines letters other than the well-documented communication with Felipe IV, including correspondence with the women of the royal family,[44] as well as with other nobles.[45] These studies enrich our critical understanding of the breadth of Sor María's circle of communication and the extent of her direct influence during her lifetime. The unpublished, yet far-reaching cosmological and metaphysical manuscript attributed to Sor María, the *Tratado de la luz y de la redondez de la tierra. . .*, is of ongoing consequence,[46] as much for the contemporaneous

42. Nogar *Quill and Cross in the Borderlands*, 136–37.

43. Nogar *Quill and Cross in the Borderlands*, 139.

44. Nieves Romero-Díaz, "Correspondencia entre la Venerable Sor María de Jesús de Ágreda y mujeres de la familia de Felipe IV." *Archivo Ibero-Americano*, 80 num. 290 (2020):33–106; and "'Lo que más nos importa': religión y política en las cartas entre la reina Mariana de Austria y sor María de Ágreda." *Bulletin of Spanish Studies*, 98.3 (2021): 335–59.

45. Consolación Baranda Leturio. *Cartas de sor María de Jesús de Ágreda a Fernando de Borja y Francisco de Borja (1628–1664): Estudio y edición* (Universidad de Valladolid: Universidad Ediciones, 201) and Nieves Romero-Díaz, "Tres cartas del príncipe Baltasar Carlos a Sor María de Ágreda," *Translat Library* 5, no. 1 (2023), accessed 10 May 2024 https://openpublishing.library.umass.edu/tl/article/id/429/.

46. Sor María de Ágreda, *Tratado de la redondez de la tierra*, ed. Judith Farré Vidal (Chapel Hill: University of North Carolina Press, 2023) and Clark Colahan, *The Visions*

astral frameworks to which the work relates[47] as for the possibilities of its present-day interpretation.[48] Contemporary interpretation of *La mística ciudad de dios* in relation to the Immaculate Conception theology illuminates both how it contributed to the doctrine's conceptual structures[49] and how its acceptance was entangled with efforts to make that theology dogma.[50] However, the Immaculate Conception was not the only apocryphal principle disclosed in *La mística ciudad de dios* that achieved popular adoption. Presented in the context of the Virgin Mary's biography, *La mística ciudad de dios* explains details of St. Joseph's life that are not found in other texts. Here, I consider the how ideas relating to St. Joseph expressed in *La mística ciudad de dios* were interpreted and applied by a worldwide readership. Within Sor María's descriptions of St. Joseph, one finds not only details of his biography, but also the enumeration of seven divine privileges granted to him, one of which relates to spiritual practices prescribed to attain a happy death.[51]

Two Mexican publications on prayers, dispositions and practices relating to St. Joseph, the *Septenario al gloriosissimo patriarca San Joseph de los siete privilegios de su Patrocinio, que refiere al V.V. María de Jesús de Ágreda en su Mística Ciudad de Dios*[52] and the *Novena mensal, de el transito de el santissimo patriarcha Sr. S. Joseph,*[53] help locate where his biography is located in *La mística ciudad de dios.* As the *Novena mensal* indicates, portions of his

---

of Sor María de Agreda: Writing Knowledge and Power (Tucson: University of Arizona Press, 1994).

47. Kathleen Cowther, "The Virgin and the Globe: The Cosmography of Sor María de Ágreda." *Early Modern Women*, 15.2 (Spring 2021):29–56 and Ran Segev, *Sacred Habitat* (University Park: Penn State University Press, 2023), 47–78.

48. Anna M. Nogar and Enrique Lamadrid. *Sisters in Blue/Hermanas de azul.* Illustrations by Amy Córdova (Albuquerque: University of New Mexico Press, 2017).

49. Rosilie Hernánedez, *Immaculate Conceptions* (Toronto: University of Toronto Press, 2019), 160–204.

50. Nogar, *Quill and Cross in the Borderlands*, 55–79.

51. The association between St. Joseph and a happy death is apocryphal, and Sor María is not the sole exponent of the idea. One source is a fifth century book called *The History of Joseph the Carpenter*, which relates that when St. Joseph was on his death bed, he was assured by the Virgin Mary and Christ that the good that he accomplished during his lifetime would be a solace to others. Knowing this, he passed peacefully. (https://www.newadvent.org/fathers/0805.htm)

52. María de Jesús de Ágreda, *Septenario al gloriosissimo patriarca Sr. San Joseph: de los siete privilegios de su patrocinio que reifere ha V.M. Maria de Jesús de Ágreda en su Mystica ciudad de Dios* (Mexico: Joseph de Jáuregui, 1785).

53. Joseph Manuel Sartorio. *Novena mensal, de el transito de el santissimo patriarcha Sr. S. Joseph: para implorar vna buena muerte: con las consideraciones sacadas de la Mystica ciudad de Dios. p 2. lib. 5.* (Mexico: En la Imprenta de la Bibliotheca [de México] y por su original reimpressa en Guatemala por Sebastian de Arévalo, 1766).

history are sown throughout the text. According to these publications, the seven privileges attributed to him can be found in Part 2, Book 5, Chapter 16, Number 893 of *La mística ciudad de dios* (*Septenario*) and St. Joseph's *feliz tránsito* is related as one of those privileges, in Part 2 Book 5 (*Novena mensal*). The important matter of St. Joseph's seven privileges was celebrated in print and in practice from the eighteenth century onward in Mexico and Guatemala.

The *Septenario al gloriosissimo patriarca San Joseph* was one of the most frequently printed excerpts of *La mística ciudad de dios* produced in colonial Mexico. As I discuss in *Quill and Cross in the Borderlands*, the *Septenario* was published at least 6 times in Mexico between 1726 and 1808: 1726, 1768, 1771, 1774, 1785, 1808.[54] It was published five times in Mexico City and once in Puebla, in 1771 by the Real Seminario Palafoxiano. The 1785 printing was published by the Congregación de San Felipe de Neri, renowned for the public preaching and prayers they carried out in the *oratorios* they occupied in Mexico City. Maintaining a consistent audience of Mexican readers and listeners for almost a century, the *Septenario* reveals important aspects of Sor María's writing on St. Joseph that were readily available to Mexican audiences.

As its title indicates, the *Septenario* draws primarily from Sor María's writing. It also references Doctor of the Church Santa Teresa de Ávila, called "La gran doctora mística" in the text. According to the *Septenario*'s preface, the two mystical women authors were channels through which the Virgin Mary communicates devotional practices dedicated to her earthly spouse: "[The Virgin Mary] took as her instruments two quills from two sober women authors from the two preceding centuries."[55] Santa Teresa's devotion to St. Joseph (attributed to her *Obras*, Tomo 1, Chapter 6), is cited as a pious example: "I wish to convince all to become devoted to that glorious Saint, because of my great experience of the glories he attains from God."[56] Both women are "enlightened quills, lighted torches, who in many senses open the eyes of knowledge and ignite the heart's affection for that admirable Saint,"[57] asserting their shared status as celebrated authors, as well as their advocacy for devotion to St. Joseph. According to its instructions,

54. Nogar *Quill and Cross in the Borderlands*, 108–09.

55. "[La Virgen María] tomó por instrumentos dos plumas de dos escritoras discretíssimas de los dos siglos antecedents." Ágreda, *Septenario*, 1.

56. "Querría Yo persuadir a todos fuesen devotos de este glorioso Santo, por la gran experiencia que tengo de los bienes que alcanza de Dios." Ágreda, *Septenario*, 9.

57. "Elevadísimas plumas, encendidas antorchas, que en muchas luces abren los ojos del conocimiento y encienden los afectos del corazón para el amor de este admirable Santo." Ágreda, *Septenario*, 10.

the *Septenario* was to be observed with mass for the seven days preceding Sta. Teresa's feast day. The meditations that accompanied each day of prayer draw from the seven privileges accorded to St. Joseph as described in *La mística ciudad de dios.*

In defining St. Joseph's seven divine privileges, the *Septenario* cites Part 2, Book 5, Chapter 16, number 892 of *La mística ciudad de dios*; specifically. The introduction states that even Sor María's text cannot encompass all there is to say about St. Joseph.[58] The *Septenario* then details the seven privileges granted to the saint. They are: 1) chastity and the conquest of carnal sensuality (including laziness); 2) the power to leave sinful ways and return to God's love; 3) devotion to the Virgin Mary;[59] 4) a happy death and defense against the Devil in the moment of transit; 5) that demons fear on hearing the name of St. Joseph; 6) to have health in one's body and succor in other work; and 7) for a succession of children in families (6). The privileges are intentions on behalf of which God permits St. Joseph to intercede.

Each day of the *Septenario* provides a meditation and prayer to St. Joseph as expressed in *La mística ciudad de dios*: seven days of prayer relating to seven privileges. The fourth privilege, that of a feliz tránsito, is the subject of reflection and prayer on the fourth day of the *Septenario.* That day's intention centers on the brevity of life, and the accompanying prayer invokes the virtues of faith, hope and charity at the time of death. It appeals for protection from the Devil like that Christ and the Virgin Mary offered St. Joseph at the time of his earthly passing.

If the *Septenario* was one channel through which Sor María's writing shaped daily devotional practices to St. Joseph in Mexico, another is the *Novena mensal.* Attributed to a member of the secular clergy of the Archbishopric of Mexico, Joseph Manuel Sartorio, the novena's nine days of prayers are intercalated with mediations on St. Joseph's life. As its title indicates, the *Novena* as whole focuses primarily on the fourth Josephine privilege outlined in the *Septenario*: a feliz tránsito or *buena muerte.* The Novena's introductory act of contrition establishes this clearly: "And how I repent and promise to never again offend you! Grant me, I pray, your grace, and concede me through the singular merits of your great St. Joseph, he who conserved your grace up unto death, that he opens for me the gates of Heaven.

58. "De las visiones y revelaciones Divinas, con que fue favorecido Señor San Joseph, he dicho algo en todo el discurso de esta Historia, y fueron muchas más que se pueden decir; pero lo más se encierra en aver conocido los Mysterios de Christo Nuestro Señor y de su Madre Santissima, y aver vivido en su compañía tantos años reputado por Padre del mismo Señor, y verdadero Esposo de la Reyna. Ágreda, *Septenario*, 5–6.

59. This section of the *Septenario* quotes directly from *La mística ciudad de dios*, Book 2, Part 6, Chapter 5, no. 1088.

Amen."[60] The novena continues with daily prayer dedicated to St. Joseph. After day one of the novena, each subsequent day includes a *consideración* that references a different passage of *La mística ciudad de dios* recounting St. Joseph's life, followed by a prayer reflecting on the virtue or quality of St. Joseph represented in Sor María's text. The passages cited are non-sequential and they derive from Chapters 14 and 15 of Part 2 Book 5 of *La mística ciudad de dios.* Taken together, they map out where text relating to St. Joseph's feliz tránsito is located in *La mística ciudad de dios*, illuminating an explicit connection between the devotional practice and Sor María's text.

The *Novena* was published at least four times in Mexico. The first edition (1766) was released by the Biblioteca Mexicana, and its cover states that the original document was printed in Guatemala on the press of Sebastián de Arévalo. Although the bibliographic record does not show a Guatemalan imprint of the *Novena* on or before 1766, the Arévalo family press did publish the *Novena* two more times, in 1797 (by the Viuda de Don Sebastián de Arévalo) and 1810 (Don Manuel Arévalo). In Mexico City, two more prints of the *Novena* emerged, one in 1773 (Felipe Zúñiga y Ontiveros) and one in 1831 after Mexican Independence from Spain. This latter edition was published on the recently emancipated lay press of "La oficina del ciudadano Alejandro Valdés." A 1793 imprint on the Puebla press of Don Pedro de la Rosa is a reprint of the 1766 Mexico City edition, perhaps reflecting the colonial-era engagement with Sor María in Puebla de los Ángeles, and the frequent republication of her writing there.[61]

But interest in Sor María's version of St. Joseph's biography was not limited to Spanish-speaking sites, nor to Franciscan interests. It sustained a worldwide presence, particularly in mission contexts. A representative example is Costanzo Gioseffo Beschi's devotional poem the *Tēmpāvaṇi* (தேம்பாவணி), known in English as "The Unfading Garland" or "A Garland of Unfading Honey-Sweet Verses."[62] Italian Jesuit missionary Beschi (1680–1747) composed the work in the South Indian language of Tamil to address the population his mission served near the southeastern town of Manapar (part of the Jesuit Madura Mission). In his theological interpretation of the nearly four thousand verse work, Francis X. Clooney, S.J., characterizes the *Tēmpāvaṇi* as expressing a "Jesuit vision of the true inculturation of the Christian story in

---

60. "¡Y como me arrepiento y prometo ya nunca más ofenderos! Dadme vuestra gracia, y concededme por los esclarecidos méritos de vuestro gran Joseph, el que conservándola hasta la muerte, me abra las puertas de la Gloria. Amen." Joseph Manuel Sartorio. *Novena mensal*, 2.

61. Nogar *Quill and Cross in the Borderlands*, chap. 3.

62. Constanzo Giuseppe Beschi, *Thembavani: A Garland of Unfading Honey-Sweet Verses*, trans. M. Dominic Raj (2018).

Tamil culture . . . and the concomitant virtues of foreign and native Christians who are invited to live according to the example of St. Joseph."[63] Clooney observes that the *Tēmpāvaṇi* retells much of the Bible "through a careful account of St. Joseph,"[64] a selection Clooney characterizes as "strategic" within the mission field. He notes that St Joseph is accessible to neophytes as an exemplary religious figure: "He is an ordinary human being . . . a pious Jew who is possessed of innumerable good human qualities, all of which are elevated by the grace of Christ, without nature or tradition eradicated in the process."[65] A major work of Tamil literature honored in its day, the *Tēmpāvaṇi* is also a noteworthy interpretation of Sor María's writing on St. Joseph, presented in poetic devotional form.[66]

In the work's preface ("Payiram"), Beschi frames the *Tēmpāvaṇi* as drawing from *La mística ciudad de dios.* Clooney remarks upon the stunning prominence of Sor María within the poem; she is the "only extra-Biblical person mentioned in Beschi's introduction, and one of the very few historical persons, other than Biblical figures, who are mentioned anywhere in the *Tēmpāvaṇi*."[67] The preface's discussion of Sor María centers on the sanctity of Sor María as author of the Virgin's autobiography: the host entrusted with inscribing St. Joseph's biography as presented by the Virgin Mary. Beschi writes in the preface's justification for basing the *Tēmpāvaṇi* on *La mística ciudad de dios*:

> In the town of Ágreda blessed with lovely gardens,
> There was virgin exalted by blessings unequalled anywhere on earth.
> Upright, exalted in her great penances,
> She touched the feet of the one who gave birth to the lord and praised her ever more fervently;
> Was she not thus shown to be worthy?[68]
>
> Mature in excellence on this earth by revelations beyond the sense,
> Mary's [of Ágreda] mouth flowered in grace, sweetness manifest in every word.
> She spoke with an excellence like that of sages perfected in speech.
> Her virtue bore with every character shown by the truth of the sacred text.[69]

---

63. Francis X. Clooney, S.J., *Saint Josephi in South India: Poetry, Mission and Theology in Costanzo Gioseffo Beschi's Tēmpāvaṇi* (Vienna: University of Vienna Press, 2022), 7.

64. Clooney, *Saint Joseph in South India*, 12.

65. Clooney, *Saint Joseph in South India*, 13.

66. Beschi employed a formal poetic structure, echoing that of other works of religious verse written in Tamil, Clooney, *Saint Joseph in South India*, 12.

67. Clooney, *Saint Joseph in South India*, 69.

68. Clooney, *Saint Joseph in South India*, 68.

69. Clooney, *Saint Joseph in South India*, 69.

Beschi cites Sor María's vision of St. Joseph expressed in *La mística ciudad de dios*, indicating that he will incorporate it into the *Tēmpāvaṇi*'s didactic narration of the life of the saint:

> To show the radiance of this fresh flowering, Mary gave to her the same name;
> To show her rich flourishing, Mary gave her unlimited graces:
> Body radiant with the sun, her feet on the crescent moon, her head crowned by lightning,
> Thus the highest mother.
>
> [...]
>
> When the girl [Ágreda] and the mother [Virgin Mary] were together,
> The mother related the ancient story of her flawless husband [Joseph]:
> "Tell others the things that I told you, that everyone can hear them."
> With courage the girl wrote down all she had been told.[70]

Beschi's description of himself as interlocutor is characterized by Clooney as a self-fashioning modeled on the mode of Sor María's mystical exegesis on Mary:

> With earnest love I too write down all there is to write.
> Even if I lack the right Tamil words, good people should lend me their ears.
> Even if they see flaws in the earthen vessel, will they not ignore them and
> Hungrily consume all there is of fine ambrosia here?[71]

Clooney is quick to point out that Beschi does not simply translate into Tamil the portions of *La mística ciudad de dios* treating St. Joseph; indeed, there is no mapping of one text on to the other in Clooney's interpretation. Yet the two texts are decisively connected. Among the *Tēmpāvaṇi*'s thirty-six cantos on St. Joseph's life, Canto 33 and Canto 34 describe his illness and death, echoing the message of a feliz tránsito advanced in the *Septenario* and *Novena*. The *Tēmpāvaṇi* demonstrates that Sor María's community of readers extended well beyond Hispanophone groups (to Italy and South India at a minimum) and outside the bounds of the Franciscan Order. One wonders how Jesuit Beschi encountered and read her work; one might also question how the Mercederians who possessed her vita read and applied it. Further study of Sor

70. Clooney, *Saint Joseph in South India*, 69.
71. Clooney, *Saint Joseph in South India*, 69.

María's writing regarding this Tamil-language devotional work is clearly necessary, as is its relationship to other worldwide Josephine practices and beliefs.

Conclusion

The reading of Sor María de Jesús de Ágreda's writing provides ample matter to explore, as her scope of influence extended around the world. From its interpretation in an early modern comedia de santos, to its incorporation into Tamil-language, Josephine devotion penned by a Jesuit, the explorations presented here open the doors to the global archive of Ágredan writing. Seen as a point of departure for future research studying the distribution, interpretation, and application of Sor María's writing, these texts illuminate the vast range of her intellectual reach.

Chapter Fifteen

The Tears in My Eyes Do Not Allow Me to Speak: A Maya Performance of the Passion

Mark Christensen, *Brigham Young University*

The Maya and the Descent from the Cross

At Christmastime, countless families perform pantomime reenactments of the Nativity, and countless churches of various denominations display Nativity scenes. In fact, live Nativity performances with animals, acting, singing, and costumes are not uncommon in many towns. Many, if not all, such performances of the Nativity involve an orator reading from Luke 2 and costumed, yet voiceless, actors who play out their individual roles. The desired result: an audible, visual, and engaging lesson on the birth of Christ.

Just as such performances exist today concerning Christ's birth, they exist concerning his death. The approach of Easter and Holy Week begins preparations for reenactments held in Christian churches all over the world. The texts that led the earliest audiences through the Passion were the Gospels, and their accounts—and modified versions of their accounts—reached countless eyes and ears over the years through various sermons and devotional works. Eventually, Nahuatl (Aztec) and Maya texts of central Mexico and Yucatan would detail Passion events throughout the colonial period; twentieth-century Guatemalans in Santiago Atitlán would develop an elaborate Passion Week celebration that blended Maya and Christian worldviews; and in 2022 over 100 actors would perform a Passion play in Trafalgar Square in London accompanied by elaborate costumes and props.[1]

1. For devotional texts, see Thomas H. Bestul, *Texts of the Passion: Latin Devotional Literature and Medieval Society* (Philadelphia: University of Pennsylvania Press, 1996); for Guatemala, see Allen J. Christenson, *The Burden of the Ancients: Maya Ceremonies of World Renewal from the Pre-Columbian Period to the Present* (Austin: University of Texas Press, 2016); for the performance in Trafalgar Square, see https://www.wintershall.org.uk/passion-jesus-london.

Some Passion performances involved detailed scripts, dozens of actors, speaking roles, scenery, props, costumes, songs, and so on. Others were more individual, personal performances as worshipers moved through the Stations of the Cross or were guided through the Passion by devotional works encouraging the reader/listener to experience Christ's suffering through imagination. Still others found a middle ground of sorts where an orator read a sermon while others acted out specific roles. Like a family or town's pantomimed re-creation of the Nativity from Luke 2, local actors, costumes, and props would provide a pantomimed accompaniment to an orator delivering a sermon on the death of Christ.

The Maya text examined here represents this type of performative sermon intended for Holy Week. The sermon describes the Deposition, or Christ's descent from the cross and burial, which occurred after his death on Friday of Holy Week, or Good Friday.[2] The text is designed to produce emotion—an "intimate script" as Sarah McNamer would have it—with the eventual result being a stronger relationship with and dedication to Christ and his sorrowing mother.[3] Certainly it falls among those medieval European Deposition texts termed "theatrical manuscripts." And certainly it aligns with the *devotio moderna* movement encouraging individuals to relate to the divine on a personal level often through pondering and contemplation.[4] The only speaking part appears to be that of the orator whose words are sometimes accompanied by specific actions performed by actors and props, thus providing a theatrical and performative element to the Maya sermon, similar to a Nativity reenactment.

As shown below, the Deposition has captured the attention of scholars over the years, particularly those interested in its appearance in painted works and sculpture. As an event, the Deposition and its historical and modern-day practice appears in various studies examining Holy Week in Spain and Latin America, although Spain receives the lion's share of attention.[5] Regarding the

---

2. For an excellent summary of the liturgy and popular events that occur during Holy Week, according to the guidelines of the Church, see Aurelio García Macías, "Armonización entre la liturgia y la piedad popular en la semana santa," in *La semana santa: Antropología y religión en Latinoamérica II*, coord. José Luis Alonso Ponga et al. (Valladolid: Ayuntamiento de Valladolid, 2010), 32–37.

3. For more on intimate scripts, see Sarah McNamer, *Affective Meditation and the Invention of Medieval Compassion* (Philadelphia: University of Pennsylvania Press, 2010), 12–14.

4. García Macías, "Armonización," 35; Joseph H. Lynch and Phillip C. Adamo, *The Medieval Church: A Brief History*, 2nd ed. (New York: Routledge, 2014), 340–41.

5. For example, see the three volumes of *La semana santa: Antropología y religión en Latinoamérica* (Valladolid: Ayuntamiento de Valladolid, 2008–2017); María Pilar Panero García, José Luis Alonso Ponga, Fernando Joven Álvarez, coord., *Palabras a la imprenta: Antropología y religión en Latinoamérica IV: Tradición oral y literatura en la religiosidad popular* (Ureña, Spain: Fundación Joaquín Díaz, 2019).

Deposition in colonial central Mexico, the work of Susan Webster (1997), Richard Trexler (2003), and Naín Alejandro Ruiz Jaramillo (2019) provide some of the more thorough treatments.[6] Yet studies on the event in colonial Yucatan are virtually nonexistent. This essay, then, endeavors to begin to fill this historiographical gap. After a general overview of Deposition texts and their appearance in Europe and colonial New Spain, this study examines a performative sermon on the Deposition written in Yucatec Maya vis-à-vis its many European antecedents to reveal how the event was presented to and familiarized by the Maya living in colonial and early post-colonial Yucatan.

The Deposition in Europe and New Spain

Passion texts can include what scholars have variously termed "postpassion narratives," "paraliturgical rites," or "extra-liturgical" dramas that oftentimes provide parishioners the opportunity of greater participation in church affairs through processions and even as actors in live reenactments.[7] Such narratives and commemorations include the portrayal of events occurring after the death of Christ including his descent from the cross and burial, or Deposition. The Gospels say very little about the time between Christ's death and his burial. Matthew, Mark, and Luke describe Joseph of Arimathea soliciting Pilate for Christ's body and subsequently removing it from the cross. To this task, John adds Nicodemus. This gap in the record was filled by later authors, thus helping give rise to the Deposition. Indeed, various Passion texts throughout medieval Europe provided the fodder for the Deposition including the *Meditationes vitae Christi*, Thomas à Kempis's *Prayers and Meditations on the Life of Christ*, the *Dialogus beatae Mariae*, and the Marian lament "Quis dabit."

Paintings of the Deposition existed by the ninth century and abounded by the late Middle Ages, and its performance of the rite appeared as early as the tenth century.[8] According to Elizabeth Parker, Charlemagne and his conquest

---

6. Although not focused on the colonial period, the work of Hilda Calzada Martínez on articulated sculptures in Mexico provides an excellent overview of the Deposition in colonial central Mexico. See her "La escultura articulada en el distrito federal: Arte, ingenio y movimiento" (master's thesis, Universidad Nacional Autónoma de México, 2011), 34–45.

7. Richard C. Trexler, *Reliving Golgotha: The Passion Play of Iztapalapa* (Cambridge: Harvard University Press, 2003), 19; Amy Knight Powell, *Depositions: Scenes from the Late Medieval Church and the Modern Museum* (Brooklyn: Zone Books, 2012), 45; Elizabeth C. Parker, *The Descent from the Cross: Its Relation to the Extra-liturgical "Depositio" Drama* (New York: Garland Publisher, 1978), ch. 2.

8. Powell, *Depositions*, 10, 46, 143; Parker, *The Descent*, 32, 119—for more on the history of the rite, see chapter 2. In paintings of the Deposition, Christ's followers typically employ a white cloth to lower his body, with the body of Christ literally appearing on the cloth. The visual association of the Deposition with the Eucharist where Christ's body is

campaigns of conversion increased the need for dramatic representations of Christianity. As Easter Saturday typically involved the baptism of catechumens, the Deposition provided additional significance to the event.[9] Moreover, as Powell argues, paraliturgical reenactments illustrate the desire for laypeople to have a role in the Church's celebrations.[10] When performed as a drama, generally the Deposition involved actors playing Joseph and Nicodemus receiving permission from Pilate to remove the body of Christ, which could be represented by an articulated sculpture hanging on a cross.[11] After receiving permission from Mary—and sometimes Christ—the two climb ladders and remove the crown and nails (and sometimes the sign attached to the cross) and present them to Mary. They then lower Christ down using a cloth and present him to Mary. From here, the body could be placed in a casket (*Santo Sepulcro*) either in the church or outside, which was subsequently employed in a procession. Each town determined the specifics of the commemoration—from the songs to the costumes to the actors—but most followed this broad outline.[12]

Spain developed a healthy repertoire of poems and plays representing the Deposition. In fact, by 1532 the *Autos del cabildo catedral* from Seville included the Deposition among a variety of other plays.[13] At times the Deposition took the form of a play with dialogue, as in the sixteenth-century *Aucto del descendimiento de la cruz* housed in Madrid.[14] On others, the Dep-

presented on the altar on the white corporal increased its popularity in paintings and images. Richard Viladesau, *The Pathos of the Cross: The Passion of Christ in Theology and the Arts—The Baroque Era* (New York: Oxford University Press, 2014), 53–54. Although many exist, an excellent work examining various artistic representations of the Deposition is Richard Viladesau, *The Triumph of the Cross: The Passion of Christ in Theology and the Arts, from the Renaissance to the Counter-Reformation* (New York: Oxford University Press, 2008).

9. Parker, *The Descent*, 82, 97.

10. Powell, *Depositions*, 45.

11. For more on the use of such sculptures in Europe and their reverence, as well as an overview of the development of the Deposition, see Pedro García González, "Ritos y representaciones de la crucifixión y su adaptación histórica y eco-cultural," in *La Semana Santa*, 3: 151–55.

12. For example, see the summary of Deposition rites in Catalan towns in Anita Louise Alvarado's "Catalan Holy Week Ceremonies, Catholic Ideology, and Culture Change in the Spanish Colonial Empire" (Ph.D. diss, University of Arizona, 1974), 105–11.

13. Charlotte Stern, *The Medieval Theater in Castile* (Binghamton: Center for Medieval and Early Renaissance Studies, 1996), 213.

14. Biblioteca Nacional de España (BNE), MSS/14711, "Colección de autos sacramentales, loas y farsas del siglo XVI (anteriores a Lope de Vega)," "Aucto del descendimiento de la cruz," f. 430–34v.; *Colección de autos, farsas y coloquios del siglo XVI*, vol. 4, ed. Léo Rouanet (Barcelona: L'Avenç, 1901), 29–46; N.D. Shergold, *A History of the Spanish Stage: From Medieval Times until the End of the Seventeenth Century* (Oxford: Clarendon Press, 1967), 31–33; J.P. Wickersham Crawford, *Spanish Drama before Lope de Vega* (Philadelphia: University of Pennsylvania, 1922), 141–44.

osition became more of a performative sermon with the orator narrating the events, as in don Vicente Catalá's mid eighteenth-century *Sentimientos tiernos.*[15] Either way, as one scholar stated, "From its inception the *Depositio Crucis* was a drama."[16] Moreover, articulated sculptures of Christ appeared in Spain allowing the dramatization of the event to include living and non-living participants.[17] And, as mentioned, the Deposition was no stranger to Spanish poetry.[18] In the end, from images to plays to sermons, the Deposition was widely familiar among European audiences despite it never officially joining the Roman liturgy and remaining a locally-shaped commemoration.[19]

Not surprisingly, the Deposition made a smooth voyage across the Atlantic to take firm root in New Spain. Indeed, the Deposition became well known to Spaniards and Indigenous alike though a variety of mediums. Cofradías emerged dedicated to the event and paintings appeared representing the Deposition allowing fray Bartolomé de las Casas to comment on the skill of Indigenous artists in depicting the holy scene.[20] Moreover, the Deposition is also embedded in popular themes and practices like the Seven Sorrows of Mary and the Stations of the Cross. Regarding the latter, the Stations typically consisted of fourteen stops that provided worshipers a mental tour of the Passion as they progressed through specific moments in Christ's trial, death, and burial. Texts dedicated to the Stations appeared in both Spanish and Indigenous languages. For example, fray Augustín de Vetancurt produced his Nahuatl *Via crucis* to assist Nahua penitents experience through imagination the Passion. Importantly, the thirteenth station concerns the Deposition with texts

---

15. Vicente Catalá, *Sentimientos tiernos* (Valencia: La oficina de Joseph, y Thomas de Orga, 1777).

16. Parker, *The Descent*, 90.

17. For a description of such in Seville, see Susan Webster, *Art and Ritual in Golden-Age Spain: Sevillian Confraternities and the Processional Sculpture of Holy Week* (Princeton: Princeton University Press, 1998), 65–68.

18. Alexander S. Wilkinson, ed., *Iberian Books: Books Published in Spanish or Portuguese or on the Iberian Peninsula before 1601* (Leiden: Brill, 2010), 144, no. 3807.

19. Powell, *Depositions*, 81.

20. For examples of cofradías, see Trexler, *Reliving Golgotha*, 35; Brian C. Wilson, "What Does Jerusalem Have to Do with Amecameca? A Case Study of Colonial Mexican Sacred Space," in *Religion as a Human Capacity*, eds. Timothy Light and Brian C. Wilson (Leiden: Brill, 2004), 210–11; Alessia Frassani, *Building Yanhuitlan: Art, Politics, and Religion in the Mixteca Alta since 1500* (Norman: University of Oklahoma Press, 2017), 60; Rubial García, *El cristianismo en Nueva España: Catequesis, fiesta, milagros y represión* (Mexico City: Universidad Nacional Autónoma de México, 2020), 224–35. For Las Casas, see Linda B. Hall, *Mary, Mother and Warrior: The Virgin in Spain and the Americas* (Austin: University of Texas Press, 2004), 108. For examples of convents emphasizing the Passion and including the Deposition, see José Guadalupe Victoria, *Pintura y sociedad en Nueva España siglo XVI* (Mexico City: Universidad Nacional Autónoma de México, 1986), 111.

Figure 1. The thirteenth station. Church of St. George the Martyr, Kaunas, Lithuania. Photo by author.

typically employing this stop to emphasize the sorrow of Mary—a central theme in the Maya sermon examined here (Figure 1).[21]

The Deposition also makes a possible appearance in the sixteenth-century *Florentine Codex*. Following his death, the body of the Aztec emperor, Montezuma, was thrown into the lake. Diana Magaloni Kerpel argues that the image of Montezuma's dead body being retrieved from the lake to be cremated reflects that of the Deposition. Admittedly, the position of Montezuma's body and how he is carried by two Nahua is like that seen in traditional portrayals of the Deposition.[22]

---

21. For an excellent overview of the Stations and their history, see John F. Schwaller, *The Stations of the Cross in Colonial Mexico: The* Via crucis en mexicano *by Fray Augustín Vetancurt, and the Spread of a Devotion* (Norman and San Diego: University of Oklahoma Press and The Academy of American Franciscan History, 2021). Schwaller likewise provides an informative overview of the impact of the Passion in New Spain, particularly chapter 2. For two of many examples of the thirteenth station, see the same 145–149, and fray Francisco Villanueva y Buytrago, *Instrucción de terceros* (Madrid: Oficina de la viuda de Manuel Fernandez, 1772), 287–89.

22. Diana Magaloni Kerpel, "Imágenes de la conquista de México en los codices del siglo XVI," *Anales del Instituto de Investigaciones Estéticas* 82 (2003): 38–42; Matthew

Regarding the Deposition's performance, the town of Huejotzingo provides one of the earliest examples. As Susan Webster notes, sixteenth-century murals uncovered in the monastery of San Miguel depict processions and the Deposition. A painted image of the Deposition appears above the north doorway. According to Webster, "the mural of the Descent ceremony . . . acts as a visual marker, reflecting and reinforcing the ritual that took place immediately beyond."[23] Performed by the Indigenous, yet Franciscan-sponsored confraternity dedicated to the True Cross (*Vera Cruz*), the Deposition of a sculpted image of Christ occurred as a sermon was read. Christ would then be carried to the altar in the church and then through the front door into the atrium where it would travel by procession to the four posa chapels. Finally, the procession would end with Christ's body being deposited in a sepulcher, likely in the cloister garth. Webster notes how similar, although not identical, processions occurred in sixteenth-century Seville.[24]

Other evidence confirms that such processions and ceremonies occurred throughout central Mexico. In 1585, Jesuits in Veracruz reenacted the Deposition, likely with articulated sculptures of Mary and Christ.[25] And the eighteenth-century Franciscan Francisco Palóu recorded that in the Sierra Gorda of Queretaro during the afternoon of Good Friday, the Deposition was reenacted with "great vividness . . . with an image of perfect stature that, for the effect, was ordered to be made with hinges."[26] Furthermore, at the church and school of San José de los Naturales—which represented the center of Indigenous religious life in the early years of Mexico City's development—Vetancurt reports the practice of numerous Easter festivals and processions.

Restall, *When Montezuma Met Cortés: The True Story of the Meeting that Changed History* (New York: Harper Collins, 2018), 199. For more insights into how Nahuas perceived the conquest through the *Florentine Codex*, see Alejandro Salafranca Vázquez, "Naturalización novohispana de la narrativa de la conquista," in *La conquista de la identidad: México y España, 1521–1910*, eds. Alejandro Salafranca Vázquez and Tomás Pérez Vejo (Madrid: Turner, 2021), 86–95.

23. Susan Verdi Webster, "Art, Ritual, and Confraternities in Sixteenth-Century New Spain: Penitential Imagery at the Monastery of San Miguel, Huejotzingo," *Anales del Istituto de Investigaciones Estéticas*, no. 70 (1997): 33.

24. Webster, "Art, Ritual, and Confraternities." See also Elena Estrada de Gerlero, "El programa pasionario en el convento franciscano de Huejotzingo," *Jahrbuch für Geschichte von Staat, Wirtschaft und Gesellschaft Lateinamerikas*, no. 20 (1983): 643–62.

25. Calzada Martínez, "La escultura articulada," 37–39. The thesis likewise exposes the continued use of such articulated sculptures in Mexico today for Deposition ceremonies.

26. Fray Francisco Palóu, *Relación histórica de la vida y apostólicas tareas del venerable padre fray Junípero Serra* (Mexico City: Imprenta de don Felipe de Zúñiga y Ontiveros, 1787), 30–31.

During Good Friday, he mentions "the sermon and Descent from the Cross, during which there are many tears."[27]

The most detailed and well-known account of the Deposition belongs to the Dominican Agustín Dávila Padilla who recorded the details of a sixteenth-century Deposition ceremony performed by a confraternity dedicated to the Descent and Burial of Christ in Mexico City. In the middle of the chapel of Santo Domingo de Mexico was a platform "nearly twenty feet long and twelve feet wide," decorated with rocks and plants and three crosses that served as Calvary.[28] And, as Estrada de Gerlero notes, it was here that the figures were placed and manipulated as a sermon was read.[29] Additionally, Dávila Padilla records how the image of Christ was made from *pasta de caña* and had joints that could move "as if it were a real body," while the image of Mary, dressed for mourning and standing with a cloth in her hand for wiping her tears, had cords attached to her that ran under her litter that, when manipulated, caused her to dry her eyes, bow her head, and tilt her body. All of this, according to the Dominican, caused much devotion among the crowd.[30] An elaborate burial procession then occurred that included the insignias of the Passion, the cross, and the various images.[31] Alessia Frassani mentions having witnessed similar productions in Yanhuitlan, Oaxaca, between 2007 and 2014.[32] In the end, a sermon accompanied by "mute actors" seemed to define many Deposition ceremonies; such performances continue to be celebrated today in various towns of central Mexico on Good Friday.[33]

---

27. Fray Agustín de Vetancurt, *Teatro mexicano, Crónica de la provincial del Santo Evangelio de México, Menologio franciscano* (Mexico City: Editorial Porrúa, 1971), part 4, 42; Calzada Martínez, "La escultura articulada," 43. For more on San José, see Jonathan Truitt, *Sustaining the Divine in Mexico Tenochtitlan: Nahuas and Catholicism, 1523–1700* (Norman: University of Oklahoma Press, and Oceanside, CA: The Academy of American Franciscan History, 2018); and Barbara E. Mundy, *The Death of Aztec Tenochtitlan, the Life of Mexico City* (Austin: University of Texas Press, 2015), 116–19.

28. Fray Agustín Dávila Padilla, *Historia de la fundación y discurso de la provincial de Santiago de México* (Mexico City: Editorial Academia Literaria, 1955), 563.

29. Estrada de Gerlero, "Programa pasionario," 649.

30. Dávila Padilla, *Historia*, 563. Trexler also gives a summary of Dávila Padilla's account in his *Reliving Golgotha*, 35–37.

31. Dávila Padilla, *Historia*, 566–67.

32. Frassani, *Building Yanhuitlan*, 103–105; see also Alessia Frassani, "Transiciones: la imagen y su significado en unas representaciones mixtecas de Cristo del siglo XVI," *Anales del Instituto de Investigaciones Estéticas*, no. 113 (2018): 117–44; and María Díeguez Melo, "Ubi est mors victoria tua. La Carrera de la Muerte en la semana santa de Yanhuitlán (Oaxaca)," in *La Semana Santa* 3: 359–71.

33. Trexler, *Reliving Golgotha*, 39. For one modern example of the Deposition, see Naín Alejandro Ruiz Jaramillo, "El Señor de la Cuevita fundacional, pieza clave que propició el origen histórico y simbólico de la representación de Semana Santa en Iztapalapa," *Rutas de Campo*, no. 5 (2019): 173–83.

The Deposition traveled beyond central Mexico to reach Yucatan, carrying with it many of the characteristics already seen. The use of religious drama and theater in Europe and central Mexico to evangelize certainly alludes to the presence of such in colonial Yucatan. And, like the Nahua, Maya culture engaged in ritual theater long before the Spaniards arrived surely facilitating the adoption of the friars' religious drama.[34] Yet although early Franciscans commented on pre-Hispanic theatrical traditions among the Maya—which oftentimes continued during the colonial period—chroniclers were largely silent on colonial religious theater in Yucatan, and no examples of colonial religious plays composed in Yucatec Maya have survived.[35] Compounding the lack of surviving plays composed in Yucatec Maya, is the lack of surviving colonial murals depicting the Deposition in Yucatecan churches.[36]

However, although such evidence is lacking, the archives provide valuable hints betraying the Deposition's presence in Yucatan. In 1784, the curate of Chunhuhub reported that the Maya under his stewardship "give special worship to the most holy cross of our redeemer Jesus, in whom they firmly believe," and that on Good Friday "although an Indian be in the most remote part of the forest, they insist on attending the Descent of Christ, Jesus, crucified."[37] The 1788 visita report of Cunduacan contained an inventory listing various items that could be used in a Deposition ceremony including images of Christ (one "with the casket"), Our Lady of Solitude, and Veronica, and a cross used specifically for the Deposition.[38] Moreover, the majority of nineteenth-century inventories made of the churches in various Yucatecan towns frequently included images of Christ crucified, sometimes with nails, shrouds,

34. For more on the pre-Columbian and colonial presence of dance, music, and theater among the Maya, see Alfredo Barrera Vásquez, Alejandro Cervera Andrade, and Leopoldo Peniche Vallado, *El teatro en Yucatán* (Mérida: Secretaria de Education del Gobierno del Estado de Yucatán, 2009); Fernando Muñoz Castillo, *El teatro regional de Yucatán*, 2nd ed. (Mexico City: Escenología/Instituto de Cultura de Yucatán/Cultura Yucatán A.C., 2012).

35. One example of a colonial play performed in Yucatan exists. It is a nativity play written in Spanish, intended for a Spanish audience, and modeled after those European. See Arturo Gamoa Garibaldi, "Historia del teatro y de la literatura dramática," in *Enciclopedia Yucatanense*, vol. 5, ed. C. Echánove Trujillo (Mexico City: Edición oficial del gobierno de Yucatán, 1946), 111–13.

36. My thanks to Amara Solari and Richard Perry for their insight on the matter.

37. Achivo Histórico de la Arquidiócesis de Yucatán (AHAY), Gobierno, Visitas Pastorales, 1784–1785, caja 622, exp. 1, Chunhuhub, 59r; Nancy Farriss, *Maya Society under Colonial Rule: The Collective Enterprise of Survival* (Princeton: Princeton University Press, 1984), 515 n.62.

38. AHAY, Gobierno, Visita Pastorales, caja 623, exp. 4.

and other items dedicated to the Passion, and most mention crosses specifically used in the Deposition.[39]

Two examples are particularly illustrative. The 1864 and 1875 inventories of Chapab list a variety of items relevant to a Deposition ceremony including "an image of Our Lady of Sorrows placed at the foot of a cross measuring six feet, with her silver diadem and a lily of gold; a *Santo Sepulcro* with its table, useable, and a *Señor de Descendimiento* with his silver crown"; and "a wooden cross for the same *Señor.*" The 1864 inventory specifies that this cross was used in the Deposition.[40] The other example comes from Teabo whose 1880 inventory included "a [Lady of] Sorrows dressed in damask with sliver dagger[s]," "a large cross of the descent," "a [Jesus] crucified of the descent measuring four feet with [his] *Santo Sepulcro,*" and other items in storage including a Saint John with the three Marys and other crosses (likely used when depicting Calvary). Finally, the inventory listed "two ladders (or stairs) for the Deposition and one with a handrail."[41]

As seen in Spain and central Mexico, all such items were likely employed to accompany a sermon, probably performative and pantomimed, given during Good Friday. Fortunately, one example of such a performative sermon intended to guide orator, actors, and audience alike through the Deposition exists. And it exists in Yucatec Maya. This is the only surviving example of a performative Deposition ceremony designed for the Yucatec Maya, and it is the strongest piece of evidence connecting theatrical performance to the evangelization of Yucatan.[42]

A Performative Sermon of the Deposition in Maya

The sermon presented here is a theatrical reenactment of the Deposition composed in Maya. Today located in the Kislak Center for Special Collections at the University of Pennsylvania, the *Discurso para el descendimiento del señor* is part of a larger collection of sermons transcribed by C. Hermann Berendt in the nineteenth century.[43] The sermon's self-proclaimed author is the priest

39. AHAY, Gobierno, Inventarios, caja 223, exp. 9, "Espita, 1897"; exp. 1, "Calotmul"; exp. 2, "Conkal"; exp. 3, "Hokaba"; exp. 4, "Abalá, 1884"; exp. 8, "Chichimila, 1870."

40. AHAY, Gobierno, Inventarios, caja 223, exp. 7.

41. AHAY, Gobierno, Inventarios, caja 228, exp. 5.

42. Some of the final, loose pages in a Maya Christian copybook from Tekom relate the final portion of a Deposition sermon. If all the pages had survived, it is likely a more complete version of the Deposition would be found. Princeton University Library, Garrett-Gates Mesoamerican Manuscripts (GGMM), no. 72, "Yucatec Prayers."

43. University of Pennsylvania, Berendt-Brinton Linguistic Collection, Colección de pláticas doctrinales y sermones en lengua maya, Ms. Coll. 700, Item 46, Discurso para el descendimiento del Señor / por Don Francisco Carvajal, presbítero.

don Francisco León Carvajal, and the manuscript's initial pages contain two conflicting biographies of the man. The first claims Carvajal to be a late eighteenth-century curate in Hocoba and Hoctun. A correction then follows stating that Carvajal was in fact someone else: the brother of the governor of Yucatan, don José Segundo Carvajal, whose nephew "well remembers his uncle Pancho (a nickname for Francisco)" and claims that Carvajal was born in Merida around 1790–1795. The correction asserts that Carvajal served the town of Temax and composed various other texts in Maya.[44] Indeed, archival records confirm Carvajal's presence in Temax as his signature can be seen on baptismal records from the town from 1820 to 1824.[45]

At the end of the sermon is another note in Spanish and Maya stating that as of 19 March 1859, the sermon belonged to the priest don Tomás Domingo Quintana Roo. An additional biographical note follows stating that Quintana Roo met Carvajal when he was little. Quintana Roo served in the parishes of Yobain, Cacalchen, Santa Ana de Merida, Hocaba, and Santiago de Merida, and he died in Merida in 1860. After acquiring the sermon from Carvajal, Quintana Roo likely brought it with him to Merida when he served at Santiago for in November 1868, the acting priest of the parish, don Nicolás Delgado, allowed Berendt to make a copy of the sermon now in his care. In the end, the sermon likely dates to the early nineteenth century.

Whether it was performed at Temax where Carvajal served is unknown. However, murals painted by colonial Maya artists on the church's walls betray a strong presence of the Passion and offer an appropriate setting for a Deposition reenactment. For example, the west wall of the sacristy shows Golgotha and its three crosses while another portrays the flagellation of Christ (Figures 2 and 3).[46]

Regardless of its performance at Temax, one of the introductory notes to the sermon claims that it "is read during Holy Week in the churches of

---

44. For more information on the sermon, see John Weeks, "Karl Hermann Berendt: una colección de manuscritos lingüísticos de Centroamérica y Mesoamérica," *Mesoamérica* 36 (1998), 645; John Weeks, *The Library of Daniel Garrison Brinton* (Philadelphia: University of Pennsylvania Museum of Archaeology and Anthropology, 2002), 109 no. 903. For more on Carvajal, see *Yucatán en el tiempo: Enciclopedia alfabética* (Mérida: Inversiones Cares, 1998), 2: 114–15.

45. *FamilySearch*, "México, Yucatán, registros parroquiales y diocesanos, 1543–1977," Temax > San Miguel Arcángel > Bautismos 1818–1846 > image 290 of 547, https://familysearch.org/ark:/61903/3:2:77TD-PVC2. I thank Michel Oudijk for finding the initial record.

46. For more on the imagery of the murals of Temax, see Amara Solari and Linda K. Williams, *Maya-Christian Murals in Early Modern Yucatán* (Austin: University of Texas Press, 2024), Chap. 4.

Figure 2. Calvary. San Miguel Arcángel, Temax. Photo by author.

Merida and of many towns."[47] Finally, and as is seen in some Spanish plays, parenthetical instructions in Spanish dictating actions to accompany the sermon indicate the presence of mute actors and articulated sculptures, thus allowing the community to more fully participate in, engage with, and own this important part of Christianity (Table 1). It is also possible, if not likely, that music would have accompanied the ritual as was done in many of its European antecedents and even Nahuatl plays.

Christianity and how it is conveyed continually changes creating different versions of the faith specific to place and time. Although Passion texts largely base the veracity of portrayed events in the synoptic Gospels, what seemed most important was helping the audience feel the Passion and draw closer to Mary and Christ. No text of which I am aware strictly adheres to the biblical account as all fill in the gaps of the narrative with dialogue, names, and events not recorded in the Gospels.[48] Thus, from their origins, Passion texts have

47. For more on Carvajal, see Alfred M. Tozzer, *A Maya Grammar, with Bibliography and Appraisement of the Works Noted* (New York: Dover, 1977), 202.

48. For more on the veracity of the portrayed Deposition, or the lack thereof, see Jerome Murphy-O'Connor, "The Descent from the Cross and the Burial of Jesus (JN 19:31–42)," *Revue Biblique* 118, no. 4 (2011): 533–57.

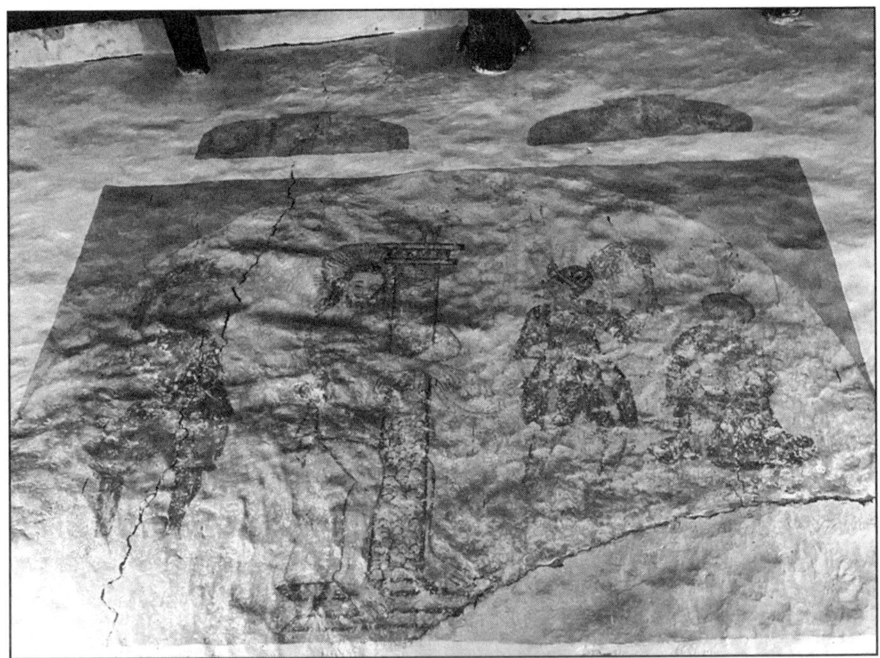

Figure 3. Flagellation of Christ. San Miguel Arcángel, Temax. Photo by author.

creatively re-created the Passion in ways best suited to the audience. Those produced in New Spain, then, continue this tradition by familiarizing the Passion to Indigenous cultures.

And so it is with sermons and plays on the Deposition. Concerning the performative sermon here, although rendered in Maya for a Maya audience, its contents also betray its Old-World origins. The intent of the sermon is to evoke a didactic and transformative sorrow in the audience. To do this, the sermon provides a brief overview of Christ's crucifixion and removal from the cross with an emphasis on the suffering of his mother, Mary, all peppered with numerous quotes from scripture and Church authorities. In truth, the text's layout, structure, and content are all right at home with its European counterparts, although its intended reception among a Maya audience certainly impacted the sermon as well. Importantly, only after understanding the literary, European well from which the Maya sermon drew can we determine the impact of the Yucatan and its Maya culture on the sermon. The general walk-through below of the performative sermon illustrates both these Old and New World influences.

Table 1. Spanish Instructions in the Maya Deposition

Spanish	English
Aqui se rasga el velo, descubriendo al Senor	Here the veil is torn revealing the Lord
Se virará el Orador hácia el Sõr.	The orator will turn toward the Lord
Aqui salen los Santos varones	Here, the holy men come forth
Aqui se hincan delante de la Senora	Here, they kneel before the lady
Moverá la cabeza la Señora en acción de conceder	The head of the Lady will nod in approval
Suben al Calvario	They climb up Calvary
Se arrodillan delante del Sõr.	They kneel before the Lord
Suben en las escaleras de la cruz	They climb the ladders of the cross
Le quitan la corona de espinas	They remove the crown of thorns
Se la llevan à la Srã	They take it to the Lady
Se la dan à besar	They give it to her to kiss
Llevan la corona de espinas al Stõ sepulcro	They carry the crown of thorns to the *Santo Sepulcro*
Desclavan el Señor	They unnail the Lord
Llevan los clavos à la Srã	They carry the nails to the Lady
Aqui se hace el descendimiento	Here, the Deposition is performed
Lo ponen en presencia de la Srã	They place him in the presence of the Lady
Se lo acercan à la Señora	They bring him closer to the Lady
Llevan al Sõr al orador, el que tomandolo en sus brazos dice	They bring the Lord to the orator, who taking him in his arms says
Se hare la ceremonia de preparer à llevar al púlpito por uno de los Santos varones la sábana santa	The ceremony of one of the holy men preparing to bring to the pulpit the Holy Shroud will be performed
Llevan al Señor al Santo Sepulcro	They bring the Lord to the *Santo Sepulcro*
Lo ponen dentro del S° Sepulcro	They place him inside the *Santo Sepulcro*
Procurara el orador con el mayor fervor y lagrimas que el Sõr le conceda hacer el siguiente acto de contricion	The orator will seek with great earnest and tears that the Lord allow him to perform the following Act of Contrition

THE MAYA DEPOSITION: A WALKTHROUGH

The orator begins with a Latin citation from Jeremiah 9:1 made familiar through the famous thirteenth-century Marian lament, the "Quis dabit." This lament that relates Mary's point of view and her suffering during her son's death was not only popular in Europe, but especially in Castille where its emphasis on emotions seemed to garner appeal.[49] In the

49. Bestul, *Texts of the Passion*, 7–14. For a translated example of the lament, see Appendix 1 of the same. See also Cynthia Robinson, *Imagining the Passion in a Multi-*

Maya sermon, Mary the mother of Christ plays the lead role and occupies much of the dialogue with her laments. This central role of Mary is common in many European Passion and Deposition plays as are her laments, or *planctus Mariae*. Although the Bible places Mary at the foot of the cross, she is speechless. But surely the sorrowing mother had something to say. And by the tenth century or so Catholic liturgy began to include phrases supposedly uttered by Mary during the Passion. Many such phrases became a common staple for Passion plays as was the encouragement for the audience to commiserate with Mary and consider her suffering, particularly during the Deposition.[50]

By the late Middle Ages, theologians had embraced the idea of Mary suffering alongside Christ, sharing in each of his agonies and torments, and, at times, surpassing him in suffering.[51] Such allowed Kempis in the fifteenth century to claim, "Dominion belongs to her, as co-redemptrix of the human race."[52] And as Jennifer Hammerschmidt noted, "Passion sermons during the fifteenth century can be characterized in part by an increased interest in Mary's suffering at the base of the cross."[53] The sixteenth-century *Aucto del descendimiento* produced in Spain seemed to follow this trend allowing Mary and her laments a significant part. Here is a small portion:

O what mortal embrace!
O what wounded person!
What dispute caused this disgrace?
Who did you defeat, my son,
so, thorns now scar your face?
   What a fierce battle, that I
and you went through, so strong:
I was tortured, for so long
to see them take your life
by those who gave you death!
   O face of radiant breadth,

---

confessional Castile: The Virgin, Christ, Devotions, and Images in the Fourteenth and Fifteenth Centuries (University Park: Pennsylvania University Press, 2013), 267–70.

50. Bestul, *Texts of the Passion*, 120, and chapter 4 in general; Karl Young, *The Drama of the Medieval Church* (Oxford: Oxford University Press, 1967), 1: 493–503. For the biblical mention of Mary during the Passion, see John 19: 25.

51. Bestul, *Texts of the Passion*, 113. For an excellent explanation of the evolution of Mary's role, see chapter 4.

52. Thomas à Kempis, *The Imitation of Mary*, ed. Albin de Cigala (Westminster: The Newman Press, 1948), 108. See also 60–69 of the same.

53. Hammerschmidt, "Beyond Vision: The Impact of Rogier Van Der Weyden's *Descent from the Cross*," in *Religion and the Senses in Early Modern Europe*, eds. Wietse de Boer and Christine Göttler (Leiden: Brill, 2013), 212.

In clarity of royal sky!
Who disturbed your holy reign?
Who gave you this much pain?
Who made your trials multiply?
  Your refulgent eyes
that were the moon of mine,
who made them terrorized?
Who bloodied your teeth divine,
and gave your blue lips brine?
  Your pierced hands,
with your arms disjointed,
your pierced feet cruelly pointed,
your flayed figure righteous stands,
torn clothes held by a Roman band.
  O you who pass
by this mountain smiling,
please see, without denying
my pain, and tell me plainly
if one can handle this grief sanely!
  Simeon was right to tell
me when I saw you in his hands
that your death would be mine as well.
O troubled Mary!
My God, what will I do without Thee?[54]

Perhaps the eighteenth-century Spanish novena of Gregorio Gago y Márquez said it best, "The pains of Mary have no comparison."[55] In the Maya sermon, the sorrow of Mary trumps all other priorities. Indeed, the orator states that "the tears in my eyes do not allow me to speak." He hesitates to relate the Passion. Why? Because his account is "stabbing the heart of the holy lady ritually prepared Mary with great sadness." Yet he presses on.

Here and throughout, Mary is referred to with the Maya phrase *cilich colel suhuy Maria*, often translated as "the holy lady virgin, Mary." However, scholars over the years have increasingly unpacked the Maya term used for "virgin," *suhuy*, to illustrate its meanings in the Maya worldview. Colonial dictionaries define *suhuy* as "virgin," true, but the term holds cultural significance that reached beyond and can be associated with female ritual power, some-

54. BNE, MSS/14711, "Colección de autos sacramentales, loas y farsas del siglo XVI (anteriores a Lope de Vega)," "Aucto del descendimiento de la cruz," 434r. The translation of this passage into an English poetic meter was done by my research assistant, Paul Guajardo. My thanks for his excellent work.

55. Gregorio Gago y Márquez, "Descendimiento de la cruz de Jesucristo nuestro redentor," BNE, MSS/15395, 64v.

thing ritually prepared or purified, and even "new." Regarding the latter, Michel Boccara argues that modern *h-men* (local Maya shamans) employ the concept of *suhuy* to incorporate new ritualistic practices and traditions among those preexisting as the *suhuy t'an*, "new word." Either way, associating the term *suhuy* with Mary allowed her to engage power and meaning far beyond the European idea of "virgin."[56]

The Maya sermon gives the crucifixion itself brief treatment. The orator begins with Christ at Calvary and the *lobil uinicob*, or "wicked people," harshly tearing away his clothes and reopening his wounds. (These wounds would have resulted from the previous scourging at Pilate's behest not mentioned in the sermon.) Christ is then given bitter wine to drink because of his great thirst. However, in the Gospels and many European Passion narratives, Christ rejects this initial drink described variously as "wine mixed with gall," "vinegar . . . mingled with gall," and "wine mingled with myrrh."[57] It seems that Rome customarily offered Jews a narcotic drink to dull the senses prior to crucifixion. Yet Christ refused, arguably to maintain his full senses.[58] Either way, the offering was not in response to Christ's thirst as stated in the sermon; this would occur later in the crucifixion.

Next, the orator asks the audience to consider the humiliation Christ endured being stripped and left quasi naked, and to consider how it would be to be laid down on a cross for crucifixion emphasizing how Christ's arms were stretched prior to their being nailed to the cross. This is all done in a very Maya way, emphasizing the heart. In Maya the words *ol* and *pucsikal* not only mean "heart," but also convey a range of emotional conditions and states. For example, "happy" or "content" is *ki' ol*, "delightful heart," or *toh ol*, "straight or just heart"; "to soothe or calm" is *sishal ol* or *sishal pucsikal*,

---

56. Various studies have examined the term *suhuy*. Those engaged here were Amy George Hirons, "The Discourse of Translation in Culture Contact: 'The Story of Suhuy Teodora,' An Analysis of European Literary Borrowings in the Books of Chilam Balam" (Phd diss., Tulane University, 2004); Pete Sigal, *From Moon Goddesses to Virgins: The Colonization of Yucatecan Maya Sexual Desire* (Austin: University of Texas Press, 2000), 123–26; Amara Solari, *Idolizing Mary: Maya-Catholic Icons in Yucatán, Mexico* (University Park: Pennsylvania State University Press, 2019), 113–24, and here I employ Solari's translation of *suhuy* as "ritually prepared"; Michel Boccara, "Tradición, improvisación y modernidad en el chamanismo maya yucateco: El arte suhuy de Juan Cob, h-men de Yaxcabá," *Salud colectiva* 13, no. 3 (2017): 429–42.

57. *Meditazione, testo breve* in Sarah McNamer, *Meditations on the Life of Christ: The Short Italian Text* (Notre Dame: University of Notre Dame Press, 2018), 141; Matthew 27:34; Mark 15:23.

58. James E. Talmage, *Jesus the Christ: A Study of the Messiah and His Mission according to Holy Scriptures both Ancient and Modern*, 3rd ed. (Salt Lake City: The Deseret News, 1916), 654–55.

"to cool down the heart."[59] In the sermon, the orator asks the audience essentially how their hearts would feel from being seen naked like Christ by many, or from being laid down on the cross. This emphasis on the heart occurs throughout the sermon.

The specifics and description of the reopening of Christ's wounds from the violent removal of his clothing, the emphasis on stretching his arms along the cross prior to being nailed in place, and his shame might initially be attributed to local, Maya influences. Yet all examples are common in medieval accounts of the Passion and, indeed, in Nahuatl Passion plays.[60] Likely created in the fourteenth century and often attributed, erroneously, to Saint Bonaventure, the *Meditationes vitae Christi* was an extremely popular and influential text that circulated widely throughout medieval Europe in manuscript form, and its Passion account influenced countless sermons and plays. A short Italian text (*testo breve*) that Sarah McNamer argues as a precursor to the *Meditationes* mentions how "the wounds were opened again, because the cloth stuck to the flesh," and how the soldiers nailing Christ "pulled so hard that it seemed the limbs and the bones were completely torn apart."[61] Certainly such European emphasis on being "stretched" influenced Maya and Nahuatl translations of the term "crucifixion": the former being *zinaan ti cruz*, "stretched on [the] cross"; the latter being *mamazoaltia*, "to cause the arms to be stretched."[62] And regarding Christ's shame, *The Golden Legend*—a popular thirteenth-century text with the Spanish adaptation being the *Flos sanctorum*—describes five pains of the Passion, "the first was its shamefulness."[63]

The Maya sermon brings attention back to Mary who nearly faints at the sound of the hammer on the first nail. The cross is then put into its place between two sinners, and the orator encourages the Maya audience to come and see the goodness of Christ crucified for their salvation. The audience is asked to consider the state of Mary's heart, stating that no one has suffered

59. *Diccionario Maya*, 4th ed. (Mexico City: Editorial Porrúa, 2001), 733, 320; David Bolles, "Combined Vocabularies," 1779. www.davidsbooks.org. See also William F. Hanks, *Converting Words: Maya in the Age of the Cross* (Berkeley: University of California Press, 2010), 256–57.

60. Bestul, *Texts of the Passion*, 65–66; Louise M. Burkhart, *Staging Christ's Passion in Eighteenth-Century Nahua Mexico* (Denver: University Press of Colorado, 2023), 170, 256.

61. McNamer, *Meditations*, 141–43. For the passages in the *Meditationes*, see Isa Ragusa and Rosalie B. Green, trans., *Meditations on the Life of Christ: An Illustrated Manuscript of the Fourteenth Century* (Princeton: Princeton University Press, 1961), 333–34.

62. For more on Maya terms for crucifixion, see Hanks, *Converting Words*, 133–34; for the Nahuatl, see Burkhart, *Staging Christ's Passion*, 170.

63. Jacobus de Voragine, *The Golden Legend: Readings on the Saints*, trans. William Granger Ryan (Princeton: Princeton University Press, 2012), 203.

as she—again, a very common theme in Deposition texts. To make the point, the orator recalls the actions of Moses who made water pour from a rock to satiate the thirsty Israelites who had been wandering in the desert for nearly 40 years.[64] The sermon asks if a rock, not having eyes, produced water, how much more water (tears) will flow from those with eyes who see Mary suffering in solitude? This example appears in various forms in European Depositions texts.[65]

Next, the Maya sermon emphasizes the solitude of Mary as she suffers by comparing her joy and company during the birth of Christ with her misery and solitude during his death. At various points the sermon asks Mary, "Where are the angels that came with the many blessed baptized? Where are those glorious shepherds? Where are the many angels that brought you happiness the day you gave birth in Bethlehem?" Attempting to make a similar point, the Passion text composed by Andrés de Li and published in 1494 in Spain similarly asks, "Where is it now, glorious Virgin, that illustrious comfort of angelic salvation that you received when you were completely full of grace? Where is that complete joy that you felt at the holy conception? Where now is that sweet song that . . . was sung at your glorious childbirth?"[66]

In the description of the crucifixion and Christ's utterances, the sermon references Saint Augustine's commentary on the Gospel of John to state how the cross served as a chair or podium of sorts from which Christ continued to teach.[67] This reference to Augustine is not uncommon in Passion and Deposition narratives, even plays.[68] What is uncommon, although not for the Maya, is the reference to Augustine as *ah bolon pixan*, or "he of the nine souls" or the "nine souled." In the Maya worldview, the number nine plays a significant role and often appears associated with deities; it also carries the meaning of "many" or even "great." The Maya pantheon demonstrates the use of *ah bolon* through the deities Ah Bolon Yocte or Ah Bolon Ahau, among others. Cer-

64. Numbers 20:1–13.

65. For example, see fray Pantaleón García, *Sermones panegíricos de varios misterios, festividades y santos* (Madrid: Imprenta de la calle de la greda, 1807), 5: 21.

66. Laura Delbrugge, *A Scholarly Edition of Andrés de Li's* Thesoro de la Passion *(1494)* (Leiden: Brill, 2011), 55–56. For the solitude of Mary emphasized in the Stations of the Cross, see Schwaller, *Stations*, 149–50. In one Deposition sermon, Mary speaks in the first person and herself makes the comparison between her joy in Bethlehem versus her pain of Calvary. García, *Sermones panegíricos*, 5: 4–5. See also Catalá, *Sentimientos tiernos*, 19.

67. See Saint Augustine, *St. Augustine: Tractates on the Gospel of John 112-24*, trans., John W. Rettig, The Fathers of the Church: A New Translation, vol. 92 (Washington, DC: Catholic University of America Press, 1995), 45.

68. For an example in a play, see Vicente Solano, *Representación de la pasión, muerte, descendimiento de la cruz y sepultura de Cristo señor nuestro* (Lérida: Imprenta y Librería de José Sol, 1847), 75.

tainly, this preexisting phrase coupled with *pixan* familiarized Catholic saints and their supernatural abilities, as *ah bolon pixan* is used consistently throughout all colonial Maya texts in reference to saints—although more frequently in those Maya authored—even appearing as *ix bolon pixan*, or "she of the nine souls," for female saints.[69]

The audience is then told to gather and see how the implements of Christ's crucifixion—the nails, spear, crown of thorns—likewise pierce the heart of Mary. Images of Our Lady of Sorrows are common throughout Yucatecan churches and likely could have served this purpose here. The Maya audience is instructed to also feel sorrow for the beating and execution of Christ. To help convey the necessary sorrow, the orator uses another biblical example sometimes cited in Spanish Deposition works.[70] When David learned of the death of King Saul, he wept and mourned bitterly. So too should the audience "seeing all these pains the only son of God suffers." Subsequently, the sermon continues through the crucifixion, addressing the seven statements Christ makes from the cross—although not in the order outlined in the Gospels—and a few lessons to be learned from them. This type of instruction from the seven statements is common in Good Friday sermons and often begins Deposition ceremonies.[71]

During this instruction, the sermon employs a phrase seen in the hymn *Stabat Mater* to assign the Maya audience as a companion to Mary while she suffers by the cross. This invitation to suffer with Mary is common in the liturgy and appears throughout the sermon multiple times, including earlier with the Latin citation of Lamentations 1:12, *O vos omnes.* This is a responsory during Holy Saturday and a common addition to Passion and Deposition sermons.[72] The orator speaks for Mary as she tries to convey her sorrow. At one point, the crucifixion renders Mary speechless and struggling for words, similar to the "Quis dabit" in which Mary states, "My voice had nearly gone, but I uttered

---

69. For more on the phrase and its colonial usage, see Mark Z. Christensen, *Nahua and Maya Catholicisms: Texts and Religion in Colonial Central Mexico and Yucatan* (Stanford: Stanford University Press and the Academy of American Franciscan History Press, 2013), 46–48; Mark Z. Christensen, *The Teabo Manuscript: Maya Christian Copybooks, Chilam Balams, and Native Text Production in Yucatan* (Austin: University of Texas Press, 2016), 48; Mark Z. Christensen, *Aztec and Maya Apocalypses: Old World Tales of Doom in a New World Setting* (Norman: University of Oklahoma Press, 2022), 133–34. Farriss likewise noted the use of this phrase in her *Maya Society*, 311.

70. See, for example, Catalá, *Sentimientos tiernos*, 29.

71. For an example in Oaxaca, see Díeguez Melo, "Ubi est mors," 367.

72. Ronald E. Surtz, ed., *Teatro castellano de la edad media* (Madrid: Clásicos Taurus, 1992), 31. For one example of a Deposition sermon, see Lucas del Olmo Alfonso, *Romance mystico a la dolorosa pasion de nuestro Señor Jesu-Christo y mysterio de el descendimiento de la cruz* (Madrid: En la imprenta y libreria de Andrés de Sotos, n.d.).

sighs of sorrow and moans of grief. I wanted to speak, but sorrow broke off the words."[73] Moreover, the Maya Deposition has Mary speaking to Christ while on the cross, pleading for him to help her, even let her die with him, following which Christ commends his mother to the care of John his apostle. This sequence also mirrors that in the "Quis dabit."[74]

Then Christ dies. The Maya women are encouraged to consider how Mary felt having lost her child, and the biblical signs of Christ's death appear including the veil in the temple tearing. At this point, the sermon inserts instructions in Spanish for someone to tear away the veil and reveal the Lord. Crosses in churches are covered during Holy Week to be progressively uncovered during the Good Friday ceremony of the Adoration of the Holy Cross.[75] Yet here, this would presumably expose an image of a crucified Christ previously covered. The orator speaks a few lines for Mary, and then the sermon emphasizes the sadness of Christ's death through signs recorded in the Bible, while also adding a few of its own. Aside from the tearing of the veil in the temple of Jerusalem, the Synoptic Gospels variously mention earthquakes, rocks breaking, and dead people emerging from their graves. They also speak of darkness covering the land from the sixth to the ninth hour when Christ died, or about noon to 3 pm, but this started prior to his death.[76]

Spanish Deposition plays and sermons consistently include these biblical signs, while augmenting them a bit with a moaning or upset ocean, typically serving as evidence for the Roman centurion and Pilate of the death of Christ. And such signs likewise appear in the Maya sermon to emphasize how the earth mourned the loss of its creator. Yet the sermon mentions additional signs not seen in European Passion or Deposition accounts including animals mourning in agony and trying to find caves in which to hide until their death, frightened birds cowering and flying above to see what is going on, fish jumping out of and leaving the water to die, and the oceans and wells overflowing.

What to make of these odd signs in the Maya text? Are they reflective of European or Maya traditions? Probably a little of both. In the Bible, Isaiah

73. "Meditacio Bernardi de lamentacione beate virginis," translated in Bestul, *Texts of the Passion*, 171. For more on the "Quis dabit," see the same, 52–53.

74. For Mary addressing the cross, see Young, *The Drama*, 1: 496.

75. Catholic Church, United States Conference of Catholic Bishops, *The Roman Missal*, 3rd ed. (Collegeville, MN: Liturgical Press, 2011), 329–31; for the liturgy of Good Friday, see 314–38. For an example in Yanhuitlan, see Frassani, *Building Yanhuitlan*, 103–105.

76. Matt. 27: 51–53; Mark 15:38; Luke 23: 44–45. For the darkness, see Kent P. Jackson, "The Crucifixion," in *From the Last Supper through the Resurrection: The Savior's Final Hours*, eds. Richard Neitzel Holzapfel and Thomas A. Wayment (Salt Lake City: Deseret Book, 2003), 330.

speaks of men seeking caves in which to hide from the Final Judgment, but not animals, and not in connection with the Passion.[77] Hosea mentions the mourning of the land, animals, birds, and fish, but in connection with Israel's apostasy from God and their resulting idolatry in the Old Testament, not Christ's Passion in the New.[78] Passion narratives, such as those in the "Quis dabit" and *The Golden Legend*, typically only speak of earthquakes, darkness, even eclipses that occurred, sometimes all over the world.[79] Spanish plays and poems likewise mention those signs found in the Gospels, sometimes elaborating the darkness with muted stars.[80] Others include the sorrow of flora and fauna. For example, one Deposition play recorded by Gregorio Gago y Márquez in 1797 and held in the Biblioteca Nacional of Spain gives ample space to the signs of Christ's death and speaks of the ocean roaring in response, and the sadness shown by men, birds, plants, and fish. Later, the text details how the sorrow for the death of Christ causes the fish to stop swimming and sob, and the birds to stop singing and come down to gaze upon the crucified Christ in the arms of his mother.[81] Yet the elaborations seen in the Maya sermon are absent in this or any other European text of which I am aware.

Maya texts do, however, favor their own redaction of a popular European text known as *The Fifteen Signs before Doomsday*, which includes signs familiar to those seen here. *The Fifteen Signs* conveys 15 ominous events that will occur prior to the Second Coming of Christ. Although never officially accepted by the Church, the text circulated widely throughout Europe and is found in the works of its most famous authors including Peter Damian, Thomas Aquinas, and Peter Comestor. Of all the texts introduced to the Maya in the schools of the friars, the Maya seemed to favor those of creation and destruction and its renewing benefits, no doubt due to their own preexisting worldview, which emphasizes period beginnings and endings. As such, Maya redactions and interpretations of Christian stories of the Creation and Final Judgment are not uncommon in their own Christian copybooks and Books of Chilam

77. Isaiah 2:10, 19, 21.

78. Hosea 4:3.

79. "Meditacio Bernardi," translated in Bestul, *Texts of the Passion*," 177; Voragine, *The Golden Legend*, 623.

80. See Gómez Manrique, "(Coplas) fechas para la semana santa," in *Teatro castellano de la edad media*, 90

81. Gago y Márquez, "Descendimiento de la cruz," 8v, 34r–34v. Another play giving ample attention to the signs is Juan de Mojica's *Descendimiento del Sagrado cuerpo de Christo nuestro redemptor, viernes santo por la tarde* (1725?) (BNE, R/24824). Mojica also includes the sorrow of fish, birds, and plants, 3, 72–73, 77–78. Typically, the inclusion of the signs serves the purpose of convincing the centurion of Christ's divinity, leading him to say, "Truly, this was the Son of God!" (Matt. 27:54).

Balam. And *The Fifteen Signs* appears in four of the few surviving Maya-authored and preserved texts extant today.[82]

In Maya redactions, the first sign is the rising of the ocean, similar to the overflowing of the ocean and wells seen here. The fourth and fifth signs speak of fish emerging to walk on the water and cry out, and birds and animals gathering together to cry also similar to the Maya Deposition sermon. And the fourteenth sign mentions humankind hiding in caves. All such actions were out of fear of the Final Judgment. Here, it is possible that these signs appear again but modified for the sorrow of Christ's death. Certainly, the signs of Christ's death found in the Maya Deposition sermon pulled from European antecedents and could be influenced by some unknown Deposition text. But it would be imprudent to ignore the likely influence of the Maya's inclination toward *The Fifteen Signs*. Whether included by Carvajal or a Maya ghostwriter is uncertain. Either way, the signs in the Maya text represent an uncommon addition to the narrative found in typical Passion and Deposition texts.

The Maya Deposition then gives instruction for the orator to address Christ doing so with a string of epithets that includes *ah menul caan y luum*, "maker of heaven and earth." The phrase engages the term *ah men* (or *h-men*), which represents the healers and diviners of precontact, colonial, and modern times. Found in every town, these individuals were a constant thorn in the side of ecclesiastics.[83] Literally translated as "doer or maker," the term *ah men* employed as an epithet for Christ certainly would have supplied additional meaning.

Continuing, the sermon redirects its attention to the audience citing sages such as Bonaventure and Aristotle to highlight again how no one suffers like Mary, pausing to give attention to the story of Jacob and Joseph. In the Bible, Jacob's preferred son, Joseph, is abducted by his brothers who tear up his coat of many colors and soak it in animal blood to sell the deception of his death, whereas in reality they sold him into slavery. Upon hearing of Joseph's "death," Jacob "rent his clothes, put sackcloth on his loins, and mourned his

---

82. I have discussed *The Fifteen Signs* and its connections to Maya and Nahuatl texts at length elsewhere. See Christensen, *Teabo Manuscript*, ch. 3; and Christensen, *Apocalypses*, ch. 3. See also Timothy W. Knowlton, *Maya Creation Myths: Words and Worlds of the Chilam Balam* (Boulder: University Press of Colorado, 2010), 81–82; Gretchen Whalen, "An Annotated Translation of a Colonial Yucatec Manuscript: On Religious and Cosmological Topics by a Native Author," Foundation for the Advancement of Mesoamerican Studies, 2002, http://www.famsi.org/reports/01017.

83. For more on the term, see Hanks, *Converting Words*, 137–38; for more on the individual, see J. Eric S. Thompson, *Maya History and Religion* (Norman: University of Oklahoma Press, 1970), 169.

son many days."[84] The sermon notes that if Jacob lamented so from just hearing of his son's death, how much more will Mary sorrow for having actually witnessed her son's torment. This example likewise appears in Spanish texts. A mid eighteenth-century sermon performed in Valencia, Spain, and addressing the Deposition and burial of Christ employs the example of Jacob in an identical way to convey the superior sorrow of Mary.[85] As do others including fray Antonio Andrés's 1785 work on the Seven Sorrows of Mary, the sixth sorrow being that of the Deposition.[86]

Mary then addresses the cross, pleading with it to lower Christ down so that she may hold him. During the liturgy of Good Friday, the *Crux fidelis* is sung during the Adoration of the Holy Cross, a verse of which appears here in both Latin and Maya, as is customary with Latin quotes in Maya texts.[87] Mary pleads with the cross to "lower your branch" and deposit Christ. This is all rather common in Deposition texts, as is the emphasis on Mary's desperation for having anyone help her remove Christ from the cross.[88] Uncommon—indeed, I have not found one example in European texts—is the Maya Mary's subsequent plea to the animals and "all that pass your life there in the forests" to detach and free Christ from the cross. Yet to emphasize her solitude, the orator responds, "Not one thing born hears your words, my holy lady." Admittedly the orator does mention the presence of "he of the nine souls" Saint John, but he is of no use as he is "really fatigued with sorrow."

Now the sermon arrives at the Deposition. As before, the scene follows a general European outline but with local and sometimes Maya influences. Mary pleads to God for help, and he sends her Joseph of Arimathea and Nicodemus. Parenthetical instructions in Spanish call for the men to come forth and kneel before Mary asking permission to touch the body of Christ and lower him down. The orator speaks for the two men, and the sermon gives instructions in Spanish for the head of Mary to nod in approval. Again, whether an actor or articulated sculpture performed this action is unknown. Yet these and subsequent instructions are similar to other Spanish reenactments, particularly

84. Gen. 37:34.

85. Catalá, *Sentimientos tiernos*, 21.

86. Fray Antonio Andrés, *Septenario doloroso de Maria SS.MA* (Valencia: Benito Monfort, 1785), 117–20. See also García, *Sermones panegíricos*, 5: 16–17.

87. For more on the liturgy during Good Friday, see Robert Atwell, "The Passion in Christian Liturgy," in *Engaging the Passion: Perspectives on the Death of Jesus*, ed. Oliver Larry Yarbrough (Minneapolis: Fortress Press, 2015), 92–98.

88. Solano, *Representación de la pasión*, 82; Catalá, *Sentimientos tiernos*, 12; Olmo Alfonso, *Romance mystico*; Francisco de la Torre y Sevil, "El descendimiento de la cruz, comedia en forma de auto," BNE, MSS/16831, 20; García, *Sermones panegíricos*, 5: 19–24.

Juan de Mojica's 1725 *Descendimiento*. Addressing the two men, the sermon gives them continual instruction, guiding their actions as they climb their ladders to take Christ down from the cross. They remove the crown of thorns, present it to Mary who then kisses it, and take it to the *Santo Sepulcro*. Then, Joseph removes the nails and presents them to Mary. Yet the orator instructs Joseph not to let her see the nails for too long, as she is already sad. Passion and Deposition texts vary in this regard, with some hiding the nails from Mary, and others presenting them to her for her to kiss.[89] The Maya sermon seems to split the difference.

The detachment of Christ from the cross includes two additions not typically seen in Spanish versions. First, Joseph and Nicodemus are told to kneel before Christ and ask permission to take him down from the cross—this is common. But then the orator tells the men to notice how he is stretched on the cross as a *hahal Dios, hahal uinici xan*, "true God, true man also," a phrase the sermon used once before in the beginning when also describing Christ. As William Hanks rightly observes, *hahal Dios* emerged as a Christian contrast to the "false" gods of the Maya.[90] The term appears widely throughout Maya texts—from Chilam Balams to last wills and testaments—and is also paired with *hahal uinic* to describe Christ's nature. For example, fray Juan Coronel's 1620 Maya *Doctrina* asks the question of "Who is Christ?" The response: "A true God, true man also."[91] Like Coronel's *Doctrina*, the Maya sermon employs the phrase didactically to remind its audience of the dual nature of Christ as being both fully human and divine. The dual nature of Christ has sparked myriad debates throughout the ages resulting in factions and splits within the Church. Indeed, many today struggle to grasp the human and divine character of Christ. The Council of Chalcedon in 451 sought to clarify the issue allowing the current catechism of the Church to state "[Jesus Christ] became truly man while remaining truly God. Jesus Christ is true God and true man."[92] And the sermon here employs the Deposition to instruct the Maya audience again on this complex topic.

---

89. For example, in Ragusa and Green, trans., *Meditations*, 341, they hide the nails; in Solano, *Representación de la pasión*, 86–87, and in Olmo Alfonso's *Romance mystico*, Mary kisses the nails.

90. Hanks, *Converting Words*, 252.

91. Fray Juan Coronel, *Doctrina Christiana en lengua maya* (Mexico: Diego Garrido, 1620), transcription by David Bolles, http://davidsbooks.org/www/Maya/CORODOCT.pdf, 200–201. The phrase also appears throughout the Maya-authored Morley Manuscript.

92. Catholic Church, *Catechism of the Catholic Church: Revised in Accordance with the Official Latin Text Promulgated by Pope John Paul II*, 2nd ed. (Vatican City: Libreria Editrice Vaticana, 2019), 117, para. 464. In general, see paras. 464–69.

The second addition not seen in Spanish renditions of the Deposition again employs the heart. Deposition texts vary on how they describe the act of removing Christ from the cross, particularly regarding his unnailing. To undo the nails, some texts mention pliers or pincers (*tenazas*), others a hammer. Some go into detail about the removal of the nails, the difficulty of the task, and its sorrow; others simply have the men remove the nails in one line of text.[93] One sermon describes the sound of Nicodemus and Joseph's hammers as so horrible that it shook the mountains and made the heart of Mary tremble as each blow pierced her heart.[94] Yet in a few Deposition texts, emphasis is placed on removing the nails quietly to not further distress Mary. In don Vicente Catalá's mid eighteenth-century *Sentimientos tiernos*, the two men are instructed not to strike with their hammers to remove the nails lest they wound and also remove the soul of Mary.[95] In an interesting addition, the orator in the Maya Deposition offers his heart to Joseph to place between the hammer and nail to muffle the sound of the strikes so Mary cannot hear. Whether Maya or European culture is responsible for this inclusion is uncertain, but it makes for a beautifully descriptive passage.

Proceeding to the lowering of the body and its presentation to Mary, the text betrays the Maya inclination toward parallel constructions for description. The orator instructs Joseph (and presumably Nicodemus) to be cautious when lowering Christ's body, "do not bang it around, do not open the wounds again." The men bring the body of Christ to Mary. At this point in Deposition texts, Mary typically performs a monologue detailing the beauty of Christ's body—his eyes, lips, neck, hands, etc.—and then the damaging effects of the crucifixion on each.[96] Indeed, Kempis's *Prayers and Meditations on the Life of Christ* includes a chapter dedicated to prayers for each body part.[97] Yet in the Maya Deposition, Mary sees the descended Christ only for the briefest of

---

93. For an example of the former, see Gago y Márquez, "Descendimiento de la cruz," 30r–31v or García, *Sermones panegíricos*, 5: 34–39; for the latter, see Olmo Alfonso, *Romance mystico*.

94. Fray Christobal de Almeida, *Sermones varios* (Madrid: Mateo de Espinosa y Arteaga, 1675), 156. The horrible sound of the hammer on the nails during the Passion is a commonly mentioned item in Passion and Deposition texts. See, for example, the famous sixteenth-century Passion play of the Spaniard Lucas Fernández, *Auto de la pasión*, in Françoise Maurizi's *Lucas Fernández: Farsas y églogas* (Rochester: Tamesis, 2015), 181.

95. Catalá, *Sentimientos tiernos*, 17–18.

96. See, for example, Gago y Márquez, "Descendimiento de la cruz," 39r–40v. This adoration of body parts could also be shared with those present including John, Mary Magdalene, Nicodemus, Veronica, Joseph, and Simon as in Torre y Sevil, "El descendimiento," 37.

97. Thomas à Kempis, *Prayers and Meditations on the Life of Christ*, trans. Michael Joseph Pohl (London: Kegan Paul, Trench, Trübner, 1904), 189–93.

moments before the orator instructs Joseph and Nicodemus to bring him Christ's body to hold. Here, the orator plays a much larger role than in typical performances of the Deposition.

Holding the body of Christ—certainly an articulated sculpture—the orator laments and presents the body to the Maya audience asking if anyone has a piece of cloth with which to bury Christ. This too appears in Spanish texts, although much more time is allotted to Mary for her lament over Christ's body.[98] Parenthetical instructions in Spanish reveal that a ceremony for carrying the Holy Shroud (*sábana santa*) to the pulpit is performed by either Joseph or Nicodemus. They then place Christ in his casket—perhaps a wooden and glass casket as is often used to represent the *Santo Sepulcro* in processions of the *Santo Sepulcro*—and the orator calls for the angels to sing and accompany the burial. Generally, all this falls in line with Deposition scenes, particularly with the angels accompanying the procession to the burial.[99] In Spain, songs were typically sung lamenting the sorrow of Mary.[100] It is possible that the Maya were led in song during specific parts of the Deposition, but it remains unclear.

However, what is uncommon—even unique!—concerns the Maya Deposition's treatment of Mary's sorrow in her final farewell to Christ. In European texts, Mary weeps profusely at having to leave Christ in the tomb, sometimes stating that she wishes to be buried with him. In *Sentimientos tiernos*, Mary exclaims, "O death, for what are you waiting to execute the final blow upon this desolate mother? Heavens, angels, men, where do I have to go without my son? How can I go leaving him shut up in this tomb?"[101] The "Quis dabit" paints an even more vivid picture with Mary pleading, "'If you wish to place the son in the grave, bury the mother . . . for why should I live after him?' They wished to bury him. She drew him to herself and sought to keep him; they attempted to bury him. And so a pious dispute and a pitiful struggle broke out among them."[102] A similar, yet somewhat less intense, struggle appears in the thirteenth-century Marian lament *Dialogus beatae Mariae et Anselmi de passione Christi*.[103]

98. For one example, see García, *Sermones panegíricos*, 5: 44.

99. For one example of many, see Catalá, *Sentimientos tiernos*, 25.

100. Cristina Laura Casado Medrano, "La música vocal de semana santa en algunas procesiones singulares de Castilla y León," in *La semana santa*, 3: 324.

101. Catalá, *Sentimientos tiernos*, 27; Torre y Sevil, "El descendimiento," likewise has Mary requesting her death.

102. "Meditacio Bernardi," translated in Bestul, *Texts of the Passion*, 183. See also Burkhart, *Staging Christ's Passion*, 114.

103. Pseudo-Anselm, *Dialogus beatae Mariae et Anselmi de passione Christi* (Passau: Johann Petri, 1485–86), unnumbered.

During the burial in the Maya Deposition, the orator abruptly asks the stars, angels, and those born (*ah sihnalob*) why they are obeying Mary's request to be buried with her child. Mary speaks, "I have no life if my holy son just died . . . all my happiness is finished." She then concludes with a farewell the likes of which I have yet to find in any European or Mexican text: "*adios* heaven, *adios* earth, *adios* forests, *adios* animals, also *adios* to those born on the earth. It is finished, it is finished, my death for all." Interestingly, in the conclusion of her farewell, Mary employs the Maya phrase *ɔoci, ɔoci*, to convey the phrase "it is finished, it is finished." This phrase originates from the biblical Christ who in John 19:30 states, "it is finished," before bowing his head and dying, and is used previously in three separate occasions in the Maya Deposition, but all in reference to Christ. Here, Mary appropriates the atoning words of her son to become a redemptrix herself boldly asserting that her suffering and death—like Christ's—is for everyone.

The orator pleads with Mary to stay and offers her his heart along with the heart of all sinners. This is not unlike a passage from *Sentimientos tiernos* where the orator asks Mary to take the audience's wounded hearts.[104] A final plea to the audience to come unto Christ, and a plea to Christ to allow the orator to recite the Act of Contrition followed by the Act itself ends the performative sermon. Here, the Act of Contrition in the Maya Deposition continues the theme of the sermon in general, which emphasizes the suffering of Mary and her role in the Passion—something not seen in other renditions of the prayer. Indeed, the penitent prays for forgiveness through not only Christ's suffering, but that of Mary's as well. Kempis's claim for Mary as co-redemptrix certainly resonates with the Maya Deposition sermon and its Act of Contrition.

Although it is uncertain whether this Maya Deposition was ever performed at Temax during the tenure of Carvajal, it is interesting to note how the town, particularly its women, held the protagonist of the sermon, Mary, in high regard. Terry Rugeley noted that Temax founded the cofradía of the Most Holy Virgin of Mount Carmel in 1819, and how in the 1870s the cofradía had become a "strictly female organization."[105] The central role of

104. Catalá, *Sentimientos tiernos*, 28.

105. Terry Rugeley, *Of Wonders and Wise Men: Religion and Popular Cultures in Southeast Mexico, 1800–1876* (Austin: University of Texas Press, 2001), 82. For the establishment and eventual changes to cofradías in Yucatan, see the same, 144–50; Farriss, *Maya Society*, 262–72. In general, see Francisco Morales, "Pueblos y doctinas en Mexico en el S. XVII," in *Actas del III congreso internacional sobre los franciscanos en el Nuevo Mundo (siglo XVII)* (Madrid: Editorial Deimos, 1991), 773–811; Gabriela Solís Robleda, "Tierra y trabajo en las haciendas de cofradías indígenas de Yucatán, siglo XVIII," *Desacatos* 13, (2003): 13–31; Murdo J. MacLeod, "Confraternities in Colonial New Spain: Mexico and Central America," in *A Companion to Medieval and Early Modern Confraternities*, ed.

Figure 4. Deposition cross. San Miguel Arcángel, Temax. Photo by author.

Mary in European Deposition texts carried over not only to this Maya sermon, but to the religious life of Temax.[106]

The Maya Deposition then ends with a list of Maya words and phrases supposedly found in the sermon and their Spanish translations. However, more than a few fail to appear in the text itself suggesting alterations to the sermon over time as it became recopied and circulated. Regardless, this Maya sermon on the Deposition remains the only example illustrating how the popular European genre of Deposition texts entered into the religious life of the Yucatec Maya and became negotiated into their worldview.

* * * * *

Today, various towns in Spain and Latin America continue to perform the Deposition in ways similar to that depicted in this Maya sermon. Regard-

---

Konrad Eisenbichler (Leiden: Brill, 2019), 280–306; and Laura Dierksmeier, *Charity for and by the Poor: Franciscan and Indigenous Confraternities in Mexico, 1527–1540* (Norman: University of Oklahoma Press, and Berkeley: Academy of American Franciscan History, 2020).

106. Perhaps they were similar to the women of Chunhuhub who the 1784 priest described as being "more devout." AHAY, Gobierno, Visitas Pastorales, 1784–1785, caja 622, exp. 1, Chunhuhub, 59r.

Figure 5. The *Santo Sepulcro* and articulated Christ. San Miguel Arcángel, Temax. Photo by author.

ing Yucatan, towns continue the tradition of the Deposition. Yet in different ways. To my knowledge, no Yucatecan town employs a Maya sermon while silent actors perform the Deposition. And Temax is no exception. Upon entering the church today, immediately to the left is a wooden cross painted black with three holes (Figure 4). This is certainly the same cross that appears listed in an inventory made in 1890 and listed as "una cruz grande pintada que sirve para el desendimiento" (a large, painted cross used for the Deposition). Entering farther into the church, the southern transept houses a wooden and glass casket, the *Santo Sepulcro*, with an articulated mannequin of Christ Crucified inside covered in a shroud. Images of Our Lady of Solitude, Veronica, and St. John also appear in the transept (Figure 5), and all such items likewise appear in the 1890 inventory.[107]

The current sacristan, Carlos Yerves, relates that the articulated sculpture of Christ is positioned on the large painted cross during Good Friday while the images of Mary, Veronica, and St. John are placed around it. The cross is removed from its current location at the entrance of the church and positioned at the front for the liturgy of Good Friday that includes a recitation of the Passion and the Adoration of the Cross. Afterwards, and in public, Christ is removed and returned to his casket. Later that night, the people of Temax

107. AHAY, Gobierno, Inventarios, caja 228, "Temax, 1890."

Figure 6. Main plaza. Acanceh. Photo by author.

gather for a procession of the *Santo Sepulcro* through the town that follows a 1-kilometer route ending back at the church.[108]

Although the Deposition in Maya seems not to have survived the twentieth century, its reenactment still clings to tradition in Acanceh. Here, the largest live reenactment of the Passion in Yucatan occurs in the town situated a little under 20 miles southeast of Merida. After a two-year hiatus due to Covid-19, Acanceh performed its forty-first reproduction of the Passion on Good Friday, 2022. Residents walked the viacrucis with the forty actors dressed to reenact the final hours of Christ's life. In the hot sun, Andrés Medina Chalé playing Christ was elevated on his cross in front of the pre-Columbian pyramid that sits in the center of town (Figure 6).

A while later, the Deposition took place and Christ was placed in the arms of an actor playing Mary who offered a few lamenting words.[109] Although the words recited were in Spanish, and although the reenactment followed an Old-World structure of events, a Maya Mary wept over the body of a Maya Christ in the shadow of a Maya pyramid. In many ways, it was a Maya Deposition.

108. Carlos Yerves, personal communication, August 5, 2023.

109. Emanuel Rincón, "Luego de 2 años regresa el viacrucis viviente a Acanceh, Yucatán," *Diario de Yucatán*, 15 April 2022, https://www.yucatan.com.mx/yucatan/2022/4/15/luego-de-anos-regresa-el-viacrucis-viviente-acanceh-yucatan-314074.html. Various videos posted on YouTube feature the Acanceh Passion. For the Deposition, see https://www.youtube.com/watch?v=MIJTdncAS8A and https://www.youtube.com/watch?v=ldlkd1S-Lb8; for more Andrés Medina Chalé and his role as Christ, see https://www.youtube.com/watch?v=VZ2EdEdlz0c.

About the Authors

Keith Ashley is an archaeologist and associate professor of anthropology at the University of North Florida. His research focuses on the deep Indigenous history of northeastern Florida, and how local Indigenous populations interacted with other communities in Florida and beyond, before, and after European arrival.

Viviana Díaz Balsera is professor of Spanish and Cooper Fellow of Arts and Sciences at the University of Miami. She has written on early modern religious theater in Spain, Mesoamerican and Iberian epistemologies in colonial Mexico, and more recently, La Florida. She is the author of *Las quimeras de la Culpa: alegoría, seducción y resistencia en tres autos calderonianos* (*Mirages of Guilt: Allegory, Seduction and Resistance in Three Calderonian Autos*, Purdue University Press); *The Pyramid Under the Cross: Franciscan Discourses of Evangelization and the Nahua Christian Subject in Sixteenth Century Mexico* (University of Arizona Press), and *Guardians of Idolatry: Gods, Demons, and Priests in Hernando Ruiz de Alarcón's* Treatise on the Heathen Superstitions (University of Oklahoma Press). Díaz Balsera has also published on Hernán Cortés, Motolinía, and Sor Juana Inés de la Cruz, focusing on the transatlantic dimensions of their writings.

Denise I. Bossy is associate professor of history at the University of North Florida and North American editor-in-chief of the *Ethnohistory* journal. Her teaching and research focus on Florida, local Indigenous history, public and digital humanities, and the Native South. Her award-winning publications include *The Yamasee Indians: From Florida to South Carolina* (University of Nebraska Press, 2018). Her forthcoming book, *Yamasee: Indigenous Mobility and Power in the Early South*, is under contract with the Omohundro Institute at the University of North Carolina Press. She is currently working with Dr. Keith Ashley on a public-facing book and digital humanities site that examine the deep history of the Mocamas, Guales, and Yamasees of Northeast Florida; see https://indigenousflorida.domains.unf.edu/. Both works are generously funded by the National Endowment for the Humanities.

George Aaron Broadwell is Elling Eide Professor of anthropology at the University of Florida. His research focuses on the Native languages of the

United States and Mexico, with a particular emphasis on Choctaw, Timucua, and Seminole Creek.

Mark Christensen is professor of history at Brigham Young University and the author of various articles and books on the colonial Nahua and Yucatec Maya. His research interests include how Christianity was conveyed and the negotiations inherent in its reception and practice. His most recent book, *Aztec and Maya Apocalypses* (University of Oklahoma Press, 2022), employs religious texts written in Nahuatl and Yucatec Maya to reveal what the Indigenous population was taught regarding the Christian Apocalypse, and how it was received and familiarized within preexisting worldviews. He lives in Mapleton, Utah, with his wife, Natalie, and their five children.

Alejandra Dubcovsky is professor of history at the University of California, Riverside. Her research focuses on early America, Native America, and the early Spanish Borderlands. She has published two books, *Informed Power: Communication in the Early American South* (Harvard University Press, 2016) and *Talking Back: Native Women and the Making of the Early South* (Yale University Press, 2023). She also leads an interdisciplinary and collaborative project on the Timucua language: https://hebuano.com/.

Helmut Flachenecker is professor emeritus for Medieval Franconian History of the Middle Ages at the University of Wuerzburg and the director of the Research Center of the Teutonic Order at the University of Wuerzburg. He was also visiting professor of history at Flagler College (2015, 2018, 2021, 2023, 2024) in Saint Augustine, Florida.

Thomas Hallock is professor of English at the University of South Florida, where he teaches on the St. Petersburg campus. He is the author/co-editor of six previous books, mostly about early American literature. The essay from this volume distills a forthcoming publication, "The Epic of Florida: Poems by Juan de Castellanos, Bartolomé de Flores, and Alonso Gregorio de Escobedo."

Doug Henning is an independent linguist and math teacher living in Jacksonville, Florida, on traditional Mocama land. He graduated with a degree in mathematics and literature from the University of North Florida. His research focuses on Timucua morphosyntax, lexicography, and language pedagogy, as well as its local Southeastern areal and historical context, drawing on philological experience and corpus work with Egyptian-Coptic, Massachusett, |Xam, Manx, Arrernte, and a number of other Indigenous and ancient languages.

Jennifer Scheper Hughes is professor in the Department of History at the University of California, Riverside. Her research focuses on the lived history of Latin American Christianity with special consideration for the religious lives of Mexican and Mexican American Catholics. Her book, *The Church of the Dead: The Epidemic of 1576 and the Birth of Christianity in the Americas* (NYU 2021) was named one of the top five academic books on religion for 2021 (*Publishers Weekly*). Hughes' first book, *Biography of a Mexican Crucifix: Lived Religion and Local Faith from the Conquest to the Present* (Oklahoma University Press, 2010) explores the affective bonds that join devotional communities to vital and agentic objects of material religion. She is co-PI of the University of California Critical Mission Studies project supporting Indigenous perspectives on the California Missions and their aftermath.

Timothy J. Johnson is Craig and Audrey Thorn Distinguished Professor of Religion at Flagler College in St. Augustine, Florida. A Senior Fulbright Scholar, he is also senior theology co-editor for *Franciscan Studies* and chair of the Research Advisory Council of the Franciscan Institute at St. Bonaventure University. Johnson is the author, co-author, editor, co-editor, and translator of numerous publications, including *Facing Florida: Essays on Culture and Religion in Early Modern Southeastern America* (2021), the third volume in the ongoing project at Flagler College on Franciscans in the Spanish Borderlands. His work has been translated into Dutch, French, German, Italian, Portuguese, and Spanish. In 2019 he uncovered the *IIII. parte de catechismo en lengua timuquana y castellana: en que se trata el modo de oyr missa, y sus ceremonias* (1628), a previously unknown liturgical catechism in Latin, Spanish, and Timucua by Fr. Francisco Pareja and his Timucuan co-authors at All Souls College Library in Oxford, England.

Seth Katenkamp is a graduate student in the Department of Linguistics at Yale University. Their research focuses on the reflexes of sociopolitical change and migration in the Indigenous languages of the Southeastern United States, especially in the Choctaw Nation. They also participate in documentation and revitalization work for Timucua and several Muskogean languages.

Lee A. Newsom is professor emerita of anthropology at The Pennsylvania State University. She is a paleoethnobotanist and environmental archaeologist with a primary interest in Florida and the Caribbean region. She has authored numerous books and articles on plant domestication, biological resource management, and related matters. Newsom is a John D. & Catherine T. MacArthur Foundation fellow, class of 2002, and was recently elected (2024) a Fellow of the International Academy of Wood Science. Her 2022 book is titled *Wood in Archaeology* (Cambridge University Press).

Anna M. Nogar is professor of Hispanic Southwest Studies in the Department of Spanish and Portuguese and associate dean for Humanities and Interdisciplinary Units at the University of New Mexico. She researches colonial Mexican literature and its readers, and engages in Mexican American cultural and literary studies, focusing on New Mexico. Among her publications are the award-winning monograph *Quill and Cross in the Borderlands: Sor María de Ágreda and the Lady in Blue, 1628 to the Present* (Notre Dame Press, 2018). She has also coedited the following works: *Colonial Itineraries of Contemporary Mexico: Literary and Cultural Inquiries* (University of Arizona Press, 2014); *A History of Mexican Literature* (University of New Mexico Press, 2016; Cambridge University Press, 2019); *Sisters in Blue/Hermanas de azul: Sor María de Ágreda Comes to New Mexico/María de Ágreda viene a Nuevo México* (UNM Press, 2017); *El feliz ingenio neomexicano: Felipe M. Chacón* and *Poesía y prosa* (UNM Press, bilingual ed., 2021); *History of Mexican Poetry* (Cambridge University Press, 2024); and the forthcoming *A History of the Mexican Novel.*

Francisco Javier Rojo-Alique, OFM, is Professor of Church history and Franciscan studies at the Instituto Teológico OFM in Murcia and the Escuela Superior de Estudios Franciscanos in Madrid, Spain. His research focuses on the Franciscans in Medieval and Early Modern Spain with a particular emphasis on relationships between friars and society. He is the editor-in-chief of *Archivo Ibero-Americano.*

Jennifer R. Saracino is assistant professor of art history at the University of Arizona. She completed her joint PhD in art history and Latin American studies at Tulane University. Her work has been published in *Imago Mundi* (coauthored with Barbara Mundy), *Artl@s Bulletin, Mapping Nature Across the Americas* (University of Chicago, 2021) and *Collective Creativity and Artistic Agency in Colonial Latin America* (University of Florida, 2023). Her work has been supported by fellowships from The Huntington Library, Dumbarton Oaks Research Library and Collection, the Newberry Library, the John Carter Brown Library, and the American Society of Environmental History. She is currently working on her book manuscript on the Uppsala Map of Mexico-Tenochtitlan (ca. 1540), the earliest known map of Mexico City painted by Indigenous artists after the Spanish Conquest.

John F. Schwaller is professor emeritus of history at the University at Albany (SUNY) and research associate at the University of Kansas. He is known for his work on the secular clergy in early colonial Mexico, Nahuatl-language manuscripts, a history of the Catholic Church in Latin America, and studies on Mexica religion, the Cortés expedition, and the Stations of the Cross. For many years he served as an academic administrator at various universities. He is also the former director of the Academy of American Franciscan History.

Jane Tar is associate professor at the University of St. Thomas in St. Paul, Minnesota. She has published numerous articles on sixteenth and seventeenth-century Spanish nun writers. She also translated the following work: *Maria Vela y Cueto: Autobiography and Letters of a Spanish Nun*, ed. Susan Diane Laningham, trans. Jane Tar (Toronto: Iter Academic Press; Tempe: Arizona Center for Medieval and Renaissance Studies, 2016). She is currently preparing an English translation and edition of the 1633 Spanish travel diary by the English Franciscan martyr, Francis Bell (British Library, Sloane MS 1572), in which he records his round-trip from the Spanish Netherlands to Toledo, Spain in 1633 to attend the order's general chapter.

Index